CW00537987

Israel and the
European Left

Israel and the European Left

Between Solidarity and Delegitimization

COLIN SHINDLER

continuum

Continuum International Publishing Group
80 Maiden Lane, New York, NY 10038
The Tower Building, 11 York Road, London SE1 7NX

www.continuumbooks.com

© Colin Shindler 2012

All rights reserved. No part of this book may be reproduced, stored in a retrieval system, or transmitted, in any form or by any means, electronic, mechanical, photocopying,
recording, or otherwise, without the written permission of the publishers.

Library of Congress Cataloging-in-Publication Data
Shindler, Colin, 1946-
Israel and the European Left : between solidarity and delegitimisation / Colin Shindler.
p. cm.
Includes bibliographical references and index.
ISBN-13: 978-1-4411-8898-4 (hardback : alk. paper)
ISBN-10: 1-4411-8898-3 (hardback : alk. paper)
ISBN-13: 978-1-4411-5013-4 (pbk. : alk. paper)
ISBN-10: 1-4411-5013-7 (paperback : alk. paper) 1. Zionism–History–20th century.
2. Zionism–History–21st century. 3. Israel–Foreign public opinion, European.
4. Israel–Foreign public opinion, British. 5. Public opinion–Great Britain.
6. Public opinion–Europe. 7. Anti-imperialist movements–Great Britain–
History–20th century. 8. Political culture–Great Britain–History–20th century.
9. New Left–Great Britain–History. 10. Right and left (Political science) I. Title.
DS149.S497363 2012
320.54095694–dc23
2011027919

ISBN: 978-1-4411-8898-4 (HB)
978-1-4411-5013-4 (PB)

Typeset by Newgen Imaging Systems Pvt Ltd, Chennai, India
Printed and bound in the United States of America

June 2016

To Jim + Ruth — with every good wish + memories of a great trip to Ireland.

John+Rose Lebow

For

Ellis Hillman 1928–1996

Lover of the Hebrew Bible and Admirer of Trotsky

Contents

Acknowledgements

This book has been a long time in the making. Although I wrote it in just over a year, I have been thinking about its subject matter for more than 40 years. The passionate and sometimes bitter debate in Europe about Israel and Zionism first emerged from the shadows in the intense discussions within the Left after the Six Day War in 1967 – and before the subsequent settlement drive on the West Bank and Gaza. It occurred during an era of decolonization when it was easier to identify with the evolving Palestinian national movement than with Israeli socialists. Since then, a lot of water has flowed under too many bridges. Convoluted and often emotional arguments replace rational analysis.

The al-Aqsa Intifada in the twenty-first century effectively destroyed the middle ground, created by the Oslo Accords of Rabin and Arafat. The peace camps in Israel and Palestine were swallowed up by an accelerating polarization, leaving the advocates of suicide bombing in Palestine and the far Right in Israel in powerful positions of authority. One sub-text of such developments was the argument that 'anti-Zionism is anti-Semitism'. This denied a long legacy in parts of the Left of ideological opposition to Zionism. Yet this was followed by the claim by many on the European Left that anti-Zionism could never be anti-Semitic. According to Lenin, anti-Semitism emanated solely from the bourgeoisie and logically therefore anyone involved in the struggle against them could not be tainted by such racism. Local reactions by some members of the European Left from the Doctors' Plot in the 1950s right up to utterances by their ideological inheritors today suggest that this is not the case. This entanglement of a whirlwind of arguments, accompanied by a megaphone war, intrigued me and dismayed me at the same time. It was all this which propelled me to revisit the episodes of my youth.

Several archives and libraries assisted in my deliberations. In London, the British Library, the British Newspaper Library, the SOAS and Senate House libraries were all extremely helpful as was the Peoples' History Museum in Manchester and Warwick University's Modern Records Centre. In addition, many classic texts with less well-known commentaries could be accessed online through sites such as the Marxists Internet Archive. In the United States, the New York Public Library, both through its Jewish division and more generally, provided a wide array of documentation. In Israel, the staff at the Hashomer Hatzair Institute for Research and Documentation at Yad Ya'ari, Givat Haviva, the Jabotinsky Institute and the Haganah Archives, both in Tel Aviv, went beyond the call of duty to assist me and to locate crucial material.

I would also like to thank Roger Lyons, Michael Ezra and Ronnie Fraser for looking at the manuscript and for their considered comments. A sabbatical year from SOAS, University of London, allowed me to devote time and effort towards the research and writing of this work. Marie-Claire Antoine at Continuum was unstinting in her willingness to provide guidance at all times.

My wife, Jean, allowed me the mental space to develop this work and supported me throughout. Her perceptive comments allowed me to look at things anew. She did this despite each gruelling day at her ailing sister's bedside. Anna passed away towards the end of work on this book. The memory of that difficult time therefore cannot easily be separated from its writing.

As in my previous books, I have used a normal transliteration system with notable exceptions where familiarity has superseded convention. Any errors of fact or interpretation are mine alone.

Colin Shindler
London September 2011

Foreword

The closing of the progressive mind

War and peace

What would have been the reaction of the British Left if Hitler had been victorious in 1940 and successfully conquered the United Kingdom?

The Labour Party leadership would probably have fled to Canada or gone underground, but what would have been the approach of the Communist Party of Great Britain? Would it have dulled any forceful reaction to the Nazi invader out of respect for the Molotov-Ribbentrop pact? Would it have limited any resistance to quiet protest such as the distribution of leaflets – as was the case in France? Was armed resistance off-limits in 1940?

Would it have regarded the German invasion forces as simply fellow workers in uniform – with whom their British counterparts should fraternize?

Leon Trotsky and many of his supporters similarly regarded World War II as a repeat of the Great War when nationalism ruled the roost and workers died in their millions in the mud of Flanders. There was a deep belief, particularly within the British labour movement that this should not be allowed to happen again. The rival imperialists of 1940, it was argued, were no better than their forebears of 1914. There was little to choose between the Axis and the Allies, between Hitler and Churchill. Why die for the cause of capitalism?

Perhaps the adversaries would fight themselves to a standstill. Perhaps a strengthened Red Army would then move into the vacuum and liberate the European masses. Perhaps the military would mutiny anyway as the war dragged on as the French did in 1917.

The unexpected, swift fall of France, however, was unsettling and changed the possible shape of things to come. Even so, time was being bought, it was argued, so that the USSR could arm itself if Hitler did decide to invade.

In contrast, the ideological purity of the Trotskyists demanded an adherence to theory. Unlike the Stalinists, they were not weighed down by the burden of state responsibilities. If the reality of 1940 did not match the theory, then reality had to be changed through making the masses aware. The conflict had to be brought to an end by workers overthrowing the regimes that had sent them to fight their brothers. Class solidarity was thicker than national allegiance.

What would have happened if the Nazis had come for the Jews in Britain in 1940? Was their fate ultimately inconsequential in the greater scheme of things? Was their sacrifice in the short term a sad necessity so that the USSR might survive? Would British Communists have remained inactive out of a rigid loyalty to the USSR and Stalin's pact with Hitler? On the other hand, would the anti-fascist inclinations of both Stalinists and Trotskyists have propelled them to save Jews?

What about anti-colonial movements which wished to rid their countries of the imperialist heel? On the basis of the enemy of my enemy is my friend, would it not make sense to make an approach for assistance to the Germans and the Italians? Suppose the IRA Chief of Staff, Sean Russell, had been successful in implementing a plan for a republican uprising in northern Ireland in preparation for a German invasion. Suppose Egyptian nationalist hopes had been realized by Rommel's conquest of Cairo. Suppose the Nazis had broken through Soviet defences and Chandra Bose had rallied Indian nationalists to oust the British from India. Suppose the Nazis had reached the Jews of Palestine.

Yet even in Palestine, there was a small group of Jewish Trotskyists, Brit Spartakus, who condemned the conflict and campaigned to halt the mobilization of the Jews of Palestine and their enlistment in the British war effort. Following the fall of France in the summer of 1940, Brit Spartakus appealed to newly arrived immigrants from Western Europe to reject the entreaties of Ben-Gurion, Weizmann and the leadership in Palestine.

> You did not save your lives from the hell of Dachau in order to die miserably in Egypt or Africa.[1]

The British like the Nazis, it was claimed, similarly oppressed 100 million people in their colonies. The British only fought for the interests of 'several thousand very wealthy families in the City of London'. The immigrants whether from 'Vienna or Berlin, Brno or Budapest' were asked to oppose mobilization and to establish a united front 'for jobs, free meal tickets, free housing, free medical assistance'.

Under Emergency Regulation 15B, the British in Palestine arrested and imprisoned political activists on charges of 'seditious conspiracy' in that they undermined the war effort. Both Avraham Stern, later of 'the Stern Gang' and Ygael Gluckstein, later known as Tony Cliff, the future mentor of Britain's Socialist Workers Party, were incarcerated at the beginning of the war.

Gluckstein and other members of Brit Spartakus analysed Lenin's example during World War I. Lenin noted the Easter Uprising in 1916 which took advantage of 'an imperialist bourgeois crisis like the war . . . which is only a minor crisis compared with the social revolution'.[2] What would Lenin have said about the war between the Nazis and the Allies? Would he have regarded the Jews, caught in-between, as expendable?

Stalinists in support of the Soviet Union, Trotskyists as exponents of revolutionary theory, colonial nationalists as ardent advocates of liberation movements, even revolutionary Marxists in Mandatory Palestine – therefore all had their own political interests. They consisted of philosemites, anti-Semites and the indifferent. The fate of the Jews was not at the top of their agenda.

In parallel, argued the Allies, the Jews would be saved, but only once the Nazis had been vanquished. The quicker the victory, the better for the Jews. Yet no British aircraft bombed the railway lines leading to Auschwitz. Neither did the Red Air Force when it was within striking distance. To be sure, there were bold declarations and dire warnings delivered to the Nazis by the Allies, but the exterminations continued and gathered apace. Some resigned themselves to the impending Jewish catastrophe. Others were indifferent to it. Communist and capitalist, Stalinist and Trotskyist, the colonized and the oppressed – not all, but many – accepted the abandonment of the Jews.

Despite the great victory over Nazism, the revelations of the death camps in the spring of 1945, profoundly shocked the surviving Jewish communities of the world. They turned to Zionism – hitherto a minority concern – with an abiding determination. The revelations of Belsen and Dachau convinced a majority of Jews that the European Left had failed them. This did not mean an automatic turn to the Right, but it made a distinction between a Jewish Left and a non-Jewish Left. It meant auto-emancipation and not emancipation by others.

The extermination of 6 million also led to a re-evaluation of what it meant to be Jewish. It raised the question of how to safeguard the Jewish future. Max Nordau's comments to the first Zionist Congress in Basle in 1897 were recalled.

> The philosophy of Rousseau and the encyclopaedists had led to a declaration of human rights. Then this declaration, the strict logic of men of the Great Revolution, deduced Jewish emancipation. They formulated a regular equation: Every man is born with certain rights; the Jews are human beings, consequently the Jews are born to all the rights of man. In this manner the emancipation of the Jews was pronounced, not through a fraternal feeling for the Jews, but because logic demanded it. Popular sentiment rebelled, but the philosophy of the Revolution decreed that principles

must be placed higher than sentiments. Allow me an expression which implies no ingratitude. The men of 1792 emancipated us only for the sake of principle.[3]

In 1945, it was clear to many that the political theories which guaranteed the future construction of heaven right here on earth did not reflect the reality of Auschwitz. By 1948, the rise of a Hebrew republic in the Land of Israel thus became a cause célèbre for many on the social democratic Left, for those who had fought fascism. For European Communists, the Soviet volte-face in early 1947 in support of a two-state solution allowed them to argue that a Hebrew-speaking people had emerged in Mandatory Palestine which satisfied Leninist norms of nationality. The Trotskyists, as good internationalists, could not deny the passage of survivors from the DP camps to build socialism in Palestine, but they also argued that it would be better if Jews emigrated to other countries instead.

The occult power of political messianism

Stalin's last years were ones which were pervaded by Jewish conspiracies and Zionist plots. The first show trial in Hungary of László Rajk in 1949 was also the first in which 'international Zionism' was invoked for crimes committed. Three out of the six of Rajk's six co-defendants were Jews. Local Communists in Western Europe parroted the official explanations. It was a principled anti-Zionism, it was stated, a stand which should not be confused with anti-Semitism. There was similarly never any doubt about Rudolf Slansky's guilt in Czechoslovakia or that a group of mainly Jewish doctors had been accused of poisoning Stalin's comrades-in-arms. The French Stalinist academic, Maxime Rodinson ardently attacked those who asked difficult questions during the period in which the Doctors' Plot was unfolding. He later related how difficult it was to come to terms with the reality that his ideological opponents including the Zionists had actually been right in their accusations – and he had been wrong.

> For the most part, however, the deeper reason is the delay in registering disillusionment is simply the visceral need not to renounce a commitment that has illuminated one's life, given it meaning, and for which many sacrifices have often been made. Hence the reluctance to recognize the most obvious facts, the desperate para-logical guile to which one resorts in an effort to avoid the required conclusions, the passionate and obstinate blindness with which the idea of any change is rejected, the refusal even to examine any document, any argument, that could imperil the delicate balance one has achieved in one's inner being.[4]

Jews like Rodinson had begun to desert the Communist parties in Europe since the Molotov-Ribbentrop pact in 1939. To this was added the invasion of Hungary in 1956, the expulsion of the remnant of Polish Jewry after 1967 and the crushing of the Prague Spring in 1968. In January 1953, an Israeli friend wrote an open letter to his friend 'Max', a Jewish Communist in Britain.

> This is what 20 years of devoted service to revolutionary socialism has led to: a regime in which wives are terrorized into demanding the deaths of their husbands and children the deaths of their fathers; a regime which in pursuit of its political and military strategy, deliberately releases one of the foulest forms of mass psychosis against your own people.

> Are you prepared, like some of the revolutionaries of a generation ago, to see Jewish blood used to grease the wheels of the Revolution? Do you really believe that, if by some extraordinary combination of events, a Communist regime were to be victorious in the United Kingdom, you yourself would escape the fate of Slansky and the rest?

> Every Jewish Communist who remains in the party today adds his grain of weight to the consideration which will influence the Kremlin to continue on the course on which it has embarked. Every Jewish Communist who leaves the party will be doing his little bit towards saving Jewish lives. You cannot escape your personal share of responsibility at this moment. Think it over, Max. Think it over.[5]

Arthur Koestler compared his time in the Communist Party to the deception practised on the patriarch Jacob in sleeping with 'the ugly Leah' rather than the lovely Rachel. He subsequently remarked that the USSR was not a socialist country. 'So let us bear in mind that "East is east" and "Left is left" and if the twain sometimes still meet, the meeting is purely coincidental'.[6]

For many Jews, 'the occult power of political messianism' had lost its potency.[7] Yet Marxism, Communism, Trotskyism – socialism and social democracy – had always exhibited a magnetic attraction for Jews. Perhaps at the root of this was a desire to repair and perfect the world, consciously and subconsciously in accordance with both Judaic teachings and Jewish experience. A desire to imitate the prophets who rebelled rather than the kings who ruled.

Yet the European Left ever since the French Revolution had preferred its Jews to be assimilated and acculturated rather than separated by national self-definition. As Clermont–Tonnerre famously exclaimed in 1789: 'We must refuse everything to the Jews as a nation and accord everything to Jews as individuals'.

Indeed not all liberals favoured looked with favour upon the Jews. Thus the Rumanian statesman, Ion Brătianu, the follower of Mazzini and Garibaldi, promulgated anti-Jewish legislation before World War I.[8]

Yet the opening up of the ghettos and the emancipation of the Jews in the wake of the Revolution allowed Jews to become members of the societies in which they lived.

Marxist Jews were heavily involved in three movements which were all founded at virtually the same point in history – the Russian Social Democratic Labour Party, the Bund and the World Zionist Organization. The latter two were specifically Jewish movements while the Russian party tended to cater for Russified Jews. Yet at Lenin's behest, it was these non-Jewish Jews who purported to speak for Jewish workers against the Bund's delegates at the London conference in 1903 which also gave birth to the Bolsheviks.

In part, the Jewish question was used by Lenin to transform the party and shape it according to his ideological wishes. In part, it was a reflection of Lenin's faulty understanding of the situation in which the Jewish masses found themselves in at the turn of the century. Lenin repeated the error of his predecessors in trying to bend the Jewish reality to fit political theory.

Yet the tradition of Jewish involvement in the European Left was a long and honourable one. While non-Jewish Jews were at the forefront of revolutionary uprisings after the end of World War I, many former Zionists and Bundists flowed into the ranks of the Soviet Communist Party and then proceeded to act with a vindictive zeal against their former comrades. This came as a revelation to Lenin and many non-Jewish Bolshevik leaders.

While the Shoah, the rise of Israel and Stalin's misdeeds persuaded many Jews that only Zionism had passed the political and survivalist test, the belief remained among a miniscule minority that Zionism was impure ideologically and a dangerous distraction. Jews were natural internationalists and should devote their energies to class solidarity.

Yet this was often caught up in the politics of identity. Isaac Deutscher, the Marxist writer, pointed out that when Jewish intellectuals are placed at 'the concatenation of various cultures', they struggle. Moreover, the alignment of a majority of Jews with Israel after 1948 often proved to be the stage upon which such questions of identity were played out. Even as late as the twenty-first century, national identity and nationalism was problematic for some Jews.

> Blackmail on the grounds of community solidarity, in order to legitimate the politics of national unity of Israeli governments, is also intolerable to us . . . it is not in spite of being Jewish that we oppose this suicidal logic of identity-based panic. We reject the deadly spiral of ethnicization of the conflict and its transformation into a war of religions. We refuse to be nailed to the wall of communal identity.[9]

The desire to be 'just Jewish', non-institutionalized, non-communal, non-religious and distant from the bourgeois lifestyle of their parents sometimes governed attitudes towards Israel. In response, there were often emotional accusations of 'jüdischer Selbsthass' (Jewish self-hatred) which polarized relations even further.

Deutscher projected himself as a non-Jewish Jew. He had left the closeted world of his Polish yeshiva for the attraction of world revolution. Deutscher never forgot his background. Even though an admirer of Trotsky, he occasionally recalled his puzzlement at the midrashic story of Elisha ben Abuya and his close friend, Rabbi Meir Baal Hanas. Ben Abuya was the classic heretic in Talmudic literature such that he was known as 'akher' – the other. While his actual misdemeanours were never revealed, he was at pains to warn his close friend, Rabbi Meir not to transgress the Sabbath when he was unwittingly in danger of doing so. Why did Elisha do this if he was the advocate of heresy? Why did Rabbi Meir maintain his friendship with Elisha when the entire Jewish community had deserted him? Such questions perplexed Deutscher who identified with ben Abuya and regarded him as the model for contemporary Jewish revolutionaries such as Rosa Luxemburg and Leon Trotsky. Yet this story and its mystery did point to the convoluted issues that faced non-Jewish Jews who had travelled outside the community yet culturally remained within. Indeed if God was the universal god, then how could he be solely the god of the Jews? Such issues of national identity and internationalism affected many Jews on the European Left who were often marooned between identities.

Some argued that they had found a place for Jewishness within socialism. The socialist intellectual, Ralph Miliband, exclaimed that his kind of socialism did not exclude Jewishness, but his kind of Jewishness did exclude that sort of Jewishness which regarded all non-Jews as enemies.

Although Deutscher welcomed the existence of the state of Israel, he regarded the nation-state as an anachronism. In a lecture in Jewish Book Week in February 1958, he pleaded with his audience 'Do you not see this yet?' Many Jews did not.

The Zionists argued that the existence of Israel has increased the sense of security among European Jews. Anti-Zionists argued the exact opposite – that Israel was in reality a source of insecurity since it was a source of contemporary misfortune, accompanied by an awakening of the anti-Semitic monster.

Leninism and Palestinian nationalism

A central contribution of Leninism to twentieth-century debate was to fuse 'the national democratic revolutionary process in the colonies with the project for socialist revolution in the advanced countries. They were two sides of the same war for the overthrow of international finance capitalism'.[10] The global nature of capitalism defined its international opposition. It was, however, the bloodletting of World War I which had, according to Lenin, demonstrated capitalism's need to survive through the exploitation of colonies. It also discredited the very nature of the nation-state – at a time when the Zionists called for one in Palestine.

By 1947, it was clear that the defeat of Nazism had not been accompanied by workers' uprisings in Western Europe as many Marxists had predicted, but instead it had ushered in an epoch of national liberation movements which were struggling for independence against their colonial masters. Indeed the ousting of the British was certainly a factor behind Soviet support for a two solution in Palestine in 1947. But Palestine was a special case. It did not fit the theoretical template since there were two national movements fighting the British – and then each other – for the same land. The Zionist Jews had won that struggle by early 1949 and the Palestinian Arabs had lost it.

The non-aligned movement in the 1950s was forced to choose between the two national movements. It could choose Israel, but it would lose the participation of the Arab world. It therefore did not do so. The rise of Palestinian nationalism in the 1960s further persuaded many that the cause of the Palestinians fitted much better into their worldview than did the Israelis. The narrative of Israel as a colonial settler state was easier to absorb than the unique complexity of the conflict.

This related to the writing of the history of 1948. It was easier to accept those historians who endorsed the Palestinian narrative. New historians such as Benny Morris who burst the bubble of both the official Israeli and Palestinian versions of 1948 were deemed unsafe. Significantly the first attack on Trotsky in 1925 by European Communist parties was a pamphlet entitled *How One Should Not Write the History of October*, with contributions by Stalin, Zinoviev and Kamenev. The past must always be controlled to meet the political exigencies of the present.

A New European Left arose in the 1960s which had never fought fascism nor lived through the establishment of Israel. It became the standard bearer of anti-colonialism and anti-imperialism. Its world outlook was fundamentally different from that of its fathers. Its causes were Algeria, Vietnam, South Africa – and eventually Palestine. All this was set in motion before the advent of the settlement drive on the West Bank and before the election of a succession of right wing governments in Israel.

Moreover, the relationship between colonialism and Zionism was never straightforward. Although it cast itself in an anti-colonialist mode, and Marxist Zionism advocated colonization without colonialism, the similarity to other models of colonialism lingered. The rise of Zionism also coincided with the ascendency of European colonialism and the expansion of empire. In a reductionist fashion, the New Left extrapolated its experience of the anti-colonialist struggle in the 1960s to the Zionist experiment of the past.

There was also an evolution of selective outrage in which some causes such as that of Chinese dissidents were glossed over since any protest would mean alignment with the imperialist camp. It was easier to react to the reactionaries than to react to the issue. Israel was therefore a soft target. Sartre detected such selectivity long ago when the Suez campaign occurred in the same year as the Soviet invasion of Hungary.

> You say the war in Algeria should be our first, our constant, worry: that is true. But the (Communist) Party reciprocates the politeness of the Right; the Right served the Party by its violence, the Party serves the Right by its pious lies: by what right should one who finds it natural for Russian soldiers to fire on Hungarian workers grow indignant when French soldiers fire on Arab peasants?[11]

There were coherent, rational arguments that modern Israel had taken a different path from the one mapped out by the dreams and aspirations of 1948. Israel had certainly changed, but the far Left in Europe had also changed dramatically. The resurrection of independent Marxist thought, mainly as a result of the student revolts in 1968, also brought in its train a second coming of Leninist practices and premises – the absence of democratic debate, the elitism of the revolutionary vanguard, the principle of revolutionary defeatism, the substitution of openness by subterfuge. This was most pronounced in the various Trotskyist groups that arose whose zeal for a return to the ideological purity of the pre-Stalinist world was unsurpassed. Unlike the increasingly pragmatic official Communist parties which had absorbed the lessons of blindly following Stalinist dictates from the Kremlin, the Trotskyists found it difficult to either brook different opinions or to accept political compromises. For both the far Left and for the state of Israel, the world had moved on.

There was also, as Robert Fine has pointed out, a transference of Europe's past misdemeanours – its racism, its violence, its colonialism – onto 'Israel' and 'Zionism'. Not Israel as a society or Zionism as an ideology, but 'as vessels into which Europe can project all that is violent in its own past and present, and to preserve the good for itself'.[12] This desire to purge the legacy of the past was felt most strongly by the European Left which saw itself as the standard bearer of anti-colonialism historically.

By the beginning of the twenty-first century, the European Left had generally become firm advocates for the Palestinian cause. In very broad terms, social democrats and socialists favoured a two-state solution while the far Left often advanced the notion of a one-state solution or a dezionized Israel. The far Left utilized the promotion of liberal ideals to attract political sympathy for the Palestinians, yet was firmly against 'the middle ground'. There was no acceptance of a compromise which many a social democrat proposed. In Leninist fashion, polarization took precedence. 'In one camp flew the flags of darkness and oppression and in the other the banners of light and freedom'.[13] The far Left shuddered at the thought of gradualism and conciliation. It preferred confrontation.

Many European left wing intellectuals, almost by definition, realized that the Israel-Palestine imbroglio was complex, not simple. In the 1960s, both Sartre and Michel Foucault refused to renounce their identification with Israel. Critics of Israeli policy in the West Bank and Gaza such as Jacques Derrida, Pierre Bourdieu, Etienne Balibar and Slavoj Zizek also believed that Israel had a right to exist as a sovereign state.[14]

The twenty-first-century Jewish problem

Israel was certainly a problem for the post-colonial reading of history.[15] Zionism was problematic since it did not slide easily into the colonial framework, reserved for it. The Zionists, for example, were unlike the white settlers in Kenya who wanted to replicate the mother country in Africa. The Zionists instead wished to create something completely different, a society which was the polar opposite of those into which they had been born.

Zionism was consequently reduced to being merely an offshoot of European imperial greed which was directed at exploiting the Middle East.

Edward Said certainly crystallized broadly held Arab perceptions of Zionism through the orientalist prism, but it did not explain the conflict. In addition, in his later years, he found it difficult to understand 'otherness' where Jews were concerned. 'Otherness' merged into Orientalism. Regardless of how they actually thought of themselves, the Jews were thus never considered to be a people, only as religious congregants. For George Antonius in his classic *The Arab Awakening*, Judaism existed but not the Jewish people per se.[16] Moreover, for many Arab nationalists, the conflict was strictly a zero-sum game whereby past proposals for partition or even a bi-national state were rejected. The Israeli Left and the Israeli Right were seen as one and the same. All this struck a chord with the European far Left which similarly dispensed with the wishy-washy nature of compromise in favour of a pristine absolutism.

Moreover, many European non-Jews resisted the temptation to stand up for either Israel or Palestine, but tended instead to support the peace camps in both Israel and Palestine against their rejectionists. Many opposed the very idea of polarization and the destruction of the middle ground. It also meant opposing boycotts of Israeli academics and criticizing the anti-normalization campaign which arose after the Rabin-Arafat handshake. They may not have approved of Israeli government policy in Gaza or Lebanon, but it did not mean that they were opposed to dialogue and negotiation.

The task of the far Left was therefore to utilize the frustration at the stagnation of the political process in the Middle East to win over adherents to its camp. Its few Jewish members subsequently discovered their ethnic voice and proclaimed their opposition 'as a Jew' to Israel per se.

All this is not new. This saga has been ongoing for well over a century and will rage unabated in the absence of peace between Israelis and Palestinians. On one level, it is fuelled by a broad desire to make the Jews conform to a specific interpretation of history as well as anger at stubborn Jewish resistance to this proposition. On another level, it is perceived as a struggle for the Jewish soul, of the Jewish outsiders against the communal establishment, of the few against the many. Above all, it pitches belief in a golden future against the lessons of the Jewish past.

While many European Jews remain idealists without illusions, there is a great reticence to believe in the construction of utopia without guarantees. The very idea of absolute obedience to an ideology has become obsolete. As the widow of one of the executed Jewish defendants of the Slansky trial in Stalinist Czechoslovakia in 1952, remembered: 'Communism was the eternal ideal of humanity, we could not doubt the ideal, only ourselves'. [17] Most Jews have now shaken off such subservience in favour of national interests.

The cry now is that the salvation of the world should also include the Jews. This plea had been expounded even before the Nazi rise to power in Germany:

> We, too, are an integral part of the world and our fate is as important and as sacred as the fate of all the other nations of the world. [18]

Some Jews do not instinctly accept this. Some prefer the path of transcending Jewishness. Others place it far down on the ladder of global priorities. But a majority today do believe that the Jews have a right to national self-determination in Israel even if they do not care for the policies of an Israeli government. The twentieth-century backwash from the utopian imagination therefore does not enthuse most twenty-first-century Jews. Although they may believe – in the broadest, often non-religious interpretation – in the coming of the messiah, they are equally perturbed by the prospect of his actual arrival. Perhaps this is the fundamental difference between most Jews who identify with Israel today and the European far Left who believe that its very existence is an obstacle in the path of universal redemption.

Notes and Works Cited

1 'An Den Einwanderer Aus Westeuropa!', Spartakusbund leaflet, 25 July 1940, Hagana archives, Tel Aviv.

2 V. I. Lenin, 'A Caricature of Marxism', *Selected Works*, vol. 19 (New York 1942), pp. 246–7.

3 Max Nordau, 'Speech to the First Zionist Congress', *The New Palestine*, 26 January 1923.

4 Maxime Rodinson, *Cult, Ghetto and State* (London 1983), p. 33.

5 Moshe Ben-Natan, 'Letter to a Jewish Communist', *Jewish Vanguard*, 30 January 1953.

6 Arthur Koestler, *The Trail of the Dinosaur* (New York 1955), p. 48.

7 Mark Lilla, Obituary of Daniel Bell, *New York Review of Books*, 7 April 2011.

8 Walter Laqueur, *The History of Zionism* (London 2003), p. 442.

9 Manifesto of a group of intellectuals of Jewish origin, *Le Monde*, 19 October 2000.

10 Neil Harding, *Leninism* (London 1996), p. 209.

11 Jean-Paul Sartre, *The Spectre of Stalin* (London 1969), p. 94. This was first published in *Les Temps modernes* in November, December 1956, January 1957.

12 Robert Fine, 'Fighting with Phantoms: A Contribution to the Debate on Anti-Semitism in Europe', *Patterns of Prejudice*, vol. 43, no. 5, 2009.

13 Harding, op. cit., p. 270.

14 Joseph Massad, 'The Legacy of Jean-Paul Sartre', *Al-Ahram*, online, 30 January–5 February 2003.

15 Avi Bareli, 'Forgetting Europe: Perspectives on the Debate about Zionism and Colonialism', *Journal of Israeli History*, vol. 20, no. 2/3 Summer/Autumn 2001; Arnon Golan, 'European Imperialism and the Development of Modern Palestine: Was Zionism a Form of Colonialism?', *Space and Polity*, vol. 5, no. 2, 2001.

16 S. Ilan Troen, 'De-Judaising the Homeland: Academic Politics in Rewriting the History of Palestine', *Israel Affairs*, vol. 13, no. 4, October 2007.

17 Heda Margolius Kovaly, *Prague Farewell: A Life in Czechoslovakia 1941–1968* (London 1988), p. 76.

18 Vladimir Jabotinsky, 'Zion and Communism', *Jewish Tribune*, December 1932.

1

The revolution and the Jewish question

The legacy of reform

Vladimir Ilyich Lenin came of political age in an epoch when Jews in the Tsarist Empire were allowed to enter the portals of higher education. The accession of Alexander II in 1855 initiated the opening up of universities to yeshiva (seminary) and gymnasia students. Indeed, the number of Jewish boys in secondary schools increased from 1.25% in 1853 to 13.2% in 1873.[1] The discriminatory barriers of the Pale of Settlement were lowered to allow Jews to cross them and pursue professional careers. Tsarist policies had also induced an urbanization of the Jews. Thus by the end of the nineteenth century, half the population of urban centres in Belarus and Lithuania was Jewish. Jews accounted for 65% of the population of Brest-Litovsk.[2] 51% of the inhabitants of Minsk were Yiddish speakers.[3] Even secondary schools saw the number of Jewish pupils increase dramatically.[4] This often provided the opportunity, not merely for Jews to escape the world of yesterday, but also to transcend their Jewishness in favour of a new identity without borders. It allowed some to move from faith in religion to faith in revolution, from the ghetto to universalism.

Unlike a majority of Jews, Vladimir Ulyanov (Lenin), a hereditary noble,[5] came from a privileged background whose immediate forbears had been middle-class professionals. His family in Simbirsk had long guarded a treasured social status in the local community. Despite this, before he had reached the age of maturity, his close family began to tragically disintegrate before his eyes. His father died of a brain haemorrhage in his early fifties. His brother, a student at the University of St. Petersburg, was hanged for plotting to assassinate Tsar Alexander III – an attempt to repeat the killing of Alexander II by the *Narodnaya Volia* in 1881. Renouncing his Christian beliefs, Lenin entered Kazan University to embark upon studies in law and to follow a well-trodden professional career path. Like other institutes of higher education, the universities were foci of intellectual turmoil and political determination in the 1880s and their students characterized by a desire to resist at all costs the heavy hand of autocracy. Kazan was a new world for Lenin. It held an honoured place in Russian imperial history since it was here that Ivan the Terrible defeated the Tartars in his push to expand eastwards. Kazan was a location where Christianity met Islam, where Tsarist imperialism met anti-colonial resistance.

Following a student demonstration for university reform, Lenin was expelled after only one year at the institution. The university refused to relent and grant him readmission and the Tsarist authorities subsequently refused to allow him to leave Russia to study abroad. This enforced interruption in his education created an intellectual space for Lenin to read Marx and Engels, Darwin and Buckle and to educate himself politically. At university, he had discovered the writings of Nikolai Chernyshevski – and in particular his novel, *What is to be Done?* This had been one of his dead brother's favourite works. It had already become required reading for any young person with a social conscience. The book and the example of its long-suffering author – in prison and internal exile for 27 years before being allowed to return to Saratov to die – became a source of inspiration for radicalizing youth with its emphasis on revolutionary discipline and ascetic puritanism. Chernyshevski rejected any suggestion of moderate reform and regarded evolutionary change as ineffective and ineffectual – a process which would eventually compromise and corrupt the reformer. Indeed *What is to be Done?* was written as a riposte to Turgenev's hopeful *Fathers and Sons*. Bakunin, Fourier and Robert Owen all influenced Chernyshevski's political philosophy as did Charles Dickens' *Hard Times* – a social commentary on early Victorian London. Chernyshevski's vision was both utopian and christological in that the truly dedicated could construct heaven right here on earth. It exuded a moral certainty. It bestowed upon a self-sacrificing elite the onerous task of shaping society in accordance with its own world outlook. Such beliefs contained 'the potential for authoritarianism as well as for liberation'.[6] Class rather than nation was the designated framework of revolutionary activity. In Switzerland many years later, Lenin commented that he regarded Chernyshevski as the greatest representative of socialism before Marx.

> I really undertook to read it and I sat over it not for several days but for several weeks. Only then did I understand its depth . . . it is a thing that supplies energy for a whole lifetime.[7]

Lenin eventually managed to reverse the restrictions placed upon him and he continued with his law studies, securing a degree at the University of St. Petersburg. His subsequent work as an affluent assistant barrister, however, took second place to his passion for revolutionary change. Even the ban on travel abroad was lifted and in 1895 Lenin embarked enthusiastically on a tour of European capitals where he met Marxist émigrés such as Georgi Plekhanov. Lenin's political views hardened as he grew older and more experienced in the ways of the world. He appreciated scholarship, intellectual discourse and the scientific nature of Marxism. Theory was all-important.

The reforms of Alexander II opened the way for those who wished to gain access to higher education. The educated elite expanded tremendously from a base of 20,000 in 1860 out of a total population of 74 million,[8] but this also created a crisis of identity.[9] Inspired by Western European norms, the newly enlightened were repelled both by the political inertia of the reactionary Tsarist state and by the depth of ignorance of the masses. Education had, in effect, been an alienating force. For the Jews who were able to gain access to higher education at this time, there was a further ingredient – a desire to escape the narrowness both of the shtetl and often Jewishness per se. For both Jew and non-Jew, revolutionary endeavour and the burning desire to repair the world became their new intellectual home and their means of self-definition. Chernyshevski appealed to those who gradually became disappointed with Alexander's reforms – those who argued that he had not gone far enough. Even the liberation of the serfs was seen as half-hearted. It was this polarized part of the intelligentsia that embraced revolutionary activity and renounced political reform.

Given this ideological milieu, the middle-class Lenin inevitably became acquainted with numerous déclassé Jewish revolutionaries who had made a conscious effort to leave their origins behind. In Switzerland, he stayed with Pavel Axelrod. Axelrod symbolized the intellectual, assimilated Jew that Lenin warmed to.

Alexander II's reforms had permitted a flowering of Jewish culture and a plethora of new periodicals. The choice of a linguistic vehicle for these new ventures was divided between Russian, Yiddish and a newly reclaimed Hebrew. The ideal for the Russifiers was that the Tsar's Jews would resemble their French brothers – Jews imbued and moulded by the values of the French Revolution. Indeed reformers had argued in the 1850s that Jews should not separate themselves from their Russian brothers and sisters and in this vein proposed the abolition of the Pale of Settlement. Educated Jews, they suggested, should assist in this process of integration and acculturation. Many Russian Jews accepted the rationale of this approach. Yiddish was to be discarded as a jargon, 'incapable of express-ing sublime thoughts . . . to cast off these old rags, a heritage of the dark Middle Ages'.[10] Yet occasionally reality intervened. The pogrom in Odessa in 1871 – and the often skewered press coverage of the events caused some Jewish intellectuals who had embarked on this path to stop and reconsider.[11]

Pavel Axelrod was caught up in this intellectual turmoil. Unlike Lenin, he came from a poor workers' household. His parents were beggars who lived in the Jewish poorhouse.[12] He had turned away from Orthodox Judaism to embrace a concern for the impoverished Jewish masses. By 1872, having read Herbert Spencer's *Basic Principles* and an anthology of Ferdinand Lassalle's writings, he remarked that he felt that it was simply too shameful to concern himself solely with the Jews:

> What significance, it seemed to me, could the interests of a handful of Jews have in comparison with the 'idea of the working class' and the all-embracing, universal interests of socialism. After all, strictly speaking, the Jewish question does not exist. There is only the question of the liberation of the working masses of all nations, including the Jewish. Together with the approaching triumph of socialism the so-called Jewish question will be resolved as well.[13]

Axelrod soon became an adherent of Bakunin. He then embraced the populist *Chernyi Peredel* before finding Marxism in the *Group for the Emancipation of Labour* in 1883. Although he made an encompassing attempt to divest him-self practically of his Jewish background, there were occasional emotional outbursts at the silence of his comrades when Jews were attacked. For example, the Dreyfus affair and the subsequent trial of Emile Zola moved him. He was unable to understand why the French labour movement remained indifferent to Zola's plight. The Beilis trial in 1913 was another example. Yet Axelrod throughout his life – like many other Jews committed to the cause of revolution – suppressed any public sentiment for the Jews. This struggle within him was most pertinently demonstrated following the assassination of Alexander II in 1881.

1881 and the Jews

The blame for the killing of the Tsar was laid at the doorstep of the Jews and manifested itself in the subsequent outbreak of pogroms in Elizavetgrad and Kiev, followed by the highly discriminatory May Laws. This confirmed for all Jews in the revolutionary movement that the Tsarist regime had to be overthrown. The widespread unrest provoked profound discussions about the way forward to a liberated Russia. A minority of Jews asked a further question – why had the movement remained silent when Jews were being assaulted and murdered by the mob?

Many Russian populists of both the *Narodnaya Volya* and the *Chernyi Peredel* perceived the pogroms as a true expression of revolutionary ardour and that this outbreak of violence, if directed towards the authorities rather than the Jews, would be the blue-touch paper for social revolution. Encouraging the peasants to evict their landlords and appropriate their land resonated with Bakunin's ideas of social anarchism and a classless, stateless society. Yet the Jews were regularly perceived by the masses as Christ killers and parasitical manipulators. The imagery of the Jew-kulak exploiting the people was a historical stereotype which the populists were eager to use – albeit covertly – to further the cause. One Ukrainian Narodnik leader, Gerasim Romanenko, issued an openly anti-Semitic manifesto, probably on his own volition.

> Who has seized the land, the woodlands, the taverns? The Yids. Whom does the peasant beg with tears in his eyes to let him near his land? The Yids. Wherever you look, whatever you touch, everywhere the Yids. The Yid curses the peasant, cheats him, drinks his blood. The Yids make life unbearable.[14]

Yet despite their opposition to the pogroms and to anti-Semitism generally, Romanenko's comrades in the movement in Russia and sympathizers abroad remained silent. They feared that the intensity of Romanenko's charges truly reflected the fury of the masses. They reasoned that any condemnation of anti-Semitism and support for the Jews could prove counter-productive – and thereby retard the cause of change.

For many Russian Jews, the situation was more than theoretical. The Hebrew writer, Moshe Leib Lilienblum, like Lenin an admirer of Chernyshevski, committed the following entry to his diary on 5 May 1881:

> The situation is terrible and frightening! We are virtually under siege. The courtyards are barred up and we keep peering through the grillwork of the court gates to see if the mob is coming to swoop down on us. All the furniture is stored in the cellars, we all sleep in our clothes and without any bedding . . . so that if we are attacked we will immediately be able to take the small children who also sleep in their clothes and flee. But will they let us flee? What does the future have in store for us? Will they have mercy on the youngsters – who don't even know that they are Jews, that they are wretches – and not harm them? Terrible, terrible. How long, O God of Israel?[15]

Yet Axelrod had warned the *Chernyi Peredel* about the dangers of idolizing the masses and the moral pitfall of exploiting a popular outburst well before the 1881 pogroms.[16] In an article in December 1881, he further argued that it had been discreditable to allow a campaign against an entire people to have been waged in which tens of thousands of proletarians had been ruined.[17]

While the Populists wished to retain their access to the masses, there was still a competing desire to work among the Jewish workers. This was particularly important to Jewish revolutionaries who hoped to acquire the loyalty of their kinsfolk. In addition there was almost a competition between the Tsarist authorities and the Jewish Populists for the soul of the Jewish community. Indeed Alexander III had cynically told a delegation of *shtadlanim* (unelected Jewish leaders) that the pogroms were due to 'anarchists'. The unsaid implication was that the involvement of Jews in revolutionary activity was a slur on the good name of the Jewish community in the eyes of the Russian people and its rulers. This was an accusation which the communal leadership wished to avoid at any cost. Indeed officially inspired pronouncements later equated Jews with revolutionaries. After all, the government could point to the fact that the number of Jewish defendants sentenced in trials for *Narodnaya Volia* actions between 1880 and 1890 was a disproportionate 17%.[18]

It was also clear on a number of occasions that the intervention of Jewish members of both the *Narodnaya Volia* and the *Chernyi Peredel* had successfully prevented Jewish workers from turning away from the cause of revolution. Even so, this privately provoked fundamental questions for many a Jewish revolutionary. Why compromise with anti-Semites and reactionaries? Why should the Jews once again be offered up as history's sacrificial lamb? Why should socialism be built with the blood of the Jews? The response that it ultimately served a higher cause and the tragic ongoing fate of the Jews would be solved through the eventual transformation of society began to ring hollow. Yet this co-existed with a belief in a perfect future overcoming the certainty of the tragic present. This conflict of loyalties affected probably all Jewish revolutionaries, regardless of their initial indifference to the pogroms. How they dealt with this inner turmoil varied from one individual to another. Some indeed believed that 'the anti-Semitic massacres to be a good omen'.[19] Others awakened to their Jewish past.

The pogroms of 1881 brought to the surface the turbulence in Axelrod's attempt to universalize his identity. Axelrod discussed with his colleagues the possibility of issuing a pamphlet that would confront the favourable, selective approach to the pogromists, taken in the revolutionary press. Axelrod approached seminal figures in the revolutionary movement for their opinion. Plekhanov was preoccupied with other work and Lavrov felt unqualified to contribute. Axelrod's inner turmoil propelled him to prepare the pamphlet himself which condemned anti-Semitism and the pogroms. It soon became clear that the executive committee of the *Narodnaya Volia* was not interested in publishing the work. Plekhanov therefore promised to publish the pamphlet in the name of a 'Group of Socialist Revolutionaries' under his own signature and those of other eminent figures in the movement.[20] Moreover Axelrod strenuously promoted the Jewish working class and argued that it should be defended against their persecutors. He drew attention to the state of mind of many shocked Jewish revolutionaries who had begun to realize that the path to acculturation and perhaps assimilation was not smooth. Axelrod wrote:

> The Jewish socialist intelligentsia suddenly realised that the majority of Russian society did, as a matter of fact, regard the Jews as a separate nation, and that they considered all Jews – a pious Jewish worker, a petit bourgeois, a money-lender, an assimilated lawyer, a socialist prepared for prison or deportation – Yids harmful to Russia, whom Russia should get rid of by any and all means.[21]

Although he was not a Zionist, Axelrod even argued that the idea of emigration to Palestine should not be dismissed. This antagonized his fellow Jewish populist, Lev Deich, who countered that this would tar the pamphlet with a nationalist veneer. Deich argued that it would be better for Russia's Jews to leave for the United States where they would disappear due to assimilation. Axelrod's initial enthusiasm was further diminished by other interventions. In response to an approach from Axelrod, the French anarchist, Elisée Réclus, argued that emigration to Palestine would not change the situation of the Jews and that it would still be dependent on others. Moreover there would be a clash with the indigenous Arabs. Pyotr Lavrov further warned against alienating the masses. In the end, even though he disagreed with Lavrov, Axelrod fell back into a revolutionary stasis and the pamphlet was never published. Despite the sore of moral ambiguity, the comfort of the revolutionary home was too seductive. While 'political expediency and ideological abstractions'[22] won the day, it was clear to many a Jewish revolutionary that a hitherto unquestioning faith in the Russian revolutionary tradition had been challenged. Subconsciously, it was no longer total.

Both Axelrod and Deich remained with the revolutionary movement. Their comrade in the preparation of the pamphlet, Grigorii Gurevich, turned towards Jewish affairs and Zionist territorialism. The rediscovery of Jewishness sometimes led to an embrace of Zionism. Axelrod's father-in-law, Isaac Kaminer joined Hibbat Zion and wrote poems of penitence after the pogroms. Even for those active in Jewish intellectual life before 1881, there was an ideological shift. Russifiers such as Leon Pinsker renounced the ideology of a lifetime and he too embraced Zionism. For all, it meant a new political beginning and not a return to their former selves as Jews, but to a new understanding of their Jewish identity. There was also a sense of 'ourselves alone'. Progressive humankind had failed in their eyes, to help the Jews in their hour of need. They were only called upon to sacrifice themselves on the altar of revolution or to disappear through assimilation. It was for this reason that Pinsker called his Zionist pamphlet *Autoemancipation*.

One of the reactions to the pogroms was the establishment of BILU which sought to organize young Russian Jews to become pioneers in Palestine. The initials of BILU were taken from the Book of Isaiah and stood for *Beit Ya'akov Lekhu ve-Nelkah* – 'O House of Jacob, let us rise up and go.'[23]

Chaim Hisin, one of the first of the BILU immigrants wrote in his diary:

> The recent pogroms have violently awakened the complacent Jews from their sweet slumbers. Until now, I was uninterested in my origin. I saw myself as a faithful son of Russia which was to me my raison d'être and the very air that I breathed. Each new discovery by a Russian scientist, every classical literary work, every victory of the Russian Empire would fill my heart with pride. I wanted to devote my whole strength to the good of my homeland, and happily do my duty. Suddenly they come and show us the door and openly declare that we are free. How pathetic is the position of those who advocated fusion with the Russian people through national self-abnegation. Life and the logic of events demand that the Jew define his position, for it has become impossible to occupy a seat between two chairs. Either one openly declares oneself a renegade or one decides to share the sufferings of his people.[24]

Cultural nationalists such as Moses Leib Lilienblum who had left his faith behind in the yeshiva in Vilkomir embodied the spiritual and ideological journey towards Zionism which many others had similarly undertaken. In an article entitled *The Future of Our People* in 1883, Lilienblum eloquently described the hopelessness of the Jewish predicament and the sense of isolation and abandonment which many Russian Jews keenly felt:

> The opponents of nationalism see us as uncompromising nationalists, with a nationalist God and a nationalist Torah; the nationalists see us as cosmopolitans, whose homeland is wherever we happen to be well off. Religious gentiles say that we are devoid of any faith, and the freethinkers among them say that we are orthodox and believe in all kinds of nonsense; the liberals say we are conservative

and the conservatives call us liberal. Some bureaucrats and writers see us as the root of anarchy, insurrection and revolt, and the anarchists say we are capitalists, the bearers of the biblical civilisation, which is, in their view, based on slavery and parasitism. Officialdom accuses us of circumventing the laws of the land – that is, of course, the laws directed specifically against us. . . . Musicians like Richard Wagner charge us with destroying the beauty and purity of music. Even our merits are turned into shortcomings: 'Few Jews are murderers', they say, 'because Jews are cowards.' This, however, does not prevent them from accusing us of murdering Christian children.[25]

The rise of the Bund

Another cultural nationalist who moved to a Zionist position after 1881 was Alexander Tsederbaum, the founder of *Hamelitz*, the first Hebrew language periodical in Russia in 1860. Born in Russian Poland, he had, like many other Jews, migrated to Odessa in the mid-nineteenth century, attracted by the port's intellectual openness and its reputation as the hub of the *Haskala* (Jewish Enlightenment). Recognizing the tri-lingual character of the Jews, Tsederbaum founded Yiddish journals such as *Kol Mevasser* and *Yidishes Folksblat* and Russian newspapers such as *Vestnik Russkikh Yevreyev* and *Rasvet*. Following the events of 1881, he became a dedicated supporter of the Hibbat Zion, one of the earliest Zionist groups. Indeed Tsederbaum was elected deputy chairman of a network of Hibbat Zion societies at the first conference of Zionists in Katowice in October 1884 and was active in its Odessa committee. The Zionist philosopher and writer, Ahad Ha'am, would never have launched his literary career, had it not been for Tsederbaum.[26] His first essay *Lo zeh haderech* (This is not the way) was republished countless times after it first appeared in Tsederbaum's *Hamelitz* in 1889.

Tsederbaum's son, Osip, distant from his father's concerns, was a Russified intellectual with a cosmopolitan outlook. Yet the assimilated Tsederbaum household, fully expected an attack during the Odessa pogrom in May 1881. One brother was ready to use a revolver and Osip's wife had at her disposal a cauldron of boiling water. Although uninterested in Judaism, she categorically refused to allow the placing of Christian icons in the window frame as a means of deceiving the crowd. On this occasion, the Tsederbaums were fortunate since the mob's fury had been spent and they never reached their doorstep. In the years to come, their children were often the target of anti-Semitic jibes and taunts from teachers and pupils alike. This accentuated

Osip Tsederbaum's detestation of the regime. Unlike his father who had turned to Zionism, his home became a focus of Russian intellectual opposition to Tsarism. The all-pervading atmosphere for all seven Tsederbaum children was thereby coloured by the writings of the political philosophers of the French Revolution and the Russian Narodniki. All of Alexander Tsederbaum's grandchildren, their cousins in the wider family and their friends became supporters of revolutionary change in Russia. Four out of the seven children became professional revolutionaries.[27]

When Lenin returned from his European trip in 1895 to St. Petersburg, he struck a up a close friendship with an assimilated Jewish Marxist, Julius Martov – otherwise known as Iulii Osipovich Tsederbaum, the second of Osip's sons. Together they organized the St. Petersburg *Group for the Emancipation of Labour*.

Unlike Axelrod, Martov did not have to make a concerted effort to transcend his Jewishness. Yet the anti-Semitism which he had experienced during his youth and his grandfather's example always remained with him. When he was arrested as a teenager, his grandfather paid 300 roubles to bail him out of prison and tried to persuade him to emigrate to the United States. Martov refused, but ironically chose Vilna as his place of two years' exile to begin his life as a political activist. It was ironically also a centre of political activism for its Jewish workers.

Already by the 1870s, there had been attempts to organize Jewish workers on an international level. Vilna, known as 'the Jerusalem of Lithuania', was a great centre of Talmudic learning with its scholar rabbis and world renown yeshivot. Enlightenment values from Western Europe began, however, to pervade Vilna. The influence of the Berlin Haskala in particular caused many yeshiva students to transcend the world of Jewish learning and to make their way to Odessa's open society.

Aaron Liebermann in particular pioneered the idea of a Jewish workers' movement in Russia and Lithuania. He placed great emphasis on using Hebrew as a vehicle to reach the yeshiva students of Vilna. Even at this early stage in the blossoming of socialism, he significantly distanced himself from the assimilationist Jewish intelligentsia. Despite his opposition to emigration to Palestine, he was still accused of fomenting nationalist separatism:

> I am an internationalist, as you equally well know, but I am not ashamed of my Jewish descent, and, among all the other oppressed, I love that part of humanity whom the ruling national and religious principles single out as Jews. And again, indeed, I do not love them all, but only the suffering masses and those capable of joining us. Otherwise I should not deserve the name of socialist.[28]

Libermann's writings influenced countless Jewish intellectuals to 'go to the people' and provide elementary education to Jewish workers. As early as 1887, a group of Jewish social democrats was established. This, in turn, evolved by the 1890s into transmitting political ideas and finally utilizing Yiddish as a vehicle of workers' agitation. Arkady Kremer's pamphlet, *On Agitation* was influential in persuading many workers across Russia to move from discussion groups to mass action. Indeed there was no mention of specifically Jewish concerns. Kremer in particular was critical of 'the abstract concern of Russian socialists with the theories of scientific socialism'.[29] Samuel Gozhansky's *Letter to Agitators*, written in Yiddish, argued that Jewish workers had to establish their own independent organization which would not only campaign for workers' rights but also for civil rights for Jews in a national sense. It was into this political turbulence that Martov waded, following his exile from Odessa.

Despite the fact that Martov regarded himself as a Russian intellectual and political activist, he made a speech on May Day 1895 which strongly promoted the idea of a separate Jewish workers' organization. The Jews, he argued, were doubly oppressed because of their nationality and because of their class. It was important therefore to create a distinct Jewish body which would lead the Jewish proletariat. But perhaps even more remarkable was Martov's comment that:

> When the Russian proletariat is forced to sacrifice certain of its demands in order to gain something, it will first give up the demands which concern only the Jews . . . such as that for equal rights.[30]

Martov never again repeated his belief that the Russian workers could potentially betray their Jewish comrades.

The original idea of training Jewish cadres for the Russian movement therefore began to fall into disuse. The 1890s bore witness to an increasing awareness of the national consciousness of the Jewish workers. By October 1897, the foundations laid by Kremer, Gozhansky and Martov bore fruit in the formation of the *Algemeyner Yidisher Arbeter Bund in Russland un Polin* – otherwise known as the Bund. A few weeks later, Bundist delegates were founder members of the Russian Social Democratic Labour Party (RSDLP). Both shared an opposition to Zionism which had formally been launched on the international stage by Theodor Herzl at the first Zionist congress in Basel a few months before. All three organizations competed for the Jewish soul. All wished to represent the interests of the Jewish worker.

The Bundists, the Jewish members of the RSDLP and socialist Zionists such as Nachman Syrkin were all hostile to the passivity of the shtetl and the docility of the rabbis. Their disdain fortified them in their initial desire to distance themselves from communal life and to change Russia – whether as Russian Jews or as Jewish Russians. Change was not always welcome. Following the attempted assassination of the governor of Vilna by Hirsch Lekert in 1902, a Minsk rabbi bemoaned the involvement of Jews in revolutionary politics:

> Oh, beware Jewish children! Look well what you are doing! God only knows what you may bring upon our unfortunate nation, upon yourself, upon your families. Our people were always proud of one thing – that they never had any rebels among them; and now you desire to wipe out this virtue too.[31]

The Bund was very clear in its opposition to conservative *shtadlanim*, rabbinical authority and the adulation surrounding Herzl. Ignoring socialist Zionism, the Bund attacked the emergence of political Zionism as merely a bourgeois movement with close ties to 'clericalism'. Zionism, the Bundists argued, had no interest in improving the lot of the Jewish worker. Herzl was indeed a Viennese liberal, both acculturated and bourgeois, who had only recently discovered his Jewish identity. Moreover, he was keen to maintain a distance from socialist movements for fear that it might damage his diplomatic initiatives. Yet Herzl's Zionism typified a condition often prevalent in central European Jewry whereby assimilation or even conversion was seen as the answer. It did not reflect East European Jewry with its deep roots in Jewish tradition. Many East European Zionists were aghast at Herzl's superficial knowledge of Judaism and Jewish life per se. Many viewed Zionism as almost a rebellion against the power of the rabbis and organized religion – whose record had been coloured by quiescence and patience in waiting for the messiah to arrive. Herzl, in contrast, looked up to rabbis as figures of authority and because he also needed to cultivate them if he was to convert the Jewish communities to Zionism.

Herzl's opponent, the Zionist philosopher, Ahad Ha'am, in contrast, came from a devout background and was well versed in Jewish learning. He understood the rise of Zionism as a transition from the past. In a letter in March 1899, he commented:

> In my opinion, the survival of Hebrew is due to the love of Torah which used to spring from religious faith, but is now the outcome of national sentiment. What we need today is not a literature of devotion, but a literature of Jewish learning and scholarship, so that anybody in search of knowledge about any aspect of Jewish life or thought will be able to find all that he needs in Hebrew.[32]

By the second Zionist congress in 1898, Nachman Syrkin was attacking the approach of Herzl and advocating a socialist Zionist alternative. By 1901, Chaim Weizmann had established the Democratic Faction within the Zionist movement which wished to bypass any consideration of the integration of Judaism into any Zionist educational programme. During the first decade of the twentieth century, individual Marxist-Zionists left Eastern Europe for Palestine in order to build a socialist Jewish society in Palestine. They regarded themselves as the Zionist wing of the Russian revolutionary movement. This was far from Herzl's Zionist dream and the Bund's response to it.

At the third congress of the Bund in Kovno in December 1899, the Bundist John Mill put forward the view that the Bund should include national as well as civil rights in their programme. This was cast aside. By the fourth congress in Bialystok in 1901, it was claimed that the territorial solutions to the national question – whether Palestine, Argentina or other potential 'Jewish homelands' – were irrelevant to the here and now of the suffering Jewish worker. In contradistinction to the otherness of Zionism, the Bund proclaimed *Doykeyt* – 'Hereness'. Even so, a debate at the Bund's congress on 'Jewish national autonomy' resulted in the conclusion that the Jews were a nationality, but that national autonomy was a premature concern. This shelved a debate which divided the Bund.

The raising of national rights also propelled a proposal within the Bund for a federal structure within the Russian party. The resolution stated:

> The conference holds that a state such as Russia, consisting as it does of many nationalities, should, in the future, be reconstructed as a federation of nationalities with complete national autonomy for each nationality, independent of the territory in which it is located. The conference holds that the term 'nation' is also to be applied to the Jewish people.

The Bund had begun to steer a middle course between the undoubtedly national character of their movement and the desire to submerge it in an undifferentiated Russian party. The southern Slavs had already proposed to the Austrian socialist movement that Franz Josef's empire should be reconfigured as a federation of nations – not as a federation of territories. This naturally appealed to the dispersed German speakers in terms of personal national autonomy. Such ideas were further developed by Otto Bauer and Karl Renner who argued for autonomous regions often within larger territorial areas. Bauer like other leading Austro-Marxists who were of Jewish origin understood Jewishness only in the imagery of the non-productive Jew and believer in religious supernaturalism in the poverty-stricken shtetl. For Bauer, the progressive solution was the assimilation of the Jews. Even so, while the

Austro-Marxists believed that their theories could not be applied to the Jews since they were not a true nationality, it did permit the Bund to develop its own concept of national autonomy.

Lenin, however, had no desire to see the Russian party go the way of the Austro Social Democrats which consisted of a federation of six parties – the German, Polish, Italian, Slovene, Czech and Ukrainian-Ruthenian.

The Bund's desire to develop separate networks for Jewish workers in Poland had already been opposed by the Polish Socialist Party. In Russia, too, the RSDLP was becoming highly critical of the Bund's drive for a federal structure within the party. It came to be seen as a rival to the Russian party – it was well organized, highly motivated and strongly supported by thousands of adherents. It was this which seemingly induced Martov to initiate the first attack against the Bund in August 1901.

Notes and Works Cited

1 Louis Greenberg, *The Jews in Russia*, vol. 1, *The Struggle for Emancipation* (New Haven 1944), p. 83.

2 Ezra Mendelsohn, *Class Struggle in the Pale: The Formative Years of the Jewish Workers' Movement in Tsarist Russia* (Cambridge 1970), p. 5.

3 Ronald Grigor Suny, 'Nationalism and Class in the Russian Revolution: A Comparative Discussion', in *Revolution in Russia: Reassessments of 1917* ed. Edith Rogovin Frankel, Jonathan Frankel, Baruch Knei-Paz (Cambridge 1992), p. 225.

4 Erich E. Haberer, *Jews and Revolution in Nineteenth Century Russia* (Cambridge 2004), pp. 12–14.

5 Richard Pipes, *The Unknown Lenin: From the Secret Archive* (Yale 1998), p. 19.

6 Michael R. Katz and William G. Wagner, *Chernyshevski, What is to be Done? and the Russian Intelligentsia*, introduction to Nikolai Chernyshevski's *What is to be Done?* (New York 1989), p. 21.

7 N. Valentinov 'Chernyshevski i Lenin', *Novyi zhurnal*, no. 27 (1951), pp. 193–4 quoted in Katz and Wagner.

8 Raymond W. Goldsmith, 'The Economic Growth of Tsarist Russia 1860–1913', *Economic Development and Cultural Change*, vol. 9, no. 3, April 1961.

9 Katz and Wagner, op. cit., p. 2.

10 Osip Rabinowich, 'Russia Our Native Land: Just as We Breathe Its Air We Must Speak Its Language', *Rasvet*, no. 16, Odessa 1861 in ed. Paul Mendes-Flohr and Jehuda Reinharz, *The Jew in the Modern World: A Documentary History* (Oxford 1995), p. 400.

11 John D. Klier, 'The Pogrom Paradigm in Russian History', in ed. John D. Klier and Shlomo Lambroza, *Pogroms: Anti-Jewish Violence in Modern Russian History* (Cambridge 1992), pp. 21–8.

12 Abraham Ascher, *Pavel Axelrod and the Development of Menshevism* (Mass. 1972), p. 9.

13 V. S. Voitinskii et al., eds., 'Iz arkhiva P.B. Aksel'roda 1881–1896' (Berlin 1924), p. 217 quoted in Erich E. Haberer, *Jews and Revolution in Nineteenth Century Russia* (Cambridge 2004), p. 68.

14 Lucy Dawidowicz, ed. *The Golden Treasury* (New York 1967), p. 406.

15 Arthur Hertzberg, *The Zionist Idea: A Historical Analysis and Reader* (Philadelphia 1997), p. 169.

16 Moshe Mishkinsky, '"Black Repartition" and the Pogroms of 1881–1882', in ed. John D. Klier and Shlomo Lambroza, *Pogroms: Anti-Jewish Violence in Modern Russian History* (Cambridge 1992), pp. 73–4.

17 P. B. Axelrod, *Volnoe Slovo*, no. 19, 13 December 1881.

18 J. L. Talmon, *Israel Among the Nations* (London 1970), p. 28.

19 Abraham Cahan, *The Education of Abraham Cahan* (Philadelphia 1969), pp. 182–4.

20 Abraham Ascher, 'Pavel Axelrod: A Conflict between Jewish Loyalty and Revolutionary Dedication', *Russian Review*, vol. 24, no. 3 (July 1965).

21 Dawidowicz, op. cit., p. 410.

22 Haberer, op. cit., p. 215.

23 Isaiah 2.5.

24 Chaim Hisin, 'Mi yoman ehad ha Biluim' (From the 'Diary of One of the Bilu Members', Tel Aviv 1925) quoted in the *Encyclopaedia Judaica*, vol. 4 (Jerusalem 1972), p. 998.

25 Moses Leib Lilienblum, 'The Future of Our People' (1883) in Arthur Hertzberg *The Zionist Idea: A Historical Analysis and Reader* (Philadelphia 1997), p. 173.

26 Ahad Ha'am, Letter to M. Raisin (New York), Odessa 19 September 1901 in ed. Leon Simon, *Ahad Ha'am: Essays, Letters, Memoirs* (Oxford 1946), p. 304.

27 Israel Getzler, *Martov: A Political Biography of a Russian Social Democrat* (Cambridge 1967), pp. 3–5.

28 Kalman Marmor, ed. *Aaron Lieberman's Briv* (New York 1951), p. 82.

29 Koppel S. Pinson, 'Arkady Kremer, Vladimir Medem and the Ideology of the Jewish Bund', *Jewish Social Studies*, vol. 7, no. 3 (July 1945), p. 243.

30 Jonathan Frankel, *Prophecy and Politics: Socialism, Nationalism, and the Russian Jews 1862–1917* (Cambridge 1982), p. 193.

31 *Die arbiter shtime*, June 1902 in ed. Koppel S. Pinson, p. 235.

32 Ahad Ha'am, Letter to Dr. S. Bernfield (Berlin), Odessa 8 March 1899 in ed. Leon Simon, *Ahad Ha'am: Essays, Letters, Memoirs* (Oxford 1946), p. 262.

2

Lenin's Jewish problem

Iskra's assault on the Bund

Martov and Lenin worked extremely closely in building a new organization for the Russian workers. At a time when political thinkers such as Bernstein, Jaurès and Millerand were advocating an adjustment of Marxism to the specific conditions and realities that they faced in their countries, Martov and Lenin embraced Marxist orthodoxy, tolerating no deviation from the chosen line. In their rhetoric, both adopted a shrill and uncompromising approach. Martov attacked those writers and intellectuals who rallied to the defence of Dreyfus in opposing the forces of anti-Semitic reaction as 'bourgeois opportunists'.[1]

Lenin left Russia in July 1900 to establish the periodical *Iskra* in order to create a network of like-minded revolutionaries. Martov followed within a year and initiated *Iskra*'s campaign against the Bund which was mimicked by Lenin. Martov's article in *Iskra* in August 1901 stemmed from the Bund's resolutions at its fourth congress which he argued contained the seeds of nationalism and separation. Jews were urged to break away from historical tradition – to overcome the barrier between 'a chosen people' and 'a non-chosen people', to amalgamate the Maccabeans with the ancient Greeks. Martov argued that the Bund should be solely a section of the all-Russian party and its specific task would be to specialize in work among the Jewish masses in the Pale of Settlement. The Bund moreover should not exercise a monopoly on Russia's Jews – indeed Martov wished them to join the ranks of the RSDLP. He hoped that the Jews would move from light industry where the Bund dominated, to heavy industry where the real struggle of the Russian workers resided.[2] To confine themselves to the provinces of Lithuania and Belarus was shortsighted, following the revolution they would be allowed to work in all areas of Russia.

The Kishinev pogrom in April 1903 accentuated the internal Jewish debate between Bundists, Zionists, territorialists and Sjemists. It also highlighted the intra-Jewish debate between Bundists and assimilated Jewish members of the Russian party. The killings of Jews in Kishinev provided the sub-text for the Bund's fifth congress in June 1903 and the RSDLP's second gathering in July and August. While Martov assailed the Bund on several occasions during 1903,[3] Lenin also wrote four articles in *Iskra* in 1903 which attacked the Bund.[4] The first foray appeared in February 1903 entitled 'Does the Jewish Proletariat need an Independent Political Party?' Lenin excoriated the Bund from moving from a position of autonomy within the Russian party in 1898 to a proclamation of virtual independence from it in 1903.

> In matters pertaining to the struggle against autocracy, the struggle against the bourgeoisie of Russia as a whole, we must act as a single and centralized militant organization, have behind us the whole of the proletariat, without distinction of language or nationality, a proletariat whose unity is cemented by the continued joint solution of problems theory and practice, of tactics and organization; and we must not set up organizations that would march separately, each along its own track; we must not weaken the force of our offensive by breaking up into numerous independent political parties; we must not introduce estrangement and isolation and then have to heal an artificially implanted disease with the aid of these notorious 'federation' plasters.[5]

Lenin's starting point was a polemical skirmish between the Bund and the Ekaterinoslav branch of the Russian party. The local branch had published a pamphlet which attacked Zionism. The Bund saw this as an encroachment on its political territory and advised the branch to stick to combating anti-Semitism among non-Jews. An additional ingredient in this dispute was the Bund's threat and desire to move into southern Russian and thereby encroach on the RSDLP's domain. The Bund raised the question of workers' participation in a pogrom in Czestochowa in Poland and the anti-Semitic behaviour of 12 scabs in Zhitomir in the Ukraine. Lenin scoffed at the idea that this was evidence of international anti-Semitism by large sections of the population. He argued that anti-Semitism was solely a product of the bourgeoisie. Lenin dismissed these claims as being unrepresentative of the wider population of working people and were identical with 'the Zionist fable about anti-Semitism being eternal'.

Iskra returned to the theme of federalism and the Bund several times during 1903, but Lenin only examined Zionism and whether the Jews constituted a nation in the latter section of an article in October.[6] Zionism was almost an incidental inclusion in an article entitled 'The Position of the Bund in the Party'. In it, Lenin famously commented that:

> Absolutely untenable scientifically, the idea that the Jews form a separate nation is reactionary politically. Irrefutable practical proof of that is furnished by generally

known facts of recent history and of present-day political realities. All over Europe, the decline of medievalism and development of political liberty went hand in hand with the political emancipation of the Jews, their abandonment of Yiddish for the language of the people among whom they lived, and in general their undeniable progressive assimilation with the surrounding population. Are we again to revert to the exceptionalist theories and proclaim that Russia will be the one exception, although the Jewish emancipation movement is far broader and deeper rooted here, thanks to the awakening of a heroic class consciousness among the Jewish proletariat? Can we possibly attribute to chance the fact that it is the reactionary forces all over Europe, and especially in Russia, who oppose the assimilation of the Jews and try to perpetuate their isolation?[7]

Clearly Lenin took the model of Western Europe of acculturation and assimilation as one to be followed in Eastern Europe as far as the Jews were concerned. Lenin believed that the French Revolution and the European Enlightenment had been successful in emancipating the Jews. The reality was that Jews in Western Europe had positioned themselves at different points along the spectrum between rebuilding the ghetto walls and outright conversion to Christianity. Each individual managed the clash between tradition and modernity in a different fashion. Some indeed divested themselves of their Jewishness, others fought hard to retain it – albeit in a different form from that of their forebears. East European Jewry, however, had evolved in an entirely different fashion due to the harsher nature of Russian orthodoxy towards Jews, its legacy of religious anti-Semitism and the repressive nature of Tsarist autocracy. Indeed the devouring and disappearance of Poland in the eighteenth century through three partitions brought an unwelcome, alien population of Jews into the Russian orbit. The evolution of the Pale of Settlement not only kept the Jews out of Russia proper, it also inadvertently encouraged a sense of nationhood and ethnic solidarity. The few contemporaries in Russia of Marx and Lassalle epitomized the transformation of the Jew as Lenin would have wished – an assimilation into a Russian cultural milieu, gradually leaving behind all traces of Jewishness. Lenin cannot have been unaware that this did not reflect the will of the Jewish masses in Russia, but it accorded with his interpretation of Marxist theory and his belief that change would only come about through the dedicated guidance of a revolutionary elite. Indeed Lenin's view was linked to his Jacobinesque idea that the programme of any revolutionary party should not emerge from the concerns of the workers or trades unions, engaged in mass action, but should be the prerogative of a group of professional revolutionaries.

In addition, Lenin certainly underestimated the power of nationalism and did not truly locate a realistic solution within Marxism to the national question

in Russia. While the Communist Manifesto certainly argued that the proletarian struggle with the bourgeoisie would initially be a national one, it also
argued unclearly if not vaguely that the national reflection of the proletariat
should not be manifested in a bourgeois interpretation. The solution to the
awkward Jewish question was in reality placed on the shoulders of the Jews
themselves. Rather than examine theory and adjust it to reflect the political
reality that the Jews found themselves in, it was better to adjust the Jews to
fit the theory. After all, Marx and Engels referred to nations rather than nationalities in Europe. Perhaps Lenin's sense of cosmopolitanism and avoidance
of the national question also resonated with his own family history in that his
maternal great-grandfather was one Moshko Blank who was indifferent to his
Jewish roots and converted to Christianity.[8] The passage from poverty and
segregation to the Russian minor nobility and acceptance could be emulated
in a revolutionary context in the drive towards socialist cosmopolitanism.

Non-Jewish Jews

Lenin's willing assistants in this venture were acculturated and assimilated
Jews who wished to consign their Jewishness to the dustbin of history. What
was right for them was deemed to be suitable for the Jewish masses as
well. Jewishness was only to be evoked for the good of the cause, to con-
vince others to follow in this path and to indicate that there was an alternative Jewish voice. Russified Jews and Russians per se distanced themselves
from the culture of the shtetl which they regarded as primitive and backward. When Lenin visited Vilna at the end of 1895, he recalled Axelrod's
comments about 'Palestinian provincialism'.[9] Any hint of Jewishness except
in a transitional sense towards eventual assimilation could be regarded as
evidence of nationalism. In his article in *Iskra*, Lenin mentioned the French
Jew, Alfred Naquet, a Comptean positivist who in a debate with the socialist Zionist, Bernard Lazare, denied that the Jews were a nation – and stated
that he personally belonged to the French nation. Admitting that he himself
did not know Hebrew, Naquet argued that as the Jews no longer had a common language and territory, it followed that the Jews were certainly not a
nation. In his article, Naquet placed anti-Semitism alongside Zionism in that
the adherents of both regarded the Jews as a nation and wanted to see an
exodus from French shores. Naquet also took issue with Edouard Drumont,
the founder of the Anti-Semitic League of France and editor of *La Libre Parole,*
who wanted Jews excluded from French society. Naquet argued that even if
it was possible to recognize the Jews as a nation, they would be 'an artificial
nation'. Naquet further offered his opinion that 'the modern Jew is a product

of the unnatural selection to which his forebears were subjected for nearly eighteen centuries.'[10]

Lenin then brought the work of the French thinker, Ernest Renan, as further evidence. Quoting Renan, Lenin argued that the French National Assembly in 1791 in emancipating the Jews was concerned less with 'the question of race' but with the abolition of the ghetto – all ghettos.

> The Jewish race has rendered the world the greatest services. Assimilated with the various nations, harmoniously blended with the various national units, it will render no lesser services in the future than in the past.[11]

Renan had written extensively on the meaning of Jewish history – and was greatly puzzled by it. He both praised the Jews and condemned them. He was unable to explain the longevity of the Jews as a people since they had outlived their usefulness. He had argued that the Jews had given the world monotheism and Christianity, but had since become redundant in the advance of humankind.

> The fanaticism engendered by the Torah survived all attempts to kill it. The best energies of the race were engaged in mad squabbles of mere casuistry. The Talmud, that bad book, which to this day is the evil genius of Judaism, took life from the Torah and then in great part filled its space, becoming the new law of Judaism.

This echo of Hegel's view was accompanied by stereotypes of the Jew as the irritant among the nations. Renan believed that Semites were inferior to Aryans, that they were history's inveterate exploiters and parasites.

Renan stood both in awe of the Jews and was repelled by them. In contrast to the racist element of his views, Renan believed that European cultures had inherited from the Greeks the notion of the immortality of the soul and therefore brought forth ideas of culture and science. The Jews, however, did not entertain such beliefs about the soul, they did not focus on the concept of a perfect future, but only in what was here and now. The Jews thus promoted the idea of justice – and it was this that supplied the missing link in the contemporary world. Liberalism was of Greek origin while socialism was of Hebrew origin.[12]

The universalism within Judaism which had given rise to Christianity logically therefore should be the catalyst in the struggle for progress. While he did not regard the Jews as an ethnic group, he praised their dispersion as a means of being able to convey their universal mission.

Renan wrote five volumes of the 'History of the People of Israel'. He concluded that Greek values and its view of the human condition were destined to survive. Judaism and Christianity would disappear as the human race moved on towards a higher and more universal stage of development. Only 'the trace of Israel would be eternal'. Such a christological view of Jews, Judaism and Jewish history appealed to Lenin in his understanding of the Jew as the yeast in the revolutionary fermentation.[13]

Lenin's third point of reference was Karl Kautsky, the editor of *Die Neue Zeit*, the German Social Democrats' theoretical journal.

In the middle of Lenin and Martov's campaign against the Bund's notions of Jewish nationalism, a massacre of Jews in Kishinev took place on 19 April 1903, Easter Sunday. Some 25 bands, averaging 35 each, attacked the city's 50,000 Jews. The official memorial album recorded 49 deaths, 495 injured and 2,000 made homeless. The police did nothing, the Christian clergy remained silent and the well-to-do looked the other way. Troops were sent in after 20 hours of killing and rioting – and dispersed the mobs within an hour.[14] The atrocities created both trauma and soul-searching within Russian Jewry – and stimulated intense debate among its intelligentsia. Chaim Nachman Bialik's angry poem blamed the victims rather than the perpetrators – with God as both narrator and berator. It urged the Jews to wake up from their slumber, to go to Kishinev and see for themselves. It commenced:

> Get up and go to the city of slaughter,
> see with your own eyes,
> feel with your hands in the courtyards,
> on trees, stones, walls
> the dried blood and brains of the dead.[15]

The international outrage and the inertia of the regime communicated itself to European Marxists. In particular, the Polish social democrats Rosa Luxemburg and Adolf Warski asked Karl Kautsky to address the question. Both were from assimilated Jewish families. Luxemburg came from a long line of Talmudic scholars, but was brought up with a respect for German culture. Moreover Luxemburg was 'strangely insensitive towards anti-Semitism'[16] and unlike even Martov appeared indifferent to anti-Semitic taunts. Even experiencing a Christmas Day pogrom in the Jewish quarter of Warsaw in 1881 left no discernible mark.[17] Her commentary on the Dreyfus affair was in essence an attack on the French revisionist socialists.[18] A passing mention in her *Junius* pamphlet on the crisis in German social democracy in early 1915 referred to 'the Kishinev air', but omitting any reference to its Jewish victims. However, she did write several articles on anti-Semitism for the weekly *Mlot* in 1910. She viewed anti-Semitism as really an attack on the workers' movement since there was a preponderance of Jews.

Yet there was an ongoing contact between the Bund and the assimilated Jewish leadership of the Polish social democrats. The latter opposed Zionism which they regarded as utopian and were averse to any sense of ethnic solidarity among Jews. Significantly both the Bund and the Polish social democrats opposed the desire for an independent Polish state, espoused by the nationalist Polish Socialist Party. Indeed Rosa Luxemburg regarded the principle of national self-determination as utterly un-Marxist. Even so, the Bund published articles by Luxemburg in their journal even though they knew that she did not support any form of national separatism. Such unsaid differences began to surface when the Polish social democrats began to seek a rapprochement with Lenin and the RSDLP. They became critical of the Bund's call for a federal structure even though they themselves were averse to submerging themselves in the Russian party because of Lenin's demand for tight centralized control. In May 1903 Warski wrote to Kautsky requesting him to address the issue of anti-Semitism after the Kishinev pogrom in an article for their theoretical journal *Przeglad Socjaldemokratyczny*.[19] Warski's rationale was that the Tsarist authorities might utilize the situation to direct workers' unrest away from the desire for revolutionary change, but to incite them against the Jews. Warski further argued that an influx of Jews from Lithuania into Poland due to Russian anti-Semitism had produced national resentment. He worried that Kishinev would be the precursor to similar atrocities in Poland. Moreover, the Kishinev pogrom had heightened national sentiment among the Jews – and also within the Bund. Warski also informed Kautsky that the Polish social democrats had condemned Tsarist anti-Semitism and called upon the Polish workers to defend the Jewish population.

Kautsky's resulting article 'The Kishinev Massacre and the Jewish Question' was published in German and Polish Marxist journals as well as in Lenin's *Iskra*.[20] It became required reading as the standard Marxist text on the Jewish question. At that point in history, Kautsky was seen as the foremost authority in the Marxist world.

Kautsky's views on anti-Semitism and assimilation were in fact inherited from Engels. Yet Kautsky lived in very different times from his mentor. Engels died before the rise of Zionism, the formation of the Bund or major Jewish socialist movements in Eastern Europe as such. Kautsky was an ardent opponent of anti-Semitism and he started writing on the question as early as October 1882. Indeed he was very aware of the ease with which the workers of Vienna would fraternize with anti-Semites and reactionaries. His two wives were Jewish as were two daughters-in-law. As much as he had recognized the growing centrality of the Jewish problem, he espoused the voluntary assimilation of the Jews. Kautsky's Jewish heroes were Spinoza, Ricardo and Marx – those who were either excommunicated or converted to

Christianity.[21] The Jews had neither a common homeland nor a common language. There were class divisions with Russian Jewry and there were growing contacts with non-Jewish workers' organizations. While he championed the Bund, the Bundists did not welcome his article on the Kishinev killings. It was not translated in Yiddish. His views on the Czech national movement were similar – national rights within Austro-Hungary, but opposition to separatism. Significantly Kautsky was born in Prague and experienced discrimination as a Czech at school. He was also a Catholic and argued that the Catholicism like Judaism had until the Middle Ages constituted an element of progress, but since then had atrophied. The Jews, confined in their ghettos, he surmised, had been 'totally untouched by this great transformation of the human mind'.[22]

Kautsky did not oppose Jewish colonization of Palestine per se, but he did not believe that a state would ultimately solve the problem of the Jewish working class. Zionist activity damaged the Bund and 'the Zionist movement was undermining the zeal of the Jewish proletariat to work for a socialist revolution'.[23] Leaving Russia and Poland for Palestine would only fortify the masses in their anti-Semitic beliefs. While he understood the raison d'être for Zionism, he still believed that it was a utopian phenomenon which would not end well. Following the Bolshevik Revolution, he argued that both the Zionist state and the Leninist state would not succeed.[24]

The ascendency of Leninism

Lenin quoted Kautsky in his *Iskra* article that 'non-native sections of the population should cease to be alien and blend with the general mass of the population'. Kautsky argued that the Jews would not disappear forcibly and tragically like the American Indians and the Tasmanians, but through an elevation to a higher level of development. Lenin, however, understood assimilation of the Jews in a less than voluntary sense. Neither did he exude Kautsky's appreciation of the Bund's struggle. Indeed he saw little difference between Bundism and Zionism.

The Bundists were also weary of the dictatorial tendencies of the *Iskra* group, defending legal norms while circumventing them.[25] Even before the establishment of the RSDLP, a meeting between the Bund's Arkady Kremer and Plekhanov had ended acrimoniously. When Lenin met Plekhanov in Switzerland in August 1900, having left Russia to establish *Iskra*, he was surprised to discover the bile which Plekhanov meted out to the Bund. 'Jews' according to Plekhanov, were all 'chauvinists and nationalists'.[26] The party must be Russian, they should not surrender to 'the tribe of Gad'. All this occurred before the Bund's conference which laid greater emphasis on the national character of the Jews.

The central task for Lenin and Plekhanov was neither to extinguish nor to marginalize the Bund per se, but to displace the Union of Russian Social Democrats Abroad and to replace its journal *Robochee delo* by *Iskra* which would then perform the role of a coordinating medium for a network of agents. The minor differences with the Bund provided the vehicle for this transformation. The idea was to change the RSDLP into a highly centralized party under the control of Lenin, Martov, Plekhanov and the editorial board of *Iskra*. The Bund's concept of a mass party did not fit into this scenario. Neither did its refusal to ignore the crucial point that the Union of Russian Social Democrats Abroad had been officially recognized by the RSDLP's founding conference in 1898.

Lenin's lifelong sense of political expediency was geared at this early stage towards creating a party in his own image. The existence of an external enemy, an ideological heretic, an 'other' provided a sense of purpose and solidarity among comrades. In this case, the Bund performed this role in the takeover strategy of Lenin and Martov, regardless of the differences about Jewish nationalism. The Bund's proposal for a federal structure became a demand in Lenin's game plan. The Bund became a pawn in the struggle between the old guard and the newcomers, between Marxist revisionists and the believers in doctrinal rigidity – a means to break out of the frustrations of émigré politics and the stagnation of revolutionary politics.

Lenin's articles 'Where to Begin?' in May 1901 and 'What is to be Done?' which was written several months later, demonstrated without ambiguity his path to revolutionary success. By early 1903, Lenin was already contacting his followers and instructing them that there would be a confrontation with the Bund. Lenin worked towards influencing the organization committee for the second congress of the RSDLP and placing the question of the Bund's relationship on its agenda as early as December 1902. The Bund, in response, by and large, bit its tongue and very rarely retaliated. In the Bund's eyes, it was *Iskra* rather than the Bund which had undermined the Russian party. The forthcoming congress had to answer the question whether the Bund was 'a regional organisation or a representative of the proletariat of a whole nation'. Should the solution be 'limited autonomy or equality in federation'?[27]

To some extent, the Bund was unsure of its own position. What was the balance between being a movement representing national interests and one proudly proclaiming its internationalist credentials? It had expected to negotiate and effect a compromise with the RSDLP. Instead it discovered that Lenin had placed the question of the Bund's position in the party as the first item on the agenda. Was the Bund no more than a state within a state within the Russian socialist camp?

The congress opened in Brussels on 17 July 1903, but then closed just as quickly, following harassment from the Belgian authorities and the Okhrana, the Russian secret police. It reopened a few weeks later in the Brotherhood Congregationalist Church in north London. 57 delegates, of which 43 had voting rights, attended. The Bund complained that given its size, it should have been accorded more than five votes. Moreover Lenin had laboured to secure the support of the Georgians who feared that a federal structure would undermine their control of smaller nationalities in Transcaucasia. The southern Russians also sided with Lenin since they did not want the Bund to expand into their domain. Lenin also moved the assimilated Jews into position so 'they could speak as Jews' and thereby imply that the Bund was not a legitimate representative of the Jewish masses. Martov led the attack by moving a resolution which restricted Bundist autonomy to the specific problem of working with Jewish workers, yet it was clearly Lenin who was directing the assault. The newly arrived Leon Trotsky, on Lenin's instigation, took the floor straight after Martov and declared that 12 'Jewish comrades' who agreed with the resolution regarded themselves as members of the Russian party. In his note to Trotsky beforehand, Lenin suggested that he state that the 12 Jews who offered their names should do so also as 'representatives of the Jewish proletariat'.[28] Martov's resolution was agreed by all the delegates with the exception of the shell-shocked Bundists. Their arguments were directed at repelling the accusations laid at their door – and omitted the bigger picture of the takeover of the RSDLP by Lenin and Plekhanov. It was, however, the very idea of assimilated Jews, belonging to a Russian party, formally posing as representatives of the Jewish working class – an idea which was both surrealistic and outrageous to the Bundist delegates – that they formally and quickly left the RSDLP in disgust and disarray. While there were neither any anti-Semitic comments nor any reference to Marx's pejorative remarks about the Jew as a parasitical capitalist, one of the foremost ideologues of the Bund, saw this in terms of a Jewish civil war, 'not an international dispute'.[29]

Lenin then moved to consolidate his hold over the party and *Iskra* in particular. This ironically now brought him into direct confrontation with Martov. Although the acrimonious debate was over seemingly unimportant party issues, the real struggle was over the sort of party that should emerge. Martov conceived of a mass movement, composed of politically aware members of the proletariat and interested members of the intelligentsia. Lenin, however, saw the party in much narrower terms as an elitist, centralized group of dedicated, professional revolutionaries – a conspiratorial movement of *Iskra* writ large. Indeed the Bund's leadership was much more homogeneously working class than that of the Russian party. With the departure of the Bundists, Lenin was able to secure a majority of votes for his candidates on the party's central committee and to eliminate Martov's supporters – Axelrod, Zasulich and Potresov – from *Iskra*'s editorial board. In protest, Martov refused to serve and thus the split into Bolsheviks and Mensheviks was cemented. Lenin's blueprint for revolutionary change and post-revolutionary rule was clear in his 'What is to be Done?' At the second congress of the RSDLP, the promotion of political expediency to reach a desired goal for the perceived greater good had made betrayal and subterfuge morally irrelevant. Martov saw this episode as merely a transient phase for the duration of the party congress. Lenin saw this as an axiom of the ongoing striving for the victory of socialism.

Lenin's behaviour and moral relativism could easily have been taken out of the pages of Sergei Nechaev's pamphlet *Catechism of a Revolutionary*. The nihilistic characterization of the soulless revolutionary, ready to sacrifice anyone and everyone, captivated anarchists such as Mikhail Bakunin, but scandalized many socialists such as Marx and members of the First International. Vera Zasulich whose long revolutionary career spanned the period from Nechaev to the Bolsheviks commented that he was 'not only against the government and exploiters, but against all society and all its cultured elements . . . against the rich and the poor, against conservatives, liberals and radicals' and even his own followers who were regarded as 'only instruments or means, but never as comrades or even disciples'.[30]

For Bundists and Zionists, the debate over the national question, utilizing non-Jewish Jews, was one issue. The question of denuding socialism of moral principle was another. It did prefigure a determination to make the Jews disappear through assimilation and to sacrifice them on Lenin's altar if he deemed it necessary. The Bund and the Mensheviks found themselves on the same side of the fence when defending the principles of social democracy against Lenin. The preponderance of Jews in the Menshevik party and at their conferences was not accidental.

Obfuscating Zionism

Zionism had arisen at virtually the same point in history as Russian Marxism. It was less attractive to the Jewish masses which preferred the 'hereness' of the Bund. The RSDLP was approximately a third of the Bund's membership in 1906. Yet both Zionism and Bundism were accidental ingredients in Lenin's drive to dominate the Russian party. The Zionists were politically irrelevant, but they played an important role in being depicted as an existential threat – a different way for the Jewish future. Since Zionism was different and could not be explained adequately theoretically, it also therefore had to be deemed wrong. This treatment of Bundism and Zionism proved to be the exemplar for the destruction of the Russian Left by the Bolsheviks 20 years hence.

Chaim Weizmann, a student in Switzerland at that time, remarked in his memoirs that while his sympathies were with the revolutionaries, he highly resented the orchestrated campaign of assimilated Jews to convert newly arrived Jewish youth to their way of thinking.

> My resentment of Lenin and Plekhanov and the arrogant Trotsky was provoked by the contempt with which they treated any Jew who was moved by the fate of his people and animated by a love of its history and its tradition. They could not understand why a Russian Jew should want to be anything but a Russian. They stamped as unworthy, as intellectually backward, as chauvinistic and immoral, the desire of any Jew to occupy himself with the sufferings and destiny of Jewry. A man like Chaim Zhitlovsky who was both a revolutionary and a Jewish nationalist was looked upon with extreme suspicion.[31]

Weizmann further remarked that already at that time – fin de siècle Europe – there was something 'significant in the autocratic spiritual attitude' of Lenin, Plekhanov and their supporters. There was little room to be different.

Although the Bund rejoined the RSDLP, Lenin remained implacably opposed to it. Despite the settling of thousands of Marxist-Zionists in Palestine and the advent of collectives such as the kibbutz, Lenin never turned his mind towards an examination of the socialist experiment in Palestine. In 1913, living in Krakow and close to the Russian border, he once more commented on the national question in Russia. This had been stimulated by the nationalism of the Balkan wars and the ideas of the Austro-Marxists on the question of national minorities. In addition, Stalin had arrived in Krakow to work with Lenin. In a series of articles including the well-known 'Critical Remarks on the National Question', Lenin again examined the Jewish question in Russia and excoriated the Bund, vehemently condemning any notion of national cultural autonomy. Once again, no analysis of Zionism was made.

Lenin believed in the amalgamation of nations – a world without national borders and national characteristics. Capitalism broke down national borders, obliterated national distinctions and thereby assimilated nations. This was 'one of the great driving forces transforming capitalism into socialism'. The Jews, in Lenin's eyes, were halfway there. Over 50% of the Jews lived in Russia and Galicia, backward locations, where the Jews lived as a segregated caste. However, in 'the civilized world' outside Russia, Lenin claimed, 'the great world progressive features of Jewish culture stand clearly revealed: its internationalism, its identification with the advanced movements of the epoch'. This explained why the Jews were disproportionately represented in the ranks of the revolutionaries.[32]

This simplified version of the Jewish world allowed Lenin to define 'Jewish-ness' through his opposition to a 'Jewish national culture'.

> Whoever, directly or indirectly, puts forward the slogan of Jewish 'national culture' is (whatever his good intentions may be) an enemy of the proletariat, a supporter of all that is outmoded and connected with caste among the Jewish people; he is an accomplice of the rabbis and the bourgeoisie. On the other hand, those Jewish Marxists who mingle with the Russian, Lithuanian, Ukrainian and other workers in international Marxist organizations, and make their contribution (both in Russian and in Yiddish) towards creating the international culture of the working-class movement – these Jews, despite the separation of the Bund, uphold the best traditions of Jewry by fighting the slogan of 'national culture'.[33]

Lenin argued that the Jews both in Russia and Galicia – as well as in 'the civilized world' outside – did not constitute a nation. Those outside had assimilated, those in the Pale of Settlement were prevented from doing so because of the oppression and discrimination meted out to the Jews. While he implicitly noted the heightened sense of ethnic solidarity of the Jews in Tsarist Russia, Lenin's knowledge of Jewish history appeared to be remark-ably superficial. It was not the historians Graetz or Dubnov who were fac-tually quoted, but Kautsky and Bauer who were lauded as authorities on Jewish history. Lenin's inability to discover flaws in the Enlightenment's emancipation of the Jews during the nineteenth century just flew in the face of reality.

Any attempt to preserve Jewish identity was viewed as anti-progressive and effectively counter-revolutionary. Lenin wanted to assist all Jews in escap-ing their Jewishness. A disenfranchised Jewish nationality was deemed to be a transient phase between being Jewish and not being Jewish. Many Jews after the October Revolution desired this path. Many more did not.

Some, however, like the non-Zionist historian Simon Dubnov understood the escape from Jewishness, not as assimilation, but as Russification. In a speech in Vilna in 1905, following a pogrom, he commented:

> In their eyes the six million Jews wedged into the body of the Russian state are Russians who only temporarily are connected with the House of Israel. They are ready and willing to grant national autonomy to all the territorial nationalities in Russia but not to the Jewish nationality. Since they believe that the Jewish river will empty into the Russian sea . . . These men do not realise that, in true lackey fashion, they are only carrying out the bidding of their masters, the bidding of the ruling nationality. They have not attained inner freedom even in revolution.[34]

Zionism also wanted to transform the Jews. It wanted the Jew to become a different type of Jew, not a different type of non-Jew. Zionism, too, was a revolt against the stultification of the ghetto and its passivity. As one Zionist leader acidly commented: 'The only true heroism of the ghetto, acknowledged, was that of self-suppression and dogged obedience to the Will above.'[35]

Lenin's commentary on Zionism in 1903 was almost an accidental adjunct to his attack on the anti-Zionist Bund. Yet he treated Zionism as monolithic – as liberal, bourgeois and quasi-religious. The only Zionism was Herzlian Zionism. No mention was made about the challenge to Herzl from Nachman Syrkin in 1898 when he published 'The Jewish Question and the Socialist Jewish State'. In this essay, Syrkin depicted the assimilating socialist Jew as merely imitating his bourgeois counterpart. He argued that the Jewish socialists of Western Europe inherited the traditions of the assimilationists of the Jewish bourgeoisie.

> To the Jewish socialists, socialism meant first of all the discarding of Jewishness, just as the liberalism of the Jewish bourgeoisie led to assimilation. And yet this tendency to deny their Jewishness was unnecessary, being prompted by neither socialism nor liberalism. It was a product of the general degeneration and demoralization of the Jews.

In another essay in 1901, Syrkin ridiculed the notion in some Marxist circles that Zionism sprang from the desire of the Jewish middle class to find new spheres for capitalist exploitation. He commented that 'such an explanation of this remarkable movement is crude and naive'.[36] He argued that Zionism arose from the consciousness of the Jewish masses that their economic situation had been destroyed and from their desire for a better life. Yet Lenin never made any attempt to challenge the ideas of Nachman Syrkin or even to mention his name. Were they unimportant or did he just not know about them? If the Bund was attacked over and over again, then why not socialist Zionism? In part, Lenin understood little about the Jews per se – about their history, traditions and culture – as well as the fragile reality of their lives. While he passionately condemned anti-Semitism, the Jews that he truly admired were those who were moving away from Jewishness. In 1913, Lenin asked Stalin to write 'Marxism and the National Question' which repeated many of Lenin's arguments. He too only understood the Jews in a one-dimensional sense.

> If there is anything common to them left, it is their religion, their common origin and certain relics of the national character. All this is beyond question. But how can it

be seriously maintained that petrified religious rites and fading psychological relics affect the 'destiny' of these Jews more powerfully than the living social, economic and cultural environment that surrounds them? And it is only on this assumption that it is possible to speak of the Jews as a single nation at all.[37]

While these comments of Stalin – and of Lenin – bore unmistakable testimony to their lack of understanding about the inner life of Jews, they paled into insignificance with the preoccupation of ensuring the success of the October Revolution in 1917 and the stability of the new regime.

The Bolsheviks in power

Ironically the Balfour Declaration and the Bolshevik seizure of power took place within days of each other. Both events governed the political odysseys of individual Jews for the rest of the twentieth century. One promised to embed Jewishness in a sovereign nation-state, the other pledged to eradicate it in the cause of a higher ideal. One promised to solve the centuries old Jewish problem, the other pledged to repair the world. Both appealed to Jews.

In Odessa, a huge demonstration of over 100,000 people in support of the Balfour Declaration took place in the presence of the British consul, Muriel Paget.[38]

The overthrow of the Tsar had catalysed the blossoming of Jewish activities and the democratic representation of competing ideological groups. The Zionists grew in strength during 1917. By the time of the October Revolution, there were 1,200 local groups, comprising a membership of 300,000 people.[39] The February revolution had lifted the ban on Zionist activities and already by early April youth groups such as Tserei Tsion were organizing meetings.[40] Zionists dominated communal elections and Hebrew language schools and periodicals proliferated. The Balfour Declaration gave these endeavours a major boost.

On attaining power, Lenin and Stalin created national commissariats to deal with the special needs of nationalities in the new Russia. The Yevkom – the Jewish Commissariat – was established at the beginning of 1918 together with the Yevsektsiya, the Jewish sections of the Communist Party. Yet they were virtually ostracized both by the Jewish intelligentsia and the Jewish working class. At the first conference of the Yevsektsiya in October 1918, its leader, Semyon Diamanshteyn, pointed out:

When the October revolution came, the Jewish workers had remained totally passive . . . and a large part of them were even against the revolution. The revolution did not reach the Jewish street. Everything remained as before.[41]

The civil war between Reds and Whites, between Bolsheviks and nationalists, resulted in the mass slaughter of Jews in the killing fields of the Ukraine.
The massacres of 1918–1920 probably took 150,000 Jewish lives and
orphaned twice as many children.[42] Such butchery drove many young Jews
into the Red Army and the emerging Communist Party apparatus. Although
not totally blameless, these were the only bodies that opposed anti-Semitism
and offered the opportunity to fight back. Jews were often more literate
than the rest of the population and filled the posts vacated by an emigrating bureaucracy. The growing permanence of the Communist Party and the
apparent success of the Bolshevik Revolution persuaded the Left from other
surviving parties to secede and throw in their lot with Lenin and his followers. In the Ukraine, the left wing of the Bund became the Kombund and then
the Komfarbund. Left wing Zionists did the same. Lenin, however, would not
permit separate parties to associate or co-exist with the Communist Party.
A one-party state meant the banning of all other parties. Democratic centralism meant an abolition of free elections, referenda and democratic norms.
It meant a crushing of the Russian Left. There was no halfway house. Thus
in 1921, the Bund dissolved itself. As ex-Bundists and ex-Zionists flooded
into the Communist Party, the Yevsektsiya and Yevkom began to exert more
influence on Communist decision making on matters concerning Jews. By
1919, the Yevsektsiya was strong enough to instigate the closure of Zionist
offices and the banning of Zionist literature. The Zionist organization was
defined as yet another bourgeois party akin to the Cadets.[43] Although the
Yevsektsiya deemed the Zionist organization to be counter-revolutionary, the
central Soviet authorities did not take any action. Significantly the VTsIK,
the all-Russian Central Executive Committee of Soviets, issued a decree
in July 1919 which stated that the Zionist organization was not counter-
revolutionary and that its activities should not be disrupted. Yet within a few
weeks, the office of the Petrograd Zionists was closed down, its leadership
and employees arrested and its publications banned. However shortly afterwards such oppressive measures were reversed and the office once more
opened.

Crushing the Zionists

All this indicated the growing influence of the Yevsektsiya and the zeal of
the newly converted. Unlike the highly assimilated Jews of the pre-1917
revolutionary movement, these Jewish Communists were Jewishly literate. Ex-Bundists could now enact their opposition to Zionism from within

the party with the full weight of the state. Ex-Zionists could prove their authenticity and devotion to the cause by condemning their former comrades. Moshe Litvakov, a long-time follower of Ahad Ha'am and devoted collector of Hebrew books now edited *Der Emes*, the periodical of the Yevkom, and through its pages demanded the suppression of Hebrew. Semyon Diamanshteyn, the Commissar for Jewish Affairs, had attended the Telz, Slobodka and Lubavitch yeshivot as a young man, yet he now vigorously directed the dismantling of traditional Jewish life.[44] Such determination proved much stronger than the vacillation of non-Jewish apparatchiks who understood little of Lenin's occasional mention of Zionism in 1903. Yet there was never an official banning of Hebrew. The distinction, however, between legality and illegality was blurred, often allowing individual officials their personal and often arbitrary interpretation. They periodically turned to the Yevsektsiya for advice and would defer to their knowledge of the subject. There were numerous examples of Soviet officials stating that they were not opposed to Palestine and did not approve of the Yevsektsiya's targeted campaign against Zionism.[45] Felix Dzerzhinskii, the head of the Cheka, questioned his subordinates on several occasions whether Zionist organizations actually challenged the Kremlin's control.[46] Lev Kamenev intervened on several occasions to assist the purveyors of Hebrew culture such as the issuing of a license for a Hebrew language periodical, *Hed Ha'am* in 1920. In 1924 Alexei Rykov published a favourable memorandum on the Hebrew language to which the Yevsektsiya strongly objected. In 1925 Georgi Chicherin told a delegation of diaspora Jews including Einstein that the Soviet government did not place any obstacles in the path of Zionist activities. Even so, a dangerous rivalry involved Zionists and Jewish Communists.

> A unique situation was created which resembled a game: if we (Zionists) succeeded in reaching the central authorities without the Jewish communists being able to say their piece first, it was usually possible to obtain what we wanted. The Yevsektsiya dictators were well aware of this state of affairs and their messengers were constantly active in the corridors of power – trying to assume responsibility for these matters, but they did not always succeed . . . every step that was taken by an individual or a group, would – if at all possible for the Yevsektsiya people to arrange – lead to the arrest of the persons involved and later to exile.[47]

By 1920, the first short-term arrests of Zionists – delegates to the all-Russian Zionist Congress – took place. The meeting was stopped by the Moscow Cheka and a female representative of the Yevsektsiya, a former Bundist.[48] It had only been the intervention of Kamenev that had stopped the Yevsektsiya from preventing the staging of the congress in the first place. The Cheka uncovered documents which purported to show contact with the Entente countries and the existence of a courier service between Moscow and London.[49] It was followed by accusations in *Izvestiya* that explosives had been found in the offices of the Petrograd Zionists.[50] By July 1921, the third Yevsektsiya conference concluded that with the victory of Communism and the crushing of all left wing parties, there was no need for reticence in moving against the Zionists – and the socialist Zionists in particular. Following arrests at a Zionist conference in Kiev in April 1922, twelve of the delegates were given two years' imprisonment. This was followed by the arrest and exile of 3,000 activists in September 1924.

Hebrew had effectively been banned in 1919 and despite a campaign by thousands to legalize the language, the Yevsektsiya was able to blunt its passion and instigate the arrest of its leadership. Even Lenin is reputed to have exclaimed that he did not know what 'a counter-revolutionary language' was.[51] Even a small group of fervent supporters of the October Revolution – the Hebrew Octobrists – who wished to speak Hebrew, found obstacles placed in their way.[52] Hebrew schools were closed down and Hebrew presses given over to publications in Yiddish. The Yevsektsiya attempted to use its influence to cut off state funds to the Hebrew theatrical group, Habima which they then branded as counter-revolutionary. Maxim Gorky's intervention prevented its liquidation. Yet Habima finally left Soviet Russia in 1926 – formally to go on tour abroad. Their last performance of *The Dybbuk* played to a theatre packed to capacity with the surrounding streets thronged with Jews. Twelve major Hebrew writers and poets including Chaim Nachman Bialik, Shaul Tchernikovsky, Ben-Zion Dinur, Yehoshua Ravnitsky and Avigdor Hameiri also chose the route of emigration. The Commissar for Education and Culture, Anatoly Lunacharsky, agreed to speak at Bialik's farewell banquet in Moscow, but was counteracted by the Yevsektsiya. Lunacharsky threatened to take them to a party tribunal. Even so, the banquet was cancelled for fear that the Yevsektsiya would be successful in having Bialik's visa revoked. Other poets stayed in the Soviet Union. Elisha Rodin and Chaim Lensky wrote their poetry behind closed doors without a readership. Lensky continued to write poems in the Gulag before his demise.[53] A letter of Rodin which was published in Palestine in 1942 included the line: 'By the rivers of sorrow our song has perished'.[54]

The Hebrew writer, Avraham Freeman, wrote a novel, *1919* which depicted the tribulations of Jews during the killings in the Ukraine. He was awarded the Bialik Prize for Hebrew literature for the work in 1936. At that point in time, he was beginning a ten-year sentence in a Soviet camp. He died in December 1953 and was never able to receive his award in Tel Aviv.[55]

In the early 1920s, the first generation of Soviet Zionists was led mainly by young people who now had access to institutes of higher education. Many had been unable to find employment. Others had become disillusioned by the Leninist dream and its inability to deal with the reality of Jewish identity. Zionist groups split into legal and underground factions – those who accepted Soviet hegemony and those who did not. The legal organizations were able to meet Stalin and Kalinin and attempted to integrate their socialist Zionism into the evolving Soviet society. Even so, their ability to organize tens of thousands of Jews galvanized the Yevsektsiya to redouble their efforts in persuading the Soviet leadership to suppress any faction of Zionism.[56] Although this generation of Zionists was highly influenced by the Soviet experiment and knew nothing of Tsarist times, its fate was sealed. One by one their organizations were eliminated by the Cheka. There were even protests about the Passfield White paper in 1930.[57] The collective farms of He-Halutz were confiscated and turned over to the KOMZET which similarly wished to settle Jews on the land. Small circles and isolated individuals existed well into the 1930s until they too – along with their persecutors in the Yevsektsiya – were swept away by Stalin's purges. In September 1934 the executive committee of Tserei Tsion was rounded up in Moscow. Its sole representative, remaining at freedom, Ben-Zion Ginsburg, survived until February 1937 when he was arrested in Proskurov. He died under torture a few months later.

The story of Zionists under Soviet rule in the twentieth century was one of persecution and liquidation. It culminated in the emergence of a Jewish national movement after 1967 and a struggle for the right to leave the USSR. It concluded in the departure of 1 million citizens for Israel in the 1990s following the fall of the Berlin Wall. Yet this struggle continued throughout the entire period of the existence of the Soviet Union. There were Jews who did not wish to disappear as Jews according to Leninist philosophy and who did not wish to renounce their ideal to build a new society in Palestine.

In 1920, Yehiel Halperin, an activist in Tserei Tsion, was stopped from crossing the Russian border. During the next couple of years, he busied himself by being active in various Zionist youth groups including a period of working on the collective farm, Mishmar, in the Crimea for those hoping to leave for Palestine. In March 1927, Halperin was arrested in Minsk and eventually sentenced to three years' exile in north Kazakhstan. In October 1931, he was arrested yet again and given three years' exile in western Siberia. In December 1934, he returned to his parents' home, but was arrested once more in June 1935. This time he was sentenced to five years' hard labour in a camp. In 1940, he was allowed to travel to Dzhambul in Kazakhstan as a free man, but not permitted to leave the area. It was only in 1955 that he received the relevant document which allowed him to depart for Kiev where he lived until September 1970. It was then that he received permission to leave for Israel in the first wave of large-scale emigration. He had commenced his personal struggle to leave as a youth of 19. He succeeded in his goal as a man of almost 70. It had taken him exactly 50 years.[58]

Notes and Works Cited

1 Getzler, op. cit., p. 43.

2 Getzler, op. cit., p. 59.

3 *Iskra*, no. 36, 15 March 1903; *Iskra*, no. 41, 1 June 1903.

4 *Iskra*, no. 34, 15 February 1903; *Iskra*, no. 46, 15 August 1903; *Iskra*, no. 49, 1 October 1903; *Iskra*, no. 51, 22 October 1903.

5 V. I. Lenin, *Iskra*, no. 34, 15 February 1903 in Hyman Lumer, ed., *Lenin on the Jewish Question* (New York 1974).

6 V. I. Lenin, 'The Position of the Bund in the Party', *Iskra*, no. 51, 22 October 1903.

7 Lumer, op. cit.

8 Robert Service, *Lenin: A Biography* (London 2000), pp. 16–18.

9 Frankel, op.cit., p. 205.

10 Alfred Naquet, 'Drumont and Bernard Lazare', *La Petite Republique*, 24 September 1903.

11 Ernest Renan, 'Judaism as a Race and a Religion', in *Discours et Conferences par Ernest Renan* (Paris 1887), p. 373.

12 Shmuel Almog, 'The Racial Motif in Renan's Attitude to Jews and Judaism', in ed. Shmuel Almog, *Anti-Semitism Through the Ages* (London 1988), p. 260.

13 Ernest Renan, *History of the People of Israel*, vol. 5 (Boston 1907), p. 189.

14 Monty Noam Penkower, 'The Kishinev Pogrom of 1903: A Turning Point in Jewish History', *Modern Judaism*, vol. 24, no. 3 (2004).

15 C. N. Bialik, *Selected Poems* ed. and tr. David Aberbach (London 2004).

16 A. Walicki, 'Rosa Luxemburg and the Question of Nationalism in Polish Marxism 1893–1914', *Slavonic and East European Review*, vol. 61, no. 4 (October 1983), p. 527.

17 Elźbieta Ettinger, *Roza Luxemburg* (Boston 1986), pp. 14–15.

18 Rosa Luxemburg, 'The Dreyfus Affair and the Millerand Case', *Cahiers de la Quinzaine* (1899).

19 Robert Wistrich, *Laboratory for World Destruction: Germans and Jews in Central Europe* (London, 2007), pp. 99–117.

20 Karl Kautsky, 'The Kishinev Massacre and the Jewish Question', *Iskra*, no. 42, June 1903.

21 Karl Kautsky, 'On the Problems of the Jewish Proletariat in England', *Justice*, 23 April 1904.

22   Karl Kautsky, *Are the Jews a Race?* (New York 1926).

23   Jack Jacobs, *On Socialists and 'The Jewish Question' after Marx* (New York 1992), p. 21.

24   Ibid., pp. 10–25.

25   Henry J. Tobias, 'The Bund and Lenin until 1903', *Russian Review*, vol. 20, no. 4 (October 1961), p. 345.

26   Frankel, op. cit., p. 229.

27   Ibid., pp. 353–4.

28   Getzler, op cit., p. 76.

29   Vladimir Medem, 'Natsionale bavegung un natsionale sotsialististie partaien in Rusland', in *Vladimir Medem tsum tsvantsikstn yortseit* (New York 1973), p. 271 in ed. Zvi Y. Gitelman, *Jewish Nationality and Soviet Politics: The Jewish Sections of the CPSU 1917–1930* (Princeton 1972), p. 43.

30   Michael Confino, *Violence dans la Violence: Le Dèbat Bakounine-Necaev* (Paris 1973), p. 64 in Aileen Kelly, *Mikhail Bakunin: A Study in the Psychology and Politics of Utopianism* (Oxford 1982), p. 262.

31   Chaim Weizmann, *Trial and Error* (New York 1949), pp. 50–1.

32   V. I. Lenin, 'Critical Remarks on the National Question', *Prosveshcheniye*, 10, 11, 12 (1913).

33   Ibid.

34   Simon Dubnov, 'The Moral of Stormy Days', in ed. Koppel S. Pinson, *Nationalism and History: Essays on Old and New Judaism by Simon Dubnov* (Philadelphia 1958), p. 207.

35   Vladimir Jabotinsky, Introduction to *Chaim Nachman Bialik: Poems from the Hebrew*, ed. by L. V. Snowman (London 1924).

36   Nachman Syrkin, 'An Appeal to Jewish Youth', *Jewish Frontier*, June 1935.

37   J. V. Stalin, 'Marxism and the National Question' (1913).

38   Arieh Rafaeli (Tsentsiper), *B'maavak l'geula* (Tel Aviv 1956), p. 29.

39   Arieh Leib Tsentsiper, *Eser Sh'not Redifot* (Tel Aviv 1930), p. 30.

40   Rafaeli, op. cit., p. 25.

41   Yehoshua A. Gilboa, *A Language Silenced: The Suppression of Hebrew Literature and Culture in the Soviet Union* (New York 1982), p. 67.

42   Howard M. Sachar, *Dreamland: Europeans and Jews in the Aftermath of the Great War* (New York 2002), p. 18.

43   Paul Mendes-Flohr and Jehuda Reinharz, eds. *The Jew in the Modern World: A Documentary History* (Oxford 1995), p. 434.

44   Salo W. Baron, *The Russian Jew under Tsars and Soviets* (New York 1976), p. 394.

45   Benjamin West, ed. *Struggles of a Generation: The Jews under Soviet Rule* (Tel Aviv 1959), pp. 140–55.

46   M. Baizer and V. Izmozik, 'Dzerzhinskii's Attitude towards Zionism', *Jews in Eastern Europe*, no. 3 (Spring 1994).

47 West, op. cit., p. 146.

48 Rafaeli, op. cit., p. 62.

49 *New York Times*, 19 May 1920.

50 *Izvestia*, 16 May 1920.

51 *Ma'ariv*, 11 February 1971.

52 Yehoshua A. Gilboa, *Oktobre'im Ivrim* (Tel Aviv 1974).

53 Gilboa, *A Language Silenced*, op. cit., p. 262.

54 *Davar*, 10 June 1942.

55 Yehoshua A. Gilboa, 'Hebrew Literature in the USSR', in *The Jews in Soviet Russia since 1917* (Oxford 1970), pp. 224–5.

56 Ziva Galili, 'The Soviet Experience of Zionism: Importing Soviet Political Culture to Palestine', *Journal of Israeli History*, vol. 24, no. 1, March 2005.

57 Benjamin West, *B'derekh l'geula* (Tel Aviv 1971), p. 239.

58 Benjamin West, *Bein yayush l'tikva* (Tel Aviv 1973), p. 89.

3

Zionists and Communists in Palestine

Moscow or Jerusalem

In 1919, the pioneering labour party, Poale Zion amalgamated with a section of its non-Marxist rival, Hapoel Hatzair, to create a new movement, Achdut Ha'avoda. The raison d'être for its birth was in part a moving away from the theories of Dov Ber Borokhov who had attempted to develop ideas on Marxism and the national question in Russia. He argued that whereas Marx had elucidated the role of stychic (unplanned) phenomena within capitalism, such factors also existed in the national dimension as well.[1] This formulation when applied to the Jewish question, it was argued, would provide a realistic answer to the inadequacy of Lenin's approach. In addition, Borokhov had personal experience of this inability to deal with the Jewish question when the Ekaterinoslav branch of the RSDLP had expelled him in 1902. By the time of his early death in 1917, Borokhov had, in fact, changed his views, even so many still held to his original analysis. The debate among the Jews of Palestine was whether Borokhov's rendition of the national question applied much more to Russia than to the political realities of the Middle East. This emerging truth became apparent to the social democratic leadership of Poale Zion in Palestine including David Ben-Gurion and Yitzhak Ben-Zvi. Even so, a small group of die-hard Borokhovists refused to go into the merger with Hapoel Hatzair and thereby presided over a rump, Left Poale Zion which preached a proletarian Zionism. This break was accentuated by Lenin's coup in Russia. Bolshevik success facilitated a clear division in Poale Zion internationally over the meaning of the October Revolution for Zionists. Should Marxism Zionism in the Middle East be abandoned for building socialism at home in Russia? Should Poale Zion affiliate to the newly formed Communist International (Comintern)? Or to Herzl's World Zionist Organization? These were questions which pre-occupied the delegates to the conference of the World Union of Poale Zion in Vienna in August 1920.

The realization of the permanence of the Bolshevik revolution persuaded many members of Poale Zion, particularly those who had spent the war years in Russia to abandon Zionism and to put their energies into building a socialist Jerusalem in Moscow instead. In Palestine, the magnetism of the success of the Bolsheviks caused a schism in Left Poale Zion to establish the MOPS, (Mifleget Ha'Poalim Ha'Sotsialistit), the Socialist Workers Party, which dreamed that the Red Army would cross the Caucasus and create a Soviet Palestine.[2] This represented the birth of a Jewish Left in Palestine which marginalized Zionism as an ideology and formally opposed Ben-Gurion's labour establishment.

The splits within Poale Zion more resembled those in Britain's labour movement than in other European countries. Such fragments eventually formed a weak party, loyal to Leninist ideals. In contrast, the social democratic parties led by Ben-Gurion over the succeeding decades became the instrument in state building and controlling a mixed economy. The distancing from Borokhovism, disdain for Soviet Communism and involvement in the increasingly intractable struggle with Arab nationalism ensured that there would always be Marxist alternatives, both Zionist and anti-Zionist, to Ben-Gurion's approach.

Changing its name three times in as many years, the fervent activities of the Mopsim proved to be an irritant for both the British and the mainstream Labour Zionists. At the founding conference of the Histadrut in 1920, they called for a joint struggle with the Arab masses against Zionism. Yet they were unable to make any headway with the Arab masses whose leadership often regarded Zionism and Communism as one and the same thing. Their lack of knowledge of Arabic and unfamiliarity with Arab culture erected a high barrier. On the other hand, they were blamed for instigating the May Day riots in 1921 when their demonstration clashed with one by Achdut Ha'avoda – whom they accused of paving the way for bourgeois Zionists to achieve economic control of Palestine. The firing of rifles in the air by the police to bring order led to rumours that Arabs had been killed. This catalysed a rampage which led to several deaths at the hands of a mob including the noted writer Yosef Chaim Brenner. The Haycroft Commission which reported on the incident remarked that Bolshevik immigrants were unwisely being allowed into Palestine. Sir Herbert Samuel, the British High Commissioner then temporarily suspended Jewish immigration and reclassified immigrants into seven new categories. The Arabs of Palestine urged the British to maintain the ban on immigration since 'the diffusion of Bolshevik principles' was a result of the Jews coming to Palestine. They also called for deporting Bolshevik Jews.[3] Even with the suppression of the Mopsim by the British who deported several activists, the leadership was divided over the balance between revolutionary and evolutionary activity. Indeed some who opposed Zionism left Palestine. They split once more to form the more radical and anti-Zionist KPP (Komunistishe Partey fun Palestine). By 1923, however, Moscow had had enough and under pressure, these factions were reunited as the Palestine Communist Party (PCP).

For some Arab leaders, there existed a belief that there was no difference between a Zionist and a Bolshevik. Remarkably, Lenin and Weizmann were mistaken for each other due to their similar facial appearance. Kibbutzim were depicted as breeding grounds for immorality and centres of Bolshevism. In Europe, there were many commentators who were keen to verify this. The Dutch diplomat, Willem Jacob Oudendijk, spoke of the 'bajonettocratie' of the mostly Jewish Bolsheviks and their associates. Even Churchill described Bolshevism as 'a Jewish movement'.[4] Yet Churchill unlike others made a distinction between Bolshevism and Zionism. It was, he argued, 'a struggle for the soul of the Jewish people'.[5] Others in the Middle East propagated the twin polar imagery of the Jew as capitalist banker and the Jew as Communist revolutionary. It was at this time that the anti-Semitic forgery 'The Protocols of the Elders of Zion' first made its appearance in the Middle East.

Unlike the Labour Zionists, the Palestine Communists subscribed to Lenin's Twenty-One theses for admission to the Comintern which were agreed at the second congress of the organization in August 1920. It called for the removal 'in an orderly and planned fashion' of reformists and centrists from all responsible positions in the workers' movement and to 'replace them by tried communists, even if, particularly at the beginning, "experienced" opportunists have to be replaced by ordinary rank and file workers'. Following the alignment of many social democrats with the national interests of their own states rather than the international proletariat during World War I, the Comintern demanded that any adherents expose social patriotism and 'also the insincerity and hypocrisy of social pacifism'. Both Europe and the United States were deemed to be on the verge of civil war and the Comintern therefore urged the creation of a parallel illegal organization, in addition to the party, 'which at the decisive moment will help the party to do its duty to the revolution'. It argued that all parties which wished to join the Comintern had to work within trade unions, workers' councils, factory committees and workers' cooperatives for the Communist cause. The Comintern preached the importance of the principle of democratic centralism where the iron discipline of the party centre had to prevail in 'the present epoch of acute civil war'. All parliamentary representatives of the party had be vetted and approved – and the work of any parliamentary faction subordinated to the centre. The centralization extended to giving 'unconditional support to any Soviet republic in its struggle against counter-revolutionary forces'. They should prevent 'the dispatch of munitions transports to the enemies of the Soviet republics . . . and carry on propaganda by every means, legal or illegal, among the troops sent to strangle workers' republics'.[6]

All this was highly reminiscent of Lenin's approach in his campaign against the Bund in 1903. The wording of the Twenty-One theses, of course, was often ambiguous and open to interpretation – and thereby to potential abuse. Who was a reformist or a counter-revolutionary? It advocated the subversion of already existing workers' movements and bitter opposition to the Second International of social democratic parties. As in Russia itself, the parties of Left were forced to disband and its adherents to either remain in the political wilderness or join the Communist Party under these terms. Many like Martov were forced to choose exile. As the Communist Party achieved its domination in Russia, no political room was available for other viewpoints. For those who carried on their political work illegally or railed against the diminishing belief in freedom of expression, the embryonic Gulag awaited them. Many Marxist Jews decided that building socialism in Palestine was a better bet than Lenin's enforced dictatorship of the proletariat. Loyalty to the Soviet Union was already emerging as a defining factor for any party which joined the Comintern. All this was formerly accepted by the Jewish Communists in Palestine in February 1924.

Moreover, the Comintern and its Eastern Department in Moscow did not view the building of socialism in Palestine in the same way as the PCP. The Comintern which contained a disproportionate number of Jews, some of whom were former Zionists, regarded the presence of Zionist Jews in Palestine as anathema. Any successful building of socialism in Palestine by their former Zionist friends was also seen as ideologically as well as psychologically threatening. Moreover, in a period of locating opponents of the Kremlin in every political nook and cranny, they felt that they still had to prove their loyalty to the regime, now under the watchful eye of Stalin. There were also a plethora of ex-Bundists who had vehemently opposed Zionism in their pre-Communist days. The growth of the Jewish settlement in Palestine, they believed, could be reversed.

The influx of Jews into the Communist Party also meant that a disproportionate number of Jews were now working in the Comintern. By the 1930s, Jews were second only to Russians in running the executive committee of the Comintern, outstripping Poles, Germans, French and English.[7] While Karl Radek, as a leading functionary of the Comintern, symbolized the cosmopolitan assimilated Jew who was at home in different cultures, former Bundists and former Zionists enthusiastically went about creating a network of Communist parties. Their antagonism towards Zionism blended in with a growing sense of Soviet nationalism rather than socialist internationalism.

Following Stalin's ascent to power in the 1920s, Zionism became even more suspect in official Soviet eyes because it had originated from Russian Jewry. Moreover, many Jews in the newly founded USSR continued to sympathize with the Zionist experiment. Stalin had been disparaging towards Jews very early on in his career. The preponderance of Mensheviks in his native Georgia led to his characterization of leaders of the party, Martov and Axelrod, as 'circumcised Yids'.[8] Trotsky, himself, had become sensitized to the prevalence and use of this kind of anti-Semitism in the USSR when he lost the power struggle to Stalin and his supporters in the mid-1920s.[9] Jews were depicted as being more involved in the Left Opposition than in either Stalin's or Bukharin's factions. The use of anti-Semitic innuendo was initiated as a party weapon to be used against highly assimilated Jews within the Bolshevik leadership who had previously given little thought to their Jewishness. This rekindled anti-Semitism among the most backward section of the population. Bolshevik Jews, such as Trotsky and Zinoviev, no matter how distant from their Jewishness, were not Russians – and therefore not qualified to lead Russia, not even a socialist Russia. A whispering campaign labelled Trotsky's followers as 'petty bourgeois from small towns'.[10] Radek, a witty litterateur even in the most adverse of situations, joked 'What's the difference between Moses and Stalin? Moses took the Jews out of Egypt; Stalin takes them out of the Communist Party.'[11]

Stalin had a long history of dislike for Jews per se – and in particular those who belonged to the intellectual elite.[12] Trotsky, despite his profound lack of identification with Jewishness, was seen as the supreme symbol of this demonic influence. Indeed, while intellectuals dominated the Soviet politburo during the early 1920s. Some years later, following the ousting of Trotsky and the ascendency of Stalin, the politburo was now constituted primarily of workers. Any sense of experimentation and innovation came to an end and a rigid conformity ruled the day. Jewish intellectuals had often given way to Stalinist apparatchiks.

By the 1930s, the Jews in the USSR were increasingly perceived as an alien element with relatives abroad. They were seen as ideologically suspect despite the disproportionate number of Jews in the Communist Party. Many former members of Poale Zion feared that they would be uncovered and worked zealously to prove their worth to the Kremlin and the authenticity of their conversion.

Into this increasingly poisonous cocktail, the Comintern came to believe that the Jews in Palestine were merely Zionist agents of British imperialism. The show trials of the 1930s which liquidated the Bolshevik old guard often referred to the Jewish origin of their defendants. Zinoviev and Kamenev appeared in the Soviet press under their original names – Radomislyski and Rosenfeld. When Arkady Rosengolts, a former Soviet diplomat, was interrogated by Vishinsky during the trial of Bukharin and Rykov in 1938, Stalin's prosecutor unexpectedly baited the doomed defendant with the revelation of a concealed amulet from his wife, containing a text from the Book of Psalms. The texts were from Psalms 68 and 91. The first was a song for King David – 'let his enemies be scattered; let them that hate him flee before him'. The second spoke of God's protection – 'thou shalt not be afraid for the terror by night'.[13] Stalin particularly loathed Rosengolts[14] and this interest in the Book of Psalms clearly did not suddenly emerge from Vishinsky's mouth.

The revolt in the East

The socialist world and Marxist theory had hardly noted the problems of the colonies and its revolutionary potential before 1914. Like Lenin on the Jewish question, the focus of European socialists was essentially on their own domestic questions. Apart from the white dominions, non-Europeans were invisible at meetings of the Second International. Socialists certainly subscribed to the mission civilisatrice.

It was Lenin, himself, who changed all that. In the spring of 1916, Lenin, then living in Zurich, wrote *Imperialism, the Highest Stage of Capitalism*. It argued that since 1860 cartels and monopolies had developed to become 'one of the foundations of the whole of economic life'. Capitalism, Lenin argued, had been transformed into imperialism. In the same year, he argued that the future of the West depended on support from the East.

> Social revolution can occur only in an entire epoch in which the civil war of the proletariat against the bourgeoisie in the advanced countries is joined with the whole number of revolutionary democratic and national liberation movements in the backward and oppressed nations.[15]

Lenin argued that in the advanced colonialist countries such as Britain, capitalism was being transformed in an age of imperialism since the period of Marx and Engels. The stage of bourgeois democratic revolution had become redundant and the conditions were now ripe for the establishment of socialism. In the colonies, however, feudalism and primitive capitalism still dominated. There the objective conditions for socialism had not come to full maturity. Hence a bourgeois revolution was required.

In a new preface to the French and English editions, written in July 1920, he vehemently assailed the French and the British. He reiterated his conviction that World War I had been an imperialist war, a predatory war, an annexationist war, a war of plunder. 'It was a war for the division of the world, for the partition and repartition of colonies and spheres of influence of finance capital.'

> Private property, based on the labour of the small proprietor, free competition, democracy – all the catchwords with which the capitalists and their press deceive the workers and peasants – are things of the past. Capitalism has grown into a world system of colonial oppression and of the financial strangulation of the overwhelming majority of the population of the world by a handful of 'advanced' countries. And this 'booty' is shared between two or three powerful world plunderers, armed to the teeth (America, Great Britain and Japan) who are drawing the whole world into their war over their division of the booty.

Both the February and the October revolutions inspired anti-colonial nationalists. Non-Europeans started to attend meetings of the Left. Indeed Russia's economic backwardness provided a model for the developing world. At the founding congress of the Comintern, nearly a quarter of the delegates came from Asia.[16] This distinguished the Comintern from the Second International. Lenin had brought the issue of colonialism to the international Left. The Revolution had first and foremost focused on the non-Russian nationalities of the Empire, stretching from Poland in the west to Mongolia in the east. This provided a template for the colonies of the imperial powers. In particular how Russia's internal colonies in the East were dealt with by the new Bolshevik regime could inspire revolutionary activity in the Middle East and India. Moreover, some 10% of the inhabitants of the Tsarist Empire were Muslims. Their liberation could be an example for Muslims worldwide. 'The Muslim weapon against the European powers' was particularly aimed at Britain because Muslims formed one of the largest groups in its colonies as well as 'the most prone towards revolts'.[17] It was therefore important for the Bolsheviks to ensure the allegiance of Muslim nationalists in their hinterland. In May 1917, the first All-Russian Congress of Muslims was staged in Moscow – and it heartily celebrated the end of Tsarism. It argued for the rights of women and an end to polygamy. In July 1917 there were attempts to convene an All Muslim Military Council which sought the allegiance of all Muslims in combat and to organize them in separate units. While there were some groups such as the Crimean Tartars who aided the Whites, the February Revolution was welcomed by Muslim reformers such as the Jadids (innovators) who were influenced by the Young Turks revolt.

Muslim nationalism unlike Jewish nationalism often meant a synthesis between religion and nationalism. While its left wing established Muslim Socialist Committees, it did not mean a distancing of religion.

A couple of weeks after the October Revolution, the Bolsheviks issued an appeal to 'All the Muslim Workers of Russia and the East' which alluded to Tsarist colonialism and depicted how Christian Moscow had suppressed Islam and Islamic culture and destroyed mosques. Lenin cultivated left wing Muslim nationalists and hoped to persuade them to enter the Communist Party. He later entertained the idea of a compromise between sharia law and the Soviet legal system. The slogan 'Long live Soviet power, long live the sharia' was heard in Central Asia. On the other hand, he was wary of embracing both pan-Islamism and National Communism. Jadid intellectuals such as the Tartar, Mirsäyet Soltangäliev, a former radical nationalist, joined the Communist Party, edited *Zhizn Natsionnalnostei* (Life of the Nationalities), sat on the Commissariat for Nationalities, but soon fell out with Lenin and Stalin over his insistence on maintaining his Muslim identity within the political arena. Soltangäliev was also clear why he joined the Bolsheviks. A few weeks after the October Revolution, he commented:

They . . . declared war on English imperialism, which oppresses India, Egypt, Afghanistan, Persia and Arabia. They are also the ones who raised arms against French imperialism, which enslaves Morocco, Algiers, and other Arab states of Africa. How could I not go to them? You see, they proclaimed the words, which have never been voiced since creation of the world in the history of the Russian state. Appealing to all Muslims of Russia and the East, they announced that Istanbul must be in Muslims' hands. They did this while English troops, seizing Jerusalem, appealed to Jews with the words: 'Gather together quickly in Palestine, we will create for you a European state'.[18]

The anti-colonial stand was paramount and there was little commitment to building socialism in such sentiments. In contrast, Marxist-Zionists viewed the Balfour Declaration as an opportunity to build socialism in Palestine. Moreover, Mirsäyet Soltangäliev warned that any anti-religious campaign should proceed with extreme caution as it was both a delicate and complex issue. Islam, he argued, was regarded as an oppressed religion which would be defended. Following the defeat and expulsion of the Arabs from Spain, contemporary European imperialism was seen as a more modern version of the Crusades. In the aftermath of a world war, there was a deep-seated fear that Britain would seize Muslim states to add to its empire. Soltangäliev therefore understood the Balfour Declaration as an appendage to British imperialism and a new addition to Muslim suffering. Indeed he argued that the real division was not based on class, between the workers and the bourgeoisie, but between the colonial exploiters and their subjugated subjects. The element of class was a product of the historical development of Europe and not of the East. It should therefore be replaced by working with all sections of the population in order to work for socialism. Soltanğäliev's heretical views on Muslim National Communism eventually led to his expulsion from the Communist Party. Indeed he came to understand Communist Russia as an imperial power. It was this different perception of the future of Palestine which governed the growth of both Jewish socialism and Arab nationalism in that territory.

The Balfour Declaration, the British had reasoned, would earn the admiration of the Jews in Russia and would actually strengthen the Kerensky regime's desire to continue with the war. In the United States, many Jewish immigrants came from Eastern Europe and detested the Tsarist regime with a deep passion. They were not opposed to a German victory over their former tormentors and oppressors in Russia. Such opposition, however, could prove an obstacle to fully involving the United States in the war. Moreover, there were strong rumours that the German government would shortly issue their own Balfour Declaration. Jews were seen as all-powerful and influential. However in an ironic twist of history, the Bolsheviks overthrew the Kerensky regime at the same time as the British issued the Balfour Declaration. The British government remarkably believed that the Declaration would influence the Jews in the Bolshevik party – that there was no difference between Jewish Jews and assimilated ones, that there was a convergence of views between Lord Rothschild, to whom the Declaration was addressed and Leon Trotsky, a central architect of the Revolution. All Jews, they believed, thought along the same lines and would fall over themselves in praise of this display of British magnanimity towards the Jews. Significantly Trotsky made his famous comment, 'I am not a Jew, I am an internationalist' to the Chief Rabbi of Petrograd just a few days after the Balfour Declaration.[19]

Shortly after taking power, the Bolsheviks were alarmed by the discovery of the Sykes-Picot agreement which was the basis for the division of the Arab world by the imperial powers. But they also saw it as an opportunity to win support for their regime. It was immediately understood that the conquest of Palestine brought the British closer to Russia's borders and would smooth the path in reversing the Bolshevik coup. The agreement was quickly published in both *Pravda* and in *Izvestia* some two weeks after the October Revolution.[20] British efforts to win over Russian Jews continued into 1918 and in particular, they wanted to disrupt Trotsky's direction of the German-Russian negotiations at Brest-Litovsk.

Both Islam and Muslim nationalism if subservient to the party could be important in ensuring the survival of Lenin's regime, given their numbers and influence in Russia and in the colonies of their British and French enemies.

The Bolsheviks instituted annual congresses of 'Communist Organisations of the Peoples of the East'. In introducing the second congress, Stalin stressed the revolutionary awakening of the East where subjugated peoples now threatened 'the wealth of imperialism'. The imperialists, Stalin claimed, were now surrounded by both the proletarians of the West and the peoples of the East.[21] However as Lenin reiterated in June 1920 at the second congress of the Comintern, it was not simply the liberation of oppressed people that was the issue at stake, but that the success of their struggle depended on the very continuation of the Soviet state.

> World political developments are of necessity concentrated on a single focus — the struggle of the world bourgeoisie against the Soviet Russian Republic, around which are inevitably grouped, on the one hand, the Soviet movements of the advanced workers in all countries, and, on the other, all the national liberation movements in the colonies and among the oppressed nationalities, who are learning from bitter experience that their only salvation lies in the Soviet system's victory over world imperialism.[22]

Any move to inflict damage on the imperial powers would therefore also assist in deflecting British imperialism in particular from its desire to strangle the fledgling workers' state in Russia at birth. The bottom line of survival soon became synonymous with the vested national interests of the state.

Lenin understood a proletarian revolution could not be carried out immediately in states where a proletariat did not exist and where feudalism persisted amidst pre-capitalist conditions. He therefore argued that Communist parties in this situation should assist in 'the bourgeois democratic liberation movement in those countries'. A temporary alliance would be entered into with such national-revolutionary movements and this would be a stage towards this goal of proletarian revolution. Nationalism which was regarded as reactionary in the West was therefore seen as progressive – at least in the public arena – in the East. Indeed Bukharin urged delegates to support 'the most outright nationalist movements . . . if it contributes to the destruction of English imperialism'.[23] Thus by 1926, the coming to power of Ibn Saud in Hijaz and Nejd was welcomed by the Kremlin and depicted as liberating.[24] It also led to Soviet agreements with nationalists and monarchists even when local Communists were being persecuted at home. Thus Russia signed treaties with both Turkey and Afghanistan in 1921.

However, Lenin was quite clear in warning against working with pan-Islamists and supporting pan-Islamic movements which sought to utilize national liberation movements for their own ideological aims. Lenin pointedly condemned social democrats and liberals who maintained their internationalism through word but not by deed 'even among parties which now call themselves communist'.[25] Lenin suggested that with the help of the proletariat in 'advanced countries, the less developed countries can arrive at soviet organisation and through a series of stages – and even avoiding the capitalist system – can arrive at Communism'. Once again, all this lay within the realm of theory and Lenin was realistic enough to point out that the means for determining this was unknown, but that 'practical experience will tell'.

Lenin's proposed theses on the national and colonial question was placed before one of the Comintern congress's commissions to list any amendments. Significantly it was suggested that after the word 'prejudices' in one clause, the following should be added 'which appear in all possible forms such as racial hatred, nationalist propaganda, anti-Semitism'. This later became the template for the bracketing of 'Zionism and anti-Semitism'. Zionism, itself, was criticized, according to Lenin's understanding from 1903.

> A glaring example of the deception practiced on the working classes of an oppressed nation by the combined efforts of Entente imperialism and the bourgeoisie of the same nation is offered by the Zionists' Palestine venture (and by Zionism as a whole), which under the pretence of creating a Jewish state in Palestine in fact surrenders the Arab working people of Palestine, where Jewish workers form only a small minority, to exploitation by England.[26]

Zionism, it seemed, was separated from the Jewish proletariat in Palestine. Yet the Jews in Palestine overwhelmingly did not disavow Zionism and many regarded themselves as socialist Zionists.

Notes and Works Cited

1 Allon Gal, *Socialist-Zionism: Theory and Issues in Contemporary Jewish Nationalism* (Boston 1989), pp. 12–14.

2 Walter Z. Laqueur, *Communism and Nationalism in the Middle East* (London 1956), p. 75.

3 Yehoshua Porath, *The Emergence of the Palestinian Arab National Movement 1918–1929* (London 1974), pp. 56–60.

4 *Times*, 5 January 1920.

5 Winston S. Churchill, 'Zionism vs Bolshevism: A Struggle for the Soul of the Jewish People', *Illustrated Sunday Herald*, 8 February 1920.

6 Jane Degras, *The Communist International 1919–1943: Documents vol. 1 (1919–1943)*, pp. 168–72.

7 Peter Huber, 'Structure of the Moscow Apparatus of the Comintern and Decision Making', in *International Communism and the Communist International 1919–1943*, ed. Tim Rees and Andrew Thorpe (Manchester 1998), p. 46.

8 Simon Sebag Montefiore, *Young Stalin* (New York 2007), pp. 130–1.

9 Joseph Nedava, *Trotsky and the Jews* (Philadelphia 1972), pp. 168–82.

10 Leon Trotsky, 'Thermidor and Anti-Semitism', *New International*, vol. 7, no. 4, May 1941.

11 Nedava, op. cit., p. 268.

12 Sebag-Montefiore, op. cit., pp. 130-1.

13 Report of the Court Proceedings in the Case of the Anti-Soviet 'Bloc of Rights and Trotskyites' (Moscow 1938), pp. 622–3.

14 Arkady Vaksberg, *The Prosecutor and the Prey: Vishinsky and the 1930s Moscow Show Trials* (London 1990), p. 342.

15 V. I. Lenin, 'On the Caricature of Marxism', in ed. Xenia Joukoff Eudin and Robert C. North, *Soviet Russia and the East 1920–1927* (Stanford 1957), p. 45.

16 Geoff Eley, *Forging Democracy: The History of the Left in Europe 1850–2000* (Oxford 2002), p. 181.

17 Mohammed Nuri al-Amin, 'The Role of International Communism in the Muslim World and in Egypt and the Sudan', *British Journal of Middle Eastern Studies*, vol. 23, no. 1 (May 1996).

18 I. G. Gizzatullin, D. R. Sharafutdinov (compilers), *Mirsaid Sultan-Galiev. Stat'I, vystupleniia, dokumenty* (Kazan': Tatarskoe knizhskoe izdatel'stvo, 1992), p. 52. Soltanğäliev's letter was published on 19 December 1917 in the newspaper *Koyash*, the same paper that had published the attack on Soltanğäliev's sympathies two days earlier, a clear sign of the openness of political debate in Kazan at that time.

19 *Jewish Chronicle*, 28 December 1917.

20 *Guardian*, 26 November 1917.

21 J. V. Stalin, *Collected Works*, vol. 4 (Moscow 1953), pp. 290–2.

22 V. I. Lenin, *Draft Theses on the National and Colonial Questions Collected Works*, vol. 31 (Moscow 1965).

23 Degras, op. cit., p. 139.

24 E. H. Carr, *Socialism in One Country* (London 1964), p. 655.

25 V. I. Lenin, *Draft Theses on the National and Colonial Questions Collected Works*, vol. 31 (Moscow 1965).

26 Degras, op. cit., p. 144.

4

Cultivating Arab nationalism

Between nationalism and socialism

The failure of the Bolsheviks in the West to defeat Pilsudski's Poland and to oust the social democrats in Germany meant a contraction of the aims of the revolution. The much promoted internationalism began in reality to take on a secondary role – the inability of the revolution to foment change in the advanced countries of Western Europe inevitably led to consolidation, the emphasis on Soviet national interests and the advent of 'socialism in one country'. Even so, there was the residual hope that taking the East would in part nullify the effects of failure in the West. Moreover, with the defeat of the Whites under Kolchak and Denikin, the regime's borders were now contiguous with Iran, Afghanistan and Turkey. There could now be 'a turn to the East'. Indeed as early as 1919, Trotsky had suggested going eastwards towards India to spread the revolution and cause problems for the British. This was blocked by Lenin who opposed armed intervention by the Bolsheviks in the colonies, but supported military assistance to the colonial masses.[1]

The developing world, however, was not the industrialized countries of the West – wherein Lenin had placed all his hopes. In September 1920, the first congress of the Peoples of the East took place in Baku. This was organized to follow through on Lenin's theses on the national and colonial question, enunciated at the second congress of the Comintern.[2] It was fronted by three Bolshevik Jews, Zinoviev, Radek and Bela Kun. Zinoviev had been appointed chairman of the Comintern by Lenin. Radek and Bela Kun had presided over failed attempts to establish Soviets in Germany and Hungary. Radek epitomized the assimilated Jewish revolutionary who was born in Poland, but became politically active in Germany and Russia and showed a great interest in Britain and France.

> And when my memory brings back images, they are not the images of Pushkin but of Mickiewicz. And when I wish to speak words of endearment to a beloved woman, it is Polish words that come to my lips.[3]

A writer and a practitioner of the black arts of propaganda, he was one of the initiators of the Comintern. In particular, he took an interest in the East following his failure to stimulate revolution in post-war Germany. Karl Radek had previously been quite clear in the rationale of Soviet policy:

> English imperialism, in particular cannot make up its mind on a definite honest policy towards us, because it is frightfully afraid of our revolutionising influence in the East. However, English imperialism is forcing Soviet Russia Eastward. It stands to reason – if Soviet Russia gets no peace, it is obliged to fight the Allies, it will fight them where it is easiest to beat them.[4]

At the conference itself, Turks, Persians and Armenians were the most numerous, followed by Russians, Georgians, Chechens and Tadzhiks. The background of Tsarist expansion into Central Asia during the previous 400 years provided an attentive audience. Yet they had been effective bystanders during the October Revolution. Moreover, the Bolsheviks knew that they faced an uphill struggle especially since Lenin's Theses on the National and Colonial Question had formerly opposed 'Pan-Islamic and Pan-Asiatic movements and similar tendencies'. Yet a large section of those who attended were precisely supporters of these ideologies and were openly anti-Communist. Indeed several delegates including those from Tunis and the Dutch East Indies referred to Lenin's hostility to pan-Islamism and argued that it damaged the cause of Communism. Moreover, the destruction of Kokand in Turkestan by the Bolsheviks was well-known.

Instead Radek described such movements as 'Russia's second sword' in preventing the encirclement of the new regime by the British. At its second session, he gave a wide-ranging speech which surveyed the plight of the colonized world from Ireland to Iraq. While he emphasized the dismemberment of the Ottoman empire, the presence of 80,000 British troops in Mesopotamia and the thirst for oil in Arabia, there was neither mention of Palestine nor the Balfour Declaration. Yet Radek labelled the Hashemite Emir Faisal as a hireling of the British. He was quite clear why the East had to rise up.

> Your destiny and ours is one; either we and the peoples of the East shall be united and consequently shall hasten the victory of the western European proletariat (over capital) or we shall perish and you will become slaves.[5]

Representatives of newly formed Communist parties in Western Europe were also present. When the British delegate spoke, he concentrated on British iniquities in Ireland and India – and again there was no mention of either Palestine or the Balfour Declaration. The final declaration of the congress was a country-by-country condemnation of British imperialism. Its appraisal of the British presence in the Arab world, but this time he did mention the Jewish settlements in Palestine.

> What has Britain done to Mesopotamia and Arabia? It has, without any ado, proclaimed these independent Muslim countries to be its colonies, driven from the land the Arabs who have owned it for centuries, taken from them the best, most fertile valleys of the Tigris and the Euphrates, taken the best pasture – land, which the people need in order to survive, taken the very rich oilfields of Mosul and Basra, and, stripping the Arabs of all means of livelihood, is trying to force them through hunger to become its slaves and its workers.
>
> What has Britain done to Palestine? There, at first, acting for the benefit of Anglo-Jewish capitalists, it drove Arabs from the land in order to give the latter to Jewish settlers; then, trying to appease the discontent of the Arabs, it incited them against these same Jewish settlers, sowing discord, enmity and hatred between all the communities, weakening both in order that it may itself rule and command.
>
> What has Britain done to Egypt? There the entire native population has for eight decades groaned beneath the heavy yoke of the British capitalists, a yoke even heavier and more ruinous for the people than was that of the Egyptian Pharaohs who built their huge pyramids with slave labour.[6]

The appeal to Islam and to the Arab world was clear. The British in Palestine were deemed to be acting solely on behalf of wealthy Jews. Their task was to engineer the dispossession of the indigenous Arabs – and then to egg on those same Arabs to attack Jewish settlers in a divide and rule strategy. The Jewish settlers were depicted as pawns in the hands of both British imperialists and Jewish capitalists – with no mind of their own. Yet the third aliyah between 1919 and 1923 had consisted mainly of Jewish socialists from Russia and Poland.

Moreover the conference organizers had to cope with the perception that the Bolsheviks had declared war on God and were opposed to Islam. Zinoviev's call for 'a holy war' and Karl Radek's praise for the military heritage of the conquering armies of Islam that had advanced into Europe were indicative of the desire of the Kremlin to win Muslim support for the October Revolution.

Marxism-Leninism, however, had very little appeal in the Arab world. It was seen as vehemently anti-religious and Russian Bolshevism itself found it difficult to relate to Arab cultural norms. Lenin had made his general position clear in a speech in March 1919.

> What, then, can we do in relation to such peoples as the Kirghiz, the Uzbeks, the Tajiks, the Turkmen, who to this day are under the influence of their mullahs? Here, in Russia, the population, having had a long experience of the priests, helped us to overthrow them. But you know how badly the decree on civil marriage is still being put into effect. Can we approach these peoples and tell them that we shall overthrow their exploiters? We cannot do this, because they are entirely subordinated to their mullahs. In such cases we have to wait until the given nation develops, until the differentiation of the proletariat from the bourgeois elements, which is inevitable, has taken place.[7]

In contrast to Lenin's cautious approach, Zinoviev and Radek argued publicly that the Islamic East could be subject to the same class basis as the Christian West. As the early Zionists discovered quickly, Palestine was not Russia, and there was no capitalist infrastructure. Lenin understood this.

Russia never viewed the Arab world as a unitary state thus setting its face against pan-Arabism. There was no common border between Russia and the Arab world. Apart from sympathy for the Palestinian Arab cause – due to the exhortations of the Jewish Communists in the Comintern and the Yevsektsiya – Russia never exhibited much interest in the Arab world in the 1920s.[8] Lenin was far more interested in the Turks – the former ruler of the Middle East. Moreover Lenin had been preceded in the Arab world by nineteenth-century reformers such as Jamal al-Din al-Afghani who proceeded to Islamize the received socialist wisdom. Al-Afghani preached an Islamic socialism where there would be no class war and where private ownership would be tolerated. 'Socialism', he wrote, 'is part and parcel of the religion of Islam'.[9] Al-Afghani was also an early advocate of opposing European imperialism. Such ideas laid the basis more for Arab nationalism than for Arab socialism. By the end of World War I, the arrival of both the British and the French in the region deepened the opposition to the Europeans.

In contrast, the Jews had been strongly influenced by the French Revolution and had bathed in the light of their own enlightenment as well, the Haskala. The path leading to nationalism had been as different for the Arabs as for the Jews. Zionism was essentially a rebellion against the rabbis and relegated faith to a lower rung. Arab nationalism, on the other hand, was a synthesis of modernity, tradition and religion – and an emphatic endorsement of faith.

The advance of Arab nationalism

The rise of nationalism in the Arab world following the Young Turks' revolt in 1908 was accentuated by the proposed cannibalization of the Ottoman Empire, according to the original terms of the Sykes-Picot agreement. This promised Greece, Italy, France and Britain a piece of the pie. Syria would go to the French and Britain would retain control over Palestine and Mesopotamia.

This also contradicted previous British promises to both the Arabs and the Jews, made in the heat of war. The earlier Sherif Hussein-McMahon correspondence in 1915 and 1916 was the basis whereby the Hashemites were led to believe that a unitary Arab state would be established if they helped the British drive out the Turks from the Middle East. Britain, of course, famously promised the Jews a national home in Palestine, through the publication of the Balfour Declaration, providing the interests of the local Arab inhabitants were not impinged upon. What 'a national home' meant was open to question by different parties at different times. The Zionists presumed that it meant a state – and it was in British interests at the height of a struggle with imperial Germany to allow that presumption to be perpetuated. Sykes significantly only heard about a proposed declaration on behalf of the Jews when he was in Petrograd in March 1916. On learning about this, Picot was immediately opposed.

Zionism was seen by Arab nationalists as an alien creed whose socialist colouring would challenge both authority and tradition in the Arab world. The Zionist did not fit the dhimmi imagery of the Jew who had to be kept in his inferior position. Moreover, the teachings of Rashid Rida and others which gave rise to modern Arab nationalism had little place for the other – and particularly if the other happened to be a Jew, an atheist and a Marxist.

The inability of the Comintern to make any headway in the Arab world finally convinced the Kremlin that the future lay in embracing Arab nationalism, regardless of its lack of progressive character. It therefore gave a wide ideological berth to national movements in the Arab world which they thought would protect the Soviet Union from its adversaries and perhaps one day foment proletarian revolution.

On the other hand, the acceptance of the Twenty-One theses allowing for adherence to the Comintern included a clause which obliged any local Communist Party

To expose the tricks and dodges of 'its' imperialists in the colonies, to support every colonial liberation movement, not merely in words, but in deeds, to demand the expulsion of their own imperialists from these colonies, to inculcate among the workers of their country a genuinely fraternal attitude to the working people of the colonies and the oppressed nations and to carry on systematic agitation among the troops of their country against any oppression of the colonial peoples.[10]

With the formation of the Comintern in 1919, Lenin's dilemma, however, was whether to fight bourgeois nationalism as part of the general struggle against capitalism or to support them – or at least its progressive wing – in their opposition to imperialism. The second congress of the Comintern in fact argued both positions.

The Comintern was surprised to discover that the May Day demonstrations in 1921 by the Mopsim with their revolutionary slogans had bewildered the Arabs of Jaffa. An appeal to revolutionary ardour and Arab-Jewish solidarity by the Mopsim had descended into pillage and killings. The Haycroft report into the disturbances commented that the Arabs did not make a distinction between the old colonists and the new immigrants – no distinction was made between Zionists and Jews. This was also food for thought for Jews on the revolutionary Left. Lenin had argued that in capitalist societies in Europe, workers would defend Jews during such periods. Was this just within the realm of theory? Did different conditions apply in Palestine and the Arab world in general?

In order to attract support in the Arab world, the Comintern argued for an 'anti-colonial front' at its fourth congress in December 1922. Moreover at the twelfth party congress in April 1923, Stalin had once more argued that the USSR needed 'a breathing space'.

Two things are possible; either we succeed in stirring up and revolutionising the far imperialist rear – the colonial and semi-colonial countries of the East – and thereby hasten the fall of capitalism, or we fail and thereby strengthen imperialism and weaken the force of our movement.[11]

This moved the PCP's leadership towards a more anti-Zionist position publicly. Zionism was projected as reactionary, counter-revolutionary and in league with British imperialism. Zionism would fail and this in turn would weaken British imperial interests in the Middle East. Radek, now head of the Comintern's Eastern department, coined a new slogan for the party – 'out of the ghetto'. This effectively meant Communist Jews desisting from working with members of the Yishuv and required instead to fraternize with Palestinian Arabs. He instructed the PCP to Arabize:

> The future of the party lies in its territorialisation. Up until now the party was composed of immigrant Jews. In the future it must become a party of Arab workers to which Jews can belong – those who have acclimatised and rooted themselves in specific Palestinian conditions, those who know Arabic.[12]

This challenged the 'theses on the Eastern Question' at the fourth congress of the Comintern in December 1922 that 'any attempt to build Communist organisations on ethnic lines contradicts the principles of proletarian internationalism'.[13] While Arabs were to be empowered and to eventually achieve dominance in the party, this was not interpreted as exalting one national group over another in Palestine. The Comintern's view in 1922 was that the task of European Communists who happened to be in the colonies was to organize the indigenous proletariat and to refrain from separating themselves in parallel organizations.

The collapse of the spread of Communism in the West catalysed a turn towards greater centralization of organization and a disciplined conformity. Communists turned inward and away from the broader Left. The Comintern's dependency on the Kremlin which was supposed to be temporary now became permanent. There would be no move to situate the Comintern in London, Berlin or Paris. The organization began to become an arm of the Soviet state, representing its national interests. International revolution began to take second place. An Anglo-Soviet Trade Pact was signed in March 1921 and there were secret agreements with the German military to supply military aid. The instruction to Arabize in 1924 also coincided with the Yevsektsiya's crackdown on Zionism in the USSR. It also took place as Stalin was beginning to consolidate his position in the party, readying himself to become the undisputed leader.

The Comintern believed that its assertion that Palestine was an Arab land would smooth the way towards persuading Soviet Muslims to join the party. There was, it argued, a symbiotic relationship between Zionism and British imperialism. The Comintern opposed Jewish immigration into Palestine and the purchase of land.

Yet the PCP understood that building socialism in Palestine was more complex. Zionism did not fall neatly into the classic 'white settler' model. In an attempt to bridge the gap between Moscow's ideology and Palestine's reality, the PCP quietly worked to develop Yishuvism as a rival ideology to Zionism.[14] This arose in spite of the fact that there was a deep rift between the broad labour Zionist movement and the Palestine Communists. The

Histadrut expelled them in April 1924 and this distanced them even further from the Jewish proletariat.

Yishuvism argued that people fleeing to Palestine from persecution was acceptable, but not if the flight was politically motivated. It also argued that the influx of capital for the Zionist enterprise would assist in undermining Arab feudalism. Zionism, however, was subservient to British imperialism and undermined the bonds between Arab and Jewish workers. The PCP therefore deemed it necessary to separate the interests of the Jewish community from the interests of Zionism and thereby to treat them as different entities. The PCP told the Comintern that it hoped to develop the true revolutionary potential of the Yishuv in that an emerging Jewish proletariat would eventually ally itself with an Arab proletariat. Yishuvism as well as Left Poale Zion regarded the Jewish proletariat in Palestine as a revolutionary vanguard – a branch of the world-wide revolutionary movement. The proponents of Yishuvism would oppose both Jewish and Arab capitalism in Palestine as well as British imperialism.

Yishuvism thereby provided the PCP with an entry point into the Jewish community of Palestine. It also provided a raison d'être for Jewish Communists remaining in Palestine. It also provided a counter-balance to the KPP faction which had advocated the departure of Jewish immigrants from Palestine. It also solved the problem of how to operate on Zionist home territory. In addition, there was a psychological factor. While seduced by the attraction of Bolshevism and world revolution, there was still a latent pride in the pioneering achievements of the Yishuv. After all, many had been former Marxist-Zionists and had immigrated to Palestine to build a new society. Even so, the party was accused of encouraging Arab attacks on Jews in Afula in 1924 when land was purchased by the Zionists from absent landlords and in Wadi Hawarit in August 1929. While it was understood that there was no real Arab proletariat, these incidents, as with the broad disturbances in 1929, could be interpreted as the first development in an agrarian revolution by the Palestinian Arab peasantry.

At its fourth congress in 1924, the Comintern urged the creation of a politically aware cadre in the Arab world. Amidst a prevailing atmosphere of apathy and disdain, the first Arab member of the PCP joined the party, followed by another eight in 1925.[15] Despite the PCP's support for the demonstrations and municipal electoral campaigns of Haj Amin al-Husseini,[16] the Mufti of Jerusalem, there was a critical lack of progress on Arabization. Even so, Yishuvism allowed the idea of 'an anti-colonial front' to advance despite the Mufti's indifference to any form of cooperation. In his address to the Communist University of the Toilers of the East in May 1925, Stalin embellished this theoretical point by remarking on the emergence of an anti-imperialist bloc in colonized countries, consisting of the workers and the revolutionary bourgeoisie which would lead the country to independence. Indeed, Lenin in 1922 and Stalin a few years later believed that the colonial countries were clearly on the eve of their own 1905 revolution.[17]

The training of Arab cadres became the task of the University of the Toilers of the East which had been established in Moscow in 1921. It originally represented 57 nationalities. The first Palestinian Arabs came in 1927, the second group in 1931 and the third in 1934. Many Jews from Palestine were on the faculty.

However this was part of a wider policy which Stalin espoused. The move towards total conformity meant the suppression of inner party discussion. It also meant ensuring that figures loyal to the Stalinist line ran the local Communist Party. Thus Thälmann and Thorez were installed as secretaries-general of the German and French parties by the late 1920s. The University of the Toilers of the East became transformed into a training ground for Stalin's new Communists. Graduates emerged with a scientific training, but unlike their predecessors – without revolutionary experience. The move towards sectarianism manifested itself in Palestine as the move towards Arabization.

The Comintern was also interested in Palestine because it had the largest Communist Party in the Middle East. It had been established and populated by mainly Russian Jews. No doubt the Comintern recruited agents to send to Palestine in order to build a strong party there. Moreover, the PCP would be able to function as a coordinating centre for Comintern activities. During the Druze uprising in 1925, the PCP acted as an intermediary between the Comintern and its leaders. In contrast to Palestine, there were no centralized Communist parties in Lebanon and Syria so Palestinian Jewish Communists were sent there to remedy the situation. Jews were among the founders and early activists of the parties in Egypt and Iraq.

In Moscow, however, the Yevsektsiya, the Jewish sections of the Communist Party of the Soviet Union were often responsible for influencing and ensuring a hard-line anti-Zionist policy. They not only opposed Zionism but also Yishuvism. Indeed there were attempts to lure Jews back from Palestine during a period of economic deprivation in the mid-1920s. However, there was a profound difference between Jewish Communists in Palestine opposed to Zionism and their compatriots in the Comintern. The former hoped to convert the Yishuv to Communism and to utilize them as a force for change within the Middle East. The Jews in the Yevsektsiya and in the Comintern simply wished to eradicate Zionism in Palestine – and perhaps disperse its adherents.

Territorial solutions on Soviet soil were mooted. After 1925, the USSR encouraged the Crimean settlements, the setting up of OZET (the Society for Settling Working Jews on the Land) and the Birobidzhan experiment to settle Jews near the Chinese border. Indeed 150 people, probably mainly PCP adherents, left Palestine for Birobidzhan under the auspices of 'The Association of Friendship with the USSR'.[18]

Stalin argued as early as 1925 that national liberation movements in the colonies had to create a link with 'the proletarian movement in the advanced countries of the West'. In the case of Palestine, this clearly meant forging a relationship with progressive elements in Britain, the colonial power. Joseph Berger-Barzilai, a leading member of the PCP, was asked to participate in a meeting of the executive committee of the Comintern in March 1925 and was introduced to delegates from the British and French Communist parties.[19] Significantly, the Middle East was not even on the agenda. A year later, the Communist Party of Great Britain (CPGB) declared its support for the Palestine Arab executive in opposing Zionism and in 'the great historic mission of establishing a united workers' and peasants' republic from Morocco to Syria'.[20]

Extinguishing the Jewish presence in the PCP

In 1928 the Comintern's broad line of cooperation with non-Communists abruptly changed. In China, miscalculation on the part of Moscow and perceived Communist subversion had forced the suppression of an uprising in Canton and a subsequent closure of Soviet consulates. Chiang Kai-Shek had then aggressively turned against the Chinese Communists.[21] There had been a precedent in Turkey when Communists were massacred following cooperation with nationalists. The situation in China was also utilized by Stalin in a speech to the Comintern to move against Trotsky and the Left Opposition.[22] The Chinese debâcle was a death blow to Trotsky's belief that the revolution was imminent in China despite all the setbacks in Europe. Karl Radek who had sympathized with the Left Opposition was similarly criticized when Stalin spoke to students of the Sun Yat-Sen University (University of the Toilers of the East).[23] Stalin believed that a more realistic policy was called for and had little faith in the Comintern which was perceived to be under Trotsky's influence. His caution and innate conservativism in preserving the USSR as a base to spread revolutionary activity manifested itself as the doctrine of 'Socialism in One Country'. The state interests of the Soviet Union were therefore paramount.

By December 1927, Trotsky, Zinoviev, Kamenev and Radek had all been expelled from the Communist Party of the Soviet Union.

The sixth congress of the Comintern 17 July–1 September 1928 naturally accepted Stalin's new direction, but it also emphasized turning its attention to the colonized East in the hope of exploiting emerging economic problems. The first period of capitalism between 1917 and 1923 had been marked by revolutionary turmoil. The second period up to 1928 was defined as years of relative stabilization. Stalin now argued that the world was entering a third period whereby capitalism would face a renewed crisis. This would provide new openings for revolutionary endeavour. It called for even more discipline and no dilution of determination by making pacts with reformists.

In Western Europe, Stalin's infamous policy of no cooperation with social democrats was laid down, but it was also argued that any such cooperation – as in the past – would now betray those in the colonies suffering under the yoke of imperialism. There would therefore be no truck with bourgeois nationalists in the colonies because their economic interests were intimately linked with colonial rule.

Palestinian Arab nationalists such as Jamal al-Husseini were now initially deemed traitors to the revolutionary cause. However, the conditions in Palestine were very different compared to other British colonies. The Communist Party was so weak and therefore had to moderate the formal stance of the Comintern, the 'class against class' strategy. It could not totally avoid cooperation with progressive bourgeois nationalists.

Moreover the PCP wished to displace the numerous parties of the notables and landed families as the leading force in Arab national politics in Palestine. New slogans were developed against the Arab bourgeoisie and its clerical leaders. The PCP thus developed a class differentiation among the Arabs.

Unlike Lenin, Stalin had to deal with the concrete reality of Zionism and a Jewish community in Palestine. Lenin never wrote about the development of the Zionist experiment in Palestine after 1917. His contribution was only about the diversionary effect of Zionism in Russia before the October Revolution. Stalin met Berger-Barzilai in 1929 and urged an accelerated Arabization of the party. Stalin showed great interest in Palestine and also suggested the publication of a new periodical in Arabic.

Stalin's new policy on colonialism and the Stalinization of the Comintern sounded the death-knell for Yishuvism. The lesson learned from the disastrous collaboration of the Chinese Communists with the Kuomintang was extended to Palestine. The PCP should no longer work with progressives within the Jewish community. The Comintern believed that attempts to influence the Jewish community had proved to be totally unproductive. Henceforth little distinction was made between the Jewish community and Zionism.

The Jewish community in Palestine was seen as monolithic and a tool of British imperialism. Indeed, the Comintern viewed the PCP itself as suspect. The Arab masses were deemed to be the only force which could produce a revolutionary situation. From the Comintern's point of view, this meant not only the full Arabization of the PCP, but a concerted and entrenched war against Zionism. Yishuvism was merely a camouflaged Zionism. Any reticence about the veracity of Yishuvism was now swept away. The PCP fell into line and it repudiated Yishuvism and thereby had to support elements of Arab nationalism, deemed to be progressive and anti-imperialist by the Comintern. Moreover, Arab cadres had to replace its Jewish ones in the party. However they were in such short supply that it was actually Berger-Barzilai who wrote the first proclamation of the Arabized PCP.

There was a new propaganda assault against Zionism – one in which its adherents were accused of aligning themselves with anti-Semites. Thus the Zionists were accused of collaborating with the Whites during the Russian Civil War. In line with its new policy towards social democrats, the Comintern labelled Mapai, 'a social fascist party'. The Histadrut became the 'Nazi Histadrut'. Later Zionism and Nazism were accused of collaborating to produce a mass hysteria which would catalyse a mass immigration of Jews to Palestine.

The killing of Jews by Arabs – mainly the anti-Zionist ultra-orthodox who lived in unfortified exposed areas – during the disturbances of 1929 became a test case for the new Comintern line. The killings recalled the terror of the Russian pogroms for many Palestinian Jews at that time. Indeed the sheer brutality of the attacks shocked the PCP – to the extent that the party approached the Labour leader, Yitzhak Ben-Zvi to tell him that it was assuming an active role in the Yishuv's defence of Jews and was placing the party's arms at his disposal. The PCP's participation in defence operations was approved by the visiting Comintern agent, Bohumil Smeral. Indeed, the PCP lamented the killings of 'Jewish workers' and further criticized the Mufti and the Supreme Muslim Council for moving from an anti-imperialist position.

The Comintern saw things differently in Moscow. Georgi Safarov, the head of the Comintern's Eastern department, had been involved in colonial questions for a long time and was responsible for the Sovietization of Central Asia. Suspected by Stalin of sympathizing with Zinoviev, he was the central person in the Comintern monitoring the Palestine situation. He understood the tales of massacres of Jews in Hebron and Safed only in terms of being undiluted imperialist propaganda. The resolution of the Comintern's executive committee cast 'the insurrectionary movement' as being distinct from 'Arab reactionaries' (feudalists and clergy who tried to respond to 'the Anglo-Zionist provocation') . . . yet 'it was still a national liberation movement, an anti-imperialist all-Arab movement'.[24] The Yishuv leadership had now become 'the Zionist-Fascist bourgeoisie'. There was now profound opposition to any Jewish immigration.

Other Communist parties including the British took its line from Moscow and portrayed the riots as an uprising of the Arab masses against British imperialism. Its anti-Jewish consequence was portrayed as a logical inevitability. In line with Stalin's third stage, this was to be expected as the world was entering a new era of revolutionary uprisings and anti-imperialist revolts.

The Communist front organization, the League against Imperialism dutifully produced a radical manifesto in line with the Comintern approach. A later apologetic communiqué in September 1929 from the PCP suggested that the Zionists themselves were responsible for the killing of Jews because 'Zionism had caused the mob in Palestine to treat the words "Zionist" and "Jew" as synonymous'. Hence they cried 'Death to the Jews!'[25] The PCP then put out a pamphlet on 'The Mufti, Mattathias and the Great Peasant Uprising 2000 years ago' which drew a parallel between the Chanukah story and the 1929 killings. Yet socialists such as Otto Bauer had long before warned that 'any mass uprising in the East would assume a reactionary form'. Both Bauer and Kautsky were quoted to suggest that what looked reactionary in the present could later be regarded as progressive in a socialist future.

The Shaw Commission report into the disturbances in 1930 was criticized as being favourable towards the Jews. Those Arabs arrested by the British for their part in the killings were now stoutly defended by the PCP. All this was directed by the Comintern's determination to prove to the Arab masses that the PCP was no longer a Jewish party. In 1930, the Comintern dissolved the central committee of the PCP and constituted a new one with a majority of Arab members. By 1932, the PCP began to cultivate progressive elements in the Istiqlal party and maintained links with 'Izz al-Din al-Qassam's Islamists.

Jewish socialists had effectively established the PCP and thus were ditched by Moscow ten years later in the hope of cultivating Arab nationalism. The Jews were allowed to advance in all the Communist parties of the world, but were denied this in Palestine.[26] Jews were subsequently purged from the PCP. Some were offered posts as assistants to the new Arab leaders. Many Jews left the PCP and joined Zionist parties. The leadership returned or was recalled to the USSR, only to perish in the Gulag several years later. Others left the country. In the United States, Jews left the Communist Party in protest. Einstein finally resigned as President of the League against Imperialism.

The fight for socialism by the Communist Jews in Palestine had been understood in terms of the struggle of the European proletariat. The early Bolsheviks recognized that any struggle in the Middle East would not necessarily be proletarian. It would essentially be a nationalist strike against imperialism.

While new generations of Jews embraced Communism in Palestine, the PCP never seemed able to bridge the gap between its Jewish members and its Arab ones – and the numerous schisms were based on accusations of being aligned with one side or the other.

Notes and Works Cited

1 Sobhanlal Datta Gupta, *Comintern, India and the Colonial Question 1920–1937* (Calcutta 1980), p. 38.

2 Jaan Pennar, 'The Arabs, Marxism and Moscow: A Historical Survey', *Middle East Journal*, vol. 22, no. 4 (Autumn 1968).

3 Karl Radek, *Portraits and Pamphlets* (London 1935), p. x.

4 Karl Radek, 'England the East', *The Call*, 1 July 1920.

5 Karl Radek, Speech at the Baku Congress of the Peoples of the East in ed. Xenia Joukoff Eudin and Robert C. North, *Soviet Russia and the East 1920–1927* (Stanford 1957), p. 80.

6 Baku Congress of the Peoples of the East (New York 1977).

7 V. I. Lenin, Speech to the Eighth Congress of the Russian Communist Party 19 March 1919. V. I. Lenin Internet Archive.

8 Carr, op. cit., p. 649.

9 Sami A. Hanna and George Gardner, *Arab Socialism* (Leiden 1969), p. 52.

10 Degras, op. cit., p. 170.

11 J. V. Stalin Speech to the Twelfth Party Congress, April 1923 in ed. Xenia Joukoff Eudin and Robert C. North, *Soviet Russia and the East 1920–1927* (Stanford 1957), p. 62.

12 G. Z. Israeli (Walter Laqueur) *MOPS-PCP-MAKI* (Tel Aviv 1953), p. 29.

13 'Theses on the Eastern Question', Fourth Congress of the Communist International, 5 December 1922, www.marxists.org

14 Jacob Hen-Tov, *Communism and Zionism in Palestine* (Cambridge, Mass. 1974), pp. 110–11.

15 Fred Halliday, review of Mario Offenberg's *Kommunismus in Palastina: Nation und Klasse in der Antikolonialen Revolution* Merip Reports no. 56 (April 1977).

16 Laqueur, op. cit., p. 79.

17 J. V. Stalin, *The Results of the Work of the Fourteenth Conference of the R.C.P (B.)* 9 May 1925, vol. 7 (Moscow 1954).

18 Shmuel Dotan, 'Birobidzhan k'alternativah l'Eretz Yisrael', *Ha'uma*, no. 114 (1993–1994).

19 Sondra Miller Rubenstein, *The Communist Movement in Palestine and Israel, 1919–1984* (Boulder 1985), p. 127.

20 Ibid., p. 193.

21 Harold R. Isaacs and Albert Treint, 'Documents on the Comintern and the Chinese Revolution', *The China Quarterly*, no. 45 (January–March 1971), pp. 100–15.

22 J. V. Stalin, *Revolution in China and the Tasks of the Comintern*, 24 May 1927, vol. 9 (Moscow 1954).

23 J. V. Stalin, *Talk with Students of Sun Yat-Sen University*, 13 May 1927, vol. 9 (Moscow 1954).

24 Degras, op. cit., p. 144.

25 Hen-Tov, Jacob, op. cit., p. 135.

26 Hen-Tov, op. cit., p. 150.

5

The new dawn

The revolution in Western Europe

The futility of the Great War had radicalized opinion in both halves of Europe as well as in the colonies. There was a tremendous growth in trade union membership after 1918. Newspaper readership began to increase, accompanied by an abiding interest in politics. Apart from the Italian PSI, all socialist parties had supported their own nation's war effort. Few supported Lenin's lonely path to Zimmerwald and did not condemn the conflict as inimicable to workers' interests. Even so, the European Left became more troubled as the war progressed. Some 49 infantry divisions of the French army staged mutinies during 1917. There were 696 strikes affecting nearly 300,000 people.[1] Yet despite the fact that there was such serious unrest, the leadership of French socialists did not want the Bolsheviks to conclude a separate peace with the Germans.

Significantly, the issue of national defence had long been an integral part of the French Left's agenda. However, by the turn of the century, a nationalist revival in France partly propelled the Left towards pacifism and a growing opposition to militarism. By 1914, the French socialists were in a real quandary. Pacifism and patriotism co-existed in the French socialist psyche and they attempted to reconcile national defence with internationalism.

While European socialists outwardly attempted to prevent war in 1914, nationalism proved politically irresistible.

When the Socialist International met in Paris in mid-July 1914, Keir Hardie and Edouard Vaillant proposed calling a general strike to prevent the outbreak of war. While the sentiment was for the motion, the reality mitigated against it. Would the move to strike be simultaneous in all countries? Were all socialist organizations sufficiently strong enough to overcome entrenched opposition? What would happen if the reactionaries triumphed in some countries and invaded their own? Would they still stand aside?

While the French socialists approved of a general strike in Europe in principle, they knew that the German SPD would probably not participate in such
an action. On 1 August 1914, German mobilization was announced and the
French working class was engulfed by a tide of patriotism and a profound
desire to march on Berlin. Desertions which were predicted at 13% were
actually a fraction of that figure.[2]

Socialists were forced to choose. In France, Gustave Hervé, for example, moved from the far Left as an 'anti-patriot' to supporting the war. Jean
Longuet (Marx's grandson), Romain Rolland and Pierre Laval were, however,
in opposition. In Germany, Karl Liebknecht led the opposition to the war. At
the meeting at Zimmerwald, the French and German delegates signed a joint
resolution, proclaiming that 'this war is not our war'. The French socialist
press ignored Zimmerwald. L'Humanité did not publish its decisions.

Lenin sided with the minority which opposed war and formulated the
doctrine of revolutionary defeatism. He called for the transformation of an
imperialist war into a revolutionary one. Lenin depicted the war as a contest
between 'two groups of predatory great powers over the division of the colonies, over the enslavement of other nations . . .'.[3]

The slaughter on the Western front had reached breaking point in 1917. On
the Eastern front, it brought revolution and Lenin.

The October Revolution therefore gave great hope to many left wing social
democrats and sketched a vision of a decent future compared to the slaughter of the recent past. The fragmentation of the Second International – like
the fragmentation of socialist Zionism – was not a clean split. While Zinoviev
made great efforts to cultivate the left social democrats in Western Europe in
1920, there were many socialists who felt both lukewarm about the Second
International and deeply uneasy about the Bolshevik take-over in Russia.
In particular they rejected Lenin's Twenty-One conditions for joining the
Comintern. For many, this sounded like the Lenin of old. Seminal figures such
as Friedrich Adler, Jean Longuet and Karl Kautsky adhered to what became
known as the 'two and a half' international.

Lenin had gathered the few European friends of the revolution, already in
Moscow, to form a Federation of Foreign Groups of the Russian Communist
Party as early as May 1918. Significantly the invitation to attend the
Comintern's founding conference in 1919 came mainly from Communist
groups in Eastern Europe. At the second congress of the Comintern, all the
delegates received Lenin's Left Wing Communism: an Infantile Disorder and
Trotsky's Terror and Communism. The unspoken agenda was not simply to
persuade the undecided about the benefits of Bolshevism, but to forge the
merger of groups which would embrace Lenin's path as the only path to
socialism. Thus, extracts in English of Lenin's article appeared just before the

Communist Unity Convention in London in 1920 in the hope of persuading its delegates to affiliate to the British Labour Party.

Both tracts promoted Leninist expediency – the adaptability of theory to achieve power. The centrality of the Communist Party rather than that of the Soviets was emphasized. Instead of free and open debate, organization and discipline became the watchwords of revolutionary endeavour. Even though there was supposed to be equality between delegations, the inability of supporters in Western Europe to achieve revolutionary success made the Russian Communists the most important and dominant group.

France and Germany

In France, the revolutionary tradition which stretched back to the Jacobin Committee of Public Safety and Babeuf's Conspiracy of the Equals was hallowed and sanctified. All Europe looked to France for it was deemed to be the living legacy of Robespierre and Buonarroti.

The French like many other Europeans had great difficulty in accepting the Twenty-One conditions and wondered how they would adapt it to French conditions. Leon Blum asked whether the principles and methods of Moscow had universal value and eventually advised against adherence to the Comintern.[4]

The French Socialists split shortly afterwards when 89 out of 96 socialist federations opted to form the Parti Communiste Française. The PCF thus started off as a mass party with a membership of 130,000 members and 880,000 voted Communist in the 1924 elections.

The PCF made a determined attempt to win over thinkers and academics. Indeed the central committee of the PCF protested against the defamation of Trotsky's name in late 1923.[5] Yet by the summer of 1924, Trotsky was condemned by the leadership of all the West European parties. One of its questioning leaders, Boris Souvarine was expelled from PCF. By the summer of 1924, it ceased to be a party of open discussion and followed the Comintern's line on a united front and then switched to a class-against-class approach in 1928. By July 1934, it once again began to cooperate with social democrats due to the rise of fascism.

Germany had long been the hope for the revolutionary future of Lenin and the early Bolsheviks. The German thinker, Ernst Meyer was at Zimmerwald.[6] Yet the German revolutionaries were perhaps the first to understand that the survival of the Soviet regime came first. Both Bukharin and Rosa Luxemburg pointed out that the separate treaty with the Germans at Brest-Litovsk effectively retarded the German revolution. Indeed the repression of the German revolution of November 1918 was made possible because Trotsky's negotiations at Brest-Litovsk had given the German military a breathing space.

The sense of primary loyalty to the Soviet Union was typified by the stand of Rotfront kämpferbund, the uniformed Red Front paramilitary organization, formed by the Communists in 1924. During the early Stalinist period in the 1920s, there was an often repeated ceremony in Berlin's Lustgarten where local Communists would swear an oath to their chairman, Ernst Thälmann, to defend the Soviet motherland.[7]

With the end of the war, there were strikes in factories and unrest in the German armed forces such as the mutiny at Kiel. Several of the revolutionary leaders were assimilated Jews, Ruth Fischer, Leo Jogiches, Arkadi Maslow, Eugen Leviné, Max Levin, who grew up in Eastern Europe. Paul Levi, the original leader of the KPD was born in Germany, but he too wished to distance himself from his Jewish origins. Although the German Communists failed on several occasions to overthrow the social democratic governments, they did help to defeat the nationalist Kapp-Lüttwitz coup by a general strike in 1920.

The violence, disillusionment, deprivation and indeed sense of humiliation that arose after Germany's capitulation gave rise to the Freikorps and eventually to the embryonic national socialists. Matthias Erzberger, the Finance Minister who has signed the Treaty of Versailles was killed at the fourth attempt in August 1921. Walter Rathenau, the Minister for Foreign Affairs was assassinated in June 1922.

It was, however, the rise of Italian fascism which proved to be of great concern to the Comintern and to the German Communists since it attracted large sections of the working class. In 1923, Radek gave a speech in which he praised German nationalists and recalled the glories and vicissitudes of German history. Radek campaigned for 'the necessary alliance between Soviet power and German nationalism'.[8]

Following the failure of revolutionary uprising in Germany, the German Communist Party, the KPD, attempted to attract the disaffected on the Right and to stop them from joining the Nazis. Ruth Fischer, a leader of the party who was also Jewish was prepared to blur the lines on the Jewish question when she addressed nationalist students in the 1920s. She called upon her followers to 'Shoot down the Jew-capitalists. Hang them from the lampposts. Crush them'.[9]

The Kremlin, however, had yet another reason for embracing German nationalism and this was moored once more in the need to ensure the survival of the Soviet regime. Radek thereby also promoted the idea of a German-Russian bloc which was designed to pose a threat to Britain and France. Strongly supported by Bukharin in Moscow, it embraced the idea of national Bolshevism and attempted to enthuse German nationalists and socialists to work towards a united front against France. Radek's ideas were interesting because of the inter-action between revolution and national liberation. German nationalists keenly resented the West European victors of the war and their imperialist designs on pre-war Germany and its former colonies.

Germany's policies in the 1920s were directed towards finding a way to revise Versailles and to regain some of its lost territories. After the French attempt to take the Ruhr and separate the Rhineland from the rest of the country, Germany entered the League of Nations. The Soviet Union, however, posed as the defender of the weak European nations against Anglo-American control and imperialism. The USSR described Germany as now being nothing more than a colony of the West. Under Stalin, the idea of national Bolshevism gained in importance in the form of Soviet nationalism. The Berlin Treaty between Germany and the Soviet Union was signed in April 1926 which pledged that each country would remain neutral in any war against the other over a five-year period. There were three votes against in the Reichstag – all dissident Communists who had been expelled from the party. They attacked Soviet foreign policy and warned of an alliance between German and Russian militarists.[10]

There had been for some years a clandestine collaboration between the Red Army and the Reichswehr. The German generals were envious of the Red Army. Radek was sent to Germany in 1921 with a proposal to build up the German army – they were offered arsenals on Russian soil which contravened Versailles. The Junkers company built factories at Samara and Saratov and an airfield in the Tambov region. The Hugo Stolzenberg company constructed a plant to produce phosgene gas. Submarines were tested in the Baltic and Black Seas. German officers were sent to Soviet Russia for training in chemical warfare. The noted assimilated Jewish scientist, Fritz Haber went to Russia and worked with the Moscow Institute for Chemical Warfare. The Krupps group received a concession for oil in the Caucasus.

There were other examples whereby the local Communists had allied themselves with local nationalists – an alliance which ended in tears. In Turkey, the Soviets had struck up a close relationship with Kemal Atatürk since the Greeks were supported by Britain and France. Stalin had founded a Turkish CP made up from Turkish prisoners of war in July 1918. While pandering to Soviet attention, Atatürk at the same time refused to support it and established his own party in 1920 which emphasized Islam far more than Western Marxism. In March 1921, a Turkish-Soviet Treaty was signed, yet only a few weeks previously, the Turkish government had been busy killing local Communist leaders. Moreover, Radek met the Turkish military leaders of World War I, Talaat Pasha and Enver Pasha. Both had been blamed for the military debacle and were implicated in the Armenian genocide. Atatürk suppressed all opposition and the TKP was eventually driven underground. In achieving an independent Turkey, Atatürk outmaneuvered the British, French and the Soviets.

In February 1921, an Afghan-Soviet Treaty had been signed, but this did not apply the break to the Afghani king's 'relentless persecution of local Communists'. M. N. Roy and other British Communists strongly opposed Saad Zaghlul and the Egyptian nationalist movement. Stalin ignored them and continued to cast a sympathetic eye on Arab nationalism.[11]

In one sense, this was part of a wider scenario to oust Britain its position in the Arab world and to substitute Soviet influence. Thus, since the British had backed the losing side in the Hashemite defeat in the Hejaz in 1924, the USSR was quick to recognize the victor, Ibn Saud, the ruler of a united Saudi Arabia.

The centrality of Britain

Only in France and Germany were the Communists able to build mass parties. This was clearly demonstrated in the elections in which they participated. Their greatest representation was in France 15.3% (April 1936) and in Germany 16.9% (November 1932). The German KPD was suppressed by Hitler with the rise of National Socialism to power in 1933 and the French PCF was banned because of its support for the Nazi-Soviet pact in 1939.

In Italy, the Socialist Party agreed to join the Comintern in 1919 and swiftly approved the Twenty-One conditions. They, too, ran into difficulties since they thought that since ousting Bissolati and Bonomi for approving the Libyan war a decade before, there would be no difficulties. But Moscow also wanted the expulsion of those who were not totally subservient. Gramsci interpreted the situation in an Italian context:

> Rising from the ashes of the old socialist parties, the Communist party repudiates its democratic and parliamentary origins and reveals distinctive features that are original in history.
>
> The Communist Party is nowadays the only institution which can be seriously likened with the religious communities of primitive Christianity . . .
>
> Rosa Luxemburg and Karl Liebknecht are greater than Christ's greatest saints; greater precisely because the purpose of their struggle was human, concrete, limited . . .
>
> The Communist party is the instrument and the historical form of the worker's process of inner liberation, the process through which the executor grows into an initiator, the mass-man becomes a leader, the arm turns into brains and will.[12]

Gramsci partly translated Marx's *Zur Judenfrage* into Italian, but otherwise showed no real interest in the Jewish question. Although his wife's mother was Jewish, he too accepted that Jews in Italy should assimilate.[13]

Unlike France and Germany, the Italian Communist Party was not a mass movement. In the only free election before it was suppressed by Mussolini, the Italian Communists achieved only 4.6% of the vote in May 1921. While Italy was soon lost to fascism, revolutionary Berlin and republican Paris began to radiate an intellectual openness which attracted many people to the Left. This cosmopolitanism appealed to many European Jews and substituted for the multi-culturalism of the great Empires that had fallen. 'The (October) revolution had released the imagination – a sense of no holds barred, of being on the edge of possibility, of "blasting open the continuum of history" in Walter Benjamin's words.'[14]

The majority of the West European parties at their most popular achieved little success in the parliamentary sphere. Their greatest representations were: Belgium 6.1% (May 1936); Holland 3.4% (May 1937); Norway 6.1% (October 1924); Spain (before the Popular Front) 4.4% (May 1931); Sweden 6.4% (September 1928).

In Britain approximately 3,000 joined – pitifully small, on a par with even the inconsequential Finnish party. British conservatism – intellectual, cultural and political – prevented Communism from rooting itself in the British Isles as it had done on the European continent proper. Unlike the French, there was no British spokesman on intellectual affairs. In contrast, the British Labour Party boasted a membership of nearly 3.5 million members. The Labour Party spoke for the British working class. Even so, all were tempted by the example of the Bolsheviks. The Communist Party of Great Britain (CPGB) had been formed from small groups such as William Morris's Socialist League. Another founding component of the CPGB was H. N. Hyndman's British Socialist Party. The party had finally split in 1916 over the wisdom of supporting the war against Germany. Hyndman and his supporters who supported the war departed. The internationalists who regarded the conflict as one between rival imperialisms remained and joined the Communist Party in 1920. As with other European parties, the left wing of the Independent Labour Party provided another component for the founding of the CPGB. In its early days, the CPGB pressed, at Lenin's behest, very strongly for affiliation to the Labour Party. Yet the party remained small and ineffectual. The weakness of the British Communists was a blow for Lenin and the Comintern. Even before the founding of the British party, Lenin had authorized funding to pro-Soviet initiatives in Britain such as the 'Hands Off Russia' campaign. Such was the centrality of Britain that the Kremlin allocated 8.5 million roubles to British sympathizers in 1919 – far more than any other country.[15] After all, Britain was the leading imperial power and a strong party was necessary to create disaffection in the colonial world. The CPGB played a pivotal role in the Soviet scheme of things, yet they were small in number and weak in revolutionary innovation.

Anti-Jewish stereotypes and anti-imperialism

Enlightened Britain in the nineteenth century was seen as the exception to the ideological certainty about Jewish machinations pervading the European continent. It had flirted with republicanism two centuries previously – and unlike the French who were torn between the attractions of Robespierre, Bonaparte and the Houses of Bourbon and Orleans – Britain remained boringly conventional. Anti-Semitism was considered by some to be uncivilized, foreign and un-British. The philosemitic Randolph Churchill occasionally remarked that he had grown up in the company of the Hirshes, Cohens, Wertheimers and Bischoffsheims. Herzl referred to England as 'the last happy isle for modern Jewry'.[16] Even so, the emancipation of the Jews was a hard fought battle. The aftermath was pervaded by a genteel anti-Semitism. The liberal conscience was undoubtedly affronted by crude acts of anti-Semitism, yet this did not conversely and automatically mean a liking for Jews. As Neville Chamberlain succinctly remarked on the eve of the outbreak of World War II, 'No doubt the Jews aren't a loveable people; I don't care about them myself; but that is not sufficient to explain the pogrom'.[17]

The omission of a typically European polarization prevented extremism and characterized nineteenth-century attitudes towards Jews in Britain. If there was dislike for Jews, it was, however, discreet, indirect and covert. In an interview in 1891, Gladstone characterized his nemesis, Benjamin Disraeli.[18]

> Palmerston had many strong and liberal convictions. On one subject Dizzy had them too – the Jews. There he was more than rational, he was fanatical. He said once that Providence would deal good or ill fortune to nations, according as they dealt well or ill by the Jews. I remember sitting next to John Russell when Dizzy was making a speech on Jewish emancipation. 'Look at him', said Russell, 'how manfully he sticks to it, though he knows that every word he says is gall and wormwood to every man who sits around him and behind him'.[19]

Liberals as well as Conservatives felt uncomfortable about Jews. Goldwin Smith, the Regius Professor of Modern History at Oxford, argued in 1881 that British liberalism was beneficent in general towards Jews because unlike Jewish power in Germany, Anglo-Jewry did not control the economy – even though some had made colossal fortunes in stock-broking. 'Israel' – as Smith termed Anglo-Jewry – 'existed as a power and an interest apart from the nations, though domiciled in them'. He suggested that the solutions to the Jewish problem were assimilation and conversion or through emigration to Palestine.[20] An observer commented on his attitude to the pogroms in Russia in 1881.

> He formulates his general accusation in a manner which must compel impartial and logical persons who accept his views to the conclusion that the Russian authorities deserve not blame, but praise, for their determined effort to expel the race of Israel from the dominions of the Tsar.[21]

Yet anti-Semitism was not only the domain of the Conservatives and Liberals. Edmund Silberner remarked in the 1950s that 'socialist anti-Semitism was almost as old as modern socialism and was not limited to any particular country'.[22] Charles Fourier, the French philosopher, regarded as one of the progenitors of left wing anti-Semitism, commented in the mid-1840s:

> Has there ever been a nation more despicable than the Hebrews who have achieved nothing in art and science, and who are distinguished only by a record of crime and brutality which at every page of their loathsome annals makes you sick.[23]

In his *Théorie des quatre mouvements et des destinées générales*, he names his well-to-do Jewish businessman, 'Iscariote'. A lifelong anti-Semite and well-known progressive, credited with coining the term, féminisme, he was also an early advocate of the Zionist solution to the Jewish problem in that Europe's Jews should reconstitute themselves in Palestine. In *La Fausse industrie* in 1835, he suggested that the Jews should have their 'own king, flag, consuls and currency' in Palestine.[24] His disciple, the utopian socialist, Alphonse Toussenel wrote *Les Juifs, rois de L'époquè* in 1845. He referred to 'Londres-Juda' in the belief that the English enemy worked together with the Jews to destroy revolutionary France. This was followed by the work of another republican socialist, Gustave Tridon who wrote *Du molochisme juif.*

The opposition to the Boer War in the United Kingdom further allowed liberals such as J. A. Hobson, the well-known economist to argue that the conflict had been instigated by international Jewish bankers and East End Jews made good such as Barney Barnato.[25] Hobson's interest in Jews had emerged from studying the wave of Jewish immigration into London's East End. He believed that such immigrants were driving down the earnings of the native British worker. He reflected both the contemporary telescoping of the dirty East European immigrant with the financial trickery of the self-made Jew. 'The clean lives of the London Jew come a long way behind his godliness.'[26] Hobson saw the Jew as unproductive since his intellectual nature created an adversity to manual labour or indeed to working the land. He believed that the London press was under the thumb of the Jews. He felt that it was wrong that the likes of Leopold de Rothschild should be hobnobbing with Lord Rosebery, a Liberal prime minister – a family into which he had married.

Influenced by the writings of Herbert Spencer, Hobson produced his own approach for the development of British society. In a similar fashion to Marx, Hobson connected Jews, Jewishness with individualistic profit-making. He reflected the contemporary belief in associating Jewish 'racial characteristics' with untoward capitalism.

In 1899, J. A. Hobson was sent to South Africa by the *Manchester Guardian* to report on the evolving crisis. Hobson believed that the stock exchange, large commercial businesses and the press in South Africa were all in the hands of the Jews.

> Until I came to examine closely the structure of industry and society upon the Rand, I had no conception of their number or their power. I thus discovered that not Hamburg, not Frankfurt, but Johannesburg is the new Jerusalem.[27]

While remarking that names such as Smith, Newman, Phillips, Gordon and Bruce masked Marks and Cohen, he referred to newly arrived Jewish immigrants as 'rude and ignorant people' in contrast to 'their highly intelligent, showy prosperous brethren' who formed the upper crust of well-to-do Johannesburg society. Hobson associated imperialism with Jewish conspiracy and Victorian capitalism. He believed that Jews hiding behind English names were the true manipulators of the Boer War.[28] Hobson's articles convinced figures such as Keir Hardie, David Lloyd-George and the TUC to find scapegoats in Jewish financiers. They were joined by early socialist writers such as H. N. Brailsford[29] and the Social Democratic Federation's H. M. Hyndman. The non-Jewish Cecil Rhodes became 'Rhodes-stein'. Indeed, while they inherited the radicalism of William Cobbett's anti-Semitism,[30] they also built on an English anti-colonial tradition stretching back to the Levellers' opposition to Cromwell's suppression of Catholic Ireland.

The English radical tradition was considerably older than its European counterparts. It stretched back to the Protestant Reformation and the

English Civil War. The debate over religious toleration had given rise to the Levellers, Agitators, Diggers, Ranters and Fifth Monarchy Men – and a host of political philosophies. The Levellers' leader, the pamphleteer, John Lilburne had first called for the King to be tried in *Regal Tyranny Discovered* in 1647. They opposed both Charles I and Cromwell. They initiated the English political tradition of open letters, petitions, political meetings and fiery speeches to the gathered. They addressed their leaders in no uncertain language:

O you Members of Parliament and rich men in the City, that are at ease and drink wine in bowls and stretch yourselves upon beds of down, you that grind our faces and flay off our skins, will no man amongst you regard, will no man behold our faces black with sorrow and famine?[31]

Such sentiments spoke to the early socialists. Edouard Bernstein, for example, had written *Cromwell and Communism* in 1895. Cromwell's re-conquest of Ireland in 1649 had provoked the ire of the Levellers. In a pamphlet entitled *Eighteen Queries* addressed to Cromwell's troops, the soldiers were asked:

Whether the land or inheritance that any nation hath for so many hundreds of years enjoyed . . . be not their right which God and nature has given them . . . How can the conquered be accounted rebels, if at any time they seek to free themselves and recover their own . . . Whether it be not the duty of every honest man to divert, what he can, the intended expedition? . . . Whether it be not England's duty to repent of the oppressions and usurpations over the Irish nation by their kings and forefathers.[32]

The sacking of Wexford and the killing of civilians in 1649 in Ireland initiated anti-colonialism as part and parcel of the English radical tradition. As the British socialist writer, H. N. Brailsford later wrote:

The *Eighteen Queries* lay down the moral foundations for the opposition of the Levellers to Cromwellian imperialism. These men are the spiritual ancestors of a long line of descendents – philosophic radicals, Gladstonian liberals, socialists – who battled for the liberties of Irishmen and Boers, Africans and Indians.[33]

Two centuries after the birth of English radicalism, the fires lit by figures such as John Lilburne and Gerrard Winstanley burned brightly in the embryonic British labour movement. In the interim, despite losing the United States, the British Empire had grown to cover large areas of the globe. Britain's colonial heritage had come a long way since John Cabot had claimed Newfoundland for the crown in 1496. All this stimulated opposition from a plethora of writers and thinkers such as Edmund Burke, Jeremy Bentham, William Wilberforce and the Abolitionists. Engels regarded Ireland in particular as the first English colony. The Chartist movement had criticized British colonialism in the 1840s while William Morris and Eleanor Marx had signed a Manifesto on Sudan some 40 years later.[34] Yet Hyndman's nineteenth-century version of anti-imperialism was that of a 'little Englander' approach while simultaneously expressing solidarity with the white races. Hyndman disliked foreigners and blamed Jewish capitalists for the Vienna riots of 1885 and the Panama Canal scandal which implicated many French politicians.[35] Jews were seen to be controlling the media and in 1893 he pointed out that Jewish newspaper owners were 'poisoners of the well of public information'.[36] The SDF's publication *Justice* frequently mirrored Hyndman's views on Jews – much to the rage of the Irish socialist James Connolly who was eventually expelled from the movement.[37] Hyndman grafted the cutting of anti-imperialism onto the tree of anti-Semitism. He spoke of an 'Imperialist Judaism in Africa'[38] and the formation of an 'Anglo-Hebraic Empire in the continent.[39] Significantly the civilization of the Zulus, Basutos and Matabele was spoken of in glowing terms while Jews were depicted as greedy capitalists. The Jews were implicitly accused of the corruption of the innocent, a desecration of an unblemished utopia. The impoverished Jewish masses of Eastern Europe remained invisible. Although the Jewish elite are not mentioned, Hobson's well-known book on imperialism was published in Britain in 1902.[40] It was not only highly regarded in Britain, but was quoted approvingly by Lenin in his own analyses.[41]

Yet many early socialists such as Sidney Webb favoured imperialism because of its 'civilizing mission' and believed that it would nullify any incipient local nationalism.[42] British workers, it was argued, could build a better empire. Yet this would increasingly become a minority-held view. Hyndman, Brailsford and Hobson effectively established the British socialist tradition of twentieth-century opposition to colonialism. Lenin, Trotsky and Rosa Luxembourg read and admired Hobson's writings on imperialism. Yet from the beginning, such opposition carried the whiff of ambivalence towards Jews.

Notes and Works Cited

1 Robert Wohl, *French Communism in the Making* (Stanford 1966) p. 87.

2 Ibid., pp. 53–4.

3 V. I. Lenin 'Manifesto on the War', *On the International Working Class and Communist Movement*.

4 Leon Blum, *L'Humanité* 24, 31 October, 13 November 1920.

5 David Caute, *Communism and the French Intellectuals: 1914–1960* (London 1964), p. 89.

6 Rose Leviné-Meyer, *Inside German Communism: Memoirs of Party Life in the Weimar Republic* (London 1977).

7 Ruth Fischer, *Stalin and German Communism: A Study in the Origins of the State Party* (Oxford 1948), p. 607.

8 Ibid., pp. 268–73.

9 Ossip K. Flechtheim, *Le Parti Communisme (K.P.D.) sous la Republique de Weimar* (Paris 1972), p. 119.

10 Fischer, op. cit., pp. 526–7.

11 Mohammed Nuri El-Amin, 'The Role of International Communism in the Muslim World and in Egypt and the Sudan', *British Journal of Middle Eastern Studies*, vol. 23, no. 1 (May 1996).

12 Antonio Gramsci, *L'Ordino Nuovo*, 4 September 1920 in Federico Mancini, *The Theoretical Roots of Italian Communism: Worker Democracy and Political Party in Gramsci's Thinking* in ed. Simon Serfaty and Lawrence Gray, *The Italian Communist Party: Yesterday, Today and Tomorrow* (Westport 1980), pp. 12–13.

13 Enzo Traverso, *The Marxists and the Jewish Question: The History of a Debate 1843–1943* (New Jersey 1994), pp. 159–66.

14 Eley, op. cit., p. 206.

15 Kevin Morgan, *Labour Legends and Russian Gold* (London 2006), p. 34.

16 Theodor Herzl, 'At the Clerkenwell Town Hall', *Die Welt*, 4 March 1898.

17 Martin Gilbert, *The Holocaust* (London 1986), p. 81.

18 Adam Kirsch, *Benjamin Disraeli* (New York 2008), pp.159–60.

19 John Morley, *Life of Gladstone*, vol. 3 (London 1903), pp. 475–6.

20 Goldwyn Smith, 'The Jewish Question', *Nineteenth Century*, no. 10 (London 1881) in J. M. Pilzer, ed. *Anti-Semitism and Jewish Nationalism* (Virginia Beach 1981).

21 Isaac Besht Ben-David, 'Goldwin Smith and the Jews', *North American Review*, vol. 217, no. 418 (September 1891), pp. 257–71.

22 Edmond Silberner, 'The Anti-Semitic Tradition in Modern Socialism', inaugural lecture at the Hebrew University, 4 January 1953.

23 Charles Fourier, *Oeuvres Completes* (Paris 1846–1848), vol. 1, p. 61.

24 Edmund Silberner, 'Charles Fourier on the Jewish Question', *Jewish Social Studies*, vol. 8, no. 4 (October 1946), p. 259.

25 Benita Parry, *Post-Colonial Studies: A Materialist Critique* (London 2004) p. 153.

26 Colin Holmes, 'J.A. Hobson and the Jews', in ed. Colin Holmes, *Immigrants and Minorities in British Society* (London 1978), p. 129.

27 J. A. Hobson, *The War in South Africa: Its Causes and Effects* (London 1900), pp. 189–93.

28 Bernard Porter, Correspondence of J. A. Hobson to C. P. Scott, 2 September 1900 in *Critics of Empire* (London 1968), pp. 210–12.

29 Stephen Howe, *Anticolonialism in British Politics: The Left and the End of Empire 1918–1964* (Oxford 1993), p. 38.

30 John W. Osbourne, 'William Cobbett's Anti-Semitism', *Historian* (August 2007), vol. 47, no. 1, pp. 86–92.

31 Fenner Brockway, *Britain's First Socialists: The Levellers, Agitators and Diggers of the English Revolution* (London 1980), p. 65.

32 Brockway, op. cit., p. 87.

33 H. N. Brailsford, *The Levellers and the English Revolution* (London 1961), p. 503.

34 Rajani Palme Dutt, *The Crisis of Britain and the British Empire* (London 1957), p. 349.

35 Claire Hirshfield 'The British Left and the "Jewish Conspiracy": A Case Study of Modern Anti-Semitism', *Jewish Social Studies*, vol. 43, no. 2, p. 97.

36 Hirshfield, op. cit.

37 Raymond Challinor, *The Origins of British Bolshevism* (London 1977), pp. 14–15.

38 H. N. Hyndman, *Justice*, 25 April 1896.

39 H. N. Hyndman, *Justice*, 7 October 1899.

40 J. A. Hobson, *Imperialism: A Study* (London 1902).

41 V. I. Lenin, *Imperialism: The Highest Stage of Imperialism* (Petrograd 1917) in *Selected Works*, vol. 1 (Moscow 1967), p. 748.

42 Peter Clarke, *Liberals and Social Democrats* (Cambridge 1978).

6

British Communism between the wars

Combating British imperialism

The Second International of social democratic parties had been relatively indifferent to questions of imperialism and colonialism. They were also held responsible for the carnage of World War I in allowing a war between rival empires to sacrifice the lives of millions of working people on the altar of nationalism and imperialism. Rosa Luxemburg bitterly referred to the Second International as 'a stinking corpse'.

By the end of the war, Britain was seen by the Bolsheviks as having been successful in keeping its empire intact whereas the Bolsheviks ruled over a much reduced imperial Russia. Moreover, Britain was viewed as the centre-piece of the anti-Soviet coalition. The miniscule CPGB therefore occupied a unique position in the pantheon of foreign Communist parties. Indeed, one of the first CPGB pamphlets was *An Introduction to the Comintern's Theses on the National and Colonial Question*.

The CPGB was from the beginning dependent on Moscow's whims. It had provided £55,000 to establish the party and some £16,000 to launch the *Sunday Worker* in March 1925. Yet its importance did not reside in the domestic situation in Great Britain, but in the fact that Britain was the world's leading colonial power. France was the only other power where colonialism became an issue. Ho Chi Minh made a speech urging the independence of Indo-China at the Congress of Tours in December 1920. Some years later, the Fédération des Jeunesses Communistes made contact with their Spanish counterparts and together they appealed to the French and Spanish soldiers to fraternize with the followers of Abd-el Krim who had organized an armed revolt in Morocco.[1]

Like the Jews in Russia, the Bolshevik dream attracted many from the Indian subcontinent who hated British imperialism and wished to see an independent and socialist India. In Britain, like the Jews, they found in the Communist Party a home free of white racism and colonial paternalism. Indeed, it was the white workers of Battersea North in London who elected Shapurji Saklatvala, scion of the well-to-do Tata family of Bombay, member of the CPGB, to Parliament as a Labour MP in 1924. He had become radicalized when working in the slums of Bombay at the turn of the century. Battersea had a radical tradition stretching back to opposing the Boer War. It also had a large Irish population who were all too willing to make their views known about British rule in Ireland.

Britain became the location where many of the Empire's elite came to receive their education. Palestine's Moshe Sharett studied at the LSE while India's Jawaharlal Nehru went to Harrow, Trinity College, Cambridge, and then practised law at the Inner Temple in London. Many forged contacts with the fledgling Labour Party and after World War I with the embryonic Communist Party. Rajani Palme Dutt and his elder brother Clemens were the sons of a middle-class Indian doctor who had settled in Britain and a Swedish mother who had defiantly challenged the prejudice of late Victorian society by crossing the racial division. Like many of his contemporaries, Rajani Palme Dutt was born into a privileged household, went to public school and Oxford University. During World War I, he opposed the conflict and was imprisoned for being a conscientious objector. The October Revolution and the triumph of Bolshevism therefore had great meaning for him. He and his brother joined the newly founded Communist Party of Great Britain and soon was regarded as the party's foremost ideologist. In 1921, he established his journal, *Labour Monthly*, funded by Comintern subsidies, and this became a vehicle to influence generations of the British Left, regardless of their affiliation to the Communist Party.[2] In the same month, the party insisted on the incorporation of Sylvia Pankhurst's independent journal, *Workers Dreadnought*. She refused and was expelled from the party.

Rajani Palme Dutt, M. N. Roy and Shapurji Saklatvala were highly involved in both British and Indian politics in the tumultuous years after the October Revolution. Roy, in particular, bestrode the international stage as a major figure in the Comintern. He publicly disagreed with Lenin and argued that India was industrializing rapidly and a local proletariat was coming into existence. Saklatvala asked pertinent questions about British colonialism in Parliament while Rajani Palme Dutt wrote *Modern India* in 1926. Both were highly involved in establishing Communism on the Indian subcontinent.

For the sectarian Rajani Palme Dutt, the centrality and survival of the USSR was paramount. In return, Stalin harnessed this deeply seated sentiment among foreign Communists in his struggle to seize power and defeat his rivals. Projecting himself as Lenin's heir at the fifth congress of the Comintern in July 1924, the German Communist, Ruth Fischer observed Stalin's machinations.

> Stalin became known to Comintern delegates for the first time. He glided silently, almost furtively, into the salons and corridors around St. Andrew's Hall. Smoking his pipe, wearing the characteristic tunic and Wellington boots, he spoke softly and politely with small groups, assisted by an inconspicuous interpreter, presenting himself as the new type of Russian leader. The younger delegates were impressed by this pose as the revolutionary who despises revolutionary rhetoric, the down-to-earth organiser, whose quick decision and modernised methods would solve the problems of a changed world.[3]

Captivated by Stalin, Dutt's deep sense of defending the USSR publicly allowed him never to dissent from the official view of the Kremlin. It became an article of faith even within the closed discussions of the central committee of the Communist Party of Great Britain (CPGB). In mid-1929, he began to receive a monthly stipend of £10 from the Comintern.[4] He was the greatest defender of Stalin during his lifetime, applauding the execution of Marshall Tukhachevsky, justifying the Moscow trials, articulating the nuances of the Nazi-Soviet pact and even in his twilight years was prepared to criticize the CPGB for its opposition to the invasion of Czechoslovakia in 1968. He was regarded by the Kremlin as the safest pair of hands in Britain and was a leading advocate in the Bolshevization of the CPGB in the early 1920s. For Dutt, there could be no half-way house.

Many intellectuals, however, gradually felt estranged from the party. In parallel with the expulsion of Trotsky from the Soviet party, intellectuals who initially were sympathetic gradually drifted away. Dutt remained, ever more devoted to the cause. The rise of Nazism, the growth of domestic anti-Semitism and the Spanish Civil War later attracted intellectuals back to the party. Yet the CPGB, unlike other European parties, never exuded an intellectual aura. It did not arise from a major split within the social democrats. British Communists were initially quite happy to associate with non-Communists. Intellectuals even if professing sympathy for the embryonic Bolshevik state, joined the Labour Party instead. The anti-colonial struggle, in particular, deeply concerned them and this brought them closer to the CPGB. Despite this involvement, the British party in the 1930s never lost its anti-intellectualism.

George Orwell's independence, for example, was resented early on. The party's secretary-general, Harry Pollitt, a former boilermaker, called Orwell 'a disillusioned little middle class boy'.[5]

Anti-Colonialism and Zionism

Dutt genuinely believed that the USSR had solved the problem of national minorities including that of the Jews. He could claim with some justification that only the Communists took an equivocal stand for Indians, Blacks and other colonized peoples against the institutionalized racism of early-twentieth-century Britain. Yet this did not mean that all on the Left were benevolent towards both Jews and colonials. Tom Quelch, a founder member of the CPGB was less than complimentary about Black labourers at the London docks.[6] H. G. Wells and the Webbs who favoured retaining the Empire were similarly less than welcoming in their approach to Jews, Blacks and Indians.

Dutt was the party's foremost expert on India and on the colonial question. All CPGB members deferred to him. This gained prominence not simply because of Dutt's pivotal position, but also because Britain after 1918 headed the greatest empire ever known. Dutt regarded the promotion of the Empire as 'a cult for popular consumption'.[7] Moreover the CPGB was 'the first political party to recognise that the alliance of the British working class with the colonial people was the key to the victory of socialism in Britain.'[8] The idea of a common struggle of the British working class and the anti-imperialist movement was promoted since they both opposed the British ruling class. This approach was strongly endorsed and promoted by Dutt.

Moreover, Muslims formed the largest group in British colonies. Although the Soviets condemned pan-Islamism at the Baku conference and lost a lot of support, the unique position of Muslims in both Palestine and in the Indian subcontinent could become a powerful revolutionary tool to be used against the British. Specific features of the anti-colonialist struggle came to define the British Left. It argued that national self-determination was the absolute right of all peoples and echoed the internationalism of nineteenth-century European national revolutionary movements, 'For Your Freedom and Ours'. It rejected the depiction of colonialism as a mission civilisatrice. Finally, it placed a special responsibility on the shoulders of the British activist in that there was a moral commitment to struggle against British imperialism across the globe – and not least in Palestine. For members of the CPGB and admirers of Lenin in general, *Imperialism: The Highest Stage of Capitalism* became required reading.[9] Zionism, however, did not fit into this broad definition.

Zionism, a minor concern both for British Jews as well as being confusing for the Bolsheviks, was viewed as having allied itself to the winning side in this war between rival imperialisms and thereby secured the issuing of the Balfour Declaration. The Zionist movement, however, was actually neutral during the war because it feared backing the wrong horse. Only Chaim Weizmann and Vladimir Jabotinsky openly sided with the British. The Zionists and the British imperialists had entirely different reasons for being in Palestine. The national interests of these two sides rapidly began to diverge.

Dutt's view of Jewish nationalism, however, was conditioned primarily by the vested interests of the Soviet Union. Zionism, moreover, was fitted into the conventional perception of anti-colonialism. It was compared to the Indian struggle. It was seen as Eurocentric and sponsored by imperialism in the form of the British Mandate. The Zionists were viewed as no more than a white settler community, imported by British imperialism. Zionism was not seen as diverse in its many political manifestations. On the other hand, the Hashemite monarchs and Arab nationalists were viewed by Dutt as leading the Arab masses towards the bright lights of socialism through the inspiration of the October Revolution.

> When, however, the national revolt of the Arab peoples was advancing to victory and was clearly directed, not to a change of masters, but to real independence, with the stimulus of the victory of the Russian revolution in 1917, the British rulers enunciated the Balfour Declaration of 1917 to take Zionism under their wing as a counter-force to Arab national liberation, and thereby sow the seeds of Arab-Jewish conflict in the Middle East as one of the main instruments of imperialist domination.[10]

The lack of any real contact between Arab and Jew in Palestine was attributed to a sense of European supremacy. Moreover, the fourth congress of the Comintern in 1922 had warned that any attempt of European Communists in countries such as Egypt and Algeria to form separate parties was 'a hidden form of colonialism' which 'furthers imperialist interests'.[11] Zionism was neatly fitted into this overarching definition.

The official Comintern line was still that of the united front with nationalist forces. It therefore argued that 'the forms taken by this alliance will be determined by the stage of development reached by the communist movement of each country or by the revolutionary liberation movement in the underdeveloped countries and among backward nationalities'.[12]

Following the Comintern's fifth congress in 1924 when the CPGB was rebuked for its negligence on the colonial question, the party was instructed to forge contacts with Indian nationalists. In addition, the CPGB argued that the British worker's standard of living was damaged by imperialism because there was a constant flow of capital to the colonies to assist in developing them. Yet the centrality of India in the Party's anti-colonial work was evident from the very beginning.[13] The following year, the CPGB also made contact with figures in Egypt, Palestine and Ireland. The CPGB's problem was that Zionism seemingly depended on British patronage. It was the British connection which angered rather than a consideration of the movement itself. Yet Zionists argued that they needed the British umbrella to build the yishuv.

Under Clemens Dutt, the CPGB established a Colonial Committee in 1925. In particular, the committee concentrated its work among Indian students – and among other students from the colonies. There were close ties with the Comintern. Roy, a founder member of the Communist Party of India was a member of the Comintern's Central Asiatic Bureau. He established an Indian military school on Tashkent with the idea of raising an army in Afghanistan to invade India.

The Labour Party and Zionism

The British Labour Party did not exhibit the same ideological hostility towards Zionism. It did not fear leakage of Jewish workers to Palestine. It did not see Zionists as reactionaries, capitalists and clerics. Neither did it have a large number of Jews wishing to subsume their identities in the quest for socialism. Following his visit to Palestine in 1922, the Labour Party leader, Ramsay MacDonald proclaimed that the new Jew in Palestine had become 'a warrior, not a moneylender or petty trader; a wild untameable mountaineer living in fortified towns; a patriot, not a cosmopolitan; one who would fight to the last hill-top, and then surrender only to fight again . . . Zionism has become the inspiration of Jewish Labour'. MacDonald differentiated between different types of Jews. He condemned the anti-Zionist ultra-orthodox as well as 'the rich plutocratic Jew'. Yet he tapped into the widespread imagery of the Jews as exploitative capitalist.

> He is the person whose views upon life make one anti-Semitic. He has no country, no kindred . . . he is an exploiter of everything he can squeeze. He is behind every evil that governments do, and his political authority, always exercised in the dark, is greater than that of parliamentary majorities. He has the keenest of brains and the bluntest of consciences. He detests Zionism because it revives the idealism of his race, and has political implications which threaten his economic interests.[14]

MacDonald, unlike Lenin, had actually seen what the Zionists were attempting to create in Palestine. While he singled out the Jewish capitalist and repeated common anti-Semitic tropes, he lauded Zionism as the antidote to this. Churchill, a lifelong adherent of British imperialism, had adopted the same approach – except that Zionism was to be the antidote to the Jew as Bolshevik.[15] In an acerbic article in 1920, Churchill wrote about 'this mystic and mysterious race' and condemned 'the schemes of the international Jews'.[16] The stereotyping of the Jew whether as capitalist or Communist was a product of nineteenth-century European society. It had led in part to the emergence of Zionism in Eastern Europe. Ironically now both British Left and Right had located an answer in Zionism to neutralize 'the malign practices of the Jews' in British society.

Lenin did not greet the possibility of a first Labour Prime Minister with joy. However, he was realistic to understand that the CPGB was highly unlikely ever to achieve power. He argued that British Communists should support the Labour Party within Parliament while still trying to win over its left wing.

By 1924, the Comintern's view of the first Labour government was one of profound suspicion because of its imperialist ties. Dutt's loyalty to the Comintern was complimented by his deep commitment to colonial issues. Labour's approach was to form an Imperial Advisory Committee comprised of mainly upper-middle-class figures with Leonard Woolf as its secretary. Labour figures such as George Lansbury and G. D. H. Cole similarly attempted to develop a policy on imperialism in the wake of the failure of the Labour government. However, they differed profoundly from the CPGB in that they advocated an Empire socialism which would come about as the British Empire became a British Commonwealth. As the Tsarist Empire had been transformed into the USSR, a multi-national entity so could the British Empire be changed. The Independent Labour Party similarly called for a socialist commonwealth of self-governing states.[17] Dutt and the CPGB vehemently opposed this. Others on the British Left did not view Zionism in such monolithic terms. The ILP's Fenner Brockway, prominent in the anti-colonialist struggle, and James Maxton did not sympathize with Dutt on this issue. On the other hand, the Fabian intellectual, Beatrice Potter famously mixed in negative stereotypical views about the Jews per se, following Renan,[18] and argued that anyone who supported the right of the Jews to return to Palestine must logically justify the colonization of Kenya by white settlers.[19] She labelled the historic right of the Jews to return as 'sheer nonsense, hypocritical nonsense'. Building socialism and the construction of kibbutzim were irrelevant and she condemned the use of the 'superior wealth' of the Jews to purchase land in Palestine. Yet her husband, Sidney Webb, in formulating the post-war Labour Party programme in 1917, included a reference to the right of the Jews to return to Palestine and to build a new society there. By 1930 as Lord Passfield and Labour's Colonial Secretary, Webb similarly pitted 'poor Arabs' against 'wealthy Jews'.[20]

Following the failure of the General Strike in 1926, the Comintern's instruction to polarize British politics was welcomed by Dutt.

By 1925, the party had become more centralized and Dutt's approach began to dominate. Indeed the ideological vagueness was clear when the party dutifully published *The Errors of Trotskyism*, a collection of attacks on Trotsky by Stalin, Zinoviev, Kamenev and others shortly after the death of Lenin. Despite the vehemence of the assault on the commander of the Red Army, J. T. Murphy, the party secretary commented:

> We knew nothing of the history of the Russian Communist Party and indeed thought little if anything at all of the party. Party conceptions were not our strong points. We saw only leaders, Soviets and masses and over all the great historical giants, Lenin and Trotsky.[21]

In the heady period following the October Revolution, few members of the CPGB had time for study and analysis. Early publications invoked the prophets Isaiah and Amos as well as the Church fathers as being proto-Communists.[22] British Communists were influenced more by the works of James Connolly than Bolshevik writings – and Lenin's work, *Imperialism, the Highest Stage of Capitalism* only appeared in English in 1926.[23] Indeed Bukharin recommended it to British Communists as a work without precedent.[24] Yet it was probably the CPGB which first conceived of a congress in Europe which would bring together nationalists and the European Left.[25] Willi Muzenberg initiated a front organization as part of the Comintern's strategy. Muzenberg who had known Lenin since his Zurich days was the genius who developed Communist agit-prop, dressed it up as literature, culture or theatre. He also recognized the importance of fellow travellers in the grand scheme of things. He understood that not everyone would wish to commit to membership while still defending the USSR. Out of this came the vehicle of the front organization.

In February 1926, the League of Oppressed People was founded which provided a vehicle to bring in Arab nationalists to work with Communists. Changing its name to the League against Imperialism, it held its first conference in Brussels in February 1927 and elected Einstein as its president. Palestine was represented by the Arab nationalist, Jamal al-Husseini, Poale Zion and the PCP. Not surprisingly, there were clashes at the very beginning.[26] Poale Zion protested that al-Husseini was a feudalist and reactionary while the PCP sought to discredit Zionism as 'a spearhead of social reformism in the revolutionary east, subservient to the Jewish bourgeoisie and British imperialism'.[27] Yet it was attended by 200 delegates including several British Labour MPs including George Lansbury, John Beckett, Ellen Wilkinson and the ILP's Fenner Brockway. At least half the British delegates were CPGB members.[28] The participants from the colonies also included Nehru, Kenyatta, Ho Chi Minh and the Nicaraguan General Sandino as well as Sarekat Islam which mixed tradition with nationalism in an attempt to oust the Dutch from Indonesia.[29]

Class against class

In May 1927, British-Soviet relations took a turn for the worst when British police entered a Russian trading company and confiscated documents. The British government accused the official Soviet Trade Legation as acting as an intermediary between the CPGB and British colonies. The USSR was further accused of military espionage and violating the trade agreement between the two countries of March 1921. Diplomatic relations were severed within a few weeks. In response, Stalin accused Britain of being behind the assassination of the Soviet Ambassador in Warsaw by a White Russian émigré. The incident was compared to the assassination of the Archduke Ferdinand at Sarajevo. Britain was also accused of being behind an attempt on Bukharin's life and linked to a series of explosions in Leningrad.[30]

The British TUC broke off relations with their Soviet counterparts shortly afterwards. Coming so soon after the failure of the General Strike, the CPGB's general disdain for social democracy and the Labour movement was sharpened. The CPGB perceived British workers as turning towards the Left. By the end of 1927, Stalin has proclaimed that Europe was entering a period of revolutionary awareness.

This change was reflected in the politics of the CPGB, following the sixth congress of the Comintern in 1928. While there were misgivings within the CPGB leadership, there was also a desire for a more militant and clear-cut approach. Dutt argued against the reticence of many on the central committee who were reluctant to ditch the hard-won alliances with people in the Labour Party, the ILP and the British Left generally. At the fifteenth congress of the CPSU in December 1927, the new head of the Comintern, Bukharin strongly attacked the British Labour Party. Stalin also did not mince his words.

> Not long ago a protest was received from the well-known leaders of the English Labour movement, Lansbury, Maxton and Brockway, against the shooting of twenty terrorists and incendiarists from among the Russian princes and nobility. I cannot regard these English labour leaders as enemies of the USSR. But they are worse than enemies.[31]

The following year, Dutt defended Stalin's position once more – this time against Bukharin and the 'Rightist' tendency. Opponents were labelled 'Rightists' and younger radicals such as William Rust and Dave Springhill were brought into the inner sanctum of decision making. The Labour Party was depicted by Dutt as the third capitalist party after the Conservatives and the Liberals. The 'class against class' about-turn was promulgated in the CPGB's retrogressive understanding of the General Strike. This was now described as raising 'the class struggle to a decisive revolutionary plain . . . a naked confrontation of class against class'. The Labour government of 1929, in accordance with the Kremlin's line, had already begun 'to show clearly its social-fascist character, namely a policy of fascism and violent suppression of the working class, concealed by legal, democratic and socialist phraseology'. The ILP was integrated into the thesis as 'an essential element in this process of fascization of the whole apparatus of imperialism'.[32]

The third period produced fundamental problems for communist parties outside of Russia. All their hard work in building alliances with social democratic parties had to be abandoned. Thus the Comintern broke with the Indian National Congress after 1928. The policy caused problems for the League against Imperialism. The CPGB attacked left wing supporters of the LAI such as George Lansbury, Ellen Wilkinson and James Maxton. Maxton left the LAI in late 1929 and Nehru a few weeks later. Dutt was hostile in particular to the ILP's colonial expert and organizing secretary, Fenner Brockway.

At the eleventh congress of the CPGB at the end of 1929, the enthusiasm for the abandonment of Yishuvism and the endorsement of the Comintern line on the killings of Jews in Palestine a few months earlier were unequivocal.

> Imperialism was trying to prevent the independent industrialisation of the colonies and sought to secure a social basis there in alliance with feudal landowners and the native bourgeoisie . . . The Arab rising in Palestine against British imperialism and its Zionist puppets, bloodily suppressed by the armed forces sent by the Labour government . . . is further proof of the growth of the anti-imperialist revolutionary movement.[33]

Dutt in turn wrote two articles under the pseudonym 'J. B.' on the 1929 'uprising' in *Labour Monthly* in 1930. It opposed land purchase, the refusal of the Histadrut to admit Arabs and the practice of solely using Hebrew labour. Dutt argued that there should be unity of Arab and Jewish workers.[34] The Palestine crisis of 1929 and the killing of Jews by inflamed Palestinian Arabs were depicted as 'the integration of social democracy with fascist imperialism'.[35]

The following year, presumably to respond to criticism and resignations from the party, the CPGB published a pamphlet by R. F. Andrews (Andrew

Rothstein) entitled *What Lenin said about the Jews*. The introduction applied the class argument to the Zionist-Arab national conflict in Palestine.

> There are two cultures among the Jews, just as among all peoples ruled by capitalism. There is the suppressed culture of the Jewish workers and peasants who have no quarrel with the Arabs of Palestine, but get no chance to develop their culture either in Palestine or in this country while capitalism rules. And there is the prevailing 'national culture' which, as in Tsarist Russia, is 'the culture of the landowners, priests and bourgeoisie' – because they have the monopoly of education and the arts, and the means of expressing them. They use it to set the Jewish workers against the Arab peasants (just as the rich Arab landowners do with the Arab poor) and this consolidates their own predominant position. For the sake of the chance to exploit the Arab workers as well as their own, the Jewish capitalists quite willingly sell their own nation and help to maintain Palestine as the 'Seventh Dominion' of their patrons and paymasters, the British capitalist class.[36]

Up until the Arab Revolt of 1936, the CPGB devoted little time to the question of Palestine, but had subsumed it as part of the wider problem of British imperialism in the Middle East. It had more pressing questions, closer to home, to attempt to answer. The Comintern's seventh congress in 1935 still supported the Arabization of the PCP and its belief that the Zionists were an imperialist pawn. The parallel call for an united front in Europe was to call for 'an anti-imperialist front' in the Arab world.

Cultivating the Jews

The formation of a national government by Ramsey MacDonald created a great sense of disillusionment within the Labour Party in 1931. Oswald Mosley defected to form the New Party, prior to establishing the British Union of Fascists (BUF). In September 1931 there was a mutiny of British sailors stationed in Invergordon in response to a 25% wage cut. All this convinced Dutt that capitalism was on the brink of crisis. The membership of the CPGB rose considerably. Between August and December, the membership trebled. Moreover many students, academics and intellectuals moved closer to the CPGB – particularly because of the hunger of the unemployed and the sight of those less privileged than themselves.

However, the rise of Hitler to power in January 1933 and the threatening presence of Oswald Mosley's British Union of Fascists introduced a new ingredient into the CPGB's approach. The CPGB wanted a solid base in a working-class community – the Jews in London's East End offered this because they appreciated the CPGB's principled stand against anti-Semitism and were deeply drawn to the idea of repairing society and creating a better world. They were attracted by the ideals of the October Revolution and the determination of the Bolsheviks to change the modus operandi of British society. For some, it offered the opportunity to escape their Jewishness. For others to reaffirm it by fighting Hitler in Republican Spain and within the anti-fascist struggle in general. The CPGB in the mid-1930s offered the possibility of escaping anti-Jewish racism, embracing anglicization, socializing with non-Jews and access to education and intellectual discussion.

Many British Jews regarded the CPGB as the university to which their impoverished parents had been unable to send them. The advent of Victor Gollancz's Left Book Club in May 1936 introduced many socialist writers and intellectuals to Jewish members of the Communist Party. In part, it was in line with the popular front strategy encapsulated by Stephen Spender's *Forward from Liberalism*.[37] This obviously appealed to a wider Jewish public who also appreciated works such as *A Philosophy for a Modern Man* by the British academic, Professor Hyman Levy.[38] The publications by Labour luminaries such as G. D. H. Cole[39] and Clement Attlee[40] could appear side by side with a legal justification of the show trial of Radek in the USSR.[41] Gollancz gave full vent to the Left's opposition to Nazism by publishing titles such as *Under the Axe of Fascism*[42] by an Italian academic or 'scientific' accounts such as *The Spirit and Structure of German Fascism*.[43] It published *The Yellow Spot* which systematically documented the persecution of the Jews living in Hitler's Germany. Accompanied by cartoons from *Der Stürmer* and photographs of humiliated Jews forced to participate in acts of self-abasement, it brought home to a wide audience what was happening under Nazism. Little-known facts such as the expulsion of Jewish children from German orphanages shocked.[44]

Opposition to Nazism, however, often characterized a political myopia towards the USSR. Thus the well-known German-Jewish writer, Lion Feuchtwanger could notoriously trumpet the good fortune of Jews to live in the USSR and be guided by Stalin – in the year of the Great Purge 1937 when millions met their deaths.[45] Significantly manuscripts submitted to the Left Book Club for publication were often read by CPGB members and discussed within party circles. George Orwell's *Homage to Catalonia* was rejected for its revelations and criticism. No work by Trotsky ever saw the light of day.[46]

In the 1930s Communist trade unionists influenced the intelligentsia rather than the other way around. Trade union leaders were viewed as authentic, genuinely working class and fighting for their members at the coal face of the class struggle. This was a world into which the intelligentsia could in reality never enter. The 'dark satanic mills', the sweatshops, the tragedy of mass unemployment was approached from the outside. When respect for the working man was translated into adherence for the Communist Party, it also meant following the twists and turns of Stalinism.

Gollancz's almost apologetic foreword to the Left Book Club edition of Orwell's *The Road to Wigan Pier*, designed to blunt as well as explain the writer's independence, illustrated the difficulty of publishing left wing authors who did not conform to the prevailing ideological pro-Soviet imagery. Orwell was particularly scathing about the attempt to gloss over class attitudes within the Left.

> Scratch the average pacifist and you find a jingo. The middle-class ILPer and the bearded fruit juice drinker are all for a classless society so long as they see the proletariat through the wrong end of a telescope; force them into any real contact with a proletarian – let them get into a fight with a drunken fish-porter on Saturday night, for instance – and they are capable of swinging back to the most ordinary middle class snobbishness.[47]

Neither was he kind to the intellectuals of the British Left.

> The Coles, Webbs, Stracheys etc., are not exactly proletarian writers. It is doubtful whether anything describable as proletarian literature now exists – even the *Daily Worker* is written in standard south English – but a good music-hall comedian comes nearer to producing it than any socialist writer I can think of. As for the Communists, it is as far removed from the common speech as the language of a mathematical textbook.[48]

Orwell's parody of his own middle-class background famously extended to a reiteration of his caricature of Jews in *Down and Out in Paris and London*. Orwell sat on both sides of the racist fence. He was given to outbursts such as describing Zionists as 'a gang of Wardour Street Jews' with a controlling interest over the British press.[49] On the other hand, he calmly argued that 'above a certain intellectual level, people are ashamed of being anti-Semitic and are careful to draw a distinction between "anti-Semitism" and "disliking Jews"'. While dampening down public anti-Semitism, Orwell remarked that Nazi persecution and atrocities seemed to have had little effect on private anti-Semitism. And he was keen to point out that the British Left in particular was not immune from such sentiments.[50]

Such iconoclasm, racist and anti-racist, could be tolerated because the Comintern at its seventh congress in 1935 had decided to embark on a Popular Front strategy to confront the spread of fascism. This meant an ending of the class-against-class approach and once more building alliances with social democrats and socialist parties in order to halt fascism in its tracks. The Labour Party and the ILP once more became touchable. Orwell while anathema to the CPGB and their sympathizers could not be completely ignored. Dutt, significantly, was still preaching the 'social-fascist' line against other sections of the Left right up to the last moment – and after the rise to power of Hitler in Germany where Nazism was more than an ideological epithet.[51] Jewish Communists were now encouraged to create a broad alliance with the Jewish community.

The influx of Jews into the CPGB created a situation whereby Jews were now disproportionately represented in the party. Significantly the party's membership trebled during the popular front period.[52]

The CPGB, faithfully replicating the Comintern's line, depicted the Zionist project as an extension of British imperialism in that it depended totally on British patronage. With the onset on the Arab revolt in the spring of 1936, there was criticism in the British press that Palestinian Arab nationalism was reactionary and that it was being influenced by European fascism. This was refuted by the *Daily Worker*.[53] The CPGB demanded a halt to Jewish immigration, a cessation of land sales and a constitution for a legislative assembly.[54]

However, many Jewish members of the CPGB, while often not identifying with Zionism, understood the attacks against Jews in Palestine in the context of attacks against Jews in Britain and in Europe generally. It raised the question of differentiating between Jewish national interests and the Comintern line. Why should attacks on Jews be fought in England but not in Palestine? It also raised the question of 'Jewishness' and Jewish identity as to whether or not an individual adhered to the party line. To what extent were sacrifices to be made in the cause of the greater good? The simplistic party line that Arab and Jewish workers should fight Zionism, Arab feudalism and British imperialism did not reflect the reality as a number of Jewish Communists understood the global situation in 1936. Were the Zionist Jews in Palestine, Marxist and Social Democrat, not attempting to build socialism? Were they not a bulwark against the spreading influence of fascism in the Middle East?

The CPGB's fight against fascism and anti-Semitism had clashed with the Comintern's anti-Yishuv policy. The CPGB's loyalty to the Comintern had to be squared with its interest in maintaining and expanding its basis within the Jewish community. Ben Bradley, the CPGB's colonial secretary commented:

> We have been driven to the situation of discussion of this question because of the apparent revolt of the Jewish population against the line of the Party. It is not only something which had happened recently but since the seventh Congress. Since the delegates from the Arab countries made their contributions there, there has been a considerable discussion in Palestine and other countries against the line laid down by the seventh world congress.[55]

In attempting to resolve the dilemma, the CPGB established a Jewish Bureau to ensure that the political leadership was informed about Jewish concerns.

The CPGB attempted to appease Jewish sensitivities by suggesting that the revolt of the Arabs was not actually directed against the Jews of Palestine and Zionism but in reality against British imperialism. Zionism was depicted as less than a safe haven for Jews. The party even erroneously depicted Jabotinsky's movement as a growing domestic 'fascist' movement in Palestine. In reality, Jabotinsky had vehemently opposed fascism and the rise of Hitler. It also promoted Birobidzhan, the Jewish autonomous region near the Chinese border as a Soviet Palestine through Jewish front organizations. This had little appeal since the Biblical resonance of Palestine conveyed much more to even the most hard-line member of the party. Despite all their reservations, there was still enormous goodwill for the CPGB by many Jews in Britain. Jewish workers in London's East End appreciated the immediate stand of the CPGB against local fascists. The party's opposition to Zionism assumed a secondary and less important relevance. Indeed, the party explained that in contrast to Britain, the Jewish problem had been solved through the eradication of anti-Semitism and the enforced equality of all nationalities in the USSR. On the eve of the Great Purge, there was little information about the Soviet reality and few British Jews were that interested. Their paramount concern was the struggle against Mosley's British Union of Fascists.

As usual, Dutt was keen on rigidly supporting the official Comintern line which gelled with his own anti-colonialist sentiments. *Labour Monthly* continued to depict the Mufti of Jerusalem as the leader of the democratic Arab masses even though he had met Admiral Canaris, the head of Abwehr, the German intelligence service and funding had been provided.[56] Following the outbreak of the Arab Revolt in 1936, *Labour Monthly* published a pamphlet, *Who is Prosperous in Palestine?* which argued that any weakening of Arab nationalism would lead to a rapprochement between Palestinian Arabs and Zionist Jews – and a two-state solution.

> The Arab landowning and capitalist class would accept the proposal (the partition of Palestine) since it would free a large area for Arab capitalist expansion, unhampered by Zionist competition; at the same time it would increase their political influence while British protection would safeguard their interests against those of the Arab masses.[57]

Such an alliance between Arabs and Jews, it was argued, would control the one through the Arab landowning and capitalist classes under an Arab prince and the other through Zionist capitalism. The Jewish state would essentially be a British puppet state since British interest in Palestine was focused on the Mosul oil pipeline and the harbour at Haifa. In the event of an Arab anti-imperialist uprising, 'England would direct it against the Jewish state. Therefore the Jews fighting for their state would actually serve the strategic interests of Britain in Palestine'.

The Peel Commission report in 1937 which advocated a two-state solution through a partition of Palestine provoked a conformist approach from the party. The CPGB argued that partition was 'a crime against Arabs and Jews' since it denied 'the inhabitants of Palestine the right of national self-determination'. The CPGB called for the end of the Mandate and the withdrawal of British troops from Palestine. There should be 'recognition of an independent Arab state with full rights of citizenship for the Jews'.

Willie Gallacher, the Communist MP, alleged that Arabs and Jews had lived in peace and fellowship for centuries past. This model of history was replicated for the present in that the Jews in Palestine would have the opportunity as 'loyal members of an Arab state' to participate in the building up of the country.[58]

Zionism was depicted as 'a harmful reactionary illusion and carried through an invasion of Palestine' which was not in the interest of Jews, but only served British imperialism. It was further suggested that the Arabs would actually have welcomed a moderate immigration of Jews. 'Whatever is offered to the Arabs or the Jews, the real power, the real control, remains with the British imperialists.'

The possibility of a Jewish state in Palestine, Gallagher believed, would be detrimental to the fight against fascism in Europe.

> The struggle to establish the rights of the Jews in Germany, Poland and elsewhere cannot be aided if the Jews allow themselves to be used by the British imperialists for the purpose of depriving the Arabs of their rights. On the contrary the greatest possible injury will thereby be inflicted on the Jewish cause.

Jewish communists were enlisted to argue that Jews should remain in Europe and not flee to Palestine. Writing in the *Daily Worker* in August 1937, the Jewish filmmaker, Ivor Montagu and son of Lord Swaythling initiated the Zionist-Nazi analogy in the aftermath of the Zionist Congress in Zurich.

> The Zionists claiming Palestine speak with the accents of Mussolini claiming an empire, or Hitler, or Japan in China . . . Jews who were not Jewish Nazis would know their only 'right' in Palestine is such that they can negotiate with liberated Arabs and share in equal and non-exclusive citizenship there with all inhabitants, not discriminating.[59]

Willie Gallacher similarly depicted the implicit fascist-like and colonial exploitative nature of Zionism by condemning the Peel Report for its proposal to
transfer Palestinian Arabs to the proposed Arab state.

> The 'best land' has been taken from the Arab peasants and 225,000 are to be
> transferred. What a blessed word, 'transferred'. Driven off the land they have
> owned and cultivated for generations, they will be 'replanted' somewhere, maybe
> to starve and die.[60]

The formal party statement in September 1937 argued that partition was
against 'the economic and commercial interests of both Arabs and Jews'
and would aggravate and not diminish the tension between the two national
groups. The creation of two separate states, it commented, would produce
friction over frontiers, tariffs and limited access to the sea.

While depriving the Jews of the right to national self-determination, it argued
that it was incumbent on the Arabs to guarantee equal, democratic, civil and
cultural rights for Jews within an independent Palestine or a wider Arab state.
Those Jews who wished to go to Palestine in 1937 should remain in their countries of origin – they should conduct the class struggle and fight fascism.

> The illusion of a national home for the Jews in Palestine is now exploded. Only
> the smallest minority of Jews could hope to escape from the terror of the fascist
> countries to Palestine. Immigration, therefore, is no solution.[61]

Yet at the same time, there was concern that the fascists were cultivating
Arab nationalists.[62] On the eve of war, the *Daily Worker* spoke positively about
the MacDonald White paper which restricted Jewish immigration to 15,000
per year for five years. Following this period, the prerogative of whether to
admit more Jews would belong to the Palestinian Arabs.

Notes and Works Cited

1 Wohl, op. cit., p. 489.
2 Francis Beckett, *Enemy Within: The Rise and Fall of the British Communist
   Party* (London 1995), p. 31; Kevin Morgan, *Labour Legends and Russian Gold*
   (London 2006), p. 36.
3 Fischer, op. cit., pp. 404–5.
4 Kevin Morgan, *Harry Pollitt* (Manchester 1993), p. 57.
5 *Daily Worker*, 17 March 1937.

6 John Callaghan, *Rajani Palme Dutt: A Study in British Stalinism* (London 1993), p. 95.

7 Rajani Palme Dutt, *Labour Monthly*, vol. 5, no. 4, October 1923.

8 James Klugmann, *The History of the Communist Party of Great Britain: Formative and Early Years 1919–1924*, vol. 1 (London 1969), p. 159.

9 Howe, op. cit., pp. 1-2.

10 Dutt, op. cit., p. 235.

11 'Theses on the Eastern Question', Fourth Congress of the Comintern, 5 December 1922.

12 Degras, op. cit., p. 139.

13 Ibid., p. 98.

14 J. Ramsay MacDonald, *A Socialist in Palestine* (London 1922), p. 24.

15 Michael Makovsky, *Churchill's Promised Land: Zionism and Statecraft* (Yale 2007), pp. 82–9.

16 *Illustrated Sunday Herald*, 8 February 1920.

17 Socialism and the Empire: Report of the Empire Policy Committee, Independent Labour Party, 1926.

18 Joseph Gorny, 'Beatrice Webb's Views on Judaism and Zionism', *Jewish Social Studies*, vol. 40, no. 2 (Spring 1978).

19 Beatrice Webb, diary entry, 2 September 1929 in *The Letters of Sidney and Beatrice Webb*, ed. Norman Mackenzie, vol. 3, 'Pilgrimage 1912–1947' (Cambridge 1978), p. 315.

20 Chaim Weizmann, Letter to Felix Warburg, 13 November 1929 in *The Letters and Papers of Chaim Weizmann* Series A Letters, vol. 14, July 1929–October 1930.

21 *The Errors of Trotskyism*, CPGB, May 1925.

22 William Paul, 'Communism and Society', CPGB November 1922.

23 Howe, op. cit., p. 55.

24 Nikolai Bukharin, 'Lenin as a Marxist', CPGB October 1925.

25 Callaghan, op. cit., p. 107.

26 J. D. Hargreaves, 'The Comintern and Anti-Colonialism: New Research Opportunities', *African Affairs*, no. 92, 1993.

27 Hen-Tov, op. cit., pp. 48–9.

28 Joyce Bellamy and John Saville, 'The League against Imperialism 1927–1937', in the *Dictionary of Labour Biography*, vol. 7, pp. 40–50.

29 Callaghan, op. cit., p. 107.

30 Gabriel Gorodetsky, *The Precarious Truce* (London 1977), p. 236.

31 Jane Degras, *Soviet Documents on Foreign Policy*, ed. vol. 2, 1925–1932 (Oxford 1952), p. 237.

32 Tasks of the CPGB: The 10th Plenum and the International Situation in 'Resolutions of the 11th Congress of the CPGB', Leeds, 30 November–3 December 1929 (London 1930).

33 Ibid.

34 Rajani Palme Dutt, *Labour Monthly*, vol. 12, no. 3 and no. 4 1930.

35 J. T. Murphy, *Communist Review*, vol. 2, no. 1, 1930.

36 R. F. Andrews, Introduction to *What Lenin said about the Jews* (London 1930).

37 Stephen Spender, *Forward from Liberalism* (London 1936).

38 H. Levy, *A Philosophy for a Modern Man* (London 1938).

39 G. D. H. Cole, *The People's Front* (London 1937).

40 C. R. Attlee, *The Labour Party in Perspective* (London 1937).

41 Dudley Collard, *Soviet Justice and the Trial of Radek and Others* (London 1937).

42 Gaetano Salvemini, *Under the Axe of Fascism* (London 1936).

43 Robert A. Brady, *The Spirit and Structure of German Fascism* (London 1937).

44 *The Yellow Spot* (London 1936), p. 239.

45 Lion Feuchtwanger, *Moscow 1937* (London 1937), pp. 100–5.

46 Callaghan, op. cit., p. 168.

47 George Orwell, *The Road to Wigan Pier* (London 1937), p. 195.

48 Ibid., p. 207.

49 D. J. Taylor, 'Orwell's Dirty Secret', *Guardian*, 13 August 2002.

50 George Orwell, 'Anti-Semitism in Britain', *Contemporary Jewish Record,* April 1945.

51 Hugo Dewar, *Communist Politics in Britain: The CPGB from its Origins to the Second World War* (London 1976), pp. 104–5.

52 Andrew Thorpe, *The British Communist Party and Moscow 1920–1943* (Manchester 2000), Appendix 2.

53 *Daily Worker*, 21 May 1936.

54 *World Views and News*, 20 June 1936.

55 Jason Heppell, 'A Question of "Jewish Politics"? The Jewish Section of the Communist Party of Great Britain, 1936–1945', in *Jews, Labour and the Left 1918–1948*, ed. Christine Collette and Stephen Bird (Aldershot 2000), p. 98.

56 Francis Nicosia, 'Arab Nationalism and National Socialist Germany 1933–1939: Ideological and Strategic Incompatibility', *International Journal of Middle East Studies*, vol. 12, no. 3 (November 1980).

57 *Who is Prosperous in Palestine?*, 'British Resident', *Labour Monthly* pamphlet, November 1936.

58 Willie Gallacher, 'Against the British Plan to Divide Palestine', *The Communist International*, vol. 14, no. 11, November 1937.

59 *Daily Worker*, 14 August 1937.

60 Gallacher, op. cit.

61 Statement of the Political Bureau of the CPGB on the Proposals of the Palestine Royal Commission in the 'The Meaning of the Palestine Partition' (NY State Buro CP, September 1937).

62 *Daily Worker*, 15 October 1938.

7

True believers and the revolutionary imperative

The origins of the pact

The Molotov-Ribbentrop pact on the eve of World War II shook the European public to its core. For members of European Communist parties, it was initially bewildering. How could the builders of a workers' bright tomorrow ally itself with the subterranean forces of the counter-revolution? How could yesterday's hated enemy become today's friend? Did the International Brigaders fight Franco in Spain and give up their lives at Jarama and Brunete for no good reason? Did German dissenters – Communists, homosexuals, Jehovah witnesses, Jews – die in Sachsenhausen for nothing?

For Jews who were party members or just sympathizers, it meant a tortured choice. Should they adhere to the cause of world revolution and relegate their Jewishness to a lower, less important, rung? Should they place their trust in Stalin and pledge their fidelity to the 'revolutionary base' of the Soviet Union? By closing off retaliation on the Eastern front, were they implicitly aiding Hitler in conquering Poland and thereby placing its 3 million Jews in mortal danger? In the longer term, suppose Hitler turned his attention to Western Europe, once he had disposed of Poland, were they encouraging the Nazi war machine and thereby positioning their own families in its path? Where were the boundaries of self-sacrifice?

Even if the pact came as a shock and lost the moral high ground for Communism, there was a sound basis for cooperation between the two states which stretched back to 1918. A few days after the publication of the pact, Molotov himself pointed out that both Germany and Russia had suffered the most during World War I. Neither country had been consulted when the world had been re-made at Versailles. Both had lost territory. The Tsarist Empire had become a reduced union of Soviet socialist republics. Imperial Germany had lost its empire and its monarchy and been transformed into the rickety Weimar republic. Both were regarded as outcasts by the international community.

Soviet Russia unlike Germany had not been defeated by the Allies. Even though 14 states had intervened to militarily eliminate Lenin's new order at birth, they retreated exhausted in 1920. A central plank of Lenin's foreign policy was to ensure the survival of the Soviet Union. With the demise of the prospect of revolution in Germany and military defeat in Poland, the early Bolsheviks feared what tomorrow might bring. Stalin understood that this meant avoiding war at all costs until the USSR was strong enough. If this meant ditching the interests of Communist parties abroad while holding up the figleaf of the Comintern, then so be it. If it meant the marginalization of ideological consistency and the refinement of the politics of expediency, then so be it. If it meant appeasement of anti-Semites and acquiescence in their deeds, in the name of Soviet survival, then so be it. It was a long road from Stalin's comment in 1931 that 'the Communists, who are consistent internationalists, cannot help but be the resolute and uncompromising enemies of anti-Semitism'.[1]

Soviet Russia's isolation and impoverishment found a remedy in the friendship of the Weimar republic. Germany exported technological skills while Russia offered a vast market for German goods. This was cemented in 1922 by the Treaty of Rapallo and four years later they signed a guarantee that if one country was attacked, the other would remain neutral. Ironically while the Bolsheviks struggled to ignite the German revolution – and failed, the Soviet military were happily cooperating with their German opposite numbers. Although the testing of weapons was banned under the terms of Versailles, Soviet Russia provided territory where the provision could be violated. A special tank unit was established at the Kama River near Kazan where the German military could carry out tests.[2] In Lipetsk, German heavy bombers could be put through trials. On one level, the USSR was attempting to destabilize Weimar Germany. On another level, it was doing just the opposite. By 1924, Maxim Litvinov replaced Chicherin to reinforce the diplomatic and pragmatic approach – as opposed – to the revolutionary option. By 1927, Stalin felt more secure in the ability of the Red Army to resist any attack from the West. Even so, the threat remained with Britain playing the role as the central antagonist. Indeed Italian fascism, for example, was not a cause for concern, compared to the threat from the British capitalists. In contrast the Soviet Union had been negotiating with Mussolini's Italy ever since November 1923.

The British cabinet had been divided as to how to relate to the USSR. Lloyd-George favoured rapprochement with Soviet Russia, but he was often opposed by his coalition colleagues. The resistance to the normalization of relations between the two countries manifested itself in the Zinoviev letter, allegations of Bolshevik instigation of the General Strike and the police raid in May 1927 on the offices of the Soviet trade delegation which brought about a severing of diplomatic relations. In the Soviet Union, Stalin openly began to talk of war. He whipped up a climate of fear and then patriotically appealed to Soviet workers to support him.

The Great Crash and the Depression forced the West to come to terms with the new Russia as it now had to seek new markets. In 1932 almost half of all Soviet imports came from Germany.[3]

When Hitler came to power in 1933, the USSR fell over backwards to assure him that it would make no difference to the relationship between the two countries – even though he decimated the KPD. Only by the end of 1933, did relations cool down. The re-alignment of Communism in 1934 to form a popular front formally endorsed Litvinov's attachment towards a collective security policy. The export of revolution was no longer a priority. However, the failure of the British and French to defend the Spanish republic suggested to the Soviets that they did not take the idea of collective security seriously. Stalin was suspicious that this was a machiavellian plan by the British to foment a war between the USSR and Nazi Germany. In 1935, Litvinov proposed to the German Ambassador, Count Friedrich von Schulenburg a mutual non-aggression pact. Throughout 1936 and 1937, there were further Soviet attempts to overcome any obstacles and to come to a compromise with Nazi Germany.

Hitler had originally wished Poland to join forces with Germany and other countries in an invasion of the USSR to destroy 'Judeo-Bolshevism'. The Poles rejected the offer and in equal measure declared their intention to refuse to allow the Red Army to cross into their country to attack Germany. In March 1939, Stalin made a speech to the eighteenth congress of the CPSU in which he suggested that the USSR would not be drawn into a war. He accused the British and French of trying to poison relations between Soviet Russia and Nazi Germany. The Nazi conquest of Prague a few days later was the first time Hitler had taken territory that did not have German inhabitants. This broke the spell of appeasement in Britain. In the USSR, it made Stalin even more aware of his regime's vulnerability. Soviet negotiations however continued apace with both Germany as well as with the British and French. Yet Stalin was discouraged by British dithering and a sense that appeasement had not totally been laid to rest. The Soviet terms were a Triple Alliance between Britain, France and the USSR which would guarantee the integrity of every state between the Baltic and the Mediterranean and to defend each other if attacked.

In a speech to the Soviet politburo on 19 August 1939, Stalin considered the possibilities for Soviet alignment. If the German offer of a non-aggression pact was accepted, modern Poland would disappear. The USSR would regain Bessarabia and exercise a sphere of influence in part of the Balkans. Moreover Stalin pointedly argued that the Bolsheviks could only come to power in Western Europe during wartime. In order to achieve a Soviet Germany and a Soviet France, an Allied victory over the Nazis had to come at the end of a long and exhausting struggle. Britain would then be in no position to oppose a Soviet Germany. Stalin continued:

> We must be prepared for the fact that in France in wartime the Communist party there must abandon legal activities and go underground. We realise that such work will require an enormous sacrifice in lives. However, we have no doubts about our French comrades. Above all their task will be to break up and demoralise the French army and police. If this preparatory work is completed in a satisfactory way, the security of Soviet Germany is assured. This will likewise ensure the sovietisation of France.[4]

If, on the other hand, Nazi Germany defeated the Allies, then although this would be an exceedingly dangerous situation, it would be in such a weakened state that it would not start a war with the USSR for at least ten years. Stalin rationalized that the Soviet Union's best option would therefore be to opt for a pact with the Nazis and to remain neutral in any conflict while supplying Germany with raw materials and foodstuffs. The Soviet Union could rearm and choose its time to intervene. According to Molotov, Stalin believed that only in 1943 would the Soviet Union be on a military par with Nazi Germany.[5]

Stalin in reality had rival bids in front of him. The British and the French refused to disclose what plans they had made to fight the Germans. They also appeared to exhibit a political lethargy in the negotiations with the Soviets. Moreover, Captain John King, a mole in the British Foreign Office was passing on information about British thinking to the NKVD[6] which it then transferred it to the German Embassy in London.[7] Stalin became convinced that all this masked British military weakness and their real policy was a continued appeasement of Hitler. He did not believe that Britain and France would really go to war over Poland.

The pact was thus agreed by Molotov and Ribbentrop, but the secret protocol in the non-aggression pact divided Poland between them as determined by the rivers Vistula, Narev and San. Bessarabia, Latvia, Finland and Estonia would be within the Soviet sphere of influence. The Germans wanted Lithuania plus Vilna.[8]

The fourth partition of Poland

Moscow congratulated Berlin on the German entry into Warsaw. The USSR invaded Poland from the East on 17 September. Molotov then called upon Britain and France to stop the war as they were now an obstacle to a just peace. Allied warplanes stationed in India and the Middle East were, according to the British Foreign Office, ready to bomb oil supplies at Baku and Black Sea ports, but only if the USSR made hostile moves first of all. The RAF vetoed such a proposal. Yet Stalin informed the Turkish Foreign Minister on 10 October 1939 that if Britain and France declared war on the Soviet Union, then he would fight on the side of Nazi Germany.[9]

Sixteen million Poles suddenly became Soviet citizens. The USSR abolished private property, nationalized industry and merged the annexed territories into the Ukrainian and Byelorussian Soviet republics. Political commissars with the Red Army urged Ukrainian and Byelorussian peasants to attack and kill Polish landlords – retribution for years of Polish rule. This developed into pogroms against Jews – and the Red Army did little to respond. This was the road to the Katyn massacre. In all, 200,000 Polish civilians were killed during the duration of the Molotov-Ribbentrop pact.[10]

When Finland refused to cave in to Stalin's territorial demands and contrary to all expectations, repulsed the Soviet forces, Hitler banned arms supplies to the Finns and supplied Soviet submarines blocking Finnish ports. The Soviets allowed the Germans to use the ice-free port of Teriberka. During the time of the pact, the Soviets handed over 1,000 people including 300 Jews to the Germans.[11] German Communists such as Margarete Buber-Neumann found herself taken from her camp in the Soviet Gulag by the NKVD, handed over to the Gestapo at Brest-Litovsk and re-incarcerated in Ravensbrück. None of her comrades believed that once deported from the USSR, their ultimate destination would be Nazi Germany.[12] The Communists already incarcerated in Ravensbrück refused to believe her story about the Soviet camps and ostracized her as a counter-revolutionary. The reality of Stalin's regime was too much to bear.

Hitler signed a non-aggression pact with Stalin some eight months after he had prophesied in his annual speech to the Reichstag that if war would break out, it would not result in the Bolshevization of the planet, but in 'the annihilation of the Jewish race' – a prophecy repeated on four subsequent occasions.[13] One month into the war, *Izvestia* told its readers that 'one cannot destroy any ideology by fire and sword . . . to undertake war for 'the annihilation of Hitlerism' is to commit a criminal folly in politics'.[14] All negative references to the 'fascist hyenas' suddenly disappeared from the Soviet press. So did plays and films with anti-fascist themes. Nikolai Shpanov's novel

The First Blow which provides an imaginary account of the first 24 hours of a war between the Soviet Union and Germany was suppressed even though it continued to be distributed abroad.[15] Wagner concerts came into prominence at the Bolshoi. Hitler was transformed into an honoured figure and his speeches were quoted extensively in the press and commented upon favourably. Quotations from the Nazi media such as the *Völkischer Beobachter* often appeared in *Pravda*. Anti-German literature disappeared from libraries and information about German contributions to Russia throughout the centuries was brought back into the school curriculum.

This added to the fact that the Soviet press had effectively downplayed reference to the Nazi persecution of Jews after 1933. Instead, the media spoke about socialists and liberals. Although there were exceptions such as the film 'Dr Mameluk' which attacked tha assault on German Jews by Nazism.[16]

Following the pact, there was an enforced silence about the treatment of Jews in Nazi-occupied Poland and beyond. The Soviets probably never discussed the Jewish question with the Nazis during this period. Even Jewish refugees who had fled to the Soviet Union and witnessed German atrocities were circumspect about communicating what they had seen for fear of arrest and incarceration. When the Nazis subsequently invaded the USSR, many Soviet Jews were remarkably ignorant about the fate of the Jews in the West.[17]

On 28 September a German-Soviet Boundary and Friendship Treaty was signed. The pact with Soviet Russia and the conquest of Poland meant that Hitler could now turn his attention to the West. On 19 October 'Operation Yellow' was issued. This was a directive to attack the West with 75 divisions.[18]

Stalin provided a port for the German navy near Murmansk. The German vessel, Komet, sailed through Arctic waters, north of the USSR and was aided by Soviet icebreakers – it went on to attack Allied shipping.

On 11 February 1940, another agreement was signed whereby the Soviet Union would supply grain, fuel and raw materials to Nazi Germany in order to circumvent the British blockade. In return, the Soviets demanded war materiel including details of latest German military developments including plans of all the prototypes for aeroplanes and warships.

During the Battle of Britain in 1940, the Soviet press was saturated by anti-British commentary.

As early as mid-September 1939, Stalin was quick to accord diplomatic recognition to Slovakia which had aligned itself with Germany. The Czechoslovak ambassador was asked to leave Moscow. When Belgium, Yugoslavia, Norway and Greece were conquered, Stalin withdrew diplomatic recognition and their ambassadors similarly were forced to leave the USSR. Stalin was careful not to over-antagonize the Allies since he was worried that they might attack the Soviet Union, therefore he was very careful in not pushing the limits of pro-German propaganda too far. While Stalin congratulated Hitler on entering Paris in May 1940, he was also surprised at the rapid collapse of France. He therefore moved very quickly to realize the gains of the pact, occupying the Baltic states, Bessarabia and northern Bukovina. All the elites – as in Poland – were deported and replaced by Russians. The ongoing arrests and passage to the Gulag included Jewish and Zionist organizations which were regarded as subversive anti-Soviet elements. The occupation of these territories, depicted originally as temporary military buffers against possible invasion, became permanent and reversed Bolshevik losses of land after the revolution.

During the period of the pact, the Soviet Army expanded two and a half times and tank production was accelerated. The Soviet Air Force was larger than the British, French and German all put together.[19] In May and June 1940, Stalin ordered Soviet industry onto a war footing, working a seven-day week.

By the end of 1940, Ribbentrop proposed another pact to Molotov based on the division of the colonial possessions of Britain and France between Germany, Italy, Japan and Soviet Russia. Hitler was determined to steer Stalin away from the Balkans which he saw as within the German sphere of influence. Instead Stalin was offered the time-old Russian dream of expanding southwards in the hope that this would provoke a clash with the British defence of India. Relations began to cool and instead Hitler authorized the first steps of Operation Barbarossa, the German invasion of Soviet Russia – and in its train the systematic extermination of Jewish communities.

The period of the Molotov-Ribbentrop pact coincided in part with the phoney war between Britain and France on one side and Nazi Germany on the other. It was terminated with the invasion of the low countries and France in May 1940. In the interim, Nazi Germany and Soviet Russia rapidly devoured Poland and several European countries practised a studied neutrality. Germany was to be appeased and Russia was not to be irritated. Thus initially Sweden refused to condemn German anti-Semitism and very few Jews were allowed into the country. Official indifference was punctuated by demonstrations at universities against 'the imput of Jews'.[20] In this period of respite, local Communist parties adjusted to the new reality.

Local Communists and the pact

Stalin's speech at the eighteenth party congress in March 1939 was utilized as the template for lauding 'this masterstroke of Soviet policy'.[21] The prospect of a second imperialist war arose, he argued, from Japan's war with China and the seizure of Manchuria, Italy's conquest of Abyssinia and Germany's switching its economy onto a war footing. The aggressor states were defined as Germany, Italy and Japan who were infringing the interests of the non-aggressor states, Great Britain, France and the United States.

> Thus an open re-division of the world and of spheres of influence is taking place before our eyes at the expense of the interests of the non-aggressor states, without the least attempt at resistance.

Stalin explained this inability to confront fascist states as a fear that any intervention would precipitate more October revolutions. Stalin further announced that the Red Army and the Red Navy would be fortified. Stalin offered to support any nation, fighting for independence against aggressors, but the USSR 'would be careful not to allow our country to be involved in conflicts by the instigators of war'.

The British were urged by the CPGB to sign a similar pact with the Soviets. Willie Gallacher told the House of Commons that Poland could be saved from German aggression and that the USSR had not deserted Poland.[22] *L'Humanité* urged Daladier to fly to Moscow and add his signature to those of Molotov and Ribbentrop. Both Latvia and Estonia had signed non-aggression pacts with the Soviet Union in June 1939. Yet the local Communist parties had not been consulted beforehand. Their initial response was to continue with their attacks on the Nazis and to exude a proud patriotism. Thus Communist parliamentary deputies in France voted for war credits and the party's secretary-general willingly joined his unit following the declaration of war.

Harry Pollitt, General-Secretary of the CPGB, wrote that Ernst Thälmann, his opposite number in Germany, then in his sixth year of solitary confinement under Nazism, 'would be delighted to know . . . that Hitler has capitulated to Stalin'. The *Rote Fahne*, the underground newspaper of the KPD, proclaimed 'Long live the peace front of the socialist Soviet Union'. Italian Communists, similarly operating in clandestine conditions, regarded the pact as 'an obstacle to war making'.[23]

The actual invasion of Poland subsequently ignited a full-bloodied desire to assault the Nazi war machine while understanding the neutrality of the USSR. The parties in countries where dictatorships ruled, Italy, Spain, Czechoslovakia and Germany, were enthusiastic about the prospect of war since they believed that any conflict would end in the overthrow of the regime. Palmiro Togliatti, the Italian Communist leader hinted that Italians should join the French Army. Other socialist and social democratic parties, however, were aghast. The French socialist leader, Leon Blum, was scathing about the PCF's position and ridiculed 'the agility of your dialectics'.[24] He regarded Stalin as the successor to Peter the Great not Lenin. The Confédération Générale du Travail voted for a resolution which condemned the pact. This also occurred in the Italian party and the Italian socialists abrogated a unity arrangement with the Communists.

All this changed when Stalin told the Comintern to define the war as one between rival imperialisms. Following a meeting with Georgi Dmitrov, the secretary-general of the Comintern on 7 September, Stalin authorized that there should be no opposition to Nazism and local Communists should argue in favour of peace and abandoning the conflict.[25] Dmitrov's diary reveals that Stalin clearly distinguished between Communists who were in power and Communists who were not. The central responsibility of the Soviet Union was to bring down the capitalist system – and Soviet war material to Germany would certainly assist in exacerbating the military tension.[26]

Molotov was even clearer in a speech to the Supreme Soviet at the end of October 1939. He argued that the war between Britain and France against Nazi Germany was 'a sort of holy war like those waged during the Middle Ages'.[27] By the end of November, Pravda was already blaming Britain and France for continuing the war.[28]

This deflating of opposition to Nazism was accentuated when Hitler, following the conquest of Poland, held out an olive branch to Britain and France in a speech to the Reichstag in early October 1939. The Belgian Communist Party launched the slogan, 'Neither London Nor Berlin' and initiated a diversionary campaign for higher pay for the mobilized conscripts. The secretary-general of the PCF, Maurice Thorez, left the French armed forces as quickly as he had joined – and decamped for the USSR. In November 1939, the party's paper, *La Voix du Peuple* was banned.[29] This was followed by the banning of *Ce Soir* and *L'Humanité* and then the party itself. The PCF now opposed conscription.

In Palestine, on the outbreak of war, the small Jewish section of the PCP declared itself in support of enlistment in the British forces. Yet within a few days, the party condemned mobilization in Palestine. The Arab majority in the party regarded the war as 'a capitalistic one'. All aspersions cast on Hitler's good name suddenly disappeared and the Jewish section of the PCP was condemned for being under the influence of 'Zionist nationalist influences'.[30] In July 1940, the party organ *Kol Ha'am* declared that the British Administration in Palestine was no different from the regimes of Hitler and Mussolini.

It would be an understatement to say that the German party was perplexed. In exile in the USSR, German Communists discussed the issue and understood their political impotence. Were incarcerated German Communists in Nazi camps now expected to cooperate with their captors for the good of the cause? Would they now have to suggest that the German people would not gain 'if they escaped Nazism in order to become subject to the British'?[31]

The KPD platform of 30 December 1939 called upon German Communists to explain to the German people the concept of rival imperialisms. Even so, there were signs that the Comintern well understood public sensibilities. Therefore the German Communist Walter Ulbricht, wrote in *Die Welt* in February 1940 that 'This war policy (of the Allies) is the more criminal because . . . (Britain) is the most reactionary force in the world'.[32] Yet this was omitted from the English language version of the article in *World News and Views* some two weeks later.[33] Ulbricht also argued in the article that the British government had established concentration camps and implemented draconian laws against the working class. If the Allies swiftly defeated the Nazis, this, Ulbricht argued, would be the pattern for the new Germany.

Yet in Germany itself, less than a month after the joint digestion of Poland, the Gestapo arrested some two thousand 'diehard' Communists.[34]

In occupied countries such as Czechoslovakia, the local party implied that the real enemy was President Benes. The Nazi army was referred to as 'German workers in uniform'.[35]

As within all local Communist parties, there were resignations and desertions at the turn of events. A score of French Communist parliamentarians resigned from the party as did the writer Paul Nizan. A statement from the Union des Intellectuels française, signed by the Joliot-Curies and other leading scientists on the Left such as Paul Langevin, Jean Perrin and Aimé Cotton, condemned the pact and termed it 'an inverted Munich'.[36] Those who went along with it found themselves overlapping with the French far Right such as Charles Maurras of *Action Française* who denounced the war as one engineered by the Jews. There were still others – long-time loyal servants of the party whose buried suspicions were brought to the surface by the pact. They made the ideological journey from Communism into the arms of the Vichy French. Some even ended up dispossessing Jewish businesses in Paris and organizing French Legions to fight the Soviets on the Eastern front.[37] The phoney war made anti-Semitism semi-respectable in France. This affected prominent figures such as Leon Blum, the former socialist Prime Minister and long-time target for anti-Semitic attack.

Roosevelt's envoy, Sumner Welles visited Europe in March 1940 in the hope of forging peace between the protagonists and met Blum in Paris. The French press published a report of his visit. A few days later, Welles received over 3,000 letters from French people, protesting at his visit to Blum.

> They were all written, however, solely because as a representative of the President of the United States, I had dared to call upon a Jew . . . (I understood) for the first time how far the penetration of Nazi ideas had already proceeded in perverting the mentality of at least a portion of the French people'.[38]

The depiction of the war as one of rival imperialisms was cast in the mould of World War I. The Molotov-Ribbentrop pact was set in the template of the prolonged negotiations at Brest-Litovsk in 1918 whereby Trotsky held off a German invasion of Russia. Just as Lenin bought time through compromise with the imperialists, now Stalin was doing the same in endorsing the pact.

The memory of World War I and its senseless slaughter in the trenches was recalled by many – and not just on the European Left. The death and destruction of that conflict had resonated down the decades. The pacifist Peace Pledge Union boasted 100,000 members in 1937 in Britain. Its deep opposition to war led to a political myopia regarding Nazism. Its journal, *Peace News*, therefore downplayed widespread attacks on Jews during the Anschluss and during Kristallnacht. The latter events were seen as no more serious than a spate of anti-Semitic occurrences in the East End of London in 1914.[39]

The lack of enthusiasm for a war over Poland was palpable. The British Left remained bitter at the betrayal of Spain and Czechoslovakia – and was less than concerned about the Poland of the reactionary colonels. It enforced Communist cries for an immediate peace and created an understanding for Hitler's peace overture. The Communist Party's stand attracted the attention of many on the British Left when no one else was opposing the war. Significantly the number of CPGB members increased from 15,781 (September 1938) to 20,000 with the onset of war. The circulation of the *Daily Worker* increased by 15,000 from January 1939 to January 1940 and that *of Labour Monthly* from 7,000 (September 1939) to 14,700 (March 1940) to 20,000 by the end of the year. The closure of the *Daily Worker* in January 1941 by the British authorities similarly created a backlash.

Harry Pollitt unlike his continental counterparts did not automatically follow Moscow. He resisted a campaign against conscription. He genuinely detested fascism, had good relations with the Jews of London's East End and was deeply affected by the Spanish Civil War.[40] Even so, he was a loyal Communist and explained away the pact as a blow against fascism. Pollitt is said to have suppressed a telegram from the Comintern informing the CPGB of the new line. The CPGB's decision to about-turn was based on a report from Dave Springhill, the party's representative on the Comintern in 1939 on his return from Moscow. Contrary to the *Daily Worker*'s editorial, 'To Betray Poland is to Betray Britain',[41] he reported that as Poland was a semi-fascist country, 'it would be regarded not as terrible misfortune if Poland were to disappear from the scene'.[42] Stalin argued that Poland could be jettisoned.

The present war is an imperialist and unjust war for which the bourgeoisie of all the belligerent states bear equal responsibility. In no country can the working class or the Communist Parties support the war. The bourgeoisie is not conducting war against fascism as Chamberlain and the leaders of the Labour Party pretend. War is carried on between two groups of imperialist countries for world domination.[43]

The war also pitched Rajani Palme Dutt against Harry Pollitt. Indeed, Pollitt had initially published a pamphlet *How to Win the War* only for it to be replaced by Dutt's *Why this War?* a few weeks later. Dutt wrote that:

This is an imperialist war, like the war of 1914. It is a sordid exploiter's war of rival millionaire groups, using the workers as their pawns in their struggle for world domination, for markets, colonies and profits, for the oppression of peoples.[44]

Dutt argued that Chamberlain and Daladier had always been on the side of fascism against democracy. Indeed Chamberlain was still trying to win over both Mussolini and Franco to his standard. Dutt called for an immediate armistice and a peace conference. Paraphrasing Karl Liebknecht in World War I, Dutt said that 'the enemy is at home'.

But if on the basis of all these arguments, you say 'Yes, we fight imperialism and we attack this imperialism'. You are not fighting imperialism, you are supporting your own imperialism. And that is why you cannot have a struggle on two fronts. It is a struggle on one front against our own imperialism.[45]

Dutt qualified his comments by arguing that this did not mean, however, that the CPGB was in favour of a Nazi victory. In the central committee debate, Pollitt juxtaposed 'English common sense' with the new line. He compared the fighting in Warsaw to that of the defence of Madrid against Franco's forces.[46] It was to no avail. Pollitt resigned his post and issued a statement of self-criticism. It spelled an end to popular front philosophy and cooperation with the Labour Party.

In no country can the working class or the Communist Parties support the war. The bourgeoisie is not conducting war against fascism as Chamberlain and the leaders of the Labour Party pretend. War is carried on between two groups of imperialist countries for world domination.[47]

Some interpreted the struggle against 'our own imperialism' as sabotaging the war effort. The CPGB set up a Workers' Music association as a front in case it was banned. They collected classified information from supporters and sympathizers about weapons and military operations.[48] In France, a powder factory at Sorques, an arms manufacturer at Bourges and an aeroplane motor plant at Boulogne were also sabotaged during the phoney war.[49]

Freedom fighters and the Nazis

A statement on the anniversary of the October Revolution in November 1939 suggested that the war was being fought for the enslavement of nations and new imperialist conquests. Its outcome would be 'the triumph of reaction'. Dutt also accepted that a war of rival imperialisms placed any struggle against colonialism into abeyance.

> How could the British government pretend it was fighting for democracy when four-fifths of the people under its control throughout the Empire had no democratic rights at all, but were as much enslaved as people under a fascist regime? Indeed, organisations campaigning for colonial liberation were already protesting that India had been declared a belligerent without any consultation whatever with representatives of the Indian people.[50]

Such arguments suggested that there could in fact be an 'understanding' for national liberation movements and figures involved in them for utilizing the argument that 'the enemy of my enemy' is my friend. There would therefore be no bar to working with the Nazis if it provided a method for ousting the imperialists and securing independence. Stalin therefore recognized the pro-Nazi regime of Rashid Ali in Iraq on 3 May 1941. Flemish and Breton nationalists thus welcomed German support. The left wing Irish Republican and commander of the Irish battalion of the International Brigade in Spain, Frank Ryan was prepared to cooperate with the Abwehr in planning operations in wartime Ireland.[51] In fact, there had been several initiatives by Sean Russell, the Chief of Staff of the IRA even before the outbreak of war. Plan Kathleen had envisaged an IRA uprising of 30,000, joined by a German invasion force of 50,000, to take Northern Ireland. This was superseded by Hitler's plan to invade Northern Ireland at the same time as the invasion of England in Operation Sealion. Northern Ireland, the Nazis argued, would provide a firm base for the Luftwaffe to bomb targets in the north of England.

Dutt referred to Gandhi's comment that many in India made no distinction between Nazism and British rule.[52] Indeed the Indian National Conference had passed a resolution in March 1940 which argued that Britain was pursuing the war for imperialist ends in exploiting the people of India and strongly disapproved of the proposed mobilization and deployment of Indian troops. It stated that the congress could not be party, in any way, directly or indirectly, to the war, 'which means continuance and perpetuation of this exploitation'.[53]

Its former president, Subhas Chandra Bose, originally wanted to go to the USSR to seek assistance in the struggle against the British. Stalin, however, refrained from provoking the British. Bose, as a second choice, decided instead to proceed to Germany and arrived in Berlin in March 1941.[54] Indeed most nationalist Indians exhibited a warmth for Bose's Indian National Army.[55] Similar sympathy for Germany had been evident during World War I when the Kaiser's forces had demonstrated its ability to inflict military defeat on the hitherto omnipotent colonial ruler.[56] Bose opposed the non-violent strategy of Gandhi and enlisted German assistance in training an Indian military force which he believed would accompany a German attack on India once the USSR had been defeated. These Indian soldiers swore an oath to both Bose and Hitler and later fought British troops in Italy.[57]

Bose requested a declaration from the Germans that they supported the movement for freedom in India – and in Arab countries.[58] He had opposed Nehru in permitting political asylum to Jews fleeing Europe in 1939.[59] He was prepared to ingratiate himself with Nazi ideology by writing for Goebells's *Der Angriff* in 1942. He argued that anti-Semitism should become a factor in the struggle for Indian freedom since the Jews had collaborated with British imperialism to exploit the country and its inhabitants.[60]

In the Middle East, German legations had consistently reported enthusiasm for National Socialism. After all, Hitler opposed the enemies of Arab nationalists – the British, the French and the Jews. Several political movements integrated elements of National Socialism and fascism. These included the Baath party, the Syrian Socialist Nationalist party, the Lebanese Kataeb, Young Egypt and the Iraqi Futuwwah movement. *Mein Kampf* was translated into Arabic and circulated widely in the Arab world.[61] The association of all Jews with Zionism by Arab nationalists, regarding them as agents of the British, led to continuing attacks on individual Jews and synagogues in Iraq despite a distancing from Zionism by the communal leadership. In Egypt, however, the intellectuals who contributed to the liberal cultural journal, *al-Risāla*, vehemently opposed Nazism and anti-Semitism.[62]

Indeed the Mufti of Jerusalem and an assembly of notables had expressed their admiration for the new Germany and its anti-Jewish policies at a meeting with the German Consul at Nebi Musa shortly after Hitler's accession to power. The Arab world like Germany saw itself a victim of the post-war settlement. This was keenly felt by the Palestinian Arabs who viewed the Balfour Declaration and the British mandate in that light. Germany, stripped of its colonies, had no presence in the Arab world. Moreover Germany was deeply aggrieved over this loss. There was, for example, a considerable resentment in forcing the German inhabitants of South West Africa to take British citizenship in 1924.

Although the Mufti pressed for a policy which would keep Jews away from Palestine, Hitler allowed a large emigration to simply get rid of Germany's Jews. This stopped in 1937 when the Nazis realized that the Peel Commission had recommended the establishment of a Jewish state. Nazi ideology then took precedence over the expediency of emigration. Hitler's racist disdain for Arabs and his unwillingness to interfere in matters concerning the British Empire, ensured that no practical support was extended. This led to a refusal to provide arms for the Palestinian Arabs despite the repeated pleas of figures such as Fawzi Qawukji.[63] The Mufti addressed a letter to Hitler on 20 January 1941, declaring the readiness of the Arab world to participate in the struggle against the common enemy, Britain. The Mufti's private secretary was dispatched to Berlin where he proposed Axis recognition of the independence of all Arab countries under the British and French Mandates as well as 'British protectorates in the Persian Gulf and South Arabia'. It also requested recognition of the right of all Arab countries

> To solve the question of the Jewish elements in Palestine and the other Arab countries in a manner that conforms to the national and ethnic interests of the Arabs, and to the solution of the Jewish question in . . . Germany and Italy.[64]

Yet even after the outbreak of war, Hitler was very reticent to go beyond expressions of sympathy for the Arab cause for fear of upsetting the colonial interests of his allies, the Italians and the Vichy French in the Middle East and obstructing negotiations which could bring Turkey into the war on the Axis side. The Mufti argued that National Socialism and Islam shared a common weltanschauung. He was not averse to extracting teachings from the Koran and adapting them to fit Hitler's latest pronouncement.[65] Moreover his involvement in the destruction of the Jews during World War II stretched beyond anti-British militancy and anti-Zionism.[66]

If Italy's forces had been successful in September 1940 and entered Cairo, they would have been welcomed as liberators by the Egyptians. Anwar Sadat commented, 'except for ill-luck, we would have joined forces with the Axis, struck a quick blow at the British, and perhaps won the war'.[67]

Had it not been for the victory at El Alamein, SS Obersturmbannführer Walter Rauff would have ordered his einsatzkommando to liquidate the Jews of Palestine. Moreover, the Nazis expected local participation in their actions.

There was therefore a profound difference of choice for Jews and for anti-colonial freedom fighters. In both cases, vested interest overcame a moral choice. For the Jews, it was often a matter of life and death which later on became an escape from a systematic extermination. Where did personal and Jewish interests lie? Was there a difference between Comintern theory and policy – and the reality in which European Jewry found itself?

For the ordinary non-Jewish party member, more often than not, it was Comintern policy, the survival of the USSR, loyalty to the Stalin and the anti-colonial struggle that mattered. As Maurice Cornforth stated during the meeting of the central committee of the CPGB to discuss the new Comintern line:

> I personally have got that sort of faith in the Soviet Union to be willing to do that, because I believe that if one loses anything of that faith in the Soviet Union, one is done for as a Communist and Socialist.[68]

Some Jews such as Eric Hobsbawm went along with party line. In February 1940, Ivor Montagu gave a talk entitled 'Jews against the War'. Yet Montagu and Hobsbawn did not know that there was a secret clause in the Nazi-Soviet pact whereby German Communists who had sought refuge in the USSR would be handed back in exchange for Nazi Germany handing back Soviet agents.

The pact effectively destroyed the alliance between the left wing of the Labour Party and the CPGB. It fragmented the united front that had been established in the 1930s in fighting the British Union of Fascists.[69] Fellow travellers such as John Strachey who had supported the CPGB throughout the 1930s now ended his association with the party. In his widely read *The Coming Struggle for Power*, he had written that 'to travel from the capitalist world into Soviet territory is to pass from death to birth'.[70] He left when he believed that the party began to identify Soviet interests with a Nazi victory over Britain, France and Norway in the spring of 1940.[71]

In an article in July 1940, following the fall of France, Strachey attacked the Communists' notion that 'a People's Government' should be established in Paris to prevent a sell-out to fascism.

> It is above all necessary for us to face the fact that this immense tragedy (the fall of France and the capitulation of Pétain and Laval) could never have taken place if the will of the French people to resist Hitler's fascism had not been fatally weakened by nine months of revolutionary defeatist propaganda on the part of the powerful French Communist party. How, after preaching defeatism, even though it was, of course, revolutionary defeatism, could the French Communists even dream that they would be in a position to stop the Fascist defeatism of Laval and Pétain?[72]

Strachey argued that the workers had had three leads from the CPGB. Wage the war on two fronts; Stop the war; Beware of counter-revolutionary attempts to stop the war. He continued:

> Can any sane man or woman doubt the appalling effect of the contraction between lines two and three? If the workers have been taught that this is an unjust imperialist war anyway, what objection will they have if anyone seeks to save them from bombing by doing what Pétain did in France? Those who cannot understand this can understand nothing.

In an acrimonious correspondence with Ivor Montagu, he argued that the Comintern was greatly underestimating the strength and importance of fascism.

> It is slurring over to a fatal extent the differences between fascism and the older forms of capitalism. It is those differences, of course which make you reject, and I accept, the view that if Hitler wins 'all will be lost'.[73]

Strachey's fury and disillusionment was further amplified by Victor Gollancz in *The Betrayal of the Left*. Gollancz summed up the Communists' argument that it therefore followed that 'it is irrelevant whether Hitler conquers Britain or Churchill conquers Germany'.[74]

Harold Laski, in the preface, suggested that the rationale for the CPGB's stand of revolutionary defeatism was:

1. The defeat of the Churchill government was a more urgent matter for British workers than the defeat of Hitler.

2. This defeat would be followed by a 'People's Government' which would sue for peace or at a later date renew the war in the hope of success.

3. The attainment of power in Great Britain would be a sign for the German and Italian workers to similarly rise up.

Laski pointed out that there was no possibility of either a parliamentary or a revolutionary take-over in Britain in 1940. It was not 1917. Moreover, if Britain lost the war, it would be unlikely that Stalin would intervene to save the United Kingdom. Arthur Koestler's *Darkness at Noon* was also published at this time and this too provided the British intelligentsia with uncomfortable reading. Yet there were Jewish Communists who vehemently opposed Gollancz such as the academic Hyman Levy and defended the two imperialisms line.

Dutt also carried on in pushing the Comintern line. He blamed the extension of the war to Norway on Britain and France. Significantly following the German invasion, the Norwegian Labour paper *Arbeiderbladet* and the Liberal *Dagbladet* did not resume publication, but the Communist *Arbeideren* did.[75] Moreover the Communist publication only appeared after Quisling had published his manifesto. The Communist Party itself in Norway blamed Britain and France for the occupation.[76] When Italy entered the war and invaded Greece, the CPGB asked the Greeks to seek peace with the invader. In France, prominent figures in the PCF such as Florimond Bonte and Francois Billoux petitioned the Vichy regime to be permitted to testify against the socialist leader, Leon Blum, at his trial.[77]

Earl Browder, the secretary-general of the CPUSA, published a pamphlet, entitled *The Jewish People and the War* in May 1940. In it, he commented that 5 million Soviet Jews lived a peaceful and tranquil life, free from persecution. In contrast

> In war torn Europe and in the rest of the capitalist world, the Jewish masses are faced with the greatest tragedy in their all too tragic history. Even the most ardent supporters of Allied imperialism in the United States are compelled to admit this. And yet there are forces in Jewish life and outside it, that are brutally and callously trading on the tragedy of a people, taking cynical advantage of the Jewish people's profound hatred for Nazi barbarism in order to bring them into the war on the side of Allied imperialism which is equally destructive.[78]

American-Jewish organizations and especially Zionist groups were castigated for supporting US entry into the war. Weizmann was attacked for writing to Chamberlain and pledging his support. The 'fascist' Jabotinsky was assaulted for calling for 'a Jewish army to fight for Anglo-French imperialism in the war under the Jewish flag'.[79]

Notes and Works Cited

1 *Jewish Telegraphic Agency*, 12 January 1931.
2 Richard Overy with Andrew Wheatcroft, *The Road to War* (London 1999), p. 216.
3 Overy with Wheatcroft, ibid. p. 224.
4 Albert L. Weeks, *Stalin's Other War: Soviet Grand Strategy 1939–1941* (Oxford 2002), pp. 171–3.
5 Felix Chuev, *Molotov Remembers: Inside Kremlin Politics* (Chicago 1993), p. 22.
6 Christopher Andrew, *The Defence of the Realm: The Authorised History of MI5* (London 2009), pp. 262–3.

7 Alan Bullock, *Hitler and Stalin: Parallel Lives* (London 1991), p. 674.

8 Bullock, op. cit., pp. 684–5.

9 Weeks, op. cit., p. 81.

10 Timothy Snyder, 'Hitler vs. Stalin: Who Killed More?', *New York Review of Books*, 10 March 2011.

11 Tzvetan Todorov, *Hope and Memory* (London 2005), p. 94.

12 Margarete Buber-Neumann, *Under Two Dictators: Prisoner of Stalin and Hitler* (London 2009), pp. 139–42.

13 Jeffrey Herf, *The Jewish Enemy: Nazi Propaganda During World War II and the Holocaust* (London 2006), pp. 52–3.

14 *Izvestia*, 9 October 1939.

15 Yehoshua Gilboa, *The Black Years of Soviet Jewry* (Boston 1971), p. 13.

16 Ben-Cion Pincuk, 'Soviet Media on the Fate of Jews in Nazi-Occupied Territory 1939–1941', *Yad Vashem Studies*, no. 11 (1976).

17 Baron, op. cit., p. 250.

18 Bullock, op. cit., p. 717.

19 Overy, op. cit., p. 249.

20 Paul A. Levine, 'Swedish Neutrality during the Second World War: Tactical Success or Moral Compromise', in ed. Neville Wylie, *European Neutrals and Non-Belligerents during the Second World War* (Cambridge 2002), pp. 324–5.

21 *Daily Worker*, 23 August 1939.

22 *Daily Worker*, 25 August 1939.

23 *Daily Worker*, 28 August 1939.

24 Joel Colton, *Léon Blum: Humanist in Politics* (New York 1966), p. 336.

25 Francis King and George Matthews, ed. *About Turn: The British Communist Party and the Second World War* (London 1990), pp. 19–20.

26 Weeks, op. cit., p. 41.

27 Pincuk, op. cit.

28 *Pravda*, 30 November 1939.

29 Alain Colignon, 'Belgium: Fragile Neutrality, Solid Neutralism', in ed. Neville Wylie, *European Neutrals and Non-Belligerents during the Second World War* (Cambridge 2002), pp. 110–11.

30 Gilboa, *The Black Years of Soviet Jewry*, op. cit., p. 16.

31 Donald Sassoon, 'The Rise and Fall of West European Communism 1939–1948', *Contemporary European History*, vol. 1, no. 2 (July 1992).

32 Walter Ulbricht, *Die Welt*, 2 February 1940.

33 *World News and Views*, 17 February 1940.

34 Allan Merson, *Communist Resistance in Nazi Germany* (London 1985), p. 217.

35 Paolo Spriano, *Stalin and the European Communists* (London 1985), p. 141.

36 Maurice Goldsmith, *Frédéric Joliot-Curie: A Biography* (London 1976), p. 105.

37 Sean McMeekin, 'From Moscow to Vichy: Three Working Class Militants and the French Communist Party', *Contemporary European History*, vol. 9, no. 1 (March 2000).

38 Sumner Welles, *The Time for Decision* (New York 1944), p. 129.

39 Mark Gilbert, 'Pacifist Attitudes to Nazi Germany 1936–1945', *Journal of Contemporary History*, vol. 27, no. 3 (July 1992).

40 Morgan, *Harry Pollitt*, op. cit., pp. 96–7.

41 *Daily Worker*, 11 September 1939.

42 Beckett, op. cit., p. 92.

43 Noreen Branson, *History of the Communist Party of Great Britain* (London 1985), p. 268.

44 Rajani Palme Dutt, *Why This War?* (CPGB 1939).

45 John Attfield and Stephen Williams, ed. *1939: The Communist Party of Great Britain and the War* (London 1984), p. 161.

46 Morgan, op. cit., p. 110.

47 Branson, op. cit., p. 268.

48 F. H. Hinsler and C. A. G. Simkins, *British Intelligence in the Second World War*, vol. 4 (London 1990), pp. 36–7.

49 Francois Fonvieille-Alquier, *The French and the Phoney War 1939–1940* (London 1971), pp. 140–1.

50 Attfield and Williams, op. cit., p. 272.

51 Enda Staunton, 'Frank Ryan and Collaboration: A Reassessment', *History Ireland*, vol. 5, no. 3 (Autumn 1997).

52 Rajani Palme Dutt, *Labour Monthly*, March 1941.

53 *Labour Monthly*, April 1940.

54 T. R. Sareen, 'Subhas Chandra Bose: Japan and British Imperialism', *European Journal of East Asian Studies*, vol. 3, no. 1, 2004.

55 Stephen P. Cohen, 'Subhas Chandra Bose and the Indian National Army', *Pacific Affairs*, vol. 36, no. 4 (Winter 1963–1964).

56 Ruth Fischer, 'The Indian Communist Party', *Far Eastern Survey*, vol. 22, no. 7 (June 1953).

57 Hugh Toye, *The Springing Tiger* (London 1959), p. 63.

58 Subhas Chandra, Bose, *The Indian Struggle 1920–1942* (New York 1964), pp. 419–32.

59 Marshall J. Getz, *Subhas Chandra Bose* (North Carolina 2002), p. 47.

60 *Jewish Chronicle*, 21 August 1942.

61 Stefan Wild, 'National Socialism in the Arab Near East between 1933 and 1939', *Die Welt des islams*, no. 1/4 (Bonn 1985).

62 Israel Gershoni, 'Egyptian Liberalism in an Age of "Crisis of Orientation": al-Risāla's Reaction to Fascism and Nazism 1933–1939', *International Journal of Middle East Studies*, vol. 31, no. 4 (November 1999).

63 Francis Nicosia, 'Arab Nationalism and National Socialist Germany 1933–1939: Ideological and Strategic Incompatibility', *International Journal of Middle East Studies*, vol. 12, no. 3 (November 1980).

64 Geoffrey Warner, *Iraq and Syria: 1941* (London 1974), p. 49.

65 Anthony R. De Luca, '"Der Grossmufti" in Berlin: The Politics of Collaboration', *International Journal of Middle East Studies*, vol. 10, no. 1 (February 1979).

66 Zvi Elpeleg, *The Grand Mufti: Haj Amin Al-Husseini, Founder of the Palestinian National Movement* (London 1993), pp. 69–73.

67 Anwar Sadat, *Revolt on the Nile* (London 1957), p. 8.

68 King and Matthews, op. cit., p. 130.

69 Bill Jones, *The British Labour Party and the Soviet Union* (Manchester 1977), pp. 50–2.

70 John Strachey, *The Coming Struggle for Power* (London 1934), p. 359.

71 Neal Wood, *Communism and British Intellectuals* (London 1959), p. 188.

72 John Strachey, 'The CP Line Now', *Left News*, July 1940.

73 John Strachey, Letter to Ivor Montagu, 16 August 1940 (Ivor Montagu archive, People's Museum, Manchester).

74 Victor Gollancz, ed. *The Betrayal of the Left* (London 1941), p. 61.

75 *Daily Herald*, 24 April 1940.

76 *Daily Worker*, 3 May 1940.

77 Spriano, op. cit., p. 139.

78 Earl Browder, *The Jewish People and the War* (CPUSA May 1940).

79 Browder, op. cit.

8

After the Shoah

Defeating the Nazis

Despite his inability to defeat Britain, the fall of France convinced Hitler that the invasion of the Soviet Union would be a relatively easy task. Hitler was now able to pursue his much desired assault on 'Judeo-Bolshevism'. The Red Army, however, despite terrible losses, refused to submit and accept defeat, but instead fought on tenaciously with great courage. Pearl Harbour also brought the Americans into the war. Within a year, Hitler's military miscalculations had suddenly altered the balance of forces. Nazi Germany was now confronted by an alliance of Stalin, Roosevelt and Churchill.

The German invasion of the USSR resolved many dilemmas and indeed saved many a Communist face in Europe. Communists could now fully engage in the struggle against fascism once more. When France had fallen to the Nazis in 1940, the PCF responded by merely distributing leaflets and staging strikes. Now they took up arms and were prominent in the resistance to the Nazi occupation. Indeed by the end of the war, local European parties emerged as the standard bearers of moral conduct and the upholders of national pride. This was rewarded by political gains and positions in government, following the post-war elections. The sacrifice and valour of the Red Army was greatly admired and valued. There was an intense desire to rebuild society without past blemishes and flaws after such devastation. The Communists passionately identified with this sentiment and were its most prominent advocates. The Molotov-Ribbentrop pact came to be seen as an aberration – a necessary time waster until the Soviet forces were ready to combat the Nazi invader. Even in Britain, respect for the USSR and a desire to build a better society, increased the membership of the CPGB from 17,756 in 1939 to 47,500 in 1944.[1]

Yet this effective rehabilitation was not inevitable. There had been no guarantee that once the Nazi war machine had been halted on Soviet soil or when the Red Army had driven back the Germans to the pre-conflict borders that the fighting would continue. The British in particular feared that Stalin would once more strike a diplomatic bargain with the Germans. Indeed the British were willing to appease the Soviets through recognition of their newly acquired territories during the period of the pact, but the Americans strongly opposed this.

Stalin, for his part, believed that true cooperation with the Allies could only be realized through a second front. As this did not materialize, Stalin asked whether Britain and the United States were trying to ensure that the Soviet Union and Nazi Germany fought themselves to an exhausted standstill leaving in place an empowered West. After the German failure at Stalingrad and the turning of the tides of war, Hitler became more amenable to a negotiated peace with the Soviets. Hitler told Goebbels that he preferred to negotiate with Stalin than with the West, even though he believed that such negotiations would be ultimately unsuccessful.[2]

Both Japan and Sweden were deemed suitable intermediaries to effect any negotiations. In addition, Mussolini had urged Hitler to make peace with the Soviets because he feared an imminent allied invasion. In the period between the encirclement of Stalingrad in February 1943 and the tank battle at Kursk in July, the Kremlin sent mixed messages as to their intentions. Stalin's initial appeals were solely directed towards the German military, recalling their previous cooperation in the pre-Hitler era. Such ambiguity ended after the German collapse at Kursk.

These twists and turns took place while millions of Jews were being systematically exterminated. They did not feature in the bigger picture of Nazi-Soviet relations. Hitler's decision to implement the final solution came shortly after his invasion of the USSR. 2.6 million Jews were murdered on Soviet territory – of whom 1.6 million had been citizens of other countries prior to the Molotov-Ribbentrop pact.[3] The USSR seemingly had no policy to save Jews. Its central desire was to increase the territory over which it had control and to impose Stalin's version of Communism. Thus the Red Army was ordered to halt its advance on the outskirts of Warsaw – to allow the retreating Germans to crush the uprising of the Polish Home Army. Stalin also prevented the Allies from providing assistance to the Poles.

Following the Nazi invasion of the USSR, the Soviet media rarely published any material to indicate that Jews specifically had been singled out by the Germans. Only general atrocities were reported. Stalin showed no great interest in the fate of the Jews.

By the spring of 1944, the Red Army was advancing on a broad front, forcing a German retreat. Majdanek had been liberated by July. Could the Soviet Air Force in the summer of 1944 have bombed the crematoria at Auschwitz or destroyed the railway lines? The front in August 1944 was 100 miles away. Stalin certain had the military wherewithal to do so. Berlin significantly had been attacked by the Soviet Air Force as early as August 1941.[4] Did any European Communist parties ask such questions once the revelations of the Final Solution had become apparent?

In London, in June 1942, the nature of the Final Solution was being conveyed to a preoccupied British government. Szmul Zygielbojm, a member of the Polish National Council and leading Bundist appealed to the British and American governments to place pressure on the Germans 'to stop the slaughter of an entire nation before it is too late. I am quite aware that my request is somewhat unusual, but these are facts without precedent in human history'. He wrote that a report recently smuggled out of Poland via Swedish businessmen revealed a new innovation in Nazi planning.

> The murder there was done by means of gas, as took place in the village of Chelmno, nine miles from Kolo, in the Kolski district. For this purpose a special car/gas chamber/was used, into which 90 people at a time were loaded. The victims were buried in special graves in the clearing of the Lubartow forest. On the average, 1000 people were gassed daily. From November 1941 to March 1942, Jewish inhabitants of Kolo, Dab, Bugaj and Izbica, 5000 in all, together with 35,000 from the Lodz ghetto and a certain number of gypsies were gassed in Chelmno.[5]

At a press conference on 9 July 1942, Brendan Bracken who headed the Ministry of Information announced that 'according to estimates, the Germans have murdered up to now 700,000 Polish Jews'. Witnesses such as Jan Karski reached Western Europe and described in harrowing detail the destruction of Polish Jewry. For the subsequent two and a half years, the killing continued essentially unimpeded and was even accelerated.

By the spring of 1945, the graphic revelations of the concentration camps and the industrialized murder of the Jews by the Nazis and their fellow travellers were communicated through film and word. Even for those who had endured the brutality of the Nazi occupation in Europe, the revelation that deportation to the East for their Jewish communities was a subterfuge for systematic extermination was numbing. For the British who were fortunate to have been isolated by a 20-mile wide cordon of deep water, there was silence and horror when the first footage of the liberation of Bergen-Belsen was shown in London's West End cinemas. But how then should the British deal with the remnant who by sheer luck had survived? How to manage those Jews who no longer wished to live with the neighbours who had betrayed them? How should the new Labour government of Clement Atlee handle the tens of thousands of displaced people who now solely envisaged Palestine under the British Mandate as the location which would offer safety, a sense of belonging and a cultural and religious familiarity?

European Jews, themselves, were too traumatized by what had come to pass, by the inability of the civilized world to save them. Jews had fought in all the Allied armies as well as in the resistance in occupied Europe. Communist, Bundist and Zionist Jews had died together in the Warsaw Ghetto Uprising in 1943. In their desire to crush Nazism and end this terrible war, neither Capitalist nor Communist had seriously deflected the ultimate fate of the Jews. In the West, saving the Jews came to be seen as a consequence of winning the war. The question – what happens if there were no more Jews to save – was addressed only marginally. In the East, saving the Soviet Union and exporting the revolution was paramount. Moreover, the international proletariat did not rise up against their masters. The circle of abandonment of the Jews was complete. The Allies may have won the war, but the Jews certainly lost it.

Division and dissension in the ranks

The different solutions to the Jewish problem in Europe after May 1945 fragmented the European Left. Indeed it was one of the many problems that Hitler had bequeathed to the victors of the war. It also essentially divided the Jewish Left from the European Left. Stalinists, Trotskyists and Marxists of different ideological hues understood that a new situation had arisen, that 'the systematic extermination of the Jews' created 'a self-awareness and solidarity of Jews wherever they may be'.[6] Moreover, just as Trotsky had realized in the 1930s that the Leninist solution of assimilation was no longer a rational solution to the Jewish problem in the context of the growth of Nazism, left wing Jews in particular had now arrived at this conclusion. As Moshe Sneh, a Polish Jew and future leader of the Israeli Communist Party, commented many years later:

Every Jew who remained alive knows and feels that he is alive only by chance – either because he was outside the area of rule of the Third Reich or because there wasn't enough time to put him into a gas chamber and furnace. Every Jew knows and feels that he was condemned to death only because of his Jewishness and that only by accident the death sentence wasn't carried out. Every Jew proudly bears in his heart the yellow patch with the star of David that our brothers were forced to carry on their backs as a sign of disgrace while being alive and as a shipping tag to the death camp. To come to this people now and advise them: 'assimilate please, forget that you were Jews, free yourselves from your Jewishness so that you will be free' – can anything more cynical and cruel be imagined? At any rate it is impossible to give our grieving people such advice in the name of communism; communism came to liberate man from alienation, not to impose it upon him and order him not to be himself.[7]

There were also changes of opinion in the Palestine Communist Party. At its congress in September 1945, the leadership argued that Palestine was now 'a country of a bi-national character'. The Yishuv – the Jewish settlement in Palestine – had changed dramatically since the British arrived. It now occupied 'the central position in the industrial development of the country'. The idea of a mass exodus from Europe and the abolition of the Diaspora were rejected. While it opposed Ben-Gurion and his Mapai party and its call for a Jewish state, such an approach aligned the PCP with left wing Zionist groups such as Hashomer Hatzair which similarly espoused the notion of a bi-national state. It also attracted Left Poale Zion which had termed partition 'a ruse of British impe-rialism' in the 1930s.[8] The PCP also took a stand against Arab nationalism:

> We fight to permeate into the Arab masses the perception and conviction that the success of the fight for democracy and independence is connected with the fight for equality of national rights and against national discriminations including the abrogation of the White Paper.

Such views from their comrades in Palestine that the situation had changed influenced other Communist parties in Europe – and particularly their Jewish members. Now it was the British Left which played a significant role in the fate and future of Palestine. As the Mandatory power, the struggle for the future was taking place in London and this relegated other European move-ments to the sidelines.

A statement from the National Jewish Committee to the International Affairs Committee of the CPGB in the summer of 1945 suggested that the Jewish community of Palestine was a firmly established one and 'as such is entitled to full rights'. The committee also argued that the rights of the Jewish people did not reside in the context of compensation for all the atrocities committed against them or for reasons of divine right or even historic claims, but simply that Palestine was one of many countries which European Jews should be allowed to go to.

Paraphrasing Stalin's definition of nationality, it argued that the Jews of Palestine were now defined by a 600,000 strong community established on a territory; an advanced economic life; a common language, Hebrew and a common psychological background. All this now fitted the traditional Leninist requirements for a nationality. The committee further pointed out that the

Jews of Palestine had enrolled in the British Armed Forces in great numbers during the war and fought fascism. 'Economically, socially, culturally and politically, they constitute the most advanced section of the peoples of the Middle East and are the most progressive force in that vital area.' The National Jewish Committee of the CPGB concluded by advocating the right of self-determination of the Jews of Palestine.[9]

The views of Rajani Palme Dutt, however, did not coincide with those of the CPGB's Jewish members. Even so, he too had to modify his approach often in line with Soviet policy and now opposed the 1939 White Paper which had proposed a quota system on Jewish immigration into Palestine and made it dependent on Arab wishes after a five-year period. At the beginning of 1946, Dutt spoke to a gathering of Jewish Communists and argued that the current problem was that in many countries Jews had no place in society. The democratic answer was therefore to change society and thereby reintegrate their Jewish citizens. The new Communist states of Eastern Europe were held up as shining examples. Zionism, he argued, played into the hands of anti-Semitism by wishing to transplant all European Jews to Palestine. The Zionists denied 'the democratic answer to the Jewish problem'.[10]

The CPGB also submitted evidence to the Anglo-American Commission of Inquiry on Palestine (AACI) which hoped to arrive at an equitable solution to the problem of displaced persons.[11] The party argued that while the sufferings of the Shoah had driven multitudes 'away from their homeland', the answer did not lie in Zionism. In fact, Zionism would contribute to an intensification of the suffering of the Jews since this would confirm the claim that they were essentially aliens in the countries in which they lived – and this would undermine the struggle for equal rights. There was, the submission stated, nothing inevitable about anti-Semitism. Through its representation of Palestine as 'a Jewish national state', the Jewish people would become 'the instrument of international and imperialist power politicians in the Middle East'. Zionism was deemed to be defeatist and was aggravating the practical problems in dealing with the DPs.

It furthered remarked that a primary aim should be to educate and encourage Jews 'to return to their country of origin' and to re-establish themselves. This should be guaranteed by the United Nations. One possibility was that a period of rehabilitation could be spent in the United Kingdom or United States under the supervision of family and friends.

The CPGB considered that the problem of the remnant of European Jewry and the problem of Palestine were separate issues. Moreover, the CPGB was strongly averse to the prospect that Jews would change their citizenship to one of colonial status.

Yet significantly the Jews of Palestine were praised by the CPGB for developing the land and industrializing Palestine. This development, it was observed, had contributed to 'a large mass of landless Arabs' who were unable to find work in the Arab sector. Once the Mandate had been terminated and Palestine given full independence, there would be:

> no hesitation on the part of the Arabs on the basis of an agreement with the Jews as equal citizens of Palestine to admit refugees from fascist persecution as freely as other free countries admit refugees to their shores irrespective of race or religion.[12]

This certainly did not reflect the desire of Arab nationalists who wished to stop Jewish immigration at all costs.

The Labour Left takes sides

Despite his reservations, Rajani Palme Dutt loyally followed the new Communist line. He was aware of the strong support for Zionism on the Labour Left in Britain and vehemently criticized its campaign for a state. He inferred privately that there were other reasons behind the political clamour for a state since 'the Labour party had previously been in the pockets of the Zionists'.[13] Dutt had never been keen on cooperating with the Labour Left and was still highly critical of those who supported the war against Nazi Germany from the outset in 1939.[14]

In early 1946, the 'Keep Left' group in the Labour Party had been formed and there was strong support for the Zionist cause. One of its prime movers was Richard Crossman who had visited the liberated camps as early as May 1945. He wrote what he had observed:

> Corpses in themselves are not particularly horrible, even half-starved corpses. After the first shock one fails to react to what is so obviously not alive and so apparently not human. Just by the crematorium there were half a dozen camp inmates sitting in the shade of a pine tree, nonchalantly watching the corpses being arranged with pitchforks on the carts. Obviously they were completely immune to any sense of horror at the sight, and even their sense of smell apparently had been deadened.[15]

Unlike Dutt, Crossman saw the reality of the post-war situation and was not addicted to making it fit theory. On visiting Dachau, he wrote:

> European civilisation was not a stable and settled way of life, but a thin crust, constantly threatened by the volcanic violence of vast and understood forces just below the surface.[16]

Atlee had ironically appointed Crossman to the Anglo-American Commission of Inquiry on Palestine as a veritable safe pair of hands who would deliver the correct verdict. Indeed, as far back as 1937, Atlee had separated immigration to Palestine from the plight of pre-war Polish Jews.[17] Crossman, an intellectual and writer, however, was his own man and carefully delved into the Jewish problem in Europe and its solution in Palestine. The Labour Left was also determined not to allow anti-Jewish sentiment to raise its head once more in Britain or elsewhere after the ravages of the Shoah. The journal of the Labour Left, *Tribune*, castigated Lieutenant-General Sir Frederick Morgan, the Chief of Operations for the UN Relief and Rehabilitation Administration in Europe, when he spoke about 'well-fed, well-dressed Jews from Poland, with pockets bulging with money' who were arriving daily in Berlin. All the arrivals, Morgan commented, told 'the same monotonous story' of pogroms and persecution – for which there was no evidence.[18]

George Orwell too bemoaned the fact that too many British citizens were indifferent. 'Their own anti-Semitism has caused this vast crime to bounce off their consciousness.'[19]

Crossman questioned whether Zionism was simply a heartfelt, but transient reaction to Nazi anti-Semitism and whether the very concept of 'a Jewish nation' was simply a reflection of this. Ernest Bevin, the British Foreign Secretary reduced Jews to their popular stereotypes, both capitalist and communist. Bevin was also concerned that any British withdrawal from Palestine would allow the Soviets to fill the vacuum. In a press conference to announce the establishment of the AACI, he jocularly remarked that the Jew should not push to the head of the queue. Crossman commented:

That might go down in Britain; in Belsen it sounded like the mouthing of a sadistic anti-Semite. Two of us had seen a Polish Jew tear up the document which promised him emigration to America, saying that he could never trust a Christian again; he would not go to America because what happened in Germany might happen there. In Washington that might sound like the raving of a lunatic: in a Bavarian assembly centre where the huddled survivors were still cooped up behind barbed wire, nine months after the day of liberation, it was the considered view of many sober and intelligent Jews.[20]

Bevin like Atlee was not well disposed to the idea of Jews immigrating to Palestine. They should remain in Europe or go elsewhere. In the 1930s, Bevin had indicated his interest in the Freeland League which advocated Jewish settlement in Australia.

Crossman became very aware of the difference between the American and British attitudes to the Jewish problem. The United States had been established by immigrants, both Jewish and non-Jewish, often fleeing European persecution. There was essentially a mass conversion to Zionism after 1945 by US Jews who felt responsible for those of their traumatized kinsmen who had survived. This in turn filtered through to American non-Jews. The English, Crossman reasoned, were unsympathetic to Zionism because their deepest fear was one of invasion. The English had been localized for centuries in their own villages and towns. Amidst the ruins of European civilization, 'the Englishman thinks of Zionism as something synthetic and unnatural'[21] and believed Zionism to be 'the product of high powered American propaganda'. The Englishman viewed the Arab as defending his 1,000-year-old civilization against the invader.

Yet the 1944 Labour Party conference had remarkably argued that there should be unrestricted immigration of Jews until they became a majority. There were even hints of transferring the Palestinian Arabs out of Palestine. All this came in the context of the first revelations of the mass murder of European Jewry. Labour Party leaders such as Hugh Dalton immediately viewed Palestine as the solution to the Jewish question. Dalton argued in 1945 that it would be 'morally wrong and politically indefensible to impose obstacles' for entry to Palestine. The Mufti and the mainstream Palestinian Arab leadership had actively been pro-German during the war. Indeed Tito had charged the Mufti as a war criminal and called for his extradition from the Middle East. In contrast, the Arabic periodical of the Palestine Communist Party welcomed him back on his arrival in Egypt with a laudatory article.[22] Labour Party members viewed the Mufti as 'the Arab Quisling'. Crossman understood the problem in more complex terms.

> Was it that we were all on the lookout in 1939 for appeasement and saw the Arabs as a fascist force to which Jewish liberty was being sacrificed? Partly, perhaps. But I suspect that six years of this war have fundamentally changed our emotions. We were pro-Jew in 1939 as part of 'anti-fascism'. We were not looking at the actual problems of Palestine, but instinctively standing up for the Jews whenever there was a chance to do so. Now most of us are not emotionally pro-Jew, but only rationally 'anti-anti-Semitic' which is a very different thing.

Crossman saw Zionism as 'the twentieth century adaptation of Jewry to a hostile world' and despite the public handwringing after Auschwitz, the Jews would remain in constant danger of persecution. Crossman believed that free Jewish immigration and the rise of a socialist Hebrew republic would be anathema to Arab nationalists who were struggling against imperialism. In both cases, an injustice would take place. He concluded, however, that Zionism as a solution was the lesser injustice.

Crossman's view and others on the Labour Left were also coloured by their admiration for the building of socialism in Palestine and the long association of many party members with the Zionist experiment. As early as December 1917, a special Labour conference met at Central Hall, Westminster to approve a War Aims Memorandum. This included a clause which advocated that Palestine 'may form a free state, under international guarantee, to which such of the Jewish people as desire to do so may return'.

Long before the rise of Nazism, the concrete developments in Palestine interested Jewish socialists whom in their youth had dismissed Jewish settlement in Palestine out of hand. Martov expressed an interest shortly before his death in 1923.[23] Pavel Axelrod wrote about it in the aftermath of the Balfour Declaration.

> When I indulge in the dream of a happy, united humanity, then it appears to me a pity that the Jews exert so much energy in colonising Palestine. But in view of the hard facts of reality, of the pogroms, and all the various forms of Jewish persecution, there stirs within me sympathy for Palestine and a wish to see in the realisation of the Zionist goal a refuge for that unhappy people.[24]

Following the rejection of the AACI report by the Atlee government, Richard Crossman and Michael Foot wrote a hard-hitting pamphlet, entitled *A Palestine Munich?* They commented on the Labour Party's profound opposition to the 1939 White Paper:

> The Labour party was fully aware of the danger of war. It realised that to permit Jewish immigration to Palestine would certainly antagonise the Arab states which had already been permeated with Nazi and Fascist propaganda. On the other hand, the party felt it impossible to connive at the sacrifice of another small ally in the interests of expediency. To limit immigration just at the moment when Palestine was the sole available refuge from Hitler would be a crime against humanity. Lastly, the party was convinced that, by appeasing the Arab League with regard to Palestine, the British government would not achieve its loyal support during the war.[25]

Between 1917 and 1945, the party conference reaffirmed its support for a Jewish National Home on no less than eleven occasions. The fight for a better life in Britain was equated with the struggle of the Jews in Palestine to build a perfect society. George Isaacs, later Minister of Labour under Atlee said at the TUC Congress in Plymouth in 1936 that:

> It seems to me that the new star of Bethlehem now shining over Jerusalem is the star of socialism and I wonder whether the British government are afraid of

this development and in doubt whether it ought to be encouraged or hindered . . . we must see to it that the door is kept open and we must give these people the opportunity of developing socialism as it is being developed there, extending to them our blessing and helping them to build a new Jerusalem in Palestine. [26]

Crossman and Foot were highly critical of Arab nationalism and ridiculed the accusation that supporting the Jews would unite the Arab world in a holy war against Britain. The Arab Higher Committee refused to recognize the rights of those Jews who came to Palestine after 1917. Crossman and Foot also assaulted the government's belief that the DPs should not be allowed to enter Palestine since this would swell the ranks of the Hagana and the Irgun. Atlee proposed the disbanding of these organizations as a condition for implementing the AACI report. Crossman and Foot concluded that partition was the only solution – with a coastal state where there would be a small Jewish majority and 400,000 Palestinian Arabs becoming part of Abdullah's TransJordan.

Out of step with the Kremlin

The leadership of the British Communists saw things differently. Rajani Palme Dutt discerned progressive features in the views of the Foreign Secretary, Ernest Bevin[27] and this led to a private exchange of correspondence with Paul Novick, the editor of the Yiddish *Morgen Freiheit*, a strong supporter of the Soviet Union and member of the CPUSA. Novick complained to Dutt that:

But the Zionist demands merge, so to speak, with the general demands of the broad Jewish masses for the abolition of the White Paper. It is also the demand of the whole working class movement in America, of the World Trade Union Federation as expressed in the resolution for a Jewish National Home. This resolution with certain reservations is being supported by the CP of the USA. Also the resolution of the Palestine Communist Party speaks of a Jewish National Home for the Yishuv in a free and democratic Palestine with equal national and citizen rights for Jews and Arabs.[28]

Novick further argued that since British policy in Palestine was an imperialist policy, Bevin's policy actually strengthened it. It was motivated by a desire to move towards the position of the Arab League, 'an imperialist anti-Soviet instrument'. How, therefore, he asked, can Bevin's attitude be progressive? Dutt responded by stating that this was in accordance with party policy and that the progressive nature of Bevin's approach was due to 'the distinction of the problem of World Jewry from the special problem of Palestine and the resistance to the reactionary Zionist clamour'.[29]

Bevin's determination to disconnect the Jewish problem from its Zionist solution in Palestine did not find favour with other Jewish Communists. Phil Piratin, however, a newly elected Jewish Communist MP, was abundantly clear in his view.

> The Jews in Palestine are in some respects as oppressed as they were under the Nazis. They have not migrated to a new free country, but to a colonial country, administered, not by freely elected representatives but by alien civil servants. They are more restricted in their development. More and more Jews are hating the British imperialist authority. These feelings they share with the Arabs who likewise have very little to bless the British administration for.[30]

In July 1946, Willie Gallacher wrote to Atlee to condemn the arrests of the leadership of the Jewish Agency on the Black Sabbath. He bemoaned past policies and argued that all the problems in Palestine might have been avoided if British politicians had considered other solutions apart from the national home for the Jews. He concluded by stating that the only solution was a British withdrawal from Palestine.[31]

The CPGB had moved a long way from pre-war positions when Zionism was deemed to be beyond the pale in that it was defined as arriving on the ideological scene too late, in an era of imperialism, colonies and empires, when Jewish aspirations were depicted as 'the helpless playthings of inter-imperial rivalries and conflicting national ambitions'.[32] There was a recognition that the Jewish settlement in Palestine now was both stable and progressive. This was a long way from Leninist preconceptions at the turn of the century.

At the beginning of 1947, Bevin effectively handed over the Palestine problem to the United Nations. The Soviet stand, mimicked by local Communist parties, did not alter. However, in May 1947, Andrei Gromyko, the Soviet representative on the UN Security Council, made a remarkable speech. He stated that Palestine was now inhabited by two peoples, each with historical rights. It had now become the homeland of both Jews and Arabs. It therefore followed that there could neither be a Jewish state without rights for Arabs nor an Arab state without rights for Jews. Gromyko therefore suggested that the only rational solution was the creation of an independent democratic Arab-Jewish state based on equal rights for both populations. This, in itself, was not dramatically different from previous Soviet utterances. Then in what was seemingly a complete ideological volte-face on the Zionist solution to the

Jewish question, Gromyko commented that if a bi-national solution proved to be impracticable then there would have to be a partition into two states.

> This solution would only be justified in the event of it being proved that relations between the Jewish and Arab populations were actually so bad that they could not be improved and their peaceful coexistence could not be ensured.[33]

In addition, Gromyko argued that the United Nations could not remain indifferent to the fate of the Jews after all that they had suffered. 'We cannot deny the right of the Jews to own a home'.

Stalin, of course, was determined to oust the British from the Middle East and to prevent the Americans from entering it. The issue of Palestine offered Moscow the opportunity of splitting the post-war alliance. Access to Middle Eastern oil was also important, following the havoc wreaked by the Nazis on the Soviet oil industry. At the Teheran Conference in December 1943, Roosevelt had rejected Stalin's request that the region's oil should be administered by the Big Three. The warm, deep sea port of Haifa was another incentive. There was also a fear at the end of 1947 that Israel would request a UN peacekeeping force if things went badly militarily. US State department officials saw this as a means of the Soviets establishing a base for themselves in Israel.[34] There was also a suspicion that the many East European immigrants to Israel contained Communist agents in their midst. If Stalin truly opened the gates to emigration, the Kremlin would infiltrate large numbers of spies. The prospect of gaining the support of the Marxist wing of the Zionist movement was important and representatives were suddenly invited to Moscow for the October Revolution celebrations in 1947.[35] Whatever the rationale, Soviet state interests prevailed over purely ideological ones. The sacrificing of Arab support and the reversal of three decades of Soviet foreign policy were deemed to be worthwhile. The Zionists, according to the Kremlin, were more likely to oust the British from Palestine than were the Arab nationalists. Local parties, however, were left to dangle at the end of their ideological rope. The new tune to be sung was deemed to be due to changed circumstances.

The Arab world was naturally taken by surprise. The Communists in Palestine were totally perplexed. Their original stand had been one of 'Arab-Jewish unity' and support for a bi-national state. In his testimony to the Anglo-American Commission of Inquiry in March 1946, Meir Vilner, a leading Jewish Communist in Palestine, had opposed partition. He said that it would strangle economic development, strengthen the dependency of both states on the British and widen the gulf between Arabs and Jews. He argued that Jewish immigration would not solve the Jewish problem, only the victory of world socialism could achieve that goal.[36]

A leading Arab member of the PCP, Emile Touma, the editor of *al-Ittihad* in Haifa, had just returned from a conference of Communist parties of the British Empire in London in January 1947 where he had opposed partition. When he heard about the Soviet about-turn, he wrote to Dutt:

> I cannot understand in particular the attitude of the Soviet Union delegation (at the UN session on Palestine) to the Palestine problem. The major point which is troubling our people is the significance of Gromyko's justification of the Jewish aspirations for a national home. Does this not help the Zionists to strengthen their hold on the Jewish masses and is this not a justification of Zionist ideology? Further, what is the significance of Gromyko's clear statement on the solutions of the Palestine problem. I cannot understand the reference for a bi-national state nor his reference to partition as a possible solution.[37]

Touma said that Gromyko's statement was not welcome and that partition was 'an imperial danger threatening peace and stability'. He then asked 'is this incorrect?' Dutt responded by surmising that perhaps the Soviet move was simply a warning to Arab states that unless they worked for an independent democratic Palestine where Jews and Arabs cooperate, then a two-state solution would be the inevitable outcome. In a rare admission of different interests, Dutt commented in his response:

> the diplomatic tasks of the Soviet Union and the political tasks of our parties do not necessarily coincide in concrete details even though they may always in practice strengthen and reinforce one another.

Dutt's explanation and justification of Gromyko's declaration was unprecedented in terms of his previous views on the Jewish question. He argued that Gromyko's comments would in fact mobilize 'extensive sections of Jewry affected by Zionist ideas' as well as Arab supporters of independence. The future of Palestine would be determined by the people themselves.

> Our aim in avoiding a definition of a bi-national state and preferring to speak in general terms of an independent democratic state based on equal rights of citizenship without laying down the type of constitution to realise this aim, was not only governed by the desire to avoid laying down from the outside the form of constitution for Palestine, but also by the necessity of the democratic fight in countries outside Palestine to present a democratic solution of the Jewish problem as against the concept of the Jews as a separate nation or aliens in the countries of their own birth.[38]

Dutt reminded Touma that Gromyko had pointed out that because the West was incapable of suppressing anti-Semitism and implementing a democratic solution, the Jews needed a national home and a state. 'The implication clearly is that if the situation of full democracy that obtains in Eastern Europe were universal, there would be no basis for such an aspiration'. Partition was held out only as 'a possibly inevitable and undesirable alternative'.

The Jewish question and the future of Palestine was clearly a sensitive and perplexing issue for all European parties. Yet Touma and *al-Ittihad* continued to oppose partition for several weeks until it decided that it was 'a constructive solution'.[39]

Soviet support for partition at the United Nation caused an attack on Communist organizations and publications in Aleppo. In Damascus, the Soviet Cultural Centre and the local party headquarters were damaged by nationalist protesters. The Syrian regime banned the party shortly afterwards.[40]

Solidarity with the Jews in the aftermath of the Shoah and the blurred approach of the Communists towards Palestine created a sense of unease on the Left. Despite disowning the Jewish underground in Palestine by Diaspora leaders, the armed struggle of Menachem Begin's Irgun catalysed attacks on Jewish shops and synagogues in the north of England. Yet Labour's *Tribune* was willing to quote from the speeches of the defendants in the trial of Dov Gruner and his compatriots:

> You have become used in the course of centuries to bring down the whip on the heads of scores of peoples which you are ruling in your colonies – and you thought we too would bow our heads to your tyranny. You were wrong. We shall break your whip; we shall put an end to the maltreatment of those to whom this country belongs. Now you know you are not going to flog the citizens of this country, Jews or Arabs, for we the soldiers of Israel revolted against your rule and its debased methods.[41]

Tribune commented that it was 'faith and fanaticism we are up against, not mere thuggery. It cannot be exorcised by the hangman's rope or by playing with words'.

In contrast, the Communist *Daily Worker* unusually published a letter from a reader asking why the paper had not protested about the execution of Dov Gruner and other members of Irgun. 'The five victims fought in the heroic way the *Daily Worker* praised the Maquis and partisans . . . to prevent the terrorism of British imperialism from using Palestine as a future war base, ostensibly against the USSR.' The editor responded by arguing that the Irgun had played into the hands of British imperialism which was used 'to justify their occupation of Palestine. It also creates anti-Semitism in the UK'.

The Jewish terrorists are in conflict with the armed invader (Britain) but wish British troops to remain in order to continue the national oppression of the Arabs. There is, moreover, no evidence that the terrorists are associated with democratic views and that they wish to defend the Soviet Union.

The policy of the *Daily Worker*, he reiterated, was to call for the withdrawal of British troops and 'the creation of a Palestinian state for equality for all its inhabitants, Arab and Jew'.[42] Dutt argued similarly two weeks later in an article in the *Daily Worker*. He strongly condemned the 'imperialist plans for the dismemberment of India' and attacked partition in Ireland, Palestine, Egypt-Sudan and the separatists' demands of the ethnic groups of Burma. He pointed out that partition was the inevitable result 'when imperialism retreats from the advance of a national movement'.[43] Dutt's article unfortunately appeared on exactly the same day as Gromyko made his speech at the United Nations, raising the possibility of partition and a two-state solution. All local Communist parties swiftly fell into line.

In May 1948 – in contrast to the year before – the central committee of the PCP, now the Communist Party of Israel, issued a stirring statement on the establishment of the state of Israel:

Just as we achieved liquidation of the mandate by a struggle for liberation of the Yishuv, so we will achieve full independence by the mobilisation of all the forces of the Yishuv for the fight for our freedom. On our side stand all progressive forces. We shall fight and we will win.[44]

Notes and Works Cited

1 *Times*, 25 February 1949.

2 Vojtech Mastny, 'Stalin and the Prospects of a Separate Peace in World War II', *American Historical Review*, vol. 77, no. 5 (December 1972).

3 Timothy Snyder, 'Nazis, Soviets, Poles, Jews', *New York Review of Books*, vol. 56, no. 19, 3–16 December 2009.

4 Jeffrey Herf, 'The Nazi Extermination Camps and the Ally to the East: Could the Red Army and Air Force Have Stopped or Slowed the Final Solution?', *Kritika: Explorations in Russian and Eurasian History*, vol. 4, no. 4, Fall 2003.

5 Letter of Szmul Zygielbojm to the British and American governments, 30 June 1942 (People's History Museum, Manchester).

6 Michael Pablo, *The Arab Revolution* (New York 1959).

7 Moshe Sneh, *Communism, Democracy and the Jewish People: Theses for the 16th Congress of the Communist Party of Israel*, Tel Aviv, October 1968.

8   Itzhak Galnoor, *The Partition of Palestine* (New York 1995), p. 105.

9   Information document, the National Jewish Committee of the CPGB January 1947, Communist Party archive, People's Museum, Manchester.

10 *Jewish Clarion*, 20 March 1946.

11 Memorandum, submitted to the Anglo-American Commission of Inquiry by Hashomer Hatzair (1946) in Paul Mendes-Flohr and Jehuda Reinharz, eds. *The Jew in the Modern World: A Documentary History* (Oxford 1995), pp. 622–5.

12 *Jewish Clarion*, 20 May 1946.

13 Rajani Palme Dutt, letter to Paul Novick, 29 January 1946 (Dutt archive, People's Museum, Manchester).

14 *Tribune*, 8 December 1939.

15 Richard Crossman, *Palestine Mission* (London 1947), p. 11.

16 Ibid., p. 13.

17 David Ben-Gurion, letter to Z. Aharonovitch, 14 February 1938 in Joseph Gorny, *The British Labour Movement and Zionism: 1917–1948* (London 1983), p. 144.

18 *Tribune*, 11 January 1946.

19 George Orwell, 'Notes on Nationalism', *Polemic*, no. 1, October 1945.

20 Crossman, op. cit., p. 76.

21 Crossman, op. cit., p. 34.

22 *Al-Ittihad*, 23 June 1946.

23 Marc Yarblum, interview with Martov, '60 shana labaaya Hayehudit Lehalakha U l'maase BeToldot HaBolshevizm', *Hapoel Hatzair*, 26 November 1963 in ed. Zvi Y. Gitelman, *Jewish Nationality and Soviet Politics: The Jewish Sections of the CPSU 1917–1930* (Princeton 1972).

24 Abraham Ascher, 'A Conflict between Jewish Loyalty and Revolutionary Discretion', *Russian Review*, vol. 24, no. 3 (July 1965).

25 R. H. S Crossman and M. Foot, *A Palestine Munich?* (London 1946).

26 Ibid.

27 Rajani Palme Dutt, Notes of the Month, *Labour Monthly*, December 1945.

28 Paul Novick, letter to Rajani Palme Dutt, 17 January 1946 (Dutt archive, People's Museum, Manchester).

29 Rajani Palme Dutt, letter to Paul Novick, 29 January 1946 (Dutt archive, People's Museum, Manchester).

30 Phil Piratin, *For Peace in Palestine* CPGB pamphlet 1946 (Communist Party archive, People's Museum, Manchester).

31 Willie Gallacher, letter to Clement Atlee, 3 July 1946 (Communist Party archive, People's Museum, Manchester).

32 George Sacks, *The Jewish Question*, New People's Library, vol. 2 (November 1937).

33 *Tass*, 16 May 1947.

34 *New York Times*, 3 December 1947.

35 Arnold Krammer, 'Soviet Motives in the Partition of Palestine 1947–1948', *Journal of Palestine Studies*, vol. 2, no. 2, Winter 1973.

36 *Political Affairs*, June 1946.

37 Emile Touma, letter to Rajani Palme Dutt, 24 May 1947 (Rajani Palme Dutt archive, People's Museum, Manchester).

38 Rajani Palme Dutt, letter to Emile Touma, 4 June 1947 (Rajani Palme Dutt archive, People's Museum, Manchester).

39 *New Leader*, 13 December 1947.

40 Martin Ebon, 'Communist Tactics in Palestine', *Middle East Journal*, vol. 2, no. 3, July 1948.

41 *Tribune*, 25 April 1947.

42 *Daily Worker*, 1 May 1947.

43 *Daily Worker*, 15 May 1947.

44 *Worker*, 15 May 1948.

9

The icy streets of Prague

East or West?

David Ben-Gurion, Israel's first Prime Minister, was a long-time admirer of Lenin because he was able to forge the Soviet state with few supporters and to secure its survival against all the odds. The model of the Soviet command economy was highly influential in Palestine where no real economic infrastructure existed. Ben-Gurion's observations of the embryonic Soviet state in the 1920s, however, led him to an anti-Communist position despite his socialist outlook. He aligned himself to the social democratic Second International rather than the Leninist Comintern. The wholesale assault on Zionism in the Soviet Union as well as the Stalinist purges in the 1930s confirmed him in this view.

Ben-Gurion was very wary of the rise of pro-Soviet opposition to his policies in Palestine. At the beginning of 1948, three groups, Hashomer Hatzair, Achdut Ha'avoda and Left Poale Zion amalgamated to establish Mapam. This arose after a visit to Moscow by party representatives as part of a delegation from Palestine to commemorate the thirtieth anniversary of the October Revolution.[1] The supporters of Mapam fought with great courage in the war of 1948 and many such as Yigal Allon, Yitzhak Rabin and Moshe Carmel achieved prominence as leading military commanders. Ben-Gurion, however, ensured that despite their military prowess, only members of his own party could achieve crucial positions in the newly established Israel Defence Forces. Indeed Allon's military force, the Palmach, was forced to dissolve.

The results of the first Israeli election in January 1949 indicated that Ben-Gurion's Mapai was the leading party and that he would form a coalition. The second placed party was Mapam and it was assumed that there would be a wall-to-wall coalition of socialist parties. Ben-Gurion, however, strongly distrusted Mapam which regarded itself as almost the USSR's representative in Israel – despite the deep hostility shown to Zionists in the Soviet Union and the imprisonment and exile of its own members in the 1930s. Ben-Gurion opted instead to form a coalition with a bloc of four religious parties – some of whom were theologically averse to the term 'Zionist'. An exasperated Mapam predicted that Israel would follow the capitalist road and this would eventually bring right wing nationalists to power.

Like Lenin, Ben-Gurion embraced realism and expediency. This formation of this first Israeli government essentially revealed that Ben-Gurion was unlikely to align Israel with the Soviet Union despite its strong support since Gromyko's UN speech positing partition. Israel's position had formally been one of non-alignment – neither East nor West. While the United States had been quick to recognize Israel, there were still lingering suspicions that Israel would evolve into a Soviet satellite – an open door for Soviet influence. Israel had been denied access to many economic aid programmes under the Marshall Plan.

The political orientation of Israel had long been a matter of debate within Mapai. Some believed that Israel should remain an independent socialist entity outside the two power blocs. There were even advocates of leaving the social democratic socialist international since its anti-Communist approach would label Israel in Soviet eyes. Others, on the other hand, believed that there should be no association with the West because of the abandonment of the Jews during the Shoah. Moshe Sharett, the Foreign Minister, believed that there was a fundamental disconnection between Soviet and Israeli concepts of democracy. Moreover, there was a belief that the Soviets would interfere or impede Israel's manoeuvrability, politically, economically and militarily.

Following Israel's admittance to the United Nations in May 1949, Soviet ardour seemed to cool. The two-year liaison had effectively seen Israel oust the British from Palestine. The Israelis had accomplished the Soviet task. The job was finished and Soviet diplomacy could return to the status quo ante in cultivating the Arab world. Moreover, throughout 1949, Soviet Jews had been arrested as 'Zionists' and the first defendants in what emerged as the Slansky trial in Prague were detained at the year's end.

In Israel, the expediency of non-alignment was increasingly seen as non-viable. In March 1950, the Mapai secretariat discussed the possibility that the Histadrut, the Confederation of Workers, would withdraw from the Soviet-led Trade Union International. This was followed in June by the outbreak of the Korean War and the Israeli cabinet's decision to support the US position. It was followed by the signing of the Israel-American Treaty of Friendship. Even so, this did not mean an automatic rejection of either the Soviet Union or the benefits of non-alignment. For example, Israel became the first non-Communist country to recognize Mao's China and to advocate its representation at the United Nations. However, the intensification of the Kremlin's assault on Jews in the USSR and in the Eastern bloc in general was numbing. The policy of keeping all options open fell into disuse. Soviet actions moved Israel away from the Soviet Union and later towards a rapprochement with the United States during the Kennedy presidency.

The Black Years

Stalin's encouragement of frenetic Jewish activity in support of the Soviet war effort did not mean a Soviet liberalization of the situation of the Jews in the USSR after 1945. Stalin's post-war campaign against 'cosmopolitans' soon degenerated into one against Jews per se. Already by the end of 1946, plans were afoot to close down the Jewish Anti-Fascist Committee (JAFC). Its chairman, Solomon Mikhoels was already receiving death threats.

Internal policy on the Jewish question in the USSR, however, had to be separated from the Kremlin's desire to support a state of the Jews within Palestine. In December 1947, in the midst of making a speech to honour the Yiddish writer, Mendele Mocher Sforim, Mikhoels referred to a character in a scene from 'The Travels of Benjamin III' who asks the way to the Land of Israel. Mikhoels remarked that 'Comrade Gromyko gave us an answer' – and received a ten-minute standing ovation from the audience. The following day the recording of the event had mysteriously gone missing. Moreover Mikhoels had met Stalin's daughter, Svetlana, in an attempt to find a way to damp down rising anti-Semitism. A month later, Mikhoels was murdered by the MGB in Minsk in 'a traffic accident'. A similar fate was to have befallen another prominent Jew, the former Foreign Minister, Maxim Litvinov, in another 'accident' between his dacha and Moscow. Unlike Mikhoels, this attempt was abandoned and Litvinov died a natural death in his bed.[2]

This was the beginning of Stalin's attempt to prevent the identification of large numbers of Soviet Jews with the cause of Israel in 1948. Despite the growing signs of the Kremlin's unease, Soviet Jews publicly addressed letters to the JAFC asking to be reunited with family in Israel. Red Army men who had fought all the way to Hitler's bunker requested to fight on Israel's behalf. Others simply wanted the right to emigrate.[3] This took place as Israeli pilots were being trained in Czechoslovakia to fly old Messerschmitts to combat the Egyptians' British spitfires. At the behest of the USSR, the Czechs also supplied 50,000 rifles, 6,000 machine guns and 90 million bullets to the Jews of Palestine.[4]

In all likelihood, there would have been a mass exodus of Jews to Israel, given the possibility. Such an event would have testified to the moral bankruptcy of the Soviet regime. The prospect of disloyalty on such a scale stoked the embers of Stalin's long-term anti-Semitism. Jews en masse were transformed into rootless cosmopolitans, purveyors of internationalism, proxies for American capitalism, Zionists.

By 1949, wholesale arrests of leading Jewish writers and intellectuals were taking place. Included in this were long-time Jewish Communists who never identified with Zionism. The demonization of Zionism and its identification with Jews per se, internationalists and old Bolsheviks served Stalin as a catch-all to eliminate imaginary opponents. Jews in Soviet industry were dismissed from their posts. Some were imprisoned, tried and shot. In Stalinsk, the discovery of an underground synagogue was connected to the local metallurgy industry. Four Jews were shot, three given twenty-five years in the Gulag followed by five years' disenfranchisement and many senior managers in the industry dismissed from their posts.[5]

The arrest and incarceration of 15 leading Jewish figures on charges of Jewish nationalism, supposedly connected with the JAFC, began with intimidation, torture and beatings and ended with their execution on 12 August 1952. The supervision of the case was initially supervised by Viktor Komarov, a deputy head of the investigative unit for such cases for the MGB. In a letter to Stalin, he wrote:

Defendants literally trembled before me. They feared me like the plague . . . I especially hated and was pitiless towards Jewish nationalists whom I saw as the most dangerous and evil enemies. Because of my hatred of them, I was considered an anti-Semite not only by the defendants but by former employees of the MGB who were of Jewish nationality.[6]

Yet Solomon Lozovsky, an old Bolshevik and colleague of Lenin, the son of a Hebrew teacher and former deputy Foreign Minister, could not easily be broken. He confronted his accusers in the courtroom. At the trial of the fifteen in the summer of 1952, he was asked why he had hired non-party staffers as head of the Sovinformburo and what percentage of them were Jews. He responded by stating that he hired people on the basis of their expertise.

I did not do that kind of calculation. I never felt drawn to Jews and never denied that I was a Jew. A person who denies his nationality is a bastard.[7]

He retracted his testimony and publicly asked Professor Lina Stern for her forgiveness for anything he may have said about her during the investigation.[8] Lozovsky and his fellow defendants were executed. Only Lina Stern was sentenced to a term of imprisonment. The news of the killings only began to leak out, following Khrushchev's speech at the Twentieth party conference in 1956, but even then it was only after the collapse of the Soviet Union in 1991 that the full details became public knowledge.

The Slansky trial

The Great Purge of the late 1930s had physically liquidated the Bolshevik old guard. Many leading East European Communists, however, who had sought refuge in the Soviet Union also perished. A disproportionate number of them were of Jewish origin. Mieczyslaw Bronski, Adolf Warski, Maksimilian Walecki of Poland, Bela Kun, Jozsef Rabinowicz of Hungary, Marcel Pauker of Rumania were executed in 1937 or shortly afterwards. Those who survived the Great Purge found themselves running the new people's democracies in post-war Eastern Europe. Many had international connections such as serving in the International Brigades in Spain. The Jews among them often had relatives abroad or in Israel. The overwhelming majority were estranged from or indifferent to their Jewishness. Many were strongly opposed to Zionism. Others such as Ana Pauker in Rumania facilitated the emigration of tens of thousands of Jews to Israel.

Stalin's next blow fell in Czechoslovakia where Kafka had been banned as a bourgeois, decadent writer and his works airbrushed from Czech literature. Soviet advisors had arrived in Czechoslovakia as early as September 1951 and within a short time, comments about Jews occupying senior positions in the party were heard at local meetings. Rudolf Slansky, the party secretary, like Lozovsky, was accused of palming out jobs to fellow Jews.[9] Artur London, the Deputy Foreign Minister of Czechoslovakia, also came across this attitude when he became a defendant in the Slansky trial in Prague in November 1952. His prison interrogator told him that Hitler was right about the Jews and 'we will finish what he started'. London was astounded.

> These words were uttered by a man who wore the party badge in his buttonhole, before three other men, in uniform who tacitly agreed. What did this anti-Semitism, this pogrom spirit, have in common with Marx, Lenin and the party? This was the first time in my adult life that I was insulted because I was a Jew and was held to be a criminal because of my race – and that by a man from State Security of a socialist country, a member of the Communist party. Was it possible that the mentality of the SS had arisen in our own ranks? This was the mentality of the men who shot my brother, Jean in 1941, who deported my mother, my sister Juliette and her husband, and dozens of my family to Auschwitz and sent them to the gas

chamber. I had concealed my race from the Nazis, should I do the same thing in my own socialist country?[10]

In Czechoslovakia alone, only a fifth of the country's pre-war Jewish community of 360,000 had survived. Three quarters of the survivors had subsequently left the country. Jews now comprised one fifteenth of one per cent of the total population.[11]

The majority of those arrested were non-Jews, but Jews were chosen to be the majority of defendants. There seemed to have been many Czech voices who believed that a multitude of Jews were in total control of the country and were serving foreign masters. They applauded this turn of events. Workers at meetings lamented the fact that Hitler had not completed his task. In the industrial district of Kladno, there was 'a pogrom-like frame of mind against the Jews . . . (believing) that it will be necessary to evict all Jews to Palestine'. In an electrical works in Kolin, a majority of workers supported the notion that 'all Jew-boys should be hung'.[12]

In terms of overt anti-Semitism, the Slansky trial far exceeded the show trials in the 1930s. In the Slansky trial, even non-Jews were being accused of 'Jewishness' since they were entrapped, according to the investigators, through their Jewish wives.[13] Eugene Loebl, another defendant in the Slansky trial similarly was greeted by anti-Semitic insults from his interrogators. In this case, a majority of those on trial were Jews, some of whom had fought in the Spanish Civil War. They were accused of 'Zionism', of being in contact with the Israeli Embassy, causing economic harm to the state and being part of a worldwide conspiratorial network.

The whole worldwide Zionist movement was in fact led and ruled by the imperialists, in particular the US imperialists, by means of US Zionists. For US Zionists who are financially most powerful and politically most influential Zionists, form part of the ruling imperialist circles of the USA.[14]

The logic of the situation suggested that the defendants were on trial not for being bourgeois nationalists, but because of their Jewishness.

The Slansky trial profoundly affected the Communist parties of Western Europe since there were personal ties through the International Brigades and the general struggle against fascism. The *Daily Worker* headlines, however, slavishly followed the Soviet presumption of guilt.

'Slansky pleads "I am guilty"'[15]; 'I worked as spy for Dulles'[16]; 'Big Business Zionists Implicated'.[17] The imagery of all-powerful, wealthy Jewish capitalists such as the London Rothschilds was invoked.

> The main aim of this plan was to enable rich Czech Jews to get out of the country, money, machinery, jewellery and other valuables, the proceeds of their businesses which had been nationalised.[18]

L'Humanité reported that the 'Zionist' defendants were spies of the United States where 'there was rampant anti-Semitism'.[19] This approach was dutifully repeated in other West European Communist newspapers including *Öesterreichische Volkstimme* (Austria), *Drapeau Rouge* (Belgium), *Vorwärts* (Switzerland) and *L'Unita* (Italy). Eleven out of the fourteen defendants were Jews who long ago had left their Jewishness behind in the cause of international revolution. They were therefore strongly opposed to Zionism. Yet they were labelled as clandestine Zionists, tied to Tel Aviv and the Israeli Embassy in Prague. *Rude Pravo*, the organ of the Czechoslovak Communist party proclaimed:

> Before the court in Pancraz prison sat eleven Jewish cosmopolitans, people without a shred of honour, without character, without country, people who desire one thing only – career, business and money.[20]

The actual indictment defined the defendants as 'Trotskyite, Titoite, Zionist and bourgeois nationalist traitors (who) created an anti-state conspiratorial centre'.[21] A long-time conspiratorial Zionist network was conjured into existence involving such Jewish public figures as the French politician, Georges Mandel, the US Supreme Court Judge, Felix Frankfurter and the Yugoslav revolutionary, Mosha Pijade. Several of the defendants were deemed to have been masquerading as Communists but in fact had actually been Zionists since their youth. Now in positions of authority, they allowed wealthy capitalists to remove their riches to Israel. Rudolph Margolius was said to have always been a Zionist and concealed this when he joined the Communist Party. Bedrich Reicin, was depicted as a one time member of a Zionist youth organization, but in fact was a Gestapo agent who betrayed Julius Fucik a hero of the Czech resistance. Reicin provided a list of others whom he had betrayed to the Nazis.

Following the example of the Soviet Yevsektsiya in the 1920s, the Jewish defendants had made great efforts to distance themselves both from their Jewish origins and from Jews per se in the present. Their abiding desire was to escape any vestige of Jewishness that resided or that they could be defined by.

> Throughout history, there have been Jews who hated themselves for what they were made to suffer, for being the perennial focus of evil and violence wherever they were. Now we wondered, how much more difficult would it have been for Hitler, had there

been no Jews? How many Germans had joined the Nazi party simply because it gave them the opportunity to snatch a share of Jewish property, to vent their frustrations? Maybe the Jews, by their very existence, had helped the Nazis to power more than anything else.[22]

Their general approach to Israel and Zionism varied from a studied indifference to controlled hostility. One defendant, Bedrich 'Fritz' Geminder was the son of a Jewish property dealer who had been the warden of the synagogue in Moravska Ostarva. He joined the Communist Party and suddenly went to Moscow where he served as Dmitrov's secretary. For years, no one heard anything about him. He suddenly reappeared in Prague after 1945. Geminder had cut himself off from past friends and had no contact with Jews. Above all, Geminder was antagonistic towards Jews who wished to leave for Israel. Now irony of ironies, he was accused of Zionism.[23]

Never again?

Jewish communities in Western Europe, Israeli public opinion and Yugoslavia's Marshal Tito labelled the trial as anti-Semitic. Coming so soon after the revelations of the Shoah, initial disbelief was supplanted by cries of 'Never Again'. The Chief Rabbis of the Eastern bloc countries, under duress, proclaimed that anti-Semitism no longer existed in their countries. The Chief Rabbi of Czechoslovakia, Dr. Gustav Sichl, gave a front page interview to the *Daily Worker*[24] which also claimed that 'an attempt was being made to turn Jewish people in Britain against the Peoples' Democracies of Eastern Europe and to support Anglo-American plans for war against these countries'.[25]

Yet Rabbi Dr Bernard Farkas was quietly arrested in Czechoslovakia and imprisoned.

Jewish Communists were mobilized by local parties in Western Europe to publicly denounce the protests of Jewish communal organizations. There was a concerted attempt to separate anti-Semitism from anti-Zionism. Jacques Duclos of the PCF refuted the accusation that anti-Semitism had played a part. Instead he pointed to the indictment of the atom spies, Julius and Ethel Rosenberg as a true example of anti-Semitism.[26] The testimony of the chief defendant, Rudolf Slansky, the former secretary-general of the party, was approvingly quoted. He told the court how he used charges of anti-Semitism to deflect opposition to Zionism.

> I deliberately shielded Zionism by publicly speaking out against the people who pointed to the hostile activities of Zionists and by describing these people as

anti-Semites so that these people were in the end prosecuted and persecuted. I thus created an atmosphere in which people were afraid to oppose Zionism.[27]

Local Communists suggested that anti-Zionism could never be labelled as anti-Semitic – and certainly not by the Left.

It is an old trick to pretend to mistake opposition to Zionism which is a political movement, for anti-Semitism. But it is an unconvincing trick.[28]

The purges of the 1930s, it was argued, had a rational basis and were therefore justified. This was simply yet another attempt by the West to destabilize the Soviet bloc.

The Soviet Union before the war and in the other peoples' democracies since the war, the dirty game of the Western intelligence services has been uncovered and scotched.[29]

Despite appeals by Einstein and Bertrand Russell as well as mass rallies in France, 11 out of the 14 were arbitrarily chosen for the hangman's noose by the local party leadership at Stalin's prompting. Their ashes were scattered on the icy roads of Prague. Their last letters revealed that they maintained their loyalty to the party and reiterated their alienation from Jewishness and Zionism.[30]

In Czechoslovakia between 1948 and 1953, 3,357 people were tried for political and economic crimes. 166 received the death sentence and 138 were sentenced to life imprisonment. In total, those who escaped the hangman were sentenced to 18,568 years in prison.[31]

This campaign against Jews was also felt in the German Democratic Republic. In the post-war years, many Jewish Communists rediscovered their Jewishness and were both members of the party and the Jewish community. Their Jewishness was both recognized and celebrated publicly. But by the time of the Slansky trial, they had begun to cancel their membership. Leo Zuckermann, under-secretary to the first President of the GDR and Julius Meyer, the head of the Jewish community in East Berlin were forced to flee to escape imprisonment. Half the Jewish population of the GDR hastily left for the West.[32]

Four days before the hanging of Slansky, the Stasi arrested a non-Jewish Communist, Paul Merker, who had been a member of the party's central committee. Unlike Walter Ulbricht, he had not marginalized the Jewish question, but made it central to his political advocacy. Indeed he was an old party member and had joined the KPD in 1920. He argued that Jews were as much a nation as any of the other nations, occupied by the Nazis, and thereby deserving of restitution. He supported the creation of the state of Israel and praised the Jewish struggle against British imperialism. A friend of one of the Slansky trial's victims, Otto Katz, he was sentenced to eight years in a secret trial in March 1955. His interrogators accused him of being a *Judenknecht* – 'a servant of the Jews'. They told him that he was 'king of the Jews' and accused him of 'selling off the GDR to the Jews'. Released in 1956 due to the advent of the revelations of Stalin by Khrushchev, he refused to go to the West and did not publicize his case. He maintained his stand on Israel and the Jewish question because this defined his understanding of Communism. Although he was readmitted to the party, he was never allowed to hold high office again.[33]

This rising crescendo of lethal threats against real Jews and mainly imaginary Zionists reached its apogee with the Doctors Plot in January 1953. Leading doctors, once again the majority of them Jewish, were accused of poisoning Soviet leaders, deliberately misdiagnosing their illnesses and sinisterly prescribing incorrect treatment. The Communist press in Western Europe once more carried headlines such as 'Plot to Murder Soviet Leaders'[34] and made the connection with Jewish organizations abroad. It demonstrated, they pointed out, the lengths to which Western intelligence agencies would go. There was, it was argued, even a precedent in the Bukharin trial in 1938 when Dr L. G. Levin had admitted that he poisoned Gorky on Yagoda's orders. Like his colleague in Prague, the Chief Rabbi of Moscow told the international media that there was no question of discrimination in such trials or prosecutions.[35] Among the Soviet public, such an idea of malevolent doctors was thought of as not being so far-fetched. Indeed at the turn of the century, there had been similar incidents such as the cholera outbreak in Makeyevka whereby doctors were accused of poisoning their patients.[36]

If Trotskyism in the 1930s had been the Stalinist smear, by the 1950s it had been transferred to Jewish nationalism along with connections to Israel and the West. Moreover the two converged through the prominence of Jews in the miniscule European Trotskyist movement. Indeed the French Trotskyist leader, Ernest Mandel commented in early 1947 that the anti-Trotskyism of the French CP was expressed not infrequently in anti-Semitic arguments.[37]

The Jews were considered to be 'a spying nation'. The Doctors Plot was the pinnacle of Stalin's broadside against the Jewish population of the USSR. The incarcerated Polina Zhemchuzhina, Molotov's Jewish wife, was now accused of being 'a leading bourgeois Jewish nationalist' and Israeli spy.[38] Any connection that could incriminate Kaganovitch, the last Jew in the politburo, was assiduously sought by Soviet investigators. The mass expulsion of the Jews from Moscow was probably a consideration. A leading academic was reported to have been asked by Stalin to provide a theoretical foundation for the deportations, based on Marxist-Leninist thought. A letter addressed to Pravda which condemned 'the killer doctors' was said to be circulating among prominent Soviet Jews. MGB officials were collecting the signatures – and few refused.[39] In December 1952, Stalin told the Presidium of the Central Committee of the party that 'every Jew is a potential spy for the United States'.[40] On 7 February 1953, an order for the arrest of the sister of Chaim Weizmann, the late President of Israel, was issued. She had last seen her brother some 40 years before. Another brother had been shot as an English spy in 1939.[41] Just over a week later, Ivan Maisky, the former Soviet Ambassador to London, was arrested. A senior diplomat, he had initiated Soviet contacts with the leadership of the Zionist movement in the early 1940s. He had several meetings with Weizmann and Ben-Gurion and visited Palestine in 1943. Ana Pauker was arrested in Rumania in preparation for a Slansky type trial in Bucharest. The USSR then broke off all diplomatic relations with Israel. The construction of camps was initiated in Central Asia in all likelihood to accommodate arrested and expelled Jews. The crescendo to this lethal drama was delayed by the refusal of one of the doctors, Sophia Karpai, kept in a refrigerated cell, to give in to her torturers and interrogators. She refused to acquiesce in the carefully constructed account of the plot. Fortunately Stalin collapsed and died at the beginning of March. A month later, Pravda announced that the arrest of the doctors had taken place without any legal validity and the accusations made against them had been false. The Communist press in Western Europe and in Israel reported the admission without comment – and without embarrassment.

The Doctors' Plot may have been due to infighting between Beria and Khrushchev within the Soviet leadership. Khrushchev may have quietly played on Stalin's escalating paranoia about Jews during the years of his physical and mental decline – indeed Beria was able to secure the Doctors' release so quickly after Stalin's demise.[42] Whether this was the case or not, the Doctors' Plot was the pinnacle of an orchestrated and bizarre campaign against Jews. This had a traumatic effect on Jewish Communists in Western Europe. It introduced uncertainty where there had been faith.

In May 1948, the PCF had organized a mass rally in support of the new state of Israel in the Vélodrome d'Hiver in Paris.[43] By January 1953, the PCF dutifully followed the Soviet line as if this political volte-face had never existed. French intellectuals such as Pierre Hervé were enlisted to support the Kremlin's charges against the Jewish doctors.[44] Anti-Zionist Jews such as Maxime Rodinson[45] and Francis Crémieux did the same. Annie Kriegel was asked to point out that it was quite possible that Jews like other human beings were capable of terrible crimes. In response Claude Bourdet wrote an article entitled 'Judéosabotage' in *L'Observateur*.[46] He queried whether doctors who were trained to save lives could have really attempted to poison the leaders of the Kremlin. Louis Le Galliant responded in an article entitled 'Les Medicins criminels ou la science pervertie' in a party journal whereby he compared the behaviour of the Soviet doctors to their Nazi colleagues in Dachau – those who had carried out terrible experiments on prisoners.[47] In *L'Humanité* ten eminent medical experts requested that the convicted defendants should be put in a place where they could no longer harm anyone.[48]

In Paris, street fighting broke out in three Jewish neighbourhoods between Communist Jews on one side and Bundist and Zionist Jews on the other. It was sparked off by carloads of Communist Jews arriving at the Belleville and Carreau du Temple areas. They proceeded to strip off Yiddish posters which announced a meeting to denounce anti-Semitism in the Eastern bloc. The PCF, itself, was said to be split with its leader, Jacques Duclos and Etienne Fajon, a party secretary condemning the plot and Francois Billoux, a member of the politburo and Auguste Lecoeur, another party secretary opposed. In Israel, the Marxist-Zionist Mapam was ideologically speechless as it watched events unfurl. Its adherents, mainly kibbutzniks, had supported the Soviet Union throughout its history, yet its emissary, Mordechai Oren had been arrested in Prague and forced to give testimony at the Slansky trial. The Mapam leader, Meir Ya'ari simultaneously thought that Oren was innocent, but believed in the rectitude of Soviet justice. The Mapam Council believed that it had been 'an accidental combination of tragic circumstances'.[49] This situation eventually created a schism on the Israeli Left and its fragmentation. A minority faction under Moshe Sneh which refused to dissociate himself from Soviet actions left Mapam and eventually joined the Israeli Communist Party. In his writings at the time, Sneh spoke about traitors to Communism from Trotsky to Slansky.[50] Sneh who had previously been a General Zionist as well as head of the Haganah believed that he could forge a strong relationship between the USSR and Israel, based on practical considerations and the national interests of both countries.[51]

Even within Ben-Gurion's Mapai, there was profound disbelief. At a meeting of the party's political committee, following the announcement of the Slansky verdict, Sharett did not mince his words:

> It is depressing that several of us still cling to an illusion . . . some cannot grow out of the feeling which they experienced in their youth towards the October Revolution. They have been struck by a blinding light, which dazzles them even today; they are unable to uproot that spiritual attitude and to understand that the light deceived, that it was false. What happened in 1917 is commonly recognised to have been a terrible calamity in Jewish and in general human history . . . the

Middle Ages are regarded as a dark era in history, its balance sheet was to all intents and purposes negative. This should be history's verdict regarding the October Revolution.[52]

A large majority of Mapai and Mapam members had been born in Russia and Eastern Europe. The reality of the Soviet Union in the early 1950s was for some politically and intellectually incomprehensible. In a private early discussion in the Mapai secretariat in August 1950, Ben-Gurion had been vehement in his denunciation of the Kremlin:

> With the exception of the Nazi regime, the world has never known so oppressive a regime of murderers and world arsonists as this one; this is a regime of a Georgian Ivan with new techniques and terminology.[53]

In the Knesset, in the aftermath of the Slansky trial, Ben-Gurion walked out when the Communists' Shmuel Mikunis discerned a rationale in all that happened.

For many European Jews who had given long years of service to the party and to the revolutionary cause, these events marked a watershed. Their loyalty had led to the Doctors' Plot. Many left their local party. Some left politics altogether. Others such as Professor Hyman Levy left the CPGB a few years later when he discovered the situation of Soviet Jewry. In France, Haim Slovès was similarly affected. The idea that anti-Semitism was a phenomenon only to be contemplated outside Communism no longer held any intellectual or moral worth. Too many illusions had been shattered.

Notes and Works Cited

1 Ebon, op. cit.

2 Nikita Khrushchev, *Khrushchev Remembers* (London 1971), p. 230.

3 Mordechai Namir, *Shlichut B'Moskva* (Tel Aviv 1971), pp. 333–54.

4 *Ha'aretz*, 9 May 2006.

5 Gennadi Kostyrchenko, *Out of the Red Shadows: Anti-Semitism in Stalin's Russia* (New York 1995), pp. 221–47.

6 Viktor Komarov, letter to Stalin February 1953 in ed. Joshua Rubenstein and Vladmir P. Naumov, *Stalin's Secret Pogrom: The Post-War Inquisition of the Jewish Anti-Fascist Committee* (London 2001), p. xii.

7 Ibid., p. 284.

8 Yakov Rapoport, *The Doctors' Plot* (London 1991), p. 250.

9 Meir Cotic, *The Prague Trial* (London 1987), p. 36.

10 Artur London, *On Trial* (London 1968), p. 50.

11 Paul Lendvai, *Anti-Semitism in Eastern Europe* (London 1971), p. 247.

12 Kevin McDermott, 'A "Polyphony of Voices"? Czech Popular Opinion and the Slansky Affair', *Slavic Review*, vol. 67, no. 4 (Winter 2008).

13 London, op. cit., p. 98.

14 Eugene Loebl, *Sentenced and Tried: The Stalinist Purges in Czechoslovakia* (London 1969), p. 110.

15 *Daily Worker*, 21 November 1952.

16 *Daily Worker*, 22 November 1952.

17 *Daily Worker*, 25 November 1952.

18 Ibid.

19 *L'Humanité*, 25 November 1952.

20 *Rude Pravo*, 30 November 1952.

21 *Jewish Chronicle*, 28 November 1952.

22 Kovaly, op. cit., p. 78.

23 *Jewish Vanguard*, 5 December 1952.

24 *Daily Worker*, 1 December 1952.

25 *Daily Worker*, 3 December 1952.

26 Ronald Radosh, *Commies: A Journey through the Old Left, the New Left and the Leftover Left* (San Francisco 2001), p. 46.

27 *Jewish Chronicle*, 28 November 1952.

28 *Daily Worker*, 28 November 1952.

29 *Daily Worker*, 29 November 1952.

30 Cotic, op. cit., p. 140.

31 Victor A. Velen, 'Czech Stalinists Die Hard', *Foreign Affairs*, vol. 42, no. 2 (January 1964).

32 Frank Stern, 'The Return to the Disowned Home: German Jews and the Other Germany', *New German Critique*, no. 67 (Winter 1996).

33 Jeffrey Herf, 'East German Communists and the Jewish Question: The Case of Paul Merker', *Journal of Contemporary History*, vol. 29, no. 4 (October 1994).

34 *Daily Worker*, 14 January 1953.

35 *Daily Worker*, 16 January 1953.

36 Khrushchev, op. cit., p. 254.

37 Ernest Mandel, *Projet de theses sur la question juive après la seconde guerre impérialiste*, 1 January 1947 published as Ernest Germain, 'Draft Theses on the Jewish Question Today', *Fourth International*, vol. 9, no. 1 January–February 1948.

38 Jonathan Brent and Vladimir P. Naumov, *Stalin's Last Crime: The Doctors' Plot* (London 2003), p. 178.

39 Rapoport, op. cit., pp. 80–1.

40 Ibid., p. 184.

41 Kostyrchenko, op. cit., pp. 298–9.

42 Amy Knight, *Beria: Stalin's First Lieutenant* (Princeton 1993), pp. 169–75.

43 *L'Humanité*, 19 May 1948.

44 *Ce Soir*, 27 January 1953.

45 Maxime Rodinson, 'Sionisme et socialisme', *La Nouvelle Critique* no. 43 February 1953. Rodinson later claimed that he foolishly agreed to add some 'intolerable' incriminating sentences by the periodical's editor-in-chief which he later regretted. See 'Maxime Rodinson on Zionism and the Palestine Problem Today', *Journal of Palestine Studies*, vol. 4, no. 3 (Spring 1975).

46 Caute, *Communism and the French Intellectuals*, op. cit., p. 202.

47 *L'Observateur*, 15 January 1953.

48 Louis Le Galliant, *La Nouvelle Critique*, no. 44, March 1953.

49 *L'Humanité*, 27 January 1953.

50 *Al Hamishmar*, 26 December 1952.

51 Moshe Sneh, 8 December 1952; 12 February 1953 in *Ketavim*, vol. 3, 1948–1954 (Tel Aviv 1999), pp. 244–7.

52 Peretz Merhav, *The Israeli Left* (New York 1980), p. 132.

53 Moshe Sharett, Speech to Mapai Political Committee, 23 November 1952 in Uri Bialer, *Between East and West: Israel's Foreign Policy Orientation 1948–1956* (Cambridge 1990), p. 51.

10

The resurrection of the outcast

Trotskyists against fascism

Trotskyism began with the development of the Left Opposition in the Soviet Union in 1923. This was subsequently reflected in different European countries. In France, Boris Souvarine, Alfred Rosmer and Pierre Monatte all began to dissent from the official PCF line. By late 1924, taking their cue from Moscow, local Communists in several countries began to criticize Trotsky's article *The Lessons of October* wherein he complained that the historical rendition of the revolution was partial and skewered.[1] By January 1926, nearly 300 French Communists complained to the Comintern about the authoritarian leadership of the PCF. Contre le Courant was an early group which supported the Left Opposition. In contrast, in Great Britain, there was little questioning and little understanding. Dutt's influence and that of his journal *Labour Monthly* became dominant at this time. Dutt promulgated any change of political line through the ranks – and no deviation would be tolerated.

Trotsky's expulsion from the USSR in 1929 and his elimination from the Soviet experiment caused grave disquiet among Marxist intellectuals and Soviet sympathizers in Europe. Moreover, there was deep unease at the ditching of allies on the Left through the adoption of the 'class against class' policy of the Comintern in 1928. To the more independently minded and politically perceptive members of the Communist Party, there was anger against the mindless 'social-fascist' label and blind acceptance of Comintern conformity. Moreover, Stalin's campaign against Right deviationism and Left sectarianism was profoundly disillusioning. It split the Left and strengthened anti-Communist tendencies. In Great Britain, many had read Trotsky's works in English before his expulsion from the CPSU and there was considerable resentment at the Labour government's refusal to grant him political asylum. Trotsky moreover had advocated a united front against fascism.

The first meeting of the International Left Opposition took place in Paris in April 1930. It established an international secretariat and started to publish an 'International Bulletin'. There were representatives from many European countries present including a French Jewish group.

Trotsky's exile in Turkey coincided with the rise of the Nazi party in Germany. The election results in September 1930 saw an increase in the Nazi vote from 2.6% to 18.3%. Nearly 6.5 million people voted for Hitler. The KPD vote also increased by 4.5 million. Trotsky was therefore preoccupied with this polarizing situation in Germany even before Hitler's rise to power.

Fascism had hitherto been marginalized by official Communism. Only Clara Zetkin in the 1920s pointedly differentiated fascism from other counter-revolutionary regimes.[2] In 1931, Trotsky significantly viewed Hitler in the same mould as the Russian Whites whom – with Western backing – had tried to eradicate Bolshevism. Hitler, Trotsky surmised, was merely part of the Western plan to bring about the downfall of the Soviet Union.

> In this enterprise, a Hitler government would be only the executive organ of world capitalism as a whole. Clemenceau, Millerand, Lloyd George, Wilson could not directly carry on a war against the Soviet government; but they were able, in the course of three years, to support the armies of Kolchak, Wrangel, and Denikin. [7] In case he is victorious, Hitler will become the super-Wrangel of the world bourgeoisie.[3]

Trotsky soon came to believe that the ultimate purpose of Nazism was to eliminate all workers' organizations. Moreover Stalin's instruction to prevent any cooperation between Communists and social democrats clearly aided the Nazis in eliminating their opponents. Trotsky was perplexed at the relative ease with which the KPD was pushed aside without a hint of revolutionary struggle. The docility of the German proletariat was similarly a matter of great puzzlement.

In Britain Dutt continued to rail against social democrats and pacifists whom he termed 'the twin ally of the bloodiest imperialism'. Yet days later the CPGB, on orders from Moscow, changed its line once more and sponsored a public appeal by the French pacifist, Henri Barbusse.[4]

As Stalin imposed his will in the 1930s, the elimination of the Bolshevik old guard was coloured by the use of anti-Semitic innuendo. This was initiated as a weapon to be used against highly assimilated Jews within the Bolshevik leadership who had previously given little thought to their Jewishness. The

real names of Zinoviev (Radomislyski) and Kamenev (Rosenfeld) suddenly sur-
faced. Even Trotsky's son became Sedov-Bronstein. Much to the incredulity
of orthodox Communists, Trotsky remarked that during the power struggle
with Stalin in the 1920s, he had received hundreds of letters from his supporters in the Left Opposition which noted the use of anti-Semitism in the
'systematic agitation' against them.[5] Indeed, he wrote to Bukharin about this
in March 1926.[6] By the 1930s, rising anti-Semitism in Europe caused Trotsky
to revise his attitude that assimilation was the answer to the Jewish problem.
He maintained that such difficulties could be overcome by dispensing with the
capitalist system.

The show trials of the Bolshevik old guard and the fabrications against
Trotsky were accompanied by shoulder-to-shoulder derision from local
European Communist parties which was directed at anyone who asked questions. The *Daily Worker* carried a headline, entitled 'Shoot the Reptiles!' The
Left Book Club maintained a diplomatic silence and critics of Stalin were rarely
published. Sympathetic British lawyers such as Dudley Collard and D. N. Pritt
were allowed to attend the trials of Zinoviev, Kamenev and Radek and proceeded to publish their legal apologia in the Left Book Club[7] and in letters
to the *Manchester Guardian*.[8] Lion Feuchtwanger was also allowed to meet
Stalin. He wrote:

> Finally, (Stalin) spoke bitterly and with feeling of the writer Radek, the most popular
> of the men involved in the second Trotskyist trial. He described his friendly relations
> with the man. 'You Jews', he said, 'have created one eternally true legend – that
> of Judas,' and it was strange to hear a man, otherwise so sober and logical, utter
> these simple, emotional words. He mentioned a long letter which Radek had
> written to him and in which he had protested his innocence on many unconvincing
> grounds. The next day, under pressure of witnesses and circumstantial evidence,
> he had confessed.[9]

Radek collaborated with the trial prosecutor, Andrei Vishinsky to construct the
trial's 'scenario' and the roles of the defendants in the drama. Stalin even edited
Vishinsky's speech for the prosecution. In this way Radek saved his life.[10]

Romain Rolland, Andre Malraux, Jean Genet and even André Gide
accepted Stalin's word and wanted to believe that his regime matched the
one of their dreams. Even Shakespeare was dragooned to condemn Trotsky
by Feuchtwanger with a selected quotation from *Coriolanus*.[11]

There was extensive coverage of the second trial in the *Manchester Guardian*
throughout January 1937 in which leading members of the CPGB defended
the verdict of the trials. Revolutionaries in exile such as the Commissar of
Justice in Lenin's first government, Isaac Steinberg, pointed to the absurdity

of the claim that the Trotskyists wished to hasten a conflict between Nazi Germany and the USSR such that a Soviet defeat would allow them to seize power.[12] The historian, A. J. P. Taylor, asked whether Lenin therefore had 'an infallible gift for choosing traitors and counter-revolutionaries'.[13]

These trials were peppered with inferences that the Jews among them had sold their services to the Gestapo. In his article, *Thermidor and Anti-Semitism*, written in February 1937, Trotsky documented the regime's utilization of anti-Semitism and raised the plight of Jews in Soviet Russia.

Trotsky had challenged an article of faith in the USSR that the Jewish problem had been solved in the USSR. This accusation irked many a Jewish Communist who wished to go along with the official line and that such a thing was unthinkable in Stalin's Russia. Trotsky's claim was considered outrageous and was simply attributed to point scoring in the struggle with Stalin.

On the coming war

Trotsky's views on how to combat Nazism were deeply coloured by the Bolshevik experience of World War I. The coming conflict was seen as a continuation of the conflict between different imperialisms. As far back as 1904, when the Russo-Japanese war commenced, Lenin instantly called for the victory of Japan. He later argued in 1915 that:

> A revolution in wartime means civil war: the conversion of a war between governments into a civil war is, on the one, hand, facilitated by military reverses ('defeats') of governments: on the other hand, one cannot actually strive for such a conversion without thereby facilitating defeat.[14]

As Liebknecht had argued 'civil war, not civil peace – that is our slogan!' Trotsky followed Lenin in espousing revolutionary defeatism. He believed that the same philosophy held in the confrontation with Hitler and adopted the theory of rival imperialisms as early as 1934 while supporting the defence of the Soviet Union.[15] Hitler's expansionist policies were attributed by Trotsky to 'an accelerated form of decadent imperialism'.

In March 1939, he responded to a letter 'A Group of Palestinian Bolshevik-Leninists' of November 1938, which argued that defeatism should be striven for only in fascist countries and not in the democratic countries. Trotsky did not make an exception and characterized this position as 'a dangerous step towards social-patriotism'.

Defeatism is the class policy of the proletariat, which even during a war sees the main enemy at home, within its particular imperialist country. Patriotism, on the other hand, is a policy that locates the main enemy outside one's own country. The idea of defeatism signifies in reality the following: conducting an irreconcilable revolutionary struggle against one's own bourgeoisie as the enemy, without being deterred by the fact that this struggle may result in the defeat of one's own government; given a revolutionary movement the defeat of one's own government is a lesser evil. Lenin did not say, nor did he wish to say, anything else. There cannot even be talk of any other kind of 'aid' to defeat. Should revolutionary defeatism be renounced in relation to non-Fascist countries? Herein is the crux of the question; upon this issue, revolutionary internationalism stands or falls.[16]

Clearly the legacy of opposition to the war between the imperial powers in 1914 loomed large. Indeed Ha'Hugim Ha'Marksistim (Marxist Circles) of Left Poale Zion in Palestine had published a collection of writings in 1934 to mark the twentieth anniversary of Karl Liebknecht's opposition in Germany to World War I.[17]

Trotsky defined the USSR as a degenerated workers' state, but the rule of the Soviets would ultimately be restored through a revolutionary uprising of the workers. The regenerated Soviets would once more rededicate itself to world revolution. The Soviet bureaucracy would be seen eventually as only an episodic relapse.

The advance of fascism and the bureaucratization of the Soviet state were both ascribed to the ideological stagnation of the proletariat.

Following the outbreak of war, Trotsky raised the prospect of practice not following theory. Trotsky speculated as to what would happen if the proletariat did not live up to its revolutionary expectations, if it did not seize the historic opportunity.

In the event that the proletariat of advanced capitalist countries, having conquered power, should prove incapable of holding it and surrender it, as in the USSR, to a privileged bureaucracy. Then we would be compelled to acknowledge that the reason for the bureaucratic relapse is rooted not in the backwardness of the country and not in the imperialist environment but in the congenital incapacity of the proletariat to become a ruling class. Then it would be necessary in retrospect to establish that in its fundamental traits the present USSR was the precursor of a new exploiting régime on an international scale.[18]

He also postulated that Hitler might eventually turn his guns on Stalin. What should the Soviet workers do? What should his supporters do?

Under these conditions, partisans of the Fourth International, without changing in any way their attitude toward the Kremlin oligarchy, will advance to the forefront as the most urgent task of the hour, the military resistance against Hitler. The workers will say, 'We cannot cede to Hitler the overthrowing of Stalin; that is our own task'. During the military struggle against Hitler, the revolutionary workers will strive to enter into the closest possible comradely relations with the rank and file fighters of the Red Army. While arms in hand they deal blows to Hitler, the Bolshevik-Leninists will at the same time conduct revolutionary propaganda against Stalin preparing his overthrow at the next and perhaps very near stage.

All this remained in the realm of theory. All this was discussed while Hitler contemplated a solution to the Jewish problem in Europe.

Yet Trotsky understood that in any war with Nazi Germany, the Jews would suffer terribly. In May 1940, before Hitler's invasion of the USSR, he predicted the annihilation of the Jews.[19] Only international revolution, he argued, would save them. Yet he also understood Stalin's rationale for keeping the USSR out of any conflict for as long as possible. The Soviet Union, in his eyes, was still a workers' state and it had to survive at all costs. It was therefore irrelevant whether Stalin allied the USSR with Nazi Germany or with Great Britain as long as the state survived. It was not a matter of morality, but one of expediency. Indeed, he was pleased with Stalin's conquest of Eastern Poland since its territory had now passed from private into public hands.

Trotskyists in places such as South Africa where the effects of colonialism were most visible and offensive, similarly saw little point in participating in an 'imperialists' war' – and thereby an unjust war. One South African activist argued in his trial in September 1940 that any support for the war was conditional.

> This war could only be transformed into a just war for the preservation of democracy and the defeat of fascism when full and unfettered democratic rights are extended to the non-European people of this country and when the oppressed peoples of India and the colonial and semi-colonial countries are granted their freedom and independence. If these conditions and rights are given them, only then, could we believe that this is a war for the preservation of democracy and the institution of a new social order; and there would be no sacrifice too great and no risk too hazardous for us, the non-Europeans, to offer for the defence of this new social order.[20]

Despite his powerful attacks against fascism in the 1930s and his dire prediction for European Jewry, Trotsky and many of his followers, Jewish and non-Jewish, ultimately chose not to identify with the fate of a doomed people. At the end of the day, there was little to choose between the views of the Stalinist ideologue Rajani Palme Dutt and the intellectual revolutionary Leon Trotsky.

Capitalist civilization was sliding towards the precipice. Differences between decaying democracy and barbarian fascism disappeared in the face of the collapse of the entire capitalist system.

> As victors, Britain and France would be no less fearful for the fate of mankind than Hitler and Mussolini. Bourgeois democracy is not to be saved. Lending aid to its own bourgeoisie against the foreign fascism, the workers would hasten the victory of fascism in their own country. The task set by history is not to support one part of the imperialist system against another but to cast the entire system over the precipice.[21]

Trotsky thus led the way in persuading Trotskyist groups in Europe as well to similarly regard the war as a conflict of rival imperialisms. While detesting fascism and its fellow travellers as well as condemning anti-Semitism, the task of revolutionaries was to make the revolution. They should only take sides if the conflict created suitable conditions for revolution.

In May 1940, the adherents of the Fourth International held an emergency conference. Trotsky wrote the manifesto which was discussed. He opened with a statement which made no distinction between the protagonists.

> The Fourth International turns not to the governments who have dragooned the peoples into the slaughter nor to the bourgeois politicians who bear the responsibility for these governments, nor to the labour bureaucracy which supports the warring bourgeoisie. The Fourth International turns to the working men and women, the soldiers and sailors, the ruined peasants and the enslaved colonial peoples. The Fourth International has no ties whatsoever with the oppressors, the exploiters, the imperialists. It is the world party of the toilers, the oppressed and the exploited.

Trotsky argued that this was no war for democracy against fascism. He blamed British policy for helping Hitler attain power.

> The butchers of the second imperialist war will not succeed in transforming Hitler into a scapegoat for their own sins.

The tragedy of the Jews was attributed to the terminal decline of the capitalist system rather than the rise of Nazism.

Today's decaying capitalist society is striving to squeeze the Jewish people from all its pores; seventeen million individuals out of the two billion populating the globe, that is less than one per cent can no longer find a place on our planet.

Some surmised that this was a reflection on his own situation. Barred from many European countries and expelled from others, Trotsky, ironically had been transformed into the wandering Jew. When France fell a few weeks later, the Nazis removed his works from libraries and bookshops.[22] Soviet-approved writings remained.

Jewish Trotskyists

A few days after Trotsky was informed that he was to be expelled from the USSR, the periodical of the Yevsektsiya, the Yiddish *Emes,* bemoaned the fact that his support among Jewish workers in Russia was far greater than among non-Jewish workers. *Emes* reported that the Jews were highly susceptible to Trotsky's ideas as 'recent incidents in Moscow, Odessa, Kiev and other cities' indicated. The Yevsektsiya concluded that it would fight 'the Left front within the Jewish masses'.[23]

Even outside the borders of the Soviet Union, Trotsky and Trotskyism attracted a disproportionate number of Jews. Trotskyism was originally viewed as a purified and independent Marxism, free of the stigma of Stalinism and the responsibility of the state interests of the Soviet Union. It imitated the idealism of the early 1920s when so many Russian Jews embraced the new Soviet dawn, following the civil war. It reintroduced creative Marxist thought. For some Jews, Trotskyism had a profound appeal. It appeared to be on a higher intellectual and moral level, promising universal redemption – something Jewish nationalism and Zionism could not offer. Indeed the latter seemed narrow and parochial, still interned in the ghetto, while Trotsky's promise of the pot of socialist gold at the end of the rainbow disposed of any restraints and was free of any boundaries. By the 1930s, Trotsky had reinvented himself as a writer, analyst and commentator. Trotskyism was anchored within the realm of theory than in actual practice. While there were aspirations, real power resided with Stalin.

This intellectual exploration into the minutiae of Marxist ideas and eventual revolutionary success appealed to traditional Jewish values of argument and debate which permeated Talmudic learning. Regardless of their religiosity and their acculturation, many young Jews followed this path, this search for the truth. Many Trotskyist leaders immersed themselves in studying Marxist texts and working full-time for the movement rather than taking on a conventional job. They often earned a pittance and lived in considerable poverty. For some, their wives took on the responsibility of being the family's bread winner – and were often happy to do so.[24] Others with well heeled and sometimes sympathetic relatives secured funding from their families. One charismatic figure of the British Trotskyist movement was reported by police surveillance to be living in a caravan in East London in 1949 and depended on funding from his sister in South Africa.[25] All this remarkably imitated the lifestyle of many a rebbe from the ultra-orthodox Jewish community.

Regardless of whether they came from an assimilated background or a traditional one, several Jews emerged as leaders of the post-war Trotskyist movement in Europe. Unlike Lenin who enforced Communist discipline and coerced opposing groups to set aside their differences, Trotsky delighted in the written word and the idealization of theory. Perhaps opposition to Stalin's centralization and brutal control had precipitated an inevitable openness. The desire to be free of the dead hand of Stalinism, however, led to splits and coalescences, spawning a plethora of Trotskyist groups. Sometimes such differences were based on ideological issues such as what sort of state was the Soviet Union? A degenerated workers' state which could be restored? Or a state capitalist one? Other times, it was a matter of strategy and tactics. Should 'entryism' into social democratic parties be encouraged and practised? On more than one occasion, matters of little consequence to the outsider loomed large to the insider – and led to fragmentation.

Trotsky's initial supporters on the International Secretariat of the embryonic Trotskyist movement included numerous Jews such as the French Marxist, Pierre Frank and the representative of the Greek section, Myrtos who began life as Oskar Rosenzweig.[26] Another member of the secretariat, M. Mill or Paul Obin in Paris was formerly Pavel Okun from the Ukraine who had spent some time in Palestine. In Paris, he had helped found the periodical, La Vérité in 1929 and organized a group of Jewish supporters of Trotsky.[27] Jan Frankel from Czechoslovakia was responsible for organizing Trotsky's affairs in Turkish exile. Such cosmopolitanism blended in with international socialism.

Names were often changed to adapt to the new environment. The South African Jew, Isaac Blank, became Ted Grant while the Palestinian Jew Ygael Gluckstein from Zikhron Ya'akov morphed into Tony Cliff. Both went on to be the ideological mentors of significant Marxist groups in Britain in the second half of the twentieth century. The South African Frank Glass appeared as Li Fu-jen in China while Max Basch emerged as Sid Frost in the United Kingdom.[28]

Several Jewish Trotskyists originated in the Marxist-Zionist Hashomer Hatzair movement which they had found limiting in terms of the immediate problems faced by European Jews in the 1930s. The poverty and hopelessness of ordinary working people in the Europe of the 1930s affected many young Jews. The rise of fascism, home-grown and foreign, was a dominant overshadowing factor. The persecutions and killings in Stalin's Russia, the sheer lack of logic by orthodox Communists in accepting the show trials and the incredulous accusations flung at Trotsky were others.

The difficulty of being a Jew in a non-Jewish society was often a cause of identity conflict. Where should one's energies best be generated? In the universalist sphere or in the particularist? Jews straddled both in the Europe of the 1930s. In these profoundly complex times which demonstrated the basest instincts in the human character, the polarization became too great for symbiosis and a choice had to be made.

South Africa and Belgium

In South Africa, the rise of Afrikaaner nationalism and the sanctification of early apartheid in the 1930s similarly pushed many Jews away from the Jewish question. After 1928, during the third period, Stalin pursued a policy in South Africa which was similar to the one in Palestine. Local Communists were ordered to focus on an 'independent native republic'. The League of African Rights, a united front grouping, was instructed by Moscow to disband in December 1929. All this persuaded many Jewish Communists to leave the CPSA and move towards Trotskyism and independent Marxism.

There was, however, an early heritage of social activism among South African Jews. Gandhi was befriended by community leaders such as Morris Alexander and his wife, Ruth Schechter.[29] Moreover the Jewish community in South Africa was continually reinforced by new arrivals from Lithuania. Thus although there were many who aspired to the comfortable lifestyle of the privileged white minority – albeit with liberal convictions – there were others who inherited the radicalism of East European Jewry. Several belonged to the local Communist Party or the Linker Kring (Leftist Circle) or the Gezerd which promoted a Jewish homeland in Birobidzhan on the Soviet border with China. The Lenin Club was established in 1933 by a few Yiddish-speaking Jews who were profoundly disillusioned with Stalinism.[30] Above all, the first Trotskyists of South Africa were energized by the land question.[31]

The Marxist-Zionist group, Hashomer Hatzair, was established in South Africa in 1935 from new arrived adherents of the movement from Lithuania.

Many were involved in clashes with the local fascists, the Greyshirts and many Afrikaaner nationalists were pro-German. Such demonstrations and groups such as the Anti-Fascist League brought together Zionists and other Jewish socialists. The foremost ideologist of Hashomer Hatzair was Nachum Sneh (Skikne) who was appalled by the Moscow show trials and Stalin's campaign against Trotskyism. He also reacted to the official Stalinist line of the movement. Within Hashomer Hatzair, he moved to a Trotskyist position and subsequently influenced many of the younger members. His library of socialist literature was on loan to many members of Hashomer.

Classic works such as C. L. R. James' *World Revolution*, Fenner Brockway's *Workers Front* and Ignazio Silone's *Fontamara* were among those read.[32] Whereas Sneh argued that the struggle for socialism had to be conducted in Palestine, the logic of Trotskyism was that according to the doctrine of permanent revolution and internationalist principles, it could in fact be conducted anywhere. Neither Stalinism nor Trotskyism favoured Zionism, therefore the choice for many was either remaining in South Africa and fighting incipient apartheid or departing for Palestine and building a socialist state. This was a very difficult choice for many. Some crossed the line, others did not.[33]

In addition to the deepening opposition to the entrenchment of apartheid, there were heated discussions about the Nazi-Soviet pact and the nature of socialism in the USSR. Koestler's *Darkness at Noon* had just been published in South Africa. There was further discussion about the policy of Hebrew labour which, it was argued, separated the Jewish worker from the Arab worker and impaired the class struggle in Palestine.

On Sneh's departure for Palestine and the absence of his restraining authority, the succeeding leadership of Hashomer Hatzair – which was more anglicized, did not speak Yiddish and tended to see things more easily in polarized terms – left the movement in 1943 and formerly embraced Trotskyism. Baruch Hirson who later spent almost a decade in prison in South Africa for his political activities and Tony Cliff's future wife, Chani Rosenberg attended a meeting to mark the first anniversary of Trotsky's assassination in 1941. In early 1943, a Trotskyist group was formed in Johannesburg which met at a trade union office connected with the African Commercial and Distributive Workers Union. A disproportionate number of Jews were involved. These included Hosea Jaffe, an active member of the Communist League of South Africa, Moshe Noah Averbach who had lived in Palestine, emigrated to South Africa where he sought work teaching Hebrew and Fanny Klenerman, the owner of Vanguard Booksellers and a veteran Leftist. Both Hirson and Rosenberg whose lives were quite isolated from the problems of South Africa met the Coloured activist, Zeid Gamiet, the Indian student Dinshaw Tavaria and John Motau who opposed the war in Europe. Jaffe who strongly identified with the Coloured community was highly influential and spoke about other anti-war groups, strikes in many countries and the need for the workers to bring the world war to an end and subsequently establish socialism. Averbach ran a grocery store in the midst of the Coloured Community's area, Cape Town's District Six. The departure of the group from Hashomer also coincided with an upsurge of political activity in South Africa. In December 1943, the Non-European Unity Movement, inspired by mainly Coloured teachers, was founded in December 1943.

The reasons for the departure of the Trotskyist Zionists from Hashomer Hatzair were several. For some, there were personal reasons, their partners went to Palestine while they remained in South Africa where they felt more comfortable. Some felt that their growing awareness about the visible injustices in South Africa compelled them to remain.

Hirson concluded that Zionism was 'colonialist', rejected Borochovism and accepted Lenin's view on national liberation movements. Unlike the Bund at the turn of the century, some understood that Zionism was not a mass movement among Jews. The kibbutz did not provide the right conditions for fighting the class struggle and no longer could form the basis for the Palestinian economy.

> The Jewish struggle for national liberation is therefore not furthering the struggle for socialism and as Zionism cannot be realised within a capitalist society, the solution of the Jewish problem must wait till the attainment of socialism . . . the kibbutz movement is degenerating because there can be no socialist utopias within a capitalist world.[34]

Chani Rosenberg went to Palestine and once there, made contact with the Trotskyists, met Ygael Gluckstein, later Tony Cliff, whose views on Zionism and a solution to the conflict seemed to harden after this encounter. Both Gluckstein and Rosenberg soon left Palestine for Britain.

In a parallel emigration to that of Lithuanian Jews to South Africa, many Polish Jews after World War I settled in Germany, Belgium and France. The economic crisis in Poland in the early 1920s prompted the fourth aliyah to Palestine of the Jewish middle class. Palestine itself was undergoing severe economic difficulties. Those Polish Jews who stayed were among the founders of the Likud in 1973. Those who left Palestine after 1926 often headed for Belgium. Abraham Wajnsztok arrived in Belgium as a child from Palestine and became a member of Hashomer Hatzair.

Ezra Mandel was a few years younger than Wajnsztok. His father, Henri Mandel spoke Yiddish and Hebrew, but taught his son neither. Ezra did not receive any religious instruction.[35] The older Mandel was, however, very interested in Jewish history and spoke very positively about the leaders of the

Labour Zionist movement such as Ben-Gurion. In the 1920s, he worked for the League for Pioneering Palestine which financially assisted Jews in the Land of Israel.[36] He also welcomed the Poale Zion leader, Yitzhak Ben-Zvi into his home. Henri Mandel worked in the diamond trade of Antwerp which was very much the domain of Orthodox Jewry. It was through his profession and his interest in Jewish affairs that he connected his family to the Jewish community. In his youth, Mandel had been interested in the October Revolution and the writings of Rosa Luxemburg. He had also known Karl Radek, Lenin's man in post-war Germany. With the rise of Hitler, many political refugees from Nazi Germany, Jewish and non-Jewish passed through the Mandel home. The deteriorating situation in the late 1930s, the war in Spain and the transparent absurdity of the Moscow trials including that of Radek persuaded Henri Mandel to use his influence and his finance to help the cause of anti-fascism. He took over a publishing house with the objective of publishing Trotsky's works in German under the Hebrew translation of his own name, Shaked – 'almond' in Hebrew. Mandel strongly opposed the Molotov-Ribbentrop pact. The schoolboy Ezra was highly influenced by his father's actions and the collapsing political world around him.

Both the younger Mandel and Wajnsztok became radicalized because of what they saw happening around them. Brussels like Paris was a hub for many a Polish-Jewish socialist en route to fight fascism in Spain. Many served in the Botwin brigade, named after the Polish-Jewish Communist, Naftali Botwin, who was executed by the Poles in 1925.[37] Zionism therefore had become a far off irrelevancy to the here and now of Nazism and Stalinism. Many young Belgian Jews such as Ralph Miliband and Marcel Liebman were affected by this situation and attempted to final a theoretical framework which would explain the world to them. Although both Mandel and Wajnsztok distanced themselves from the Jewish community, they remained culturally coloured by Jewishness. Wajnsztok took control of the decimated miniscule Belgian Trotskyist movement, Parti Communiste Révolutionnaire, edited *La Voie de Lénine* and involved Mandel in its activities. Abraham Wajnsztok was eventually arrested, deported to the East and perished as Abram Leon in Auschwitz. Ezra Mandel was also arrested, but his father was able to secure his release for 100,000 francs.[38] Mandel's grandfather and uncle failed to escape to Switzerland. They all managed to live under false identities due to Henri's connections and wealth. Ezra was arrested again, survived and was liberated from Flössenberg concentration camp. He emerged as Ernest Mandel, a major Marxist theorist, academic and writer in the second half of the twentieth century.

Tony Cliff originated in the bosom of the Zionist aristocracy as Ygael Gluckstein in Palestine. His parents came to Palestine with the wave of immigration of the first socialist Zionists that also brought Ben-Gurion, Ben-Zvi and Tabenkin at the turn of the century. His uncle, Chaim Kalvarisky who was known for his efforts to secure reconciliation between Jews and Arabs,[39] arrived in Palestine years before even Herzl embraced Zionism. Cliff's piano teacher was Chaim Weizmann's sister and his father's partner in the construction business was Weizmann's brother. His father was a well-known builder. He studied at Jerusalem's gymnasium and then entered the Haifa Technion which specialized in technology. He dropped out and enrolled instead to study economics at Jerusalem's Hebrew University. He joined Mapai at 14 and flirted with Stalinism and the PCP at 15 when he regarded his former social democratic comrades as 'social fascists'. At 16, he left for Ha'Hugim Ha'Marksistim B'Eretz Yisrael (the Marxist Circles of the Land of Israel) of Left Poale Zion which was close to the ILP in Britain. In addition, many were affected by the show trials of the late 1930s and Hashomer Hatzair's relative silence.[40]

Ha'Hugim Ha'Marksistim published *Bamifneh* which contained articles by Borochov and Lenin as well as poetry from Maxim Gorky and Avigdor Hameiri.[41] Cliff also contributed to *Bamifneh*, extolling the virtues of Zionist immigration and its benefit to the Land of Israel.[42] By the late 1930s, Cliff had renounced Marxist-Zionism altogether for Trotskyism.[43] Like his counterparts in other countries, he had been influenced by the rise of Nazism and was impressed by Trotsky's early writings on the subject.

At the beginning of World War II, he was arrested by the British and imprisoned in Acre prison in 1940. He left Ha'Hugim Ha'Marksistim because he too viewed the war as one of rival imperialisms and vehemently opposed the campaign to mobilize the Yishuv in support of the British war effort. By October 1940, he was a leading light in the Jerusalem branch of Brit Spartakus which attempted to persuade Hebrew University students to oppose all attempts at mobilization and enlistment. In the pages of its journal, *Dapei Spartakus*, reports of student opposition to the war were quoted. In Britain, the actions of students at Cambridge who opposed Churchill were approvingly quoted as were the publications of the pro-Soviet Labour MP and admirer of Stalin, D. N. Pritt. Brit Spartakus condemned the arrest of Professor Paul Langevin at the Sorbonne by the Vichy government and the dismissal of Jewish academics at the universities of Delft and Utrecht in Holland.[44] Social Democrats were reviled for their participation in the war – an echo of their betrayal of the working class in World War I.[45] Brit Spartakus argued for 'an end to the imperialist war and for a peoples' peace'.

The group was also active in trying to win over members of the Marxist-Zionist Hashomer Hatzair to the cause of international revolution and thereby joined organizations such as the Socialist League and the League for

Arab-Jewish Cooperation.[46] Hashomer Hatzair was considered fertile territory by Brit Spartakus. One member wrote to a friend in Amsterdam several weeks before the German invasion of Holland:

> The workers of Palestine are fighting for their existence. This war is not ours. The fight is of the working masses. The fight of the Red Flag will bring victory. All of us are for the revolution. The whole East and Near East, in particular, eg Palestine and India, are prepared to fight against British imperialism.[47]

The group also strongly opposed the activities of the Irgun Zvai Leumi. In particular, it condemned the example of David Raziel, the head of the Irgun who like Cliff had been imprisoned at the beginning of the war. Raziel who had originally been the Jerusalem Commander of the Irgun agreed to collaborate with the British against the Nazis. This led to a split in the Irgun with Avraham Stern forming Lehi (the Stern Gang) which continued the military struggle against the British in Palestine and attempted to contact the German Legation in Beirut on the rationale of 'the enemy of my enemy is my friend'. When the Irgun's Raziel was killed on a mission for the British in Iraq, the members of Brit Spartakus did not mourn for him.

Cliff's precarious existence during the war years led to a sequence of detention and release by the police plus occasional searches of his home in Aza Street in the well-to-do suburb of Rehavia. In 1942, he left Jerusalem for Haifa where his parents lived.[48]

By 1946, after 8 years of political activity, the Trotskyists in Mandatory Palestine numbered 30 members – 23 Jews and 7 Arabs. In September 1946 as tens of thousands of Jews from the DP camps were trying to illegally enter Palestine, Cliff was going in the opposite direction to Britain. Although he was allowed to remain in Britain for a short time, the British soon refused him a residence permit and forced him to live in Dublin for several years. The Irish welcomed him, in the mistaken belief that the British had enforced his departure from Palestine because he was a Zionist.[49]

Jewish Trotskyists and the question of Palestine

The Trotskyists exhibited a profound distaste for any form of nationalism – no doubt in reaction to Stalin's policies within the USSR and the denigration of internationalism. Those who emerged from Hashomer Hatzair or Left Poale

Zion also reacted to the hero-worship of Stalin and adulation for the achievements of the Soviet Union of these Marxist-Zionist organizations. They placed great emphasis on revolutionary uprisings occurring in the colonies. This also led them to an entrenched position on Zionism and opposition to a state of the Jews in the Middle East.

Trotsky was the mentor and model for many Jews with a troubled conscience in troubled times. Trotsky had attempted throughout his life to rationalize human conduct and to insert reason into its deliberations. This governed the logic in not investigating his Jewishness. In 1903, he had even attended the sixth Zionist congress when the Uganda debate had taken place. The lesson that he drew from this was that Zionism was an unworkable dream and would soon fade away. It could not be accommodated by reason or theory. It was not as ideologically wholesome as world revolution. Indeed, his article, following the congress, was entitled *The Decay of Zionism and its Potential Successors*.[50]

Trotsky's interest in Palestine was reawakened in 1929 in the aftermath of the killings in Hebron and Safad. These had occurred at a time when Trotsky had lost power and was in exile in Turkey. From here, he closely followed the evolution of the Stalinist state. In an interview with the Yiddish periodical, *Unzer Kamf*, he suggested that Arab nationalism had to some extent been tainted by 'Islamic reaction and Jewish pogromism'.[51] He added that he still opposed Zionism because it separated the Jewish workers. Yet throughout the 1930s, Trotsky became acutely aware of the Zionist answer to the rise of anti-Semitism. There were times when it seemed impossible that Zionism would be successful such as after the publication of the MacDonald White Paper in 1939. Such episodes simply confirmed Trotsky's contention that Zionism was a non-starter.[52] At other times, such as his day long conversation with Beba Idelson, a socialist Zionist, in 1937, he seemed deeply interested.

> I noticed that my words penetrated deep into his heart, that he was glad to hear about a world from which he had dissociated himself. I sensed that he was listening not like a man who placed himself above all nationality, and that our great idea found an echo in his heart. At the end of our conversation, Trotsky asked me not to publish the fact of our meeting and its contents.
>
> 'Let the matter remain between us. The world will not understand. People will seek in this, too, grounds for accusing me of harbouring alien views and perhaps even sympathy for Zionism.'[53]

Although Idelson waited 20 years before publishing her account of the meeting with him – and long after his assassination – Trotsky had taken to using the term 'Jewish nation' and did not appear ideologically opposed to the Jews moving en masse once the victory of socialism had been achieved. While accepting the migration of workers, he really did not believe that the Jews would be able to reconstitute themselves in Palestine.[54]

Trotsky was increasingly concerned by the deepening bitterness of the Jewish-Arab conflict in Mandatory Palestine. There, Trotsky's small band of followers condemned the influx of funds and propaganda from fascist sources 'to strengthen this ideological reactionary influence and so gain control of the (Arab) nationalist movement' since it encouraged the spread of anti-Jewish ideas and anti-Semitic imagery. Gluckstein-Cliff significantly took a line which seemed close to Yishuvism.

> The Arab nationalists and their Stalinist supporters claim that the collision is between the Arab liberation movement and Zionism . . . It does not take into consideration that there really is a conflict between feudalism and capitalist development. Secondly that inside the nationalist movement there is an Arab bourgeoisie which is in competition with the closed Jewish economy, develops exclusivist Arab tendencies. Thirdly that the Jewish population is no integral part of the imperialist camp.[55]

Indeed Cliff's articles in the *New International* which centrally blamed the British for the dire situation in Palestine were fiercely attacked by the Workers Party of South Africa in their journal, *The Spark*.[56] It argued that Zionism was attempting to exploit Jewish persecution in Europe. Marxists should take an unequivocal stand in support of colonial people and oppose Jewish immigration into Palestine.[57] Zionism, it was argued, was the major cause of the problems in Palestine.

> It is evident that the authors have been swept off their feet by the widespread anti-Semitic wave and have fallen victims to nationalism. A clear, unambiguous stand in support of the colonial people in their struggle against imperialism is the first duty of revolutionary socialism.[58]

It criticized the Palestine Communist Party for permitting even a limited Jewish immigration in 1939. The article exhorted any struggle for national liberation in Palestine not to follow the lead of Gandhi in India, but to pursue 'active revolutionary mass struggle'.

In a second attack, *The Spark* accused Cliff of supporting the Zionist policy of 'unrestricted Jewish immigration'.

> Unfortunately Comrade Rock (Gluckstein-Cliff) is not an internationalist and nothing could illustrate it more clearly than this last article, where after much juggling with Marxist phraseology and centrist sophistry, he comes out openly for the all-Zionist

national slogan of unrestricted Jewish immigration! He is not in a position to refute a single one of our arguments against this immigration which we maintain is not immigration under the protection of, and for the strengthening of imperialism, with the avowed aim of trampling upon and destroying the rights of the native population of that country, with the aim of reducing the Arabs to a minority in a then Jewish state.[59]

Cliff attacked the authors of the articles for pandering to Arab nationalism rather than taking an independent class position. An independent state in Palestine could only be attained with the support of the Jewish workers. This would not come about if there was anti-Jewish terror, instigated by Arab nationalists and an end to Jewish immigration.

There were other Trotskyists in Palestine and those close to them who similarly recognized that placing the future of the Jews of Palestine in the hands of Arab nationalists and in enacting the cause of revolutionary defeatism might end in unexpected ways.

In June 1939, the journal *Ha'or* published 'A Programme of Action in Palestine' which drew attention to the increase in Nazi influence in Palestinian Arab nationalism. It argued that if such sympathies gained the upper hand in Palestine, the Jewish community would face 'complete destruction'.

The persecutions of the Jewish community will be carried out not only with the greatest barbarity and cruelty, but systematically and continuously. The talk about guarantees on the part of the leaders of the Arab national movement, as rulers, of the rights of the Jewish minority in Palestine, are but empty words, not regarded as being at all serious even by those who talk of them, who do not expect anyone to take them seriously.

Notes and Works Cited

1   *Imprecorr*, February 1925.
2   Robert Wistrich, *Trotsky: Fate of a Revolutionary* (London 1979), p. 178.
3   Leon Trotsky, 'Germany, the Key to the International Situation', *Bulletin of the Opposition*, nos 25–26, November–December 1931.
4   Reg Groves, *The Balham Group: How British Trotskyism Be*gan (London 1974), p. 62.
5   Leon Trotsky, 'Thermidor and Anti-Semitism', *New International*, vol. 7, no. 4, May 1941.
6   Stephen F. Cohen, *Bukharin and the Bolshevik Revolution* (London 1974), p. 239.
7   Collard, op. cit.

8 *Manchester Guardian*, 5 February 1937.

9 Feuchtwanger, op. cit., p. 128.

10 Vaksberg, op. cit., pp. 79–80.

11 Feuchtwanger, op. cit., p. 138.

12 *Izvestia*, 24 January 1937.

13 *Manchester Guardian*, 2 February 1937.

14 V. I. Lenin, 'The Defeat of One's Own Government in the Imperialist War', *Collected Works*, vol. 21, pp. 275–6.

15 Leon Trotsky, *War and the Fourth International* (New York), June 1934.

16 Leon Trotsky, 'A Step Towards Social Patriotism', *Writings of Leon Trotsky (1938–39)* (New York 1974), p. 209.

17 *Milkhama b'milkhama 1914–1934*, Hashomer Hatzair archives, Yad Ya'ari, Israel.

18 Leon Trotsky, 'The USSR in War', *New International*, vol. 5, no. 11, November 1939.

19 *Die Presse*, 22 May 1940.

20 Y. M. Dadoo, statement before the court, 6 September 1940 in Allison Drew, ed. *South Africa's Radical Tradition: A Documentary History*, vol. 1, 1907–1950 (Cape Town 1996), p. 338.

21 Leon Trotsky, 'Imperialist War and the World Proletarian Revolution, Manifesto of the Emergency Conference of the Fourth International', May 1940, in *Documents of the Fourth International: The Formative Years 1933–40* (New York 1973).

22 Robert Black, *Stalinism in Britain: A Trotskyist Analysis* (London 1970), p. 142.

23 *JTA*, 5 February 1929.

24 *Yediot Aharanot*, 4 October 1991.

25 HO45/25486: A Special Branch Report on the Revolutionary Communist Party and the Trotskyist Movement. www.marxists.org/history/etol/revhist/brittrot/ho45.htm

26 Albert Glotzer, *Trotsky: Memoir and Critique* (New York 1989), p. 30.

27 Glotzer, op. cit., p. 83.

28 Baruch Hirson, 'The Trotskyist Groups in South Africa', *Revolutionary History*, vol. 4, no. 4, Spring 1993.

29 Baruch Hirson, *The Cape Town Intellectuals: Ruth Schechter and Her Circle 1907–1934* (Cape Town 2001), pp. 37–50.

30 Drew, op. cit., pp. 134–46.

31 Baruch Hirson, *A History of the Left in South Africa* (London 2005), p. 92.

32 Baruch Hirson, *Revolutions in My Life* (Johannesburg 1995), pp. 108–9.

33 Chaim Shur, *Shomrim in the Land of Apartheid: The Story of Hashomer Hatzair in South Africa 1935–1970* (Givat Haviva 1998), pp. 46–7.

34 Ruth Rosenberg, letter to the Kibbutz Ha'artzi Actions Committee, 4 November 1943 in Shur, pp. 144–5.

35 Jan Willem Stutje, *Ernest Mandel: A Rebel's Dream Deferred* (London 2009), p. 3.

36 Ibid., p. 10.

37 Gerben Zaagsma, *Jewish Volunteers in the Spanish Civil War: A Case Study of the Botwin Brigade*, MA thesis, SOAS, University of London September 2001.

38 Stutje, op. cit., p. 31.

39 *Jewish Times,* 28 November 1939.

40 Shmuel Dotan, *Adumim: Hamiflagah hakommunistit b'Eretz Yisrael* (Tel Aviv 1991), pp. 241–8.

41 *Bamifneh*, 1934, Yad Ya'ari Archives, Israel.

42 *Bamifneh*, 20 March 1936.

43 *Yediot Aharanot*, 4 October 1991.

44 *Dapei Spartakus*, no. 4, June 1941.

45 *Dapei Spartakus*, editorial no. 1, June 1940.

46 Extract from letter 9 April 1941, no. 11/1/pj., CID files, Haganah archives, Tel Aviv.

47 Letter from David Metusak of Rishon L'Zion *Davar*, 19 February 1940.

48 Shai reports for Ygael Glikstein (not Gluckstein), 24 April 1941; not dated 1942, Haganah archives, Tel Aviv.

49 Jim Higgins, *More Years for the Locust* (Chapter 2) www.marxists.org/archive/higgins/1997/locust

50 *Iskra*, 1 January 1904.

51 Leon Trotsky, 'On the Jewish Problem', *Class Struggle*, vol. 4, no. 2, February 1934.

52 *JTA*, 25 January 1937.

53 Nedava, op. cit., p. 207.

54 *New York Tag*, 26–27 January 1937.

55 L. Rock (Tony Cliff) 'Roots of the Jewish-Arab Conflict', *New International* November 1938.

56 Articles in *The Spark* were unattributed. However, it is likely that those about Zionism were written by Yudel (Jacob) Burlak, a Jewish immigrant from Eastern Europe, who arrived in South Africa in the early 1930s.

57 Robert Fine with Dennis Davis, *Beyond Apartheid: Labour and Liberation in South Africa* (London 1991), p. 64.

58 'Zionism and the Arab Struggle', *The Spark*, February 1939.

59 'Rebuttal on the Palestine Question', *The Spark*, 8 May 1939.

11

Leon, Mandel and Cliff

Leon's book and its legacy

Abram Leon's book, *The Jewish Question* was first published in Paris in 1946. Ernest Mandel, writing as 'Ernest Germain', wrote a short biographical sketch of Leon as way of an introduction. The book was subsequently resurrected after the Six Day War by the former Stalinist Maxime Rodinson for an English-speaking audience and it became in due course an authoritative text on the Jewish question for Marxists. It began with the sentence 'The scientific study of Jewish history is yet to transcend the stage of idealist improvisation'. Taking issue with the conventional rendition of Jewish history and the myriad opinions of historians, Leon dismissed the issue of religion and defined the Jew solely and monolithically in terms of his economic and social role. The idea of Jewish civilization – religion, culture, literature, language – was of lesser importance, it was only a reflection of the economic role. Leon surmised that the history of the Jews could be better understood if its central actor was viewed as a people-class and that in reality there was a socio-economic basis for membership.

According to Leon, Jews essentially adhered to specific professions in medieval Europe out of choice rather than having them imposed. Some professions therefore became 'Jewish'. The Jews were deemed to be remarkably unproductive during the feudal period. Jews were always traders and then became usurers. Leon then depicts Jews as exploiters and managers.[1] Effectively the Jews only had themselves to blame. 'Long before the first attempts of the Polish cities to struggle against the Jews, all commerce and all banking in that country already lay in their hands.' Why did the Jews never take to the land? Who stopped them?[2] Anti-Semitism therefore arose as a result of Jewish behaviour. Marx touched upon this, Leon argued, when he wrote that the Jew had survived not in spite of history, but by virtue of history. All this was considerably different from Trotsky's view – he saw the Jews as victims of circumstances.

Similarly Leon argued that the Jewish people would disappear as a histori-
cal necessity – a notion Trotsky had come to reject, given the reality of the
1930s. Leon praised Stalin's USSR, since it had shown the way in this respect.
The flowering of Jewish culture and the establishment of Birobidzhan, the
Jewish Autonomous region on the border of China, testified to its success.
For Trotsky, this was Stalinist propaganda.

Leon believed that wherever the Jews had integrated into the capitalist
system, they assimilated. Judaism had only been rescued from oblivion in
Western Europe and the United States through learned immigrants from
Russia and Eastern Europe. Yet these Jews too eventually took part in the
process of assimilation.

> But the development of history is dialectical. At the same time that the bases for
> a new Jewish nationality were being elaborated all the conditions were likewise
> being created for their disappearance. Whereas the first Jewish generations in
> the countries of immigration still remain firmly attached to Judaism, the new
> generations rapidly lost their special customs and language.[3]

Capitalism therefore created the conditions both for 'nationalization' and
for assimilation. The Jews were involved in the industrialization of the
Russian economy in the mid-nineteenth century which offered them
opportunities to integrate themselves into the capitalist economy. There
was therefore a migration of the Jews to urban areas. On the one hand,
capitalism favoured the assimilation of Jews. On the other hand, the
urbanization of the Jews led to anti-Semitism and to the rise of Jewish
nationalism.

> The (Jews were the) first to be eliminated by decaying feudalism; the Jews were
> also the first to be rejected by the convulsions of dying capitalism. The Jewish
> masses find themselves wedged in between the anvil of decaying feudalism and
> the hammer of rotting capitalism.[4]

Leon's own life had been coloured by the economic crisis of the Grabski era
in Pilsudski's new Poland. This was then compounded by a similar crisis in the
mid-1920s after emigrating to Palestine. Finally he confronted such problems
in Belgium in the late 1930s. No doubt, reflecting on his own background,
Leon wrote that:

> The general decay of capitalism manifested itself in crises and unemployment
> within the countries of Eastern Europe; by the closing of all the outlets for emigration
> outside their frontiers. Seven to eight million peasants were landless and almost

without work in 'independent' Poland. Placed between two fires, the Jews were exposed to the hostility of the petty bourgeoisie and the peasantry who sought to find a place for themselves at the expense of the Jews.[5]

According to Leon, it was the combined decay of feudalism and capitalism in Eastern Europe which led to a mass emigration to Western Europe and this in turn led to the rise in anti-Semitism. He gave as an example the ruin of the bourgeoisie by the rise of monopoly capitalism and the mass influx of Jews to Vienna. Their competition gave rise to anti-Semitism.

> Racism is therefore in the first place the ideological disguise of modern imperialism. The 'race struggling for its living space' is nothing but the reflection of the permanent necessity for expansion which characterizes finance or monopoly capitalism.[6]

From being a leader of Marxism-Zionism in Belgium on the eve of the Shoah, Leon moved to a position of accepting World War II as a war of rival imperialisms. He attacked the notion that it was impossible to assimilate and that anti-Semitism would always be present in human society. Zionism, he argued, was the result of the petrification of capitalism. Zionism only wished to resolve the Jewish problem without destroying capitalism which was the main cause of Jewish suffering.

> The refutation of the ideological fantasies of Zionism does not naturally refute the real needs which brought them into being. It is modern anti-Semitism and not mythical 'eternal' anti-Semitism which is the best agitator in favour of Zionism. Similarly the basic question to determine is: 'To what extent is Zionism capable of resolving not the "eternal" Jewish problem but the Jewish question in the period of capitalist decay?'[7]

The idea that the Jews were a people was simply a romantic notion, based on 'an imaginary, poetic base'. Written under German occupation, he argued that the Jewish Diaspora did not need a country of its own at present and hence had no deep desire to aid in the construction of the Yishuv.[8] The creation of a small Jewish state in Palestine would not change anything for the Europe of 1940.

He argued that whereas national movements were the product of the ascending period of capitalism, Zionism came on the scene late in the day and was the product of the imperialist era. In contemporary Palestine, Jewish nationalism frequently collided with 'increasingly aggressive Arab nationalism'. For Leon, this seemingly only commenced in 1933 and he did not write about attacks on Jews in Palestine before the rise of Nazism. Large-scale immigration, following Hitler's accession to power had produced 'a storm of anti-Jewish demonstrations and massacres'.[9] Arab feudal elements feared being deluged by this capitalist wave. This suited the British whose sole intent was to polarize Arabs and Jews in Palestine. It was merely a question of divide and rule.

The centrality of the British exploitation of the conflict in Palestine dovetailed with Leon's understanding of the British struggle against Hitler. It had to be placed in its rightful context. 'The Zionists have a great deal of faith in a victory of Anglo-American imperialism.'

> Zionism wishes precisely to resolve the Jewish question independently of the world revolution. By misconstruing the real sources of the Jewish question in our period, by lulling itself with puerile dreams and silly hopes, Zionism proves that it is an ideological excrescence and not a scientific doctrine.[10]

Although the sympathetic Maxime Rodinson praised the work in 1968, he also pointed out that it was not a scientific work. Leon, as Mandel noted, had been forced to leave higher education in the late 1930s. Secondary sources were utilized and selected quotes were fitted to his thesis. While well written and astute, Leon's rendition and analysis of Jewish history stereotyped and demonized the Jews. For Leon, it was 'the petty bourgeois character of Judaism which makes it so odious to the petty bourgeoisie'. For the masses, the Jew remained the icon of 'money-power'.[11] One writer, well acquainted with Trotsky's writings, commented:

> Except for Marx himself, I have found no Marxist writer, before the late 1960s, to be as disparaging of the Jewish people as Leon.[12]

Mandel's inheritance

Ezra Mandel took up Abram Leon's mantle. Unlike his older mentor, he was defined by his father's household and its pre-war activities as well as his work for the miniscule Belgian Trotskyist movement. His Jewish identity was forged by the Jewishness of his acculturated family before and during the Nazi occupation and by his imprisonment in Flössenbürg concentration camp where tens of thousands died. This was mainly a camp for political prisoners and for Soviet and Polish prisoners of war. Few Jews were incarcerated there until the last few months of the war when the contraction of the Reich and the forced marches brought slave labour within its gates. For some, such experiences led assimilated and acculturated Jews towards Zionism and the road to Palestine. Mandel however required a theoretical framework for his experiences whereas others such as Primo Levi believed that the Shoah was beyond any rational explanation. Mandel viewed the destruction as a product of the era of imperialism. Institutionalized racism such as the anti-Semitism of the Nazi period was ultimately linked to institutionalized colonialism and imperialism – although the outcome did not necessarily have to be mass extermination.

> Once large groups of human beings are considered to be intrinsically inferior – as sub-human – as untermenschen, as some species of animal – then it only takes one more ideological-political step to deny them, not only the right to liberty and the pursuit of happiness, but the right to life itself.

> The seeds of the Holocaust are not to be found in traditional semi-feudal and petty bourgeois anti-Semitism . . . the seeds of the gas chambers resided in the mass enslavement and killing of Blacks via the slave trade, in the wholesale extermination of the central and south American Indians by the conquistadors. In such cases, the term genocide is fully justified: millions of men, women and children were killed just because they belonged to a supposedly 'inferior', 'subhuman' or 'wicked collective group'. It is true that these crimes of colonialism/imperialism occurred outside Europe. But it was precisely German imperialism's 'manifest destiny' to colonize Eastern Europe.[13]

While he argued that the Shoah was 'a unique crime in mankind's sad criminal history', he also pointed out that it was not only the Jews who were to be enslaved and exterminated. The first to be exterminated, he wrote, were 200,000 'mentally insane' Germans in 1940–1941. He feared that the Jewish tragedy was a harbinger of what was to come for other peoples.

Mandel's universalism and ambiguity in identifying personally with both the Jewish fate and future coloured his views on the Jewish question after the war. Mandel and his father grew apart because of political differences[14] and he was influenced by another Jewish Trotskyist, Ernst Federn who had been imprisoned by the Nazis as early as 1938. He believed that the Germans per se as a people were not responsible for this catastrophe and wrote under the pseudonym of Ernest 'Germain' to signify this.

In the summer of 1946, a year after his liberation from Flössenbűrg by American troops, Mandel added a conclusion to his introduction to Leon's book. He felt no need to challenge Leon's analysis, written in the dark days of occupation. He did remark that the Jews had allowed themselves to be carried away by 'the psychosis of despair and demoralization' and this was producing a turn towards Zionism. He recognized that not only was this the product of Nazi persecution, but also 'the relative passivity of the world proletariat.'

Most Jews therefore had little faith in the ability of the world proletariat to resolve their situation and many concluded that they had to take their destiny, personal and national, into their own hands. The 23-year-old Mandel, however, believed that the workers of the world should struggle for the freedom of immigration into their own countries, to persuade their governments to allow Jews in since this would be the best way to divert them from believing in the Zionist utopia. Jews wanted to go to Palestine, he argued, because the doors to most countries were closed to them.

The Palestinian economy would be able to absorb a 100,000 immigrants a year. Even with the influx of American capital, 'this problem will prove insoluble'. He also believed that the forces ranged against them would have 'a crushing superiority over the Palestinian Jews and over world Zionism'.

> The illusion of building a prosperous country in the midst of a world in decline becomes the absurd illusion of building a 'Jewish state' in the midst of an Arab nation twenty times as populous and in process of reaching the same state of advancement.[15]

He argued that it was a matter of crucial importance for a declining Western capitalism therefore to align themselves with the Arab bourgeoisie which was uniting the Arab world. The Americans, he suggested, cared little for the Jews, but only wished to gain access to Middle Eastern oil – and the same could be said for the Soviets.

Mandel returned to the Leninist argument that Zionism prevented the integration of the Jewish and Arab proletariat. If it did not give up the right of free immigration, then the Jews would suffer their fate.

> Only the Arab masses, once they are freed from the imperialist yoke, will have the right to decide whether or not they are opposed to the immigration of Jewish workers. But the division of the Palestinian working class movement along nationalist lines, can only act to stimulate opposition by the Arab masses to this immigration. The Jewish workers of Palestine must be forewarned! If they do not integrate themselves into the workers' movement of the Middle East in time, the unity of the Arab world against imperialism may take place over their heads, with the complete destruction of their position.[16]

At the beginning of 1947, Mandel wrote *Projet de theses sur la question juive après la seconde guerre impérialiste*. This essentially became the formal approach of the united Trotskyist movement, the Fourth International, on whose secretariat Mandel sat. Like Leon – but without his Jewish background – Mandel attempted to explain the course of recent Jewish history. Like Lenin, he believed that West European Jewry had been in the process of assimilation rather than of acculturation – and that East European immigrants, squeezed out by industrialization in Russia, had saved them from oblivion by injecting them with both Judaism and Jewishness.

Mandel's critique of Zionism focused on the belief that it was possible to develop 'a closed economy' in Palestine while capitalism generally was undergoing a tremendous crisis. Jewish nationalism, he argued, provoked Arab nationalism – and this in turn therefore undermined any cooperation between Jewish and Arab workers. Writing only of Arabs rather than Palestinians, he argued that the Jews were in an impossible situation. They were outnumbered 70:1 by a hostile Arab world and that the higher Arab birth rate would erase the effects of mass Jewish immigration. Arab notables bought their land from the peasants and sold it on to the Jews, often at inflated prices. The Jews should therefore fight for the redistribution of land among the Arab masses, but to do so, Mandel pointed out, would mean the end of land purchases. Mandel's harshest criticism was directed at socialist Zionists – a category which Lenin had omitted and Trotsky had expressed interest in.

Mandel labelled them as reformists, social patriots and defenders of imperialism.

Yet Mandel recognized, probably through his own experience, that many Jews now wished to affirm their own Jewish nationality. 'The desire of the Jews to leave a continent which for them is nothing but a vast graveyard finds its expression primarily in a Zionist desire to go to Palestine.' Mandel's answer to the Jewish problem in post-war Europe was not an immediate solution, but one based in theory which would be realized in an indeterminable future.

> The Fourth International, basing itself firmly on its program and on a scientific analysis of the situation in Palestine but at the same time taking into account the actual state of mind of the Jewish masses, must recognize that their desire to lead their own national existence is a legitimate one. The Fourth International must show concretely that the winning of their nationality cannot be realized within decaying capitalist society, and is especially unrealizable and reactionary in Palestine.[17]

It had to be demonstrated to the Jews that a closed state or a closed economy would not work, but only 'a planned world socialist economy' was the answer. 'The Jewish masses must be made aware of the terrible catastrophe that awaits them if the decay of capitalism continues its course.'

> When the Jewish masses have gone through their disillusioning experience with Zionism and have learned the futility of their efforts and sacrifices, they will turn

toward us – provided we understand how to move toward them today with our solutions as well as with an intransigent criticism of Zionism.[18]

Mandel too placed his faith in the Arabs masses rather than socialist Zionists since he believed that it constituted the central revolutionary force of the Middle East. This was because of 'their numbers, their social conditions and the material conditions of their existence which set them in direct conflict with imperialism'.

Mandel asserted that there had been no armed struggle against British interests because the British militarily protected the Jews against an increasingly hostile world. The Zionists simply exerted pressure on British imperialism to produce concessions – and did 'not to strive to expel British imperialism from Palestine'.

The actions of Menachem Begin and the Irgun Zvai Leumi were, Mandel argued, simply a pretext to allow British troops to remain in Palestine in large concentration. He qualified this by stating that:

> The terrorist movement and the so-called 'Hebrew Committee of National Liberation' do set forth the objective of expelling British imperialism from Palestine. But they cannot conceive of such expulsion except in the form of a general arming of the Jews in Palestine who would hold the Arab world in check until such time as large-scale immigration of Jews would give them the military strength to oppose the 'Arab menace.' These ideas, an abstraction formed out of complete utopianism, are ultra-reactionary and can only deepen still further the gulf separating the Jewish and the Arab workers in Palestine.[19]

Mandel understood the prospect of mass Jewish immigration from Europe in the context of the two separate economies in Palestine. The Arabs, he pointed out, regarded the arrival of new immigrants as 'the arrival of enemy soldiers'. Immigration therefore widened the gulf between Arab and Jewish workers – and consequently strengthened and prolonged the presence of British imperialism. This 'cannot but prepare the ground for the complete extermination of the Jewish minority when the Arab uprising comes in the next stage'.

All solutions had to start from 'the sovereignty of the Arab population'. Only the Arabs had the right to determine whether Jews could enter Palestine after the Shoah. In the current political climate, the Fourth International would therefore do everything, he argued, to dissuade Jews from going to Palestine.

Yet at the same time, the Fourth International should condemn and combat 'the British repression of Jewish immigration and denounce all their police measures'.

> It will not be hard to explain to the Arab masses that this imperialist repression, now limited to the Jews, is only the preparation for much more savage repression of future Arab movements. It is in the interest of the Arab masses that every protest movement against British police terror should be utilized to bring forward concretely the question of withdrawal of British troops.[20]

All solutions, proposed by imperialism, such as partition, the limited immigration of 100,000, the surrender of the Mandate, would prolong the presence of British troops in the country. The tasks and tactics of the Trotskyists were to communicate the suicidal tendencies of the Zionists which, he argued, entrapped the Jews and would lead to another catastrophe.

> But as the bankruptcy of Zionism becomes more and more strikingly revealed to the masses; as immigration slows down and the terrible danger of the Arab explosion comes nearer; as our propaganda helps in getting the masses to realize that it is a life-or-death question for them to find a common ground with the Arab masses, even at the price of temporarily giving up certain privileges – under these conditions our slogans will be able to pass from the propaganda stage to the stage of agitation, and will help in bringing about a split between the workers' movement and Zionism. This is the condition sine qua non for the realization of Jewish-Arab unity of action against imperialism. This alone can prevent the Arab revolution in the Middle East from passing over the corpse of Palestinian Judaism.[21]

A starting point for this approach was to cultivate the left wing of the Zionist movement – and like Abram Leon – bring them to universalism by transcending their specifically Jewish Marxism.

Tony Cliff and the question of Palestine

Tony Cliff had similarly identified with the Trotskyist movement after moving away from Left Poale Zion in the late 1930s and making contact with the Socialist Workers' Party in the United States. Unlike Leon and Mandel, Cliff wrote about the problems of Palestine as someone who actually lived there.

Cliff's journey to the United Kingdom was by way of Paris and the offices of the Fourth International. Cliff was not particularly impressed by the direction of Mandel and the Fourth International. In particular, the adherence to the idea that Stalin's regime was on the verge of collapse and that capitalism was decaying dramatically. In Britain and Ireland, Cliff began to work on his own theories of state capitalism and the deflected permanent revolution. Indeed in September 1947, he published *All that Glitters is not Gold* which rebuked Mandel's approach. In doing so, he moved away from orthodox Trotskyism towards a Trotskyist-derived independent Marxism. It also heralded the inability of Trotskyism to produce a unified movement.

Cliff's pre-war writings significantly belie a fundamental difference with his somewhat harsher writings on Zionism after 1945.

Before the outbreak of hostilities in September 1939, Cliff's writings clearly indicated their ideological pedigree in the Zionist Left, even though he often castigated his former comrades in Mapai, Hashomer Hatzair, the Palestine Communist Party and Left Poale Zion. He repeatedly condemned Arab nationalism and exhibited an understanding of the issues which concerned the Jews of Palestine. After 1945, he wrote almost as an outsider, more supportive of Arab nationalism, regardless of leadership, a severe critic of Zionism with apocalyptic views of the Jewish future. He emerged as an opponent of immigration solely into Palestine from the DP camps. There was far less a willingness to recall past history and to analyse it.

His radicalization during the war years was influenced by his imprisonment in Acre prison by the British in 1940 and his frustration that his repeated appeals to Hebrew University students in Jerusalem not to enlist in the British war effort fell on deaf ears. Thousands of Jews volunteered, but few Arabs. Despite his noted individualism and influential arguments, he had achieved little. Instead he had witnessed the polarizing situation between Arabs and Jews and his belief in cooperation between Jewish and Arab workers against the imperialists seemed further off than ever. Despite his political irrelevance, the police periodically looked for him and searched his room. His political activities became more restricted and this eventually led to a return to Haifa from Jerusalem. He later reacted strongly to the revolt of Menachem Begin's Irgun Zvai Leumi against the British.

In contrast, in 1938, he had held the British responsible for many of the problems of Palestine. The divide and rule policy, he maintained, was designed to create a manageable friction between Arab and Jew. It prevented any joint workers' action. The Zionist movement saw in immigration the basis for paradise in the country. The feudal leadership of the Arab national movement saw in it the basis for hell in the country.

Both views are false. Marxists cannot be for immigration or against it, just as they cannot be for or against immigration from country to city. Marxists must only record that in the capitalist order it is necessary to fight for free migration, without falling into illusions about the 'liberating role' and the 'creation of happiness' attributed to this migration, without adopting a chauvinistic attitude towards this migration ('Jewish majority', 'Jewish products', 'Jewish labour', etc.). The same view must be adopted by the Marxists with respect to settlement.[22]

The immigration of Jews was utilized not only to stimulate the growth of capitalism in Palestine but also to foment Arab anger against the Jews. He did not regard the Jews as an integral part of the imperialist camp and he attributed any comparison with South Africa to 'extreme Arab nationalists and Stalinists'. Commenting on the utilization of this comparison by both social democrats and Communists in Palestine, he wrote that it was especially dangerous that 'such a perverted analogy should take root among the Marxists of South Africa'. According to Cliff, the official Communists in Palestine considered that the Jews were part and parcel of the imperialist camp whereas they were in fact a part of the general working class.

Cliff was scathing about leading figures in the Palestinian Arab national movement such as Haj Amin al-Husseini who feared modernization. Their leadership of the Palestinian Arabs provided fertile ground for the spread of fascism and profound anti-Jewish settlement. He documented the series of attacks on Jews during the inter-war period including the Arab accusation that many Jewish immigrants from Eastern Europe after 1917 were in reality Bolsheviks. Cliff made a distinction between the Arab notables and the masses.

While the opposition of the Arab upper classes to the Jews is reactionary, the struggle of the Arab masses against Zionism is absolutely progressive. The upper classes are today successful in diverting the national struggle of the masses into anti-Jewish channels by means of the fact that the predominant majority of the Jewish population is Zionist.[23]

Yet he maintained that the Arab national movement in Palestine, like its parallels in other colonial countries, was historically essentially an anti-imperialist movement. This premise was accepted not only by Marxists, but also by Stalinists. This was true, Cliff argued, even if such a movement was led by feudalists – and gave the examples of Abd-el Krim in Morocco and the national movements in Syria and Egypt at their inception.

Cliff and indeed other Jewish Trotskyists were deeply bothered by the desire of the early Marxist-Zionists to develop their policy of Hebrew labour which had effectively separated them from Arab workers. This violated the cardinal principle of the workers of the world uniting against their capitalist overlords and class enemies. Such theory did not translate well into fin de siècle underdeveloped Palestine with an embryonic, unstructured economy. What constituted a living wage for the Jewish workers was different for the Arab workers of Palestine. In 1894 in Zikhron Ya'akov, both Jews and Arabs were paid six piastres, but the Jewish workers received an extra four piastres from a charity fund.[24] When Baron de Rothschild withdrew his financial support from the plantations in Palestine in 1900, the subsidy was discontinued and the Jewish workers were ruthlessly displaced by cheaper Arab workers by the Jewish management. In 1908, the managers at the settlement of Petach Tiqva attempted to replace their Jewish workers with imported Arab labour from Egypt. The economic argument therefore often took precedence over one of ethnic solidarity. The idea of Hebrew labour was essentially based on the struggle for the survival of the Jewish proletariat and that cheap Arab labour should not be pitted against Jewish labour. In 1905 there was no state or institution which could subsidize the Jewish workers. An overwhelming majority of the Jewish workers who had arrived in Palestine in the years of the second aliyah (1903–1914) left again because of the dire economic and employment situation. The initiative of Hebrew labour was formulated to meet the reality of the changing situation in Palestine. It essentially failed and this led to the more successful idea of the collective settlement. The labour market evolved such that the less-skilled Arab workers were confined to 'the simplest jobs'. Moreover as capital came to Palestine due to the Zionist experiment, an Arab middle class was slow to develop whereas the Jewish sector developed dramatically. Both Marxist and Marxist-Zionist solutions did not work. In addition, the rise of Arab nationalism pushed Jewish workers closer towards institutions with Jewish managers. Trotskyist interpretations, however, often simplified and telescoped a complex chain of events. As one commentator has pointed out:

> In aspiring to split the labour market, European workers were, especially in the early stages of the conflict, not motivated by any inherent racism, but by a desire to protect their European standard of living and to prevent their potential displacement.[25]

However, for Cliff, the imperialist yoke could only be thrown off if Jews and Arabs worked together, unless the Jews renounced both Zionism and the closed economy.

He was also critical that the Palestinian Arab workers placed nationalism before class.

> The Jewish toiling masses will not, however, support the anti-imperialist movement if no class differentiation takes place in the Arab national movement. What is so terrible in the situation in Palestine is that, on the one hand, there is a strong national differentiation between Jews and Arabs and, on the other, the national unity in the Arab camp is very firm.[26]

Cliff also attacked Zionism because it seemingly did not believe in the inevitable victory of the international working class and seemed fatalistic in accepting 'the continuation of world reaction and its consolidation'. Cliff distinguished, however, between the Jewish community of Palestine and the Zionist leadership. He believed that the former could always be won over to the cause of world revolution, to Arab-Jewish cooperation and to a ditching of Zionist ideology. Moreover, the negation of Zionism did not mean 'the negation of the right to existence and extension of the Jewish population in Palestine'. In this sense, he came close to espousing Yishuvism which the PCP had advocated in the early 1920s. He commented that the PCP in the 1920s vociferously opposed Zionism, but demanded 'the maximum freedom of movement for Jewish immigration into Palestine'. The Communists also requested material aid for the establishment of Jewish immigrants in Palestine. The struggle against Jewish immigration shifted the focus of anti-imperialist struggle towards something which was patently anti-Jewish – and that this was only helpful to British imperialism. The PCP declared that any struggle against Jewish immigration would only strengthen 'Zionist chauvinism among the Jewish masses'.

> Before 1926–27, the Comintern in Palestine was for tenant protection and the recognition of his right to the land, but at the same time demanded that Jewish settlement on uncultivated land be made possible; it repeatedly declared that there are still large areas of land in the hands of the government and the Arabian effendis which are cultivable but uncultivated. This attitude was genuinely internationalist.

Following Stalin's dominance and the suppression of the Left Opposition in the USSR, Comintern policy on both the colonial question and Palestine changed. In addition to a policy of Arabization of the PCP, Cliff pointed out that the Stalinists in Palestine subsequently wanted a stop to Jewish immigration, an expropriation of land owned by the Jews and to arm the Arabs. 'The PCP preens itself before the Arab population with anti-Jewish terrorist actions', he commented.

Cliff depicted the conflict as a collision between 'two national exclusivist movements'. On the one hand between Zionism and the feudal, semi-bourgeois Arab leadership and on the other the struggle of the Arab masses against Zionism.

In the months before the outbreak of war in 1939 and the subsequent mass killing of Jews, Cliff argued that the Jewish question could only be solved by a socialist world revolution. Zionism remained a factor that weakened the class struggle of the Jewish masses, and strengthened the reactionary forces in Palestine. Jewish immigration on the one hand strengthened the working class in Palestine and the cause of anti-imperialism since the immigrants were mainly workers. On the other, because the immigration was deemed to be Zionist, it strengthened 'the exclusivist positions and the forces of imperialism in Palestine'. He argued both for the right of Jews to leave Europe for Palestine as well as for Arabs to leave the surrounding countries to come to Palestine.

Following the London conference in February 1939 whereby the Palestinian Arabs refused to sit in the same room as the Palestinian Jews, some Trotskyists in Palestine clearly agreed with the demands of the Arab delegates that there should be halt to Jewish immigration into the country and a prohibition on land sales to Jews.[27] On the eve of war, few countries were then willing to take in Jews, fleeing from Hitler's Germany. Such ideas found their way – partly and wholly – into the MacDonald White Paper which was published a couple of months later.

Tony Cliff after 1945

Six years later, Cliff returned to the question of Palestine in the full knowledge that 6 million Jews had been exterminated and that the world proletariat had not risen up against the Nazis and the Stalinists. The world revolution had not broken out. While he was open to free immigration before the war, after it he – like the British – hoped that the Jews would go to other countries. Indeed, he called upon both British and American workers to urge their governments to open the gates of their countries to the victims of fascism including the Jews. Cliff never advocated the idea of Palestine as a haven for the persecuted. There was no redemption through Zionism.

> It is impossible for the Palestinian Jews to save the displaced Jews in Europe by bringing them to Palestine. Their task will be to save themselves from the abyss into which they are being driven. This can be done only by their renunciation of

Zionism, by breaking down their isolation in the Middle East, and by extending their hand to the Arab masses who fight against imperialism.[28]

The emphasis on the reactionary nature of Arab nationalism was downgraded. Cliff described any future Jewish state as being both a buffer between British imperialism and the Arab world as well as an actual pillar of imperialism. The Jews of Palestine could only save themselves if they embraced national revolution in the Arab world against the imperialists.

He also argued that the Jews would never join the struggle against British imperialism. Yet Begin had repeatedly written that the Irgun was fighting against British imperialism. Cliff rejected this by arguing that Palestine could not be liberated from imperialism without the liberation of the entire Arab East. Moreover, the leaders of the Irgun's Revolt were the same, he argued, as those who boycotted Arabs. Acts of violence on the part of the Zionists widened the gap between Jewish and Arab workers.

Cliff's frustration at the growing polarization and the almost inevitability of a conflict between the two national movements was palpable. Despite this, he continued to argue for a class-based cooperation.

Cliff's views hardened during the war at a time when there was growing understanding for the Zionist solution to the Jewish problem. In contrast to his pre-war writings, he blamed the Zionists for not protesting about the British suppression of the Arab Revolt between 1936 and 1939 and for subsequent acts against the Arab national movement in Palestine. Moreover, he gave this as a reason for the multiplicity of Arab attacks on Jews. In October 1938, he had spoken about 'the bloody attacks on the Jews'. In November 1945, it had become a national uprising which had been diverted from its real aims by feudal leaders who were 'agents either of British imperialism or of Germany and Italy'.

The British were still seen as promulgating a divide and rule policy after the war in order to hang onto their colonies. Cliff argued that the possibility of granting 100,000 immigration permits, following the Anglo-American Commission of Inquiry, was actually designed to divert Arab criticism of British imperialism towards the Jews. On the other hand, he commented that the British were fostering the development of the reactionary Muslim Brotherhood in the Middle East to cause further problems. The British were accused of being responsible for everything that had come to pass solely by encouraging the Jews.

This is the result of the criminal imperialist policy of goading the Jewish minority to struggle for a Jewish State, of helping them to erect a closed Zionist economy which turns the anti-imperialist ire of the Arab masses against the Jews.[29]

Tel Aviv, a city founded by Jews in 1909 as a Jewish outpost of Arab Jaffa, expanded and had been populated by Jews ever since. Cliff stated that the metropolis of Tel Aviv did not have one Arab worker.

Before 1939, Cliff wrote little about the Zionist purchase of land from absentee landlords. By 1945, he compared Zionist actions to Nazi ones and spoke of their desire for ethnic cleansing. His uncle, Chaim Kalvarisky, had spent much of his adult life in land purchase and was involved in acquiring the Jezreel valley.

> If at one stroke twenty villages in the Jezreel valley were wiped out when the land was bought from a Syrian banker, Sursuk, if thousands of evicted peasants were prohibited from looking for work as wage labourers on the land on which their families had toiled for generations, if there were constant 'purges' of Arabs from the economy, so strongly reminiscent of the 'purges' practised by the Nazis against the Jews from 1933–39, if from such 'innocent' acts the Zionists pass over to speaking about making Palestine a Jewish State and expelling all the Arabs from the country – then is there any wonder that the Arabs oppose Zionism to the very death?[30]

Cliff argued that the Jews, of all people after the Shoah, had become militarists and chauvinists, 'the blind tool of imperialism in subjugating the Arab masses'.

> In the same way that the existing social order is to be blamed for the calamity of the Jews, so is it to be blamed for the exploitation of their catastrophe for reactionary, oppressive aims.[31]

Cliff's vehemence was tempered by a plea to see the light. If things went well for the Zionists, the British would offer the Jews 'a pocket state in a small part of Palestine'. There would be two irredentist movements and an economically weak Palestinian state. This would end, he argued, in terrible sacrifice and Zionism's burial. Cliff believed that the Jews of the world were doomed if imperialism continued to rule, but would only be saved if there was world revolution. All the minorities – Jews, Kurds and others – would be given a wide autonomy in the regions inhabited by them, within the all-embracing framework of a Republic of Workers and Peasants of the Arab East.

A few weeks after his arrival in Britain at the end of 1946, Cliff was confronted by several articles that had appeared in the internal bulletin of the US Socialist Workers Party.[32] They, in part, reiterated numerous points which Cliff himself had made as a member of the Trotskyist group in pre-war Palestine. Now, he was prepared to bury such views and ridicule its proponents. One, entitled *A Revolutionary Programme for the Jews* by Leo Lyons was deemed as 'bringing the superficial tourist approach to the Palestine question . . . an absolute lack of any understanding of the theory of the Permanent Revolution and the colonial question'. Its tendency, according to Cliff, was Zionist in all but words.[33]

Cliff further commented that he feared that the position expressed in all the articles would cause infinite harm to the cause of the Fourth International in all the Arab countries and might even bring about a cleavage between the colonial sections and the SWP. Cliff's primary concern was the centrality of mobilizing the Arab masses, regardless of the political hue of their leaders, as a means of ousting imperialism from the Middle East. The Jews of Palestine were a secondary matter.

Cliff's new approach to the Israel-Palestine conflict in 1946 – before the establishment of the state of Israel and the war of 1948 – as an authoritative, authentic Palestinian Jew set the tone among sections of the European Left for decades to come.

Trotskyists and Palestine after 1945

The differing views of Mandel and Cliff reflected the views of many Jewish Trotskyists after 1945. Few could separate themselves from the emotional trauma of the Shoah and the self-evident desire of many survivors to reach Palestine and to leave behind the charred legacy of Europe. There was also a deep need to locate an encompassing Marxist theory which would rationalize their thoughts – not to surrender to Zionism, but to recognize the plight of European Jews. Moreover, it was now conceded that Jews had become one of two distinct nationalities in Palestine.

> The surviving Jews are not only tired in the sense of physical and spiritual exhaustion; they are tired in a historical sense – tired of flight. After Belsen and Buchenwald, the prospects of finding a home in surroundings that promise to be merely less inhospitable evoke little enthusiasm from those who must build anew their shattered lives.
>
> But given even this state of mind of Europe's Jews, the question remains: But why Palestine? Because it is the one place where they can expect – not the freedom and equality they yearn for – but a fair chance to fight for it.[34]

Yet flight to Palestine, it was argued, would not solve the problem of the Jew. Only the fight for socialist freedom in all countries would achieve that. Yet many Jews would refuse to heed such advice to fight for socialism in their countries of origin.

Lenin, it was acknowledged, had been wrong as far as the answer of assimilation to the Jewish question was concerned. The Jews of Germany, a Leninist ideal of assimilation and acculturation, had been expunged from their fatherland. Their thirst for acceptance and absorption had ended at Auschwitz. There was a widespread recognition that the situation had changed.

> Revolutionary Marxists recognise that the perspective of assimilation under capitalism is utopian and can only lead the Jewish masses to underestimate the catastrophic weakness of their position in bourgeois and Stalinist society.[35]

Lenin was found to have erred by uncritically relying on Kautsky's views 'in considering the Jews a social caste and not a socially heterogeneous national-ity'. The Comintern's characterization of Zionism as merely 'an agent of British imperialism' ignored, it was argued, 'the intense anti-imperialist temper and activities of the Palestinian Jewish masses'. The Stalinists' approach was viewed as 'oversimplified and outdated'.

It was further understood that there were many bars to Jews being per-mitted to enter a range of countries. Enlightened Canada placed Jews in the 'least desirable' category. The Jews of Europe faced 'a world of walls'.

American Trotskyists appealed to their English comrades to become cham-pions of the slogan 'Open the doors of Palestine'. This would be achieved, not by bargaining with British imperialism, but by mobilizing the masses for a revolutionary struggle against it. Whereas the Zionists demanded solely Jewish immigration into Palestine, revolutionary Marxists advocated both Arab and Jewish immigration into the land. This was therefore not a narrow Jewish nationalist position, but an internationalist one.[36]

Some argued that 'critical but unambiguous support' should be given to 'the Jewish resistance movement' in its efforts to circumvent British attempts to stop illegal immigration into Palestine. It was even suggested that 'an under-ground railroad' should be constructed to facilitate the passage of survivors into Palestine.[37]

Yet all of this had to compliment the rights of the Arabs in Palestine. Their rights would not be compromised by Jewish immigration, it was argued. They would only be jeopardized if a Jewish state emerged as a result of such immigration.

> To deny the right of the Jews today to immigrate to Palestine on the grounds of the possible consequences it will have on the Arabs is to deny them the right to go anywhere.[38]

There should be unrestricted Jewish immigration into Palestine to create an autonomous bi-national socialist Palestine within a Near East Federation of Socialist Republics.

Other Marxists took a different view and endorsed a call for Jewish emigration from Europe to any country which would take them – except Palestine. There would inevitably be a clash between Jews and Arabs, but that revolutionaries should solely support the Arabs.

> The Arab world is awakening. It is only a question of time when a powerful movement for national liberation and unification will set in. It will be a progressive movement whether it is led by feudal capitalists or not; whether it can or cannot succeed without a victorious socialist movement. We will have to support it unconditionally as we did even Haile Selassie, or any oriental despot, in their struggle for national independence from imperialism.[39]

The ideological contortions to make theory fit reality were profound. The complexity of the situation, the anti-Nazi sympathy for the Jews, the anti-imperialist fervour for the Arabs plus the fractious nature of debate within Marxist groups, all conspired to produce a pot-pourri of confused choices.

In Palestine, following the departure of Tony Cliff for British shores, his miniscule movement, the Revolutionary Communist League, followed a Leninist policy of revolutionary defeatism in the war of 1948 between Zionist Jews and Palestinian Arab nationalists. Neither side, it argued, exhibited progressive tendencies. It weakened the proletariat and strengthened imperialism.

> 'The main enemy is in our own country!' – this was what Karl Liebknecht had to say to the workers (during World War I) when imperialists and social democrats were inciting them to the slaughter of their fellow workers in other countries. In this spirit we say to the Jewish and Arab workers: the enemy is in your own camp! . . . The only way to peace between the two peoples of this country is turning the guns against the instigators of murder in both camps.[40]

In 1948, the Israeli war for independence or the Palestinian nakhba were therefore viewed through the eyes of World War I Europe.

This did not conform to the mindset of either of the combatants in this war. The Jews believed that they were fighting for their very existence and defeat would spell annihilation once more. The Arabs believed that they were fighting for the independence awarded to other Arabs. Defeat would mean domination and a colonial settler state in their midst. No one heeded the call to place class solidarity above national solidarity.

Notes and Works Cited

1   Abram Leon, *The Jewish Question: A Marxist Interpretation* (New York 1970), pp. 195–6.

2   Ibid., p. 138, no. 12.

3   Ibid., p. 222.

4   Ibid., p. 226.

5   Ibid., p. 227.

6   Ibid., p. 236.

7   Ibid., p. 248.

8   Ibid., p. 252.

9   Ibid., p. 254.

10   Ibid., pp. 255–6.

11   Ibid., p. 236.

12   Werner Cohn, 'From Victim to Shylock and Oppressor: The New Image of the Jew in the Trotskyist Movement', *Journal of Communist Studies*, vol. 7, no. 1, March 1991.

13   Ernest Mandel, *The Meaning of the Second World War* (London 1986), pp. 91–2.

14   Stutje, op. cit., p. 44.

15   Ernest Germain, 'The Jewish Question since World War II', *Fourth International*, vol. 8, no. 4, April 1947.

16   Ibid.

17   Ernest Germain, 'Draft Theses on the Jewish Question Today', *Fourth International*, vol. 9, no. 1, January–February 1948.

18   Ibid.

19   Ibid.

20   Ibid.

21   Ibid.

22   L. Rock, 'Class Politics in Palestine', *New International*, June 1939.

23   L. Rock, 'The Jewish-Arab Conflict', *New International*, November 1938.

24   Gershon Shafir, *Land, Labour and the Origins of the Israeli-Palestinian Conflict 1882–1914* (Cambridge 1989), p. 61.

25   Ibid., p. 82.

26   L. Rock, 'Class Politics in Palestine', *New International*, June 1939.

27   Nathan Weinstock, *Zionism: False Messiah* (London 1979), p. 199.

28   Tony Cliff, 'Terrorism in Palestine: Are the Terrorists Anti-Imperialists?', *Socialist Appeal*, December 1946.

29   Ibid.

30   Tony Cliff, 'The Middle East at the Crossroads', *Fourth International*, vol. 7, no. 1, January 1946.

31 Ibid.

32 *Internal Bulletin of the SWP*, no. 11, October 1946; no. 12, October 1946.

33 Tony Cliff, 'On the Irresponsible Handling of the Palestine Question', *RCP Internal Bulletin*, early 1947.

34 Notes of the Month, *The New International*, November 1946.

35 Edward and Albert Findley, 'Assimilation Utopian: Self-Determination of the Jews', *The New International*, November 1946.

36 Resolution of the Socialist Workers' Party, USA, May 1946, *The New International*, November 1946.

37 Findley and Findley, op. cit.

38 Notes of the Month, *The New International*, November 1946.

39 W. Brooks, 'No Immigration to Palestine: Arab Freedom the Main Issue', *The New International*, November 1946.

40 Translated from *Kol Hama'amad* in *Fourth International*, vol. 9, no. 3, May 1948.

12

The non-aligned

The road to Suez

The central prerogative of Israel's political orientation by 1950 was not a preference towards the Communist East or towards the capitalist West, but a flexible policy whereby there was freedom of manoeuvre. It was a question of being able to act independently and if necessary unilaterally. Ben-Gurion's view was dominated by the profound weakness of the Jewish people historically. Alliances in the real world were often transient and temporary. Moshe Sharett, however, viewed it as a question of civil liberties.

> The interests of the Jewish people determine our position here. It sets the choice and leaves no room for deliberation, not because democracy is pro-Jewish, not because Communism is anti-Jewish . . . but because in a democratic regime there are liberties that enable Jewish self-defence, Jewish self-action, links among various Jewish communities in the world.[1]

The early Soviet Union had been shaped and had survived through Lenin's implementation of the politics of expediency. Ben-Gurion, for this reason, respected Lenin. However, he also realized that Soviet national interests did not necessarily coincide with Israeli ones. There were intense debates between 1948 and 1953 in Ben-Gurion's party, Mapai. These were not only about neutrality in the debate between East and West, but about neutrality between democratic socialism and Communism. Moreover, if it was decided to support the forces of democratic socialism, then this did not automatically mean an alignment with the West. Sharett shrewdly differentiated between the ideological and the diplomatic. He observed that there was a subtle difference between relations with Communism and with the state interests of the USSR. Ben-Gurion, in contrast, had been ultra-cautious and distanced

Labour Zionism from the forces of the October Revolution. He did not wish Zionism to be submerged by the Bolshevik experiment and swept away by the revolutionary fervour that accompanied it. He was keenly aware of the persecutions that Zionists in the USSR had suffered – and continued to suffer even during the period of Soviet support after 1947. As a Marxist-Zionist who had visited Soviet Russia in 1923, Ben-Gurion clearly understood the role which Jewish Communists had played and their deep hostility towards Zionism – and in particular the Zionist Left. He attacked what he termed 'the Jewish Yevsektsiya' – both Zionist and anti-Zionist, who believed in Stalin and desired the triumph of Stalinism in Israel. In November 1949, in an address to the Mapai secretariat, he did not mince his words:

> This is an internal Jewish debate in which there can be no agreement . . . their conception conflicts with ours, and hence there can be no contact, no provisional agreement between us and the Yevsektsia.[2]

His venom in particular was directed at Mapam which had come second in the first Israeli election at the beginning of 1949. The party's belief that Mapam was truly international Communism's representative in Israel led to many revolutionary proclamations despite the fact that the Kremlin had sent many of its members in the USSR to their deaths. One of its constituent parties, Hashomer Hatzair, had dutifully translated Stalin's *Problems of Leninism* into Hebrew and published them.[3] Ben-Gurion regarded Mapam as a fifth column and following the first elections, he refused to form a socialist bloc with them. Instead he brought into government a bloc of four religious parties – some of whose views were ideologically light years away from his own.

Despite this, Israel's foreign policy was designed to serve the national interest and not to deliberately antagonize the USSR. By 1950, Israel's approach in the United Nations was one of independent action on a case-by-case basis. Israel therefore often abstained on Cold War issues and the United States was not mightily pleased. Thus Sharett supported the United Nations' attempt to bring about a ceasefire in Korea as well as the US position in actually dispatching military forces to halt the North Korean invasion. Yet Israel opposed US attempts to secure the reunification of the two Koreas. It also supported China's representation at the United Nations and opposed the United States in refusing to overturn the boycott of Franco's Spain. Sharett instructed its UN representative to vote against granting independence to Italian Somaliland since he needed good relations with the Vatican.[4]

The Slansky trial, the Doctors' Plot and even the temporary break in diplomatic relations with the USSR certainly pushed Israel towards London and Washington. Even Mapam was fragmenting into its constituent parties. It was weighed down by the revelations of these events and the dragooning of its own representatives into the machinations of the Slansky trial. Even so, by 1954, Eisenhower's Republican administration still questioned Israel's adherence to the West and refused to sell arms to her. It was the calculated swing of Nasser's Egypt towards the USSR after 1955 that polarized the situation and truly moved Israel towards Washington.

From Ben-Gurion's point of view, Israel's collusion with the imperial powers, Britain and France, was deemed to be essential if Nasser's bellicose intention towards Israel was to be stopped before it was too late. Yet Israel's determination to forge its own independent path and to serve its own national interest during the Suez crisis of 1956 cast the first shadow over its internationalist credentials and dented the socialist imagery perceived in many a Western capital.

In late 1951, the Egyptian government declared its intention to eject the British from the Canal Zone and to reinforce its claim to Sudan. Three years of instability and struggle ended with Colonel Nasser taking control of the newly established Egyptian republic in 1954. It was also marked by an increasingly bitter confrontation between Egypt and Israel. By the mid-1950s, there had been a dramatic rise in the number of Israelis killed by infiltrators from Gaza. In response, there were increasingly hard Israeli retaliations – and were decidedly unrestrained following Ben-Gurion's return to government.

Nasser's triumph over his rivals manifested itself at the beginning of 1955 with a turn to the East. In April 1955, Western fears deepened when Egypt concluded an agreement to sell cotton to Mao's China which was seen as the leading power in the developing world despite its Communist rulers. Nasser's desire to topple pro-Western regimes in the Middle East such as those in Beirut, Amman and Baghdad accelerated efforts by Britain and the United States to entice the Egyptian leader to pull back from the Soviet embrace. The Kremlin had not only approached Cairo, but also Damascus and Riyadh.

The Soviet Union in the post-Stalin era retained its historic fear of encirclement by the West. In the political space opened up by the death of Stalin, the new Soviet leadership resolved to reach out to the emerging developing world. By looking to the Arab world and to Latin America, the Kremlin hoped to disrupt US alliances. 'The Communist world' therefore became superseded by 'the progressive world'. The US attempt to construct an alliance of pro-Western states in Turkey, Iraq and Iran moved nationalist regimes in Egypt and Syria closer to the USSR. India's Nehru which had once been regarded as 'a lackey of the imperialists' was now befriended by the Kremlin.

Yet the Kremlin pursued the same sort of policy towards the Arab nationalist regimes that had failed with Atatürk's Turkey three decades previously.

Taking what he could from Lenin to oust the British and the French, Atatürk then harshly suppressed the local Communists. This pattern was repeated in supporting Nasser, welcoming the Egyptian union with Syria and maintaining good relations with the FLN once Boumedienne had come to power. In each case, the local Communists were purged from positions of influence and the party banned.

Yet the Kremlin viewed Nasser's rise as an opportunity to revive its interests in the Middle East and announced that it would sell arms to the Egyptian nationalists. This manifested itself in September 1955 through a Czechoslovak arms deal with Egypt. All this alarmed the West and initiated a period of intense cultivation of the Arab world in the hope of salvaging its interests in the Middle East and preventing the entry of the Soviets. Sudan was awarded its independence and Britain agreed to withdraw from the Canal Zone. Although British relations with Israel had always been frosty and restrictive, this was exacerbated by Ben-Gurion's refusal to allow British military bases on Israeli territory. The developing situation in the Middle East now meant an even greater distancing from Israel than previously. By early 1956, the United States decided not to supply arms to Israel.

By May 1956, $250 million worth of Soviet arms were in transit to Egypt. Heavy-duty tanks, submarines, fighter aircraft, anti-aircraft guns, bombers, torpedo boats and minesweepers were rolling out of East European factories destined for Egyptian ports. The Soviets promised 48 Ilushin-28 bombers to match Israel's 2. The Egyptians now possessed twice as many fighter aircraft as Israel.

Ben-Gurion with his supporters Moshe Dayan and Shimon Peres had always believed that a second round of fighting after 1948 was inevitable. Ben-Gurion believed that Israel should choose the time and place for such a confrontation. The arms build-up in Egypt and the refusal of both Britain and the United States to match it, however, had thrown all such calculations to the winds. In addition, the presence of Moshe Sharett, the Foreign Minister and former Premier, was seen by Ben-Gurion and his supporters as a formidable obstacle to any Israeli unilateral action. In the polarizing atmosphere of attack and counter-attack, Sharett's influence withered until he was ousted from the government. Ben-Gurion now had a free hand to proceed with an attack on Egypt before Nasser had accumulated a critical mass of weaponry which might be utilized to attack Israel.

An unlikely ally was located in the social democratic government of France's Guy Mollet. France began to supply arms on a large scale including the Dassault Mystere fighter to Israel clandestinely in the spring of 1956. France had only recognized Israel in May 1949, a year after the state's establishment. The reticence was due to opposition from the French colonial administrations in north Africa which deferred to local religious and national-ist sensitivities. Indeed the French Foreign Ministry attempted to thwart the arms deal with Israel.

The French national interest was to hang onto the remnants of its empire despite its defeat at Dien Bien Phu by the Vietnamese and its departure from Indo-China. It was determined more than ever to proclaim Algérie française and to inhibit Nasser's attempt to aid the FLN. Yet the closing of the imperial era was clear to see even as the pro-British King Hussein dismissed Glubb Pasha in March 1956.

The Kremlin's support for the Aswan Dam project was symbolic of the Soviet move to open up a new front in the Middle East. Not to be outdone, the Americans also offered to help. At this point, the British were in two minds about Nasser. In July 1956, however, both the British and the Americans with-drew their offer to fund the Aswan Dam. A week later Nasser nationalized the Suez Canal. A 100-year concession had originally been given to the Universal Suez Maritime Canal Company which was due to expire in 1968. For the British, this was the tipping point. For Eden, Nasser became the Mussolini of the 1950s. As he exclaimed so graphically, 'The Egyptian has his thumb on our windpipe'.[5]

The British now doubted Nasser's good faith in that he would impede the passage of selected shipping through the Canal. Israeli shipping had been banned for some years. Ironically the British who were then occupying the Canal Zone did nothing at all. Now they thought that this might happen to their ships as well. Nasser planned to utilize the funds gained from nationaliza-tion to finance the building of the Aswan Dam.

Some 70 million tons of oil from the Persian Gulf passed through the Suez Canal each year. Of this, 60 million tons were destined for Western Europe and represented two thirds of its oil consumption. To move this volume of oil via the Cape of Good Hope would require twice the tonnage of tankers. If Nasser attempted to interfere with the passage of oil through the canal, it would also affect the export trade to India. Britain had enough oil supplies to last six weeks. Other European countries had even smaller reserves of oil. As Eden commented to Eisenhower:

> The Canal is an international asset and facility which is vital to the free world. The maritime powers cannot afford to allow Egypt to expropriate it and to exploit it by using the revenues for her own internal purposes irrespective of the interests and the Canal and the Canal users. Apart from the Egyptians' complete lack of technical qualifications, their past behaviour gives no confidence that they can be trusted to manage it with any sense of international obligation. Nor are they capable of providing the capital which will soon be needed to widen and deepen it

so that it may be capable of handling the increased volume of traffic which it must carry in the years to come.[6]

Eden concluded by telling Eisenhower that force would be used as a last resort to bring Nasser to his senses. Even so, he had already instructed the chiefs of staff to draw up plans.

The nationalization of the Suez Canal thus brought together the different interests of Britain, France and Israel in the commonality of toppling Nasser's regime.

Ben-Gurion, Mollet and Selwyn Lloyd met at Sèvres outside Paris between 22 and 24 October 1956. Ben-Gurion viewed the coming conflict as a continuation of the war of 1948. He wanted a reordering of the Middle East. He postulated that following the destruction of the Egyptian army in Sinai, Israel would annex Gaza and other parts of Sinai to prevent future infiltration by fedayeen. Jordan would disappear with the East Bank being awarded to Hasehmite Iraq and the West Bank to Israel. Lebanon would lose its Muslim areas and become a Christian republic. Israel would annex Lebanon up to the Litani. Ben-Gurion was dissuaded from this grandiose scheme by the British and the French as well as by Dayan.

The plan which was proposed to Ben-Gurion was that the Israelis would launch the attack on the Egyptians on 29 October. The following day, the British and the French would call upon both sides to cease all acts of war and to withdraw their troops to 10 miles from the Suez Canal. The Egyptians would then be requested to accept the temporary presence of Anglo-French troops to ensure free passage of shipping until a solution would be arrived at. Israel would occupy the Gulf of Akaba and the small islands within it to ensure freedom of navigation in that area. Israel would agree not to attack Jordan. This effectively allowed Israel to occupy Sinai to within 10 miles of the canal while Egypt was forced to retreat.

Ben-Gurion clearly did not like Israel effectively doing the dirty work for the imperial powers and being branded as the aggressor. Yet he was also worried about the potential bombing of Tel Aviv by the Egyptian air force equipped with Soviet fighters.

While Israel fulfilled its obligations militarily, the British and French subterfuge was incompetent, transparent and amateurish. British military action was confused. Canberra bombers attacked Cairo military airport and accidentally also hit the civilian airport – this caused a lot of criticism in the British press.

Eden's greatest mistake was acting without informing either the Americans or the Labour opposition in Britain. It was now the turn of the United States to press its thumb on the British windpipe – and this came in the shape of US economic pressure. The British balance of payments and therefore the gold and dollar reserves had been under considerable strain anyway and needed both US and Commonwealth support. The shortfall of oil would cost $800 million a year to replace from US controlled sources.[7]

The United States felt a profound responsibility for Western interests and was determined to prevent Soviet infiltration in to the Middle East. It therefore needed to win over the Arab world. Although Israel had won a convincing military victory over the Egyptians, Nasser, through his control of the media, persuaded the Arab world that the reverse was true. He subsequently enjoyed enormous prestige in the Arab and developing worlds. Even so, the Sinai campaign stopped fedayeen raids into Israel after 1957. It marked a huge advance for Soviet national interests in the Middle East. For the British, it finally put paid to the faded dreams of a bygone age and marked the end of empire and the beginning of commonwealth. American action over Suez in halting both Britain and France in their tracks signified the new role which the United States would now play in the Middle East.

The British Labour Party and the Suez crisis

The Suez crisis coincided with the invasion of Hungary by the Soviet Union. The European Left was deeply affected by both events, but none more so than the British and French. The British Labour Party leader, Hugh Gaitskell initially did not welcome the nationalization of the Suez Canal. At the beginning of August 1956, he argued that Britain should take the matter to the United Nations and to the International Court. He said that force should be used as a last resort and only then with a UN mandate. The leader of the Labour Left, Aneurin Bevan had strong feelings about Israel and was distinctly unsympathetic to Nasser's rule. He accused Nasser of 'stirring the pot of nationalist passions' and was critical of the progressive nature of his rule:

> If a social movement elects to take the path of revolution, it must pursue it to the end and the end is a complete transformation of society, accompanied by a transference of power from the old to the new social forces. Judged by this criterion, the movement first led by General Neguib and then by Nasser has not as yet added up to a social revolution or anything like it.[8]

His comparison of 'the semi-medieval institutions of the Arab nations' with progressive Israel reflected the broad support for Israel within the Labour Party.[9]

Indeed it was far more supportive than the Conservative party – and Eden was deemed to be a placater of the Arabs. Eden's approach attracted some strange bedfellows such as the Conservative MP, Sir Thomas Moore, a one-time admirer of the British Union of Fascists and a member of the Council of Anglo-German Fellowship in the 1930s. Indeed many Conservatives made it clear to Jewish Labour MPs that the crisis would not alter the policy of aloofness towards Israel.[10] Bevan wrote two articles opposing Eden's approach to Nasser's action in which he argued that all waterways should be nationalized.[11] In Parliament, he compared Britain's ultimatum to Egypt with Hitler's to Norway.

The British Labour Party had been distinctly unimpressed by Egypt's hiring of a raft of former SS officers and Gestapo officials. Many of these were employed in the secret police and were deeply implicated in the extermination of Jews during World War II. SS Obersturmbannfuehrer Bernhard Bender was the head of the political department of the secret police and had been involved in hunting Jewish resistance fighters in occupied Poland. SS Obersturmbannfuehrer Joachim Daümling had headed the Gestapo in Dusseldorf and was believed to have used the template of the SS Reichssicherheitshauptamt – Himmler's Reich Security Main Office – to establish the Egyptian secret service. Another employee was Friedrich Karl Weseman, an SS officer who took part in the liquidation of the Warsaw ghetto and was wanted by the British as a war criminal.[12] The Egyptian secret police had also been involved in suppressing the local Communist Party which contained a disproportionate number of Jews.

There were 17 Jewish Labour MPs of whom a majority aligned themselves with the Left. Several of them made the distinction between the government's motives and those of Israel. This broadly mirrored the party's position. Yet Gaitskell himself had implicated Israel in the Suez affair. He commented that rather than act as a policeman, Eden had gone to Suez 'to help the burglar and shoot the householder'.[13]

Aneurin Bevan led the anti-war protests in London's Trafalgar Square. He argued that because Eden was wrong, this did not mean that Nasser was right. The Israelis, he believed had been provoked. In general, such protests were not specifically directed at Israel, but against the duplicity of the Eden government in its pretence that it was merely some sort of neutral referee in this affair. Moreover, Labour believed that Israel was not an equal partner in the attack on Egypt and that the country's vulnerability had been exploited by the British and the French for their own purposes.[14] In a BBC broadcast, Gaitskell commented that 'you do not separate two sides by bombing airfields and landing troops a hundred miles behind one side only.' Gaitskell accused the British action of violating the charter of the United Nations and dividing the Commonwealth. He called upon Eden to resign.[15] In Parliament, Bevan gave one of his finest speeches.

What happened? Did Marianne take John Bull to an unknown rendezvous? Did Marianne say to John Bull that there was a forest fire going to start and did John Bull then say, 'We ought to put it out' but Marianne said, 'No, let us warm our hands by it. It is a nice fire.' Did Marianne deceive John Bull – or seduce him? . . . The social furniture of modern society is so complicated and fragile that it cannot support the jackboot. We cannot run the processes of modern society by attempting to impose our will upon nations by armed force. If we have not learned that, we have learned nothing.[16]

The Kremlin did not conceal its anger. Premier Nikolai Bulganin sent Ben-Gurion a message in which he wrote that 'we are fully determined to crush the aggressors by the use of force and to restore peace in the East'. He accused Britain and France of wishing to re-establish 'the regime of colonial slavery rejected by the peoples'. Bulganin also questioned the legitimacy of Israel.

(The attack) was sowing hatred for the state of Israel among the peoples of the East such as cannot but make itself felt with regard to the future of Israel and which puts in jeopardy the very existence of Israel as a state.[17]

While there was a certain hypocrisy in Bulganin's missive as the Soviet troops were crushing the Hungarian revolt as well as pandering to the Arab world in the hope of furthering Soviet national interests, the hint of delegitimization indicated that while the overt anti-Semitism of the last years of Stalin was now deemed both ideologically embarrassing and politically counter-productive, there was still a sense that the Jews should not over-reach themselves.

The road to Bandung

Ben-Gurion had seemingly allied Israel to the colonial powers and the resulting opprobrium, albeit indirect, was a turning point in the relations between Israel and the European Left. Aneurin Bevan was clear how Eden's action was tantamount to a godsend to Nasser.

When Britain and France appeared to take upon themselves the role of champions of world rights over the Suez, they converted the crisis not into a conflict between Egyptian nationalism and the legitimate claims of world commerce, but into the old acid struggle between imperialism and the new nations.[18]

India and Yugoslavia had been advocating a bloc of non-aligned countries who would kowtow to neither East nor West since the early 1950s. This would consist of the newly independent from colonial rule and those who wished to follow an independent path, unfettered by Moscow's control. The Arab states were quite lukewarm to the idea and Nasser had to be cajoled by a visit to Cairo by Nehru before accepting.

The Bandung conference came in the wake of the debacle of the Lavon affair whereby a network of Israeli agents and Egyptian Jewish youth were discovered. Two were hanged, many were tortured and imprisoned. As a result, Prime Minister Moshe Sharett was forced to bring back Ben-Gurion into the Israeli cabinet as Minister of Defence. The gulf between them was wide and growing. Whereas Sharett looked towards a diplomatic solution and desired a policy of military self-restraint, Ben-Gurion believed in retaliation and military prowess and exuded the conviction that a second round of fighting was inevitable. Although Sharett approached Nasser via Eden for a renewal of a dialogue, fedayeen infiltrators, often abetted by Egyptian intelligence, simultaneously killed civilians in Israel. Ben-Gurion resolved to mount Operation Black Arrow to strike at Egyptian military facilities in Gaza. Although Sharett had been informed that there would be minimal casualties, it proved to be 'the bloodiest operation on the Egyptian front since 1949'.[19] Ben-Gurion even authorized a false IDF statement that Israeli forces had been attacked in Israel itself and had merely chased their assailants across the border into Gaza. Ben-Gurion's next attempt was a cabinet proposal to attack the Gaza Strip with the accompanying probability of annexing it. Sharett defeated Ben-Gurion's proposal by a vote of 9 to 5.

From the other side, Sharett's attempts to rekindle contacts were not reciprocated by Nasser. Just a few months before, Nasser had overthrown his predecessor, Neguib, banned both the Communist Party and the Muslim Brotherhood and was attempting to stabilize his regime. Espousing first a localized nationalism and then a pan-Arabism proved to be powerful tool in solidifying his rule. Ben-Gurion's belligerency assisted him. Sharett was gradually politically marooned in this polarizing situation.

The Israeli raid was viewed in the Arab world as simply being a premeditated attempt to weaken Nasser's opposition to the pro-Western Baghdad pact. It moved Nasser towards greater support for the fedayeen infiltrators and closer to the discredited Mufti of Jerusalem.[20] Moreover Nasser propagated the idea that it was really Israeli collusion with Britain which was really behind the raid. He coupled this with promoting 'positive neutralism' which allowed Egypt to align itself with the developing world and the cause of liberation from imperialism and colonialism.

The visit of Nehru to Cairo thus came at an opportune time and Nasser agreed to attend the Bandung conference in April 1955 in order to establish the non-aligned movement. The US deposing of the government of Jacoba

Arbenz in Guatemala by the United States, the insurgencies in the Philippines and Malaya, the revolt of the Viet Minh in Indo-China and the Mau-Mau uprising in Kenya all fuelled the desire of many new countries to aid those who had not achieved independence. The Israel-Palestine conflict was, however, more complicated. On the one hand, the Palestinian case was rarely heard. On the other, the Zionists had fought the British and seen them leave their country.

The campaign to exclude Israel from developing world forums had commenced even before the UN proposal of a two-state solution and before Soviet acceptance of it. In March 1947, Zionist representatives had participated in an Asian Relations Conference in New Delhi. Although an invitation was extended to both the Jews and Arabs of Palestine, the latter plus all the Arab states boycotted it as well as the Indian Muslim League. At the second conference in January 1949, Israel was not invited and consequently all the Arab states attended.[21] At the first Asian Socialist Conference in Rangoon in January 1953, the Egyptian delegate refused to sit at the same table as the Israeli delegate. In April 1954 in Colombo, the Pakistani Prime Minister forced a discussion on the Israel-Palestine conflict at the outset of the preparatory conference for the formation of a non-aligned bloc. Pakistan had always counted on Arab support in its ongoing struggle with India. The final communiqué was watered down by Nehru and U Nu of Burma.

Burma, Ceylon and India, however, all argued for Israel's attendance at the Bandung conference. Although both Vietnams agreed to come, Pakistan and Indonesia opposed any invitation to Israel, arguing that if Israel attended then the Arab states would refuse to come.[22] Nehru reluctantly concluded that an Arab boycott would sink the movement at its very birth and therefore Israel reluctantly had to be excluded. Nine Arab states eventually came to Bandung including representatives of the feudal regimes of Saudi Arabia, Libya and Yemen.

Nasser persuaded the Bandung conference of the non-aligned nations in April 1955 to condemn the Baghdad pact, but he also raised the question of Palestine and the conference duly supported the rights of 'the Arab people of Palestine' and the implementation of UN resolutions. The Grand Mufti of Jerusalem, Haj Amin al-Husseini, arrived uninvited and insisted on taking part in the political committee's deliberations. This was refused by the conference organizers on the basis that he did not represent any country. Instead the Mufti was permitted to join the Yemeni delegation and speak. He argued that Israel intended to annex all the land between the Nile and the Euphrates. This included the northern Hejaz and the holy city of Medina.[23]

Although China was still allied to Moscow at that stage, Chou en-Lai was invited to the conference wherein he compared Palestine to Formosa (Taiwan) – and argued that neither conflict could be settled peacefully unless interventions by outside forces were excluded. In the debate on Palestine, Pakistan and

China were far more vociferous in their condemnations of Israel than several Arab states.[24] Yet a memo, submitted by 'The Moslem Nations under Soviet Imperialism' was never debated. It spoke of 'oppression, torture, massacres and mass deportation in Azerbaijan, north Caucasus, Crimea, Idil-Ural and Great Turkestan'.[25] The Arab states turned a blind eye to the suppression of Islam and the banning of Arabic script in Soviet Central Asia. The internal and external policies of the Soviet Union towards the Arab world bore an uncanny resemblance to the Kremlin's approach towards Soviet Jews and Israel in 1948. Internal oppression coupled with external support. Soviet national interests were primary. Therefore 'Positive Neutralism', Nehru's defining catchphrase for the non-aligned movement was now linked to opposing Israel.[26]

Nasser's approach and the alignment of the non-aligned was a watershed in both excluding Israel and viewing the conflict in monolithic terms. It fortified Ben-Gurion and his supporters and weakened Sharett. It prepared the ground to oust Sharett from Israeli political life altogether and for both Ben-Gurion and Nasser to confront each other. The Soviets saw another opportunity to move into the Middle East and perhaps envious of its potential rival, China, began the first attempts to cultivate Nasser and the countries of the developing world. Indeed they attended the Afro-Asian People's Solidarity Conference in Cairo in January 1958. This approach continued at the first conference of independent African states in Accra in December 1958. The Egyptians wanted a condemnation of 'world political Zionism' and spoke of 'Palestine's and Algeria's martyrdom', but did not gain a great deal of support. Instead the conference urged a just solution to the Palestine question.[27]

The very presence of British and French troops in Suez allowed Nasser to portray himself as a victor despite the vanquishing of Egyptian forces and to depict the Israeli military success in Sinai as a defeat of an imperialist campaign against Egypt. Suez boosted Nasser's prestige in the Arab and Muslim worlds and within the non-aligned movement.

Israel's isolation in the international arena continued dramatically until the early 1970s when 20 African states broke off diplomatic relations after the Yom Kippur war. As the Senegalese leader, Leopold Senghor commented 'The Arabs have the numbers, space and oil. In the third world, they outweigh Israel.'[28] Yet Israel's attempts to help newly emergent African countries initially met with sympathy from pan-Africanists such as George Padmore, the former head of the Negro Bureau of the Communist International of Labour Unions as well as grudging respect from founding fathers such as Tom Mboya, Julius Nyerere, Hastings Banda and Kenneth Kaunda. Like Nehru, these figures eventually realized that the Arab world and the non-aligned bloc would serve their national interests far more than any ties to Israel. Although quiet contacts continued, identification with the rise of Palestinian nationalism and the Arab defeat in the Six Day War translated into even greater pressure on African states in such bodies as the Organisation for African Unity by the countries of the Maghreb. It also moved those countries with sizeable Muslim minorities to cement their ties with the Arab world. Other states also bowed to their national interests. Japan depended on Arab oil supplies while in Cambodia, Prince Sihanouk wanted to play a bigger role in the developing world and thereby moved his country's policy closer to the Arab line. In reaction to all this, Israel began to shelter more and more under the US umbrella and subsequently came to heavily rely on political and economic aid from Washington.

The conquest of East Jerusalem including the Haram and the al-Aqsa mosque in the Six Day War in 1967 intensified international Muslim resentment. Its annexation and 'the Judaization of Jerusalem' gave rise to the Islamic Summit Conference (Rabat September 1969) and a meeting of the Secretariat of International Islamic Organisations (Mecca, February 1971). At a meeting of the Islamic Conference of Foreign Ministers in Libya in March 1973, the participants called for the opening of offices in all Muslim states whereby volunteers could enlist for a jihad against Israel.[29] This increasingly shrill attitude towards Israel coincided with the growth of Muslim communities in Western Europe in the 1970s. It also coincided with the early activities of Palestinian Islamists such as Sheikh Ahmad Yassin.

Notes and Works Cited

1 Moshe Sharett, address to Mapai's Central Committee 3 March 1951 in Uri Bialer, *Between East and West: Israel's Foreign Policy Orientation 1948–1956* (Cambridge 1990), p. 42.

2 David Ben-Gurion, address to the Mapai Secretariat, November 1949, in Bialer, op. cit., p. 47.

3 *Jewish Herald*, 8 June 1945.

4 Gabriel Sheffer, *Moshe Sharett: Biography of a Political Moderate* (Oxford 1996), p. 499.

5 Hugh Thomas, *The Suez Affair* (London 1986), p. 38.

6 Message from Eden to Eisenhower, 27 July 1956 in *The Suez Crisis*, ed. Anthony Gorst and Lewis Johnman (London 1997), pp. 61–2.

7 Ibid., p. 133.

8 *Tribune*, 3 August 1956.

9 *Jewish Vanguard*, 29 January 1954.

10 Leon D. Epstein, *British Politics in the Suez Crisis* (London 1964), pp. 177–8.

11 *Tribune* 3, 10 August 1956.

12 'The Arabs and the Nazis: A Study in Complicity', Fact Sheet 1, Labour Friends of Israel 1970.

13 *House of Commons Debates*, 3 December 1956.

14 June Edmunds, *The Left and Israel: Party Policy, Change and Internal Democracy* (London 2000), pp. 44–5.

15 Gorst and Johnman, op. cit., p. 120.

16 Michael Foot, *Aneurin Bevan 1945–1960*, vol. 2 (London 1975), pp. 529–30.

17 Gorst and Johnman, op. cit., p. 297.

18 *Tribune*, 14 September 1956.

19 Sheffer, op. cit., p. 786.

20 Zvi Elpeleg, *The Grand Mufti, Haj Amin al-Husseini: Founder of the Palestinian National Movement* (London 1993), pp. 57–8.

21 Ran Kochan, *Israel in Third World Forums* in *Israel in the Third World* ed. Michael Curtis and Susan Aurelia Gitelson (New Brunswick 1976), pp. 248–9.

22 George McTurnan Kahin, *The Asian-African Conference* (London 1956), p. 7.

23 Kochan, op. cit., p. 253.

24 David Kimche, *The Afro-Asian Movement: Ideology and Foreign Policy of the Third World* (Jerusalem 1973), p. 67.

25 *The Muslim Nations under URSS Imperialism*, Bandung, April 1955.

26 Michael B. Oren, *The Origins of the Second Arab-Israeli War: Egypt, Israel and the Great Powers 1952–56* (London 1992), pp. 70–1.

27 Colin Legum, *Bandung, Cairo and Accra: A Report on the First Conference of Independent African States* (London 1958), p. 22.

28 *Le Monde Diplomatique*, no. 23, February 1974.

29 Kochan, op. cit., p. 265.

13

The watershed of 1956

The birth of the New Left

The events of 1956, the invasions of Suez and Hungary, gave birth to an independent anti-colonialist Left and sounded the death-knell for unthinking obedience to the Kremlin. It also marked the development of a new ideological opposition to Zionism and the start of a haemorrhaging of support for the state of Israel on the European Left.

The Movement for Colonial Freedom became an influential group in British political life – and many leading members of the British Left supported it. It wrote resolutions and framed policy for the British trade union movement. The Labour Left identified with Nasser's efforts at the Bandung conference and effectively turned a blind eye to his domestic policies. Michael Foot concluded that Israel's action in 1956 had been morally wrong and he had become thoroughly disillusioned with the Zionist experiment through the marginalization of figures such as Moshe Sharett by Ben-Gurion.[1] In the late 1950s, the British Labour Party began to make contact with socialist parties in the Arab world including the Syrian Ba'athists and to explore the Palestinian refugee problem.

The line of the CPGB was to support the USSR's pro-Arab position in 1956.[2] The British Communists accused Israel of serving the interests of imperialism and that it was solely motivated by a desire for territorial expansion.

The Suez crisis simultaneously created a debate about Soviet anti-Semitism within the party. This did not happen overnight as there had been growing concern following the Slansky trial and the Doctors' Plot. Hungary occupied a special place in the Soviet denunciation of 'Zionism'. The first mention of Zionism as an agent of US imperialism had occurred in the first show trial in Eastern Europe when Laszlo Rajk, the Foreign Minister, was tried in Budapest in 1949. The defendants were asked if they were 'Zionists'. One,

András Szalai, told the prosecution that he had participated in 'a Trotskyist Zionist movement' since 1930. Along with Rajk, he was executed.

The CPGB's National Jewish Committee, led by Chimen Abramsky and Hyman Levy, began to challenge Dutt's unquestioning belief that the Soviet Union had solved its Jewish problem. Levy wrote *Jews and the National Question* and Abramsky published it. Their eventual departure from the CPGB on the issue of Soviet anti-Semitism was part of the much wider exodus after the Soviet invasion of Hungary and the establishment of questioning periodicals such as *The New Reasoner*. Abramsky and Levy also wanted a reconsideration of Jewish nationalism. Dutt refused and was unmoved. He described Khrushchev's revelations about 'the negative cult of the individual' as 'spots on the sun'.[3] His acerbic review of Levy's book was entitled *An Anti-Marxist Book on the Jewish Question.*[4]

1956 was a year when many Communists discovered that its gods were in fact idols. Despite Khrushchev's revelations about Stalin, the Kremlin found Imre Nagy's views in Hungary too much to bear – reinstating the multi-party system and withdrawal from the Warsaw Pact were both heretical and against Soviet state interests. 1956 also bore witness to the return of the ragged survivors of Stalin's Gulag after decades of incarceration and maltreatment. Khrushchev even visited Tito in an attempt to patch up the Moscow-Belgrade rift. Suddenly the CPGB withdrew their approval for James Klugmann's *From Trotsky to Tito* as required reading for members.

The leadership of Communist parties in Europe were deeply troubled, but they had invested their political lives and circumvented too many inconvenient truths to leave now. British Communist leaders, for example, received no answers about its members who had disappeared in the USSR. They inquired about Rose Cohen who had married the Comintern's representative in the United Kingdom in the 1920s and returned with him to Moscow. She had actually been shot in November 1938. The missing *Daily Worker* correspondent in post-war Eastern Europe, Edith Bone, was more fortunate – she spent seven years in prison and was released after Stalin's death. While the leadership of the British party was struck dumb by its lies and compromises, the rank and file spoke with their feet. The Soviet invasion of Hungary persuaded nearly a quarter of the party's membership to depart including many industrial workers and trade union officials. 400,000 left the Italian party. It marked the end for wall-to-wall Stalinism. It was both a fragmentation and a reinvention of the Marxist Left in Europe.

The events of 1956 also symbolized the bankruptcy of social democracy to many a European socialist. Guy Mollet, one of the architects of the Suez fiasco was a social democrat – and social democrats in Europe had given no real lead on the problems of colonialism. For the adherents of Communism and its fellow travellers, the convoluted explanations which were offered for the invasion of Hungary, was an ideological and moral summersault too far. This sense of disillusionment with the expounders and justifiers of both Suez and Hungary created a third space for a New Left.

In Britain, the upsurge and disillusionment of 1956 manifested itself in the emergence of two journals, *Universities and Left Review* and *The New Reasoner*. The latter was published by two party intellectuals, E. P. Thompson and John Saville, as an independent publication outside the party in mid-July 1956. The publication proclaimed that it would embellish 'a rebirth of social-ist principles ensuring that dogmatic attitudes and theoretical inertia do not return'.[5] The party leadership moved quickly to try and shut down *The New Reasoner*. It finally suspended Thompson and Saville when they called upon the CPGB to dissociate itself from the Soviet intervention in Hungary.[6] These periodicals provided a home for the ideologically shell shocked.

During the 1950s, Europe began to emerge from austerity of the immediate post-war years. This was also marked by a deepening generational conflict. The Old Left in Britain which defined itself by resistance to Nazism and the culture of class warfare believed that nothing had really changed since 1945. The same certainties were in place. The succeeding generation, however, was not so sure. It argued that post-war capitalism was actually profoundly different from what had gone before and that this new situation required a new analysis. In particular, the rise of consumerism had affected cultural atti-tudes which the Left had to recognize. Thus, E. P. Thompson and Raphael Samuel debated Stuart Hall's article *A Sense of Classlessness*.[7]

The two periodicals merged to form *New Left Review* in 1959 under Stuart Hall's editorship and modelled the offspring on Sartre's *Les Temps modernes*. Subsequently under Perry Anderson's editorship, there was an emphasis on 'continental Marxism' and the work of Gramsci. Yet some had doubts about the merger of the two periodicals and this led to yet another publication.[8] Together with Thompson and Saville, Ralph Miliband, a disciple of Harold Laski and a Jewish refugee who had fled to Britain from Belgium in 1940, began to edit the *Socialist Register* in the early 1960s.

Miliband argued that 'the deepening and the formal institutionalisation of the split between Communism and Social Democrats' left little room for free think-ing and intellectual discourse within the Marxist tradition.[9] Trotsky's writings were now being re-read. Rosa Luxemburg's ideas were now being rediscov-ered. Marxism was also being distanced from Marxism-Leninism. Indeed one of the founders of the *Universities and Left Review*, Charles Taylor, considered Leninism to be 'one of the great political disasters of the twentieth century'.[10]

The first issue of *Socialist Register* contained an appraisal of Egyptian Marxism and noted that the European Left was still seeking 'a way out of its confusion' regarding 'Arab socialism'.[11] After all, Nasser, Qassem and Ben Bella had suppressed their Communist parties. Yet the USSR had awarded Nasser the title of 'Hero of the Soviet Union'.

This first New Left was keen to see Britain's secession from the superpower bloc and for it to co-exist with the non-aligned countries of the developing world. On the one hand, it viewed support for orthodox Communism as being synonymous with unquestioning solidarity with the USSR. On the other, support for the Atlanticist strain of social democracy led to alignment with American policy. The British Labour Party was divided between the Atlanticists who looked to Washington and the 'positive neutralists' who admired Nehru, Tito and Nasser.

Yet this desire to leave behind the ideological straitjacket that had incarcerated many an inquisitive mind was not shared by all who emerged from the traumatic soul-searching of 1956. Failed revolutionaries such as Trotsky, Luxemburg and Gramsci were reclaimed. They were not only viewed as martyrs to the cause of revolution, but unheeded prophets who could have guided it into different channels.

The Trotskyist Revolutionary Communist Party in Britain had split into several factions in 1950. Independent Marxist thinkers such as Gerry Healy, Tony Cliff and Ted Grant established their own groups – and their own ideological certainty. In addition, the International Marxist Group (IMG) officially represented the Fourth International in Britain. IMG's approach of 'from the periphery to the centre' placed great faith in revolutionary endeavour in the developing world. It was able to successfully develop single issue campaigns such as the Vietnam Solidarity Campaign. In contrast, despite the recruiting slogan 'From Palestine to Vietnam: One Enemy! One Fight!',[12] a similar attempt to initiate a Palestine Solidarity Campaign at the end of the 1960s failed abysmally.[13]

Tony Cliff was the moving force behind the *Socialist Review* in the 1950s and he wrote widely about Stalin and the USSR. He denounced the Soviet Union as a 'state capitalist' regime while remaining loyal to the tenets of Leninism whereas the Fourth International believed in the official definition of a degenerated workers' state. For Cliff, there was no possibility that the Stalinists could form workers' states. Yet there was virtually no mention of the use of 'Zionism' in the show trials or that many of the defendants were Jews. In February 1962, a sympathetic article about the plight of Soviet Jews appeared in the periodical under the pseudonym of M. Ben-Reuben. No mention was made in it of Zionism or Israel.[14]

Healy, more than his Trotskyist rivals, capitalized on the unease felt over Hungary and Suez. His Socialist Labour League (SLL) benefitted from defections from the CPGB and the Marxist group of the Labour League of Youth. The SLL was known even on the far Left in Britain for its sectarianism. Healy was a highly controversial leader with authoritarian beliefs – in the 1930s he had been an avid Stalinist, known for his assaults on Trotskyists.

Both Healy and Cliff cultivated people in the theatre and the arts. Vanessa and Corin Redgrave joined Healy while Cliff made headway among students and youth after 1968. Cliff recruited the writer and polemicist Christopher Hitchens and the poet James Fenton. He also implemented a more central-ized Leninist approach which resulted in several splits.

Such groups were prone to denunciations, defections and schisms. All attempted entryism into the Labour Party at one time – with Ted Grant's Militant Tendency exhibiting the deepest ideological belief in such an approach. This was a legacy from the earliest days of Trotskyism in the 1930s when it was realized that the early groups would not mushroom into mass parties. All eventually broke with the Labour Party when the leadership judged the time to be right – and formed their own parties. Cliff's Labour Socialists became the International Socialists and then the Socialist Workers' Party. The number of IS branches increased dra-matically in the early 1970s and the circulation of its publication, *Socialist Worker* increased by 70% in 1972 to 28,000.[15] The paper also attacked Zionism in conspir-atorial language. Healy transformed his Socialist Labour League into the Workers' Revolutionary Party. Its publications compared Israel to Nazi Germany and during the invasion of Lebanon in 1982 accused the Israelis of using poisonous gas 'such as the ones used by the Nazis against the Jewish people'.[16]

Militant lasted until 1991 before it became the Socialist Party a few years later. All developed ties with sister groups in Europe. Militant had equivalents in Spain, France, Ireland, Greece, Sweden, West Germany and Belgium.[17]

The first New Left, emerging out of the intellectual openness of the lecture halls of Oxford in the 1950s found their approach, difficult and disconcerting.

> This (first New Left) was in sharp contrast to the 'hard' Left and Trotskyist sects, who by and large adopted a cynical but classically sectarian practice towards CND. They treated the peace movement as a 'soft' recruiting ground: to them, it was a movement dominated by misguided moral and religious enthusiasts, a few of whom could, however, be picked off for a more 'serious' enterprise and parachuted into the nitty-gritty of 'real politics' somewhere else. In this conception, 'real politics' is so often not where everybody else is, but always 'somewhere else'.[18]

In addition, the Old Left of the pre-war years was growing more affluent by the 1960s and found itself distinctly at odds with the New Left. There now existed a different culture and a different mentality. A new generation was defining itself outside the political gridlines, laid down by the victory of 1945. By 1968, the year of student revolt, the political agenda was not sim-ply one of class warfare and economic betterment, but of additional issues such as sexuality, feminism, peace, ecology, racism, community politics, music – and 'the politics of the personal'.[19] The advocacy of such issues was often defined by direct action and a broad antagonism towards parliamentary politics. In Europe, social democratic, socialist and Communist parties gradually began to absorb these new ideas and themes.

In addition, there were anti-colonial struggles in the Belgian Congo, Portuguese Africa, Rhodesia and South Africa. The fight for national liberation in the Arab world was personified by the struggle of the FLN in Algeria against France. The cause of decolonization and anti-imperialism loomed large. The struggle of the FLN for Algerian independence was certainly the cause célèbre in France. Ben Bella, later President of Algeria, had also spoken of liberating Palestine from foreigners. All this struck a deep chord within the European Left and it had a profound effect on its previous identification with socialist Zionism.

In Israel, it had initiated an eventual split in the Communist Party when Shmuel Mikunis, one of the party leaders, responded to Ben Bella in August 1964. He condemned the contamination of the anti-imperialist movement by 'the bacteria of Arab chauvinism'. The Arabic publication of the party, *al-Ittihad*, refused to publish it.

The double legacy

For non-Jews on the French Left of the pre-war generation, the question of Israel became more and more perplexing. Jean-Paul Sartre supported the Algerian struggle and was a proponent of Nasser's programme for 'Arab socialism'. He also criticized Britain and France over Suez but like many members of the French Left, he was the bearer of a 'double legacy'. He was scarred by the memory of what had happened to the Jews in France, following the defeat in 1940 – the discrimination, the betrayals, the deportations, the exterminations. He recognized the struggle of the Jews in 1947 in Palestine and argued that, following the withdrawal of British troops, the United Nations should have armed the Jews. He feared another massacre of the Jews by 'Arab mercenaries awaiting the departure of the English'.[20] In 1949, he commented that the establishment of the state of Israel was one of the few events 'that allows us to preserve hope'.[21] Yet he was silent about Israel's collusion with the imperial powers in the Suez affair. His solidarity with the Jews stemmed from the time of the Nazi occupation. His solidarity with the Arabs grew out of the Algerian War.

This 'double legacy' of the Algerian struggle and fidelity to Israel was the predicament of the entire French Left. Sartre argued that the Left was unable to take a position between right and right and that it was up to the Jews and the Arabs to resolve this seemingly intractable situation through discussion. Sartre rationally therefore tried to create a space for a dialogue between the Arab Left and the Israeli Left. As an intellectuel engageé, Sartre's neutrality was not always appreciated. As he commented in 1976:

> I will never abandon this constantly threatened country whose existence ought not to be put into question . . . I know that my stance earns me the enmity of certain Arabs who cannot understand that one is able to be at the same time for Israel and for them.[22]

Yet Sartre was of a generation that had experienced the past. The mindset of the succeeding generation in France did not have that experience. Their ideological agenda was forged through opposition to 'Algerie Française' and the struggle of the NLF against the Americans in Vietnam. Socialist advocates for Israel such as Leon Blum were long dead. The mentors of the post-war generation were Frantz Fanon and Regis Debray. Their icons were Che Guevara and Ho Chi Minh.

Yet there were exceptions. Michel Foucault's pro-Israel stance caused a deep rift with his close friend, Gilles Deleuze.[23]

Even so, Frantz Fanon's *The Wretched of the Earth* made a tremendous impact on the generation of the 1960s with its assault on the evils of colonialism. Its first chapter, 'Concerning Violence' commenced:

> National liberation, national renaissance, the restoration of nationhood to the people, commonwealth: whatever may be the headings used or the new formulas introduced, decolonisation is always a violent phenomenon.[24]

Fanon was contemptuous of the French Left and the PCF in particular. The latter had supported the liberation struggle in Indo-China, primarily because the Viet Minh were Communists. In the case of Algeria, the PCF called for peace, but not independence. It was believed that this was partly due to the PCF's pandering to the white working class's disdain for Arab workers in France and that there were often family ties to the colons.[25] Fanon in particular had close relationships to individual Jews in Algeria and he was well aware of the FLN's appeal to Algerian Jews in November 1956 – and the non-committal response of a 'wait and see' attitude despite the anti-Semitism of the colons.[26]

The post-war generation of the European Left also rejected their parents' cultural and political values in a search for self-definition. In part, this search included evaluating the significance of the rise of Israel in 1948. Their commitment to repairing the world was viewed through the prism of decolonization and anti-imperialism. The situation of the Arab world – and France's colonial role in it – was both closer in time and of more immediate importance to the succeeding generation than the resistance of the Maquis and the deportation of the Jews.

As the New Left in France had neither experienced the assault on the Jews during the Nazi occupation nor witnessed the rise of the state of Israel in 1948, many adherents became politically desensitized on issues about Jews and Israel. This became more accentuated with the rise of Palestinian nationalism in the 1960s and when it became a cause for identification by sections of the Left.

The New Left could immediately identify attacks on Jews if they came from the Right. When the right wing press made comments that Daniel Cohn-Bendit, one of the leaders of the student revolt in 1968, was both a Jew and a German, there was a student demonstration around the statement that 'Nous sommes tous des juifs allemands'. When the Left began proposing that the veteran socialist, Mèndes-France should replace De Gaulle, the right wing cry was 'Mèndes Jerusalem'. When De Gaulle stopped the Left in its tracks in 1968 and turned the political tide, the Right came onto the streets to support him, chanting the slogan, 'Cohn-Bendit à Dachau'. It seemed that the Vichy mentality had not been entirely abandoned, but merely been put into abeyance.

Yet whereas the Left reacted instinctively to right wing anti-Semitism, it was reticent to recognize it when it emerged from its own ranks – and especially if such an incident involved any mention of Israel. There was little comment about attacks on the remnant of Jewish communities in Arab states before, during and after the Six Day War. Reports in the press noted that Jews had been thrown from rooftops and balconies in Tripoli[27] and that 600 Jews had been arrested in Egypt.[28] In Aden, British troops intervened to save and evacuate the Jewish community – a community that had existed for almost two millennia. Boumedienne's nationalist regime in Algeria did little to prevent discrimination against Jews and attacks on synagogues. Moreover, Fanon's stature was diminished and his contribution marginalized. As neither an Arab nor a Muslim and not even a believer, he was accused of underestimating the power of Islam.[29]

The Six Day War and the intellectuals

Israel's victory in the Six Day War over Nasser's Egypt in June 1967 was particularly hard to digest in France. There were just too many stereotypes to absorb and it confused the French Left. On the eve of the Six Day War, amidst talk of another massacre of the Jews – the imagery was that of the emaciated Jew in the striped pyjamas and his post-war liberated successor, the socialist kibbutznik who made the desert bloom. During the war, the jackbooted Jewish conqueror emerged, aided and abetted by a coordinated Jewish lobby which was centrally pulling the political strings in a multitude of countries. Which image was correct? Was Nasser a third world liberation hero, struggling to liberate his people from the colonialist past or a expansionist reactionary nationalist who had crushed his progressive rivals? Moreover, the United States strongly supported Israel but was deemed responsible for waging war in Vietnam. Added to all this was a growing sense of guilt over colonization and the war in Algeria. There was a belief that even if some aspects of liberation movements were reactionary, they generally belonged to the movement of progressive anti-imperialism. *L'Humanité* selected the images which accorded with the PCF's policy in supporting De Gaulle's pro-Arab stance in 1967 and thereby attempted to connect Israelis with Nazis and with the war in Vietnam. The Six Day War whipped up all these conflicting images into an emotional whirlwind. Wartime anti-Nazism against contemporary anti-colonialism.

Sartre challenged the dejudaization of the Israeli Jews and the separation from their Diaspora counterparts. The Six Day War deeply affected many assimilated Jews who had distanced themselves from Jewishness. The writer and filmmaker, Claude Lanzmann who strongly opposed the Algerian war commented: 'without Israel I feel naked and vulnerable'.[30]

The Cubans referred to Israel as 'the spearhead of Yankee imperialism' and treated the Middle East crisis as merely another instance of American irresponsibility as in Vietnam and Latin America.[31] While this impressed many, other French intellectuals in 1967 did not subscribe to the anti-colonialist narrative of the generation of Algeria. Sartre signed a manifesto with other French intellectuals, which was published in *Le Monde* on 1 June 1967. This clearly opposed the view that Israel was the aggressor and an agent of US imperialism. It disputed the view that Arab nationalists were also socialists and solely wanted peace. It pointed out that Israel was the only state whose right to exist had been put in question. In response to this initiative, Sartre's books were subsequently censured in some Arab states. Frantz Fanon's widow asked the publisher, Maspero, to withdraw Sartre's introduction to *The Wretched of the Earth*. Yet even *L'Humanité* condemned the Algerian Minister of Justice when he argued before a symposium of Arab jurists that 'Israel must be liquidated as a nation'.[32]

The situation was even more complex for Jewish Marxists who opposed Zionism. In London, the historian, Isaac Deutscher, a Polish ilui (a child prodigy learned in Jewish religious texts) from Chrzanów chided Sartre for effectively allowing his judgement to be clouded by 'emotions and memories, however deep or haunting. We should not allow even invocations of Auschwitz to blackmail us into supporting the wrong cause'. Deutscher whose family had perished in the Shoah was dismissive of 'the confusion on the Left'. He was particularly disparaging about Jews on the Labour Left in Great Britain. 'Scratch a Jewish left-winger and you find only a Zionist'. In an interview,[33] given just a few weeks after the Six Day War, he argued that Israel had played up fears of another final solution in the run-up to the war and believed that the Arabs in reality were actually incapable of any victory on the battle-field because of their military weakness. He was particularly scathing of 'the frenzy of belligerence, arrogance and fanaticism' in the aftermath of victory. He decried the scenes of joyous rabbis celebrating the taking of the Western Wall in Jerusalem. For him, it conjured up the imagery of a past life which he had left far behind. He felt 'the ghosts of Talmudic obscurantism' tapping him on the shoulder. There was therefore a clear difference between the Jewish Marxist historian Deutscher and the non-Jewish existentialist phi-losopher Sartre in the manner in which they interpreted the events of June 1967 in terms of the recent traumatic past – a past which had impinged on both their lives.

Deutscher's analysis hinged on the belief that the United States had changed from an anti-colonialist power during the rise of Israel in 1948 and during the Suez campaign in 1956 – and its subsequent desire to penetrate Africa and Asia. Deutscher offered the examples of the overthrow of Nkrumah in Ghana, the mass killing of Indonesian Communists and others – real and imaginary – as indications of US determination not to permit the vacuum, created by the withdrawal of the old imperial powers from their colonies, to be filled by the Soviet Union. Israel had become merely a tool in the cold war between the superpowers and this had inculcated reactionary trends in Israel and exacerbated the Arab-Jewish conflict. Israelis had become 'protégés of neo-colonialism'. Moshe Dayan – to whom he attributed Israel's victory – was simply 'a kind of Marshal Ky' (of South Vietnam) of the Middle East.

Like India and China, Israel, he believed, had passed through its revolu-tionary phase towards 'exclusiveness, national egoism and racism' and now appeared as the Prussia of the Middle East.

Yet Deutscher tempered such commentary with criticism of the Arab states and he berated them for their 'verbal excesses' and refusal to rec-ognize Israel. He believed that Arab workers should have appealed over the heads of the government leaders to Israeli workers and kibbutzniks. He argued for a different Israel and not for its abolition. Indeed he had once commented in 1954 that if he had urged European Jews to go to Palestine in the inter-war years, then 'I might have helped to save some of the lives that were later extinguished in Hitler's gas chambers'.[34] Moreover there was neither comment about the existence of a Palestinian people nor the rise of the PLO.

Like Deutscher, the Belgian Marxist, Marcel Liebman reacted strongly to the Six Day War. During the Nazi occupation of Belgium, an elder brother had been deported to Auschwitz and never returned. He was hidden in Catholic institutions for the duration of the war. His experience led him to embracing Judaism with fervour and a desire to become a rabbi. This proved to be a temporary phase. He ditched this and instead embraced Marxism, joining the Parti Socialiste Belge. Although his parents were sympathetic to the Zionist experiment in Palestine, he became a strong opponent of Zionism during the Algerian struggle and feared that Israeli action would fortify the radical forces in the Arab world. He hoped in vain for a declaration of support for the FLN from Algerian Jewry.[35] Yet as Albert Memmi explained in his *The Colonizer and the Colonized*, the situation was complicated.

> Their (the Jews of north Africa) constant and very justifiable ambition is to escape from their colonised condition, an additional burden in an already oppressive status. To that end, they endeavour to resemble the coloniser in the frank hope that he may cease to consider them different from him. Hence their efforts to forget the past, to change collective habits and their enthusiastic adoption of western language, culture and customs.[36]

Memmi, a Tunisian Jew, wrote that the Jews of north Africa – and especially in Algeria – lived in 'painful and constant ambiguity'. The Jews of Algeria feared both the French colons and the Arab nationalists – and this placed the communal view in abeyance. Between 1950 and 1970, 220,000 Jews migrated to France from north Africa. This reality disappointed Liebman in Brussels.

Liebman's core belief was that Jews should not separate themselves. Israel's victory during the Six Day War thus renewed his view that the Jews of Israel should renounce Zionism and integrate into the Arab Middle East. He therefore opposed 'the Jewish character of the Jewish state'. He spoke of 'a ghetto-nation which regards itself as ethnically, socially and politically differ-ent' which was 'an alien element in the region'.[37] He believed that the identi-fication of Diaspora Jews with Israel would justify the classical assertion of double loyalty by anti-Semites. If the Jews of Israel would only de-Zionize and stretch out their hand to their Arab brothers, they would be heartily welcomed into the Middle East.

Liebman was an early exponent of Palestinian nationalism on the European Left and the absolutist interpretation of the right of return. He defended the PLO's advocacy of 'a democratic and secular Palestine' to replace the state of Israel. He believed that the PLO should cultivate the Jews of Israel and bring them around to its way of thinking and supported 'the superiority of the Palestinian solution over the Zionist one'. Israel, he argued, would find their support in 'circles possessed of enormous financial resources' which was influential in the Western media. The Palestinians, by contrast, would find their support among left wing youth for a progressive bi-national Palestine.

> In this connection, it is essential to stress that all the Palestinian organisations have turned their backs on that earlier nihilism which, basing itself on a single consideration, the unjust origin of Israel, formerly refused to contemplate the possibility of co-existing with the Jews, now settled in Israel. Today, these organisations openly acknowledge that the positions they formerly defended and the language they used were symptoms of their political immaturity. Now they call upon the Jews of Israel to agree to co-operate in building a new state in which they would not have to suffer any discrimination but in which also they would enjoy no privileges.[38]

This advocacy of a one-state solution was in contrast to the outlook of one of the leaders of the Israeli Communist Party, Moshe Sneh. He made a distinction between anti-imperialism and pan-Arabism – and pointed out that Arab proclamations of equality with other groups, Armenians, Assyrians, Kurds, were not always realized. His colleague, Shmuel Mikunis was scathing about the apparent Arab blueprint to end Israel's existence, suggesting that the old cry of the European fascists, 'Judeo-Bolshevism', had been updated to one of 'Judeo-Colonialism'.

> We have been repeatedly told not to pay heed to the threats against Israel. It was explained to us, over and over again, that these were mere words, which would disappear 'with time'. . . we had been preached at to be lenient with the Arab anti-imperialists, at least, notwithstanding their warmongering because they were not only progressive but also on friendly terms with the Soviet Union . . . And even more: because of – what is called 'the general interests of peace and socialism'.[39]

Liebman was accused of utopianism and wishful thinking. Unlike his close friend and colleague, the Marxist academic, Ralph Miliband, he regarded Arab nationalist regimes as progressive. He attacked suggestions that the PLO really wanted an Arab Palestine and that Arafat's pitch to the New Left in Europe was little more than a public relations exercise.

The Miliband-Liebman correspondence

There was a remarkable exchange of letters between Miliband and Liebman during the period of the Six Day War in June 1967. They were good friends, came from similar Polish-Jewish families and examined contemporary events from a Marxist perspective. Yet while they agreed on most issues, there were profound differences on the question of Israel, especially on the eve of the war. Miliband who rarely touched on the Middle East conflict argued for Israel's right to exist whereas Liebman espoused Arab nationalism with a passion. The correspondence was both civilized and acrimonious.

Miliband differed profoundly with Liebman on the part of the European Left's willingness to accept 'the rhetoric of Arab socialism' emanating from Cairo. Nasser's regime was, he pointed out, 'a semi-military, bureaucratic dictatorship' and the independent Egyptian Left had been brutally suppressed by it – 'often with the help of former Gestapo officials'.[40]

Miliband argued that the European Left should be more discerning. While it should undoubtedly support Nasser's moves against imperialism and colonialism, some of his undertakings against Israel left much to be desired. Liebman in turn argued that while Israel did not prevent the economic and socialist development of the Arab world, it did in essence fetter it and inhibit it. Miliband did not agree:

> The sad thing is that this sterling Left is incapable of distinguishing anything from anything, and reacts with a truly Pavlovian predictability to the slogans used to make it drool on cue. I repeat, someone would have to demonstrate very clearly to me just how Israel is a break on the Arab socialist revolution, or rather hinders it, in order to justify the avowed intention of Nasser etc to put an end to the state itself. I don't believe that there is any way to demonstrate this.[41]

Miliband accused Arab regimes of utilizing nationalist feeling towards Israel not as a means of moving towards socialism, but for deflecting attention away from other issues. 'If Israel did not exist, they would have to invent it' he wrote. Israel was the only country where a certain degree of freedom of expression existed in the Middle East – there was not one, but two Communist parties. While some Israelis protest against discrimination against Arabs, how many Arab protests, he asked, have there been against persecution of Jews in the Arab world?

> It is no duty of socialists to support pseudo-socialist revolutions unconditionally; they should do it in a nuanced way. But the rottenness of official Marxism in our

_time makes this kind of attitude impossible, even leaving aside the role of state interests.[42]

Liebman replied that Israel was an American pawn – and Miliband, to some extent, agreed. It therefore followed that Israel would therefore do everything in its power to prevent revolution in the Middle East. Liebman contended that Israel's view stemmed from innate reactionary attitudes and allegiance to the US. Israel helped imperialism whenever the opportunity arose.

Miliband responded by pointing to Liebman's inclination 'to neglect anything that might extenuate Israel's faults and crimes or even explain them'.

> Once the state of Israel was established, over the Arab world's opposition, the idea that they shouldn't have gone looking for alliances etc is rather abstract. It is in fact Israel's great historic misfortune, which may yet cost it its existence, that no alliances were available to it outside the imperialist camp. Even then, they should have looked for another way out. But we are dealing with people who aren't socialists, or not the right kind.[43]

Miliband saw the fundamental issue on the eve of the Six Day War as one of life and death for Israel. Socialists, he argued, should not support the elimination of the state and all its citizens. Liebman, to some extent, concurred and pointed out that Arab socialists had ended up by challenging the very existence of Israel. He believed that this was because the state of Israel was not simply viewed as a foreign implant on Arab soil, but it constituted 'the very symbol of their humiliation and furthermore an auxiliary of imperialism and therefore a danger'.

Yet Liebman queried the Arabs' claim that the state of Israel must be destroyed. He asked what was actually meant by this and argued that they had a responsibility to clarify such commentary.

> Do they mean physical destruction; does 'state' here mean 'nation'?

> Do they mean destroying the Israeli political entity as it exists today and replacing it with a different set-up: for example, transforming it into a federative component of a Middle Eastern federation, in which the Israeli nation would take part?

> Do they mean creating a Palestinian state in which Jews would be nothing more than citizens with individual rights, without national representation? (But in that case there would be two million Jews and one million Arabs in this state, after the necessary and legitimate return of the refugees.)

> Do they mean creating a Palestinian state from which the Jews would be expelled?[44]

Liebman was certainly more emotional in his approach and his correspondence was peppered with assaults on local Jews and Israelis per se. Miliband was also not spared this. He accused Miliband of reacting 'as a European and a Jew rather than as a socialist'.

Both Miliband and Liebman understood the brutality of the Nazi occupation of Belgium. Yet Liebman pointed out that the Arab experience in World War II was not the Jewish one. The Arabs, therefore, had 'the right to give a low priority to this (Auschwitz) factor which is so foreign to their own direct or indirect experience'.

Liebman railed against support on the European Left by figures such as Sartre.

> (Why) does the fate of the Jews weigh so on Europeans' consciences, didn't they take on the task of succouring and hosting the survivors themselves? Did all those Jewish survivors want to go to Palestine, by the way? No matter – to Palestine they went.[45]

Many Europeans, Liebman argued, believed that Israel was a European beachhead and a bastion of civilization surrounded by 'a sterile landscape and a dark continent'. Miliband was much more sanguine about the Jewish presence in Palestine.

> What right do the Jews have to be in Palestine? . . . Their right stems from the fact that the world is what it is, from Hitler's persecutions etc etc. All this doesn't amount to an answer. But the fact is there.[46]

Miliband went further. The old ideas about Zionism were now out of date with the establishment of the state of Israel – 'this makes what the great thinkers of the Comintern said of little relevance'.

A Jewish New Left?

Within a few weeks of the end of the war, a few prominent Jews such as Britain's Chief Rabbi, Immanuel Jakobovits[47] and the academic, Max Beloff,[48] argued that the conquered territories should be given up. Most Diaspora Jewish organizations preferred to take their cue from the approach of the Israeli government. This was certainly unacceptable to many young Jews as well as to the Jewish intelligentsia. Such events and the student revolt in France initiated a Jewish New Left whose agenda was to democratize local Jewish communities, revitalize Zionism and recognize the emerging Palestinian national movement as a partner for peace based on the partition of the land. The 'Critical Zionists' of Holland and their journal *Kova Tembel*, the British Israel-Palestine Socialist Action Group, the German Borokhovbund, and the pan-European Comité Israël-Palestine were indicative of the new thinking. Many became involved in Jewish student politics and injected a new radicalism such that they found themselves in a majority at the World Union of Jewish Students' conference in Arad, Israel in July 1970. Their resolution stated:

> Zionism is the national and, also by virtual of its territorialist aspect, the social liberation and emancipation movement of the Jewish people; it is to be realized in Israel. This goal can only be realized if the national rights of the Palestinian Arabs are considered so that they may be recognized to be a consequence of Zionist ideology.[49]

A few months later a seminar was organized by the Comité Israël-Palestine at Choisy-le-Roi, near Paris which attracted such diverse bodies as the Young Liberals (UK), Theorie und Praxis (Austria), Siah (Israel), Matzpen (Israel) and the Organisation des Jeunes Juifs Révolutionnaires (France). This meeting brought together representatives of the Fourth International with members of the World Union of Jewish Students.[50] The Democratic Front for the Liberation of Palestine sent observers. There was a broad criticism of Fatah with its belief that the Jews were solely defined by religion and its advocacy of a democratic secular state. The resolutions condemned the Israel government's refusal to recognize the existence of a Palestinian people and called upon all Palestinian organizations 'to recognise the right of the Israeli nation to self-determination'.

Sartre subsequently supported this initiative. He commented that he rejected the idea of one side as good and the other as evil and argued that the task of intellectuals was to reproach such thinking.

This third way anticipated the emergence of peace camps in both Israel and Palestine. While there were severe disagreements between Zionists and anti-Zionists, for many young Jews, it was a unique occurrence in the politics of the Jewish Diaspora. It aligned many Jewish students with the embryonic Israeli peace camp and often earned them the opprobrium of their elders and opponents. It also issued into existence a group of people that had to struggle on two fronts – against the ultra-Zionism of the Israeli Right which propelled the settlement drive on the West Bank and against the anti-Zionism of some sections of the European New Left which wished to delegitimize and then erase a state with a Jewish majority in the Arab Middle East.

Such ideas began to influence social democratic parties in Europe particularly in the 1970s. The settlement drive on the West Bank and Gaza by the Israelis after 1968 was a reflection of the political immobility of the Labour Alignment which included both the dovish Mapam and the hawkish Rafi. It pitted liberals such as Abba Eban and Pinchas Sapir against military heroes of the Right such as Moshe Dayan. Golda Meir's guiding belief was to hold this pantomime horse of ill-suited allies together – and in so doing, allowed the zealous advocates of colonizing the newly conquered territories to squeeze into the political interstices and establish new settlements. The question of recognizing the emerging existence of a Palestinian people was readily accepted by the younger generation of Labour activists and writers such as Amos Oz,[51] but hotly resisted by the old guard. This was personified by the Prime Minister, Golda Meir who proclaimed that there was no such thing as a Palestinian people.[52]

Notes and Works Cited

1 Edmunds, op. cit., p. 61.

2 *Daily Worker*, 31 July 1956.

3 John Callaghan, *Socialism in Britain* (Oxford 1990), pp. 186–7.

4 Rajani Palme Dutt, *World News*, 8 March 1958.

5 *The New Reasoner*, no. 1, July 1956.

6 *The New Reasoner*, no. 3, November 1956.

7 *Universities and Left Review*, no. 5, Autumn 1958.

8 Ralph Miliband, 'Thirty Years of Socialist Register', *Socialist Register*, 1994.

9 Ralph Miliband, 'Socialism and the Myth of the Golden Past', *Socialist Register*, 1964.

10 Charles Taylor, 'Marxism and Socialist Humanism', in *Out of Apathy: Voices of the New Left 30 Years On*, ed. *Oxford University Socialist Discussion Group* (London 1989), p. 66.

11 Anouar Abdel-Malik, 'Nasserism and Socialism', *Socialist Register*, 1964.

12 *Socialist Worker*, 15 May 1969.

13 *Black Dwarf*, 26 November 1969.

14 M. Ben Reuben, 'Gagarin and the Jewish Problem', *A Socialist Review* (London 1965), pp. 249–53.

15 Jim Higgins, *More Years for the Locust* (Chapter 11) www.marxists.org/archive/higgins/1997/locust

16 Ben Cohen, 'A Discourse of Delegitimisation: The British Left and the Jews', Institute for Jewish Policy Research, http://www.axt.org.uk/HateMusic/ essay_cohen_delegitimisation.htm

17 John Callaghan, *The Far Left in British Politics* (Oxford 1987), p. 199.

18 Stuart Hall, 'The "First" New Left', in *Out of Apathy: Voices of the New Left 30 Years On*, ed. Oxford University Socialist Discussion Group (London 1989), p. 32.

19 Eley, op. cit., p. 338.

20 Jonathan Judaken, *Jean-Paul Sartre and the Jewish Question: Anti-anti-Semitism and the Politics of the French Intellectual* (Nebraska 2006), pp. 187–8.

21 Jean-Paul Sartre, *Hillel*, no. 7, June 1949 in www.marxists.or p.41.g.reference/ archive/sartre/1949/israel.htm

22 Jean-Paul Sartre, *La Terre Retrouvée* 49, no. 4, November 1976 in Judaken p. 184.

23 Edward Said, *London Review of Books*, August 2000.

24 Frantz Fanon, *The Wretched of the Earth* (London 1967), p. 27.

25 David Caute, *Fanon* (London 1970), p. 48.

26 Norman A. Stillman, *The Jews of Arab Lands in Modern Times* (New York 1991), pp. 537–41.

27 *Corriere della Sera*, 14 June 1967.

28 *New York Times*, 14, 15 June 1967.

29 Alice Cherki, *Frantz Fanon: A Portrait* (London 2006), p. 187.

30 *Le Monde*, 2 June 1967.

31 *Agence France-Presse*, 30 May 1967.

32 *Morgen Freiheit*, 11 August 1967.

33 *New Left Review*, July–August 1967.

34 *The Reporter*, April–May 1954.

35 Marcel Liebman, *Born Jewish: A Childhood in Occupied Europe* (London 2005), pp. 169–170.

36 Albert Memmi, *The Colonizer and the Colonized* (London 2003), p. 59.

37 Marcel Liebman, 'Israel, Palestine and Zionism', *Socialist Register*, 1970.

38 Ibid.

39 Shmuel Mikunis, 'Against Arab Chauvinism', in *War and Peace: Articles Published by Morgen Freiheit* (New York 1967), p. 12.

40 Gilbert Achcar, ed. *Ralph Miliband and Marcel Liebman: The Israeli Dilemma; A Debate between Two Left Wing Jews* (Monmouth 2006), p. 16.

41 Ibid.

42 Ibid.

43 Ibid., p. 43.

44 Ibid., p. 33.

45 Ibid., p. 30.

46 Ibid., p. 45.

47 *Guardian*, 24 June 1967.

48 *Jewish Chronicle*, 30 June 1967.

49 *New Outlook*, September–October 1970.

50 *Le Monde*, 25 March 1970.

51 Amos Oz, 'Meaning of Homeland', *New Outlook*, December 1967.

52 *Sunday Times*, 15 June 1969.

14

The post-Stalinists and the anti-Stalinists

Zionism revisited

Following the invasion of Hungary, it became increasingly difficult for even the most loyal of European Communists to align themselves with the Kremlin's policies. The state interests of the USSR did not always coincide with local desires to build international socialism. The revelations of the Gulag survivors and the official denunciations of Stalin produced an ideological fragmentation. Some left the Communist movement. Others became independent Marxists or morphed into a more open Euro-communism. Within the USSR, writers such as Solzehnitsyn, dissidents such as Daniel and Sinyavsky and an embyronic movement of Soviet Jews in protesting against thinly disguised discrimination all came to the fore in the years following the invasion of Hungary.

Even so, in the 1960s, the Kremlin turned its attention to the Arab world in the growing belief that victory in the Cold War depended on victory for liberation movements in the developing world. The Americans, in turn, supported reactionary regimes in many parts of the world in the hope of preventing anti-Western, pro-Soviet regimes from coming to power. Much hope in particular was placed in Nasser's Egypt by the Soviets who considered it to be 'progressive' despite the suppression of local Communists. This strategy was promoted in particular by Aleksandr Shelepin, the head of the KGB such that 'the agenda of Soviet intelligence' was totally transformed.[1] An acerbic anti-Zionism, which depicted Israel as being linked to American imperialism evolved as part and parcel of Soviet strategy in the 1960s. It contrasted dramatically with its approach a decade before when Stalin had been partly responsible for the establishment of the state of Israel. Anti-Zionism had become a tool in aligning the public face of Soviet policy with Arab nationalist aspirations – and thereby furthering the USSR's interests in the Arab world. Thus the Great Soviet Encyclopaedia commented in 1979 that:

> Zionism's main policy has always been the struggle, both open and covert, against socialism, the international communist and national liberation movements, the Soviet Union and other socialist countries. Immediately after the victory of the October Revolution of 1917 in Russia, Zionism unleashed an active struggle against the Soviet state . . . as a shock detachment of imperialism, colonialism and neo-colonialism, international Zionism opposes the national liberation movements of the peoples of Africa, Asia and Latin America . . . many means of mass information are controlled or influenced by Zionist organisations including many publishing houses and radio, television and film companies in the USA, western Europe, Latin America, Africa and Australia.[2]

While there was no desire to repeat the overt anti-Semitism of Stalin's last years, the temptation to appeal to time-honoured anti-Jewish canards such as the control of the international media could not be resisted. This had both external and internal consequences. Within the USSR and the Soviet bloc, the whiff of anti-Semitism, with or without Jews, carried in its train a certain populism which deflected any criticism of the regime. Moreover, this campaign became accentuated following Nasser's defeat during the Six Day War and the open desire of many thousands of Soviet Jews to leave the USSR for Israel. In the Arab world, Soviet anti-Zionism could be viewed as an act of solidarity with liberation movements – a bond of friendship between the Soviet and Arab peoples.

Moreover Yuri Andropov, the head of the KGB after 1967, was said to be increasingly obsessed with the campaign in Western Europe for the free emigration of Soviet Jews. This manifested itself in the arrest and imprisonment of Jewish refuseniks as well as human rights activists – all accompanied by an ongoing campaign of denigration in the Soviet media. Even the heads of the First Chief Directorate of the KGB, responsible for foreign intelligence, Vladimir Kryuchkov and L. P. Zamoysky, were strong believers in conspiracy theory. Opinions that the US military-industrial complex was dominated by the Jews were firmly implanted and such a view was not unusual even at the beginning of the Gorbachev era.[3]

In February 1958, *Literaturnaya Gazeta* attacked the writer, Howard Fast, following his break with the CPUSA after Hungary and the publication of his book *The Naked God: The Writer and the Communist Party*. Significantly the attack highlighted his Jewish origins which up until that point have never been publicized in the Soviet press. The following year, Ivanov and Sheynis published *The State of Israel* which also conjured up anti-Jewish stereotypes, thought to have been long buried. In 1963, the Ukrainian writer, Trofim Kichko, published his *Judaism without Embellishment* which caused a storm of outrage in Western Europe. The book's cover featured a swarthy Jew in a prayer shawl, standing in a pulpit, nonchalantly jingling coins in his hands. Such illustrations were a common feature in the Soviet press. They bore an uncanny resemblance to anti-Jewish cartoons which were published in Nazi-occupied Ukraine during World War II.[4]

Indeed in a celebrated court case in Paris in 1973, an edition of the Soviet Embassy publication, *URSS*, was shown to be based on Tsarist anti-Semitic literature. Robert Legagneux, the deputy mayor of Nanterre and a member of the PCF was formally indicted despite his protestations that he had simply allowed his name to be used, but never saw the contents beforehand. Grigory Svirsky, a recent Soviet emigrant to Israel, submitted as evidence a pamphlet by the Okhrana and 'the Black Hundreds' which had been published in 1906. Svirsky demonstrated that the 'quotations' from the Talmud and other religious tracts which had been published in *URSS* were taken 'word for word, including spelling mistakes, from the 1906 anti-Semitic pamphlet. There was only one change: the term "Zionist" had been substituted for the word "Jew".'[5]

Jews living outside of Israel were connected to Israeli Zionists in a conspiratorial fashion. There were references to the 'Zionist inclined Jewish bourgeoisie of various countries'[6] and accusations that Jews were encouraged to be disloyal to the states in which they lived.[7]

Soviet publications increasingly began to link Zionism and Nazism following the Eichmann trial in Jerusalem in 1961. Yevgeny Yevseyev subsequently wrote *Fascism under the Blue Star* which depicted Zionism as an octopus with tentacles, stretching into every nook and cranny, controlling everything from afar. Yuri Ivanov in *Beware Zionism* spoke about Zionist power over the banks, the media and Western governments. In a report from Cairo, a few months after the Six Day War, quoting Arab sources, *Sovetskaya Estonia* stated that:

> The Israelis turned the town of El Arish into a large concentration camp in which the Arab population is the object of terror, torture and humiliation, no less cruel and bestial than the crimes perpetrated by the Hitlerite executioners in the Jewish ghettos.[8]

Palestinian militants who participated in the armed struggle against Israel were depicted as 'anti-Nazi partisans'. The expansion of Israel's territory

<u>almost fourfold</u> as a result of the war was characterized as premeditated and an example of Zionist 'lebensraum'. As evidence of this closeness between Zionism and Nazism, the 'Jews for trucks' dialogue between Adolf Eichmann and Rudolf Kastner, was often invoked.

Zionism was depicted as reactionary and inherently anti-Soviet since 1917.[9] Its treatment of Arabs was compared with treatment of Blacks in South Africa.[10] The attack on Nasser's Egypt was solely an assault on 'one of the progressive movements'.

A McCarthyite aspect of all this was locating 'Zionists' among rivals and opponents. Thus Zionists were involved in the subversion of socialist Czechoslovakia in 1968. The presence of Jews within the administration in Dubček's Czechoslovakia such as Eduard Goldstuecker and Frantisek Kriegel led to anti-Semitic jibes from Soviet leaders[11] and accusations that these life-long Communists were working for the Jewish organization, the Joint.

'Zionists' were demonized and held responsible for all the wickedness in the world. Thus Jack Ruby who shot Lee Harvey Oswald, the assassin of President Kennedy, was labelled 'a Zionist'. Inevitably Trotsky was unmasked as a 'Zionist' in Ivan Shevtsov's bestselling novel, *In the Name of the Father and Son*.[12]

Israeli Jews were essentially stripped of their Jewishness and their recent history when 'Zionists' were said to have collaborated with Nazis during World War II to murder Jews. A separation opened up between those Jews who perished in the Shoah and 'Zionists' who were the embodiment of all evil and oppressors of the Palestinians.

Anti-Semitism without Jews

A tipping point for many a European Communist was the determined assault on the remnant of Polish Jewry. It became a useful scapegoat in an internal power struggle in the Polish party. There was a virtual contest as to who could unmask 'Zionists' in Poland. Official demonstrations bore banners which read 'Clean the Party of Zionists'. *The Protocols of the Elders of Zion* was printed twice. One academic in a lecture in Gdansk stated that:

> The ideological sources of Zionism are derived from the monstrous double ethics of the Talmud which divided humanity into 'the chosen people' and the so-called 'goyim' (non-Jews), beasts with human faces who should be totally subordinated to the interests of the 'Supermen' – the Jews.[13]

In view of the small number of Jews in Poland, non-Jews who were on the wrong side of the debate were occasionally turned into Jews. The non-Jewish wife of one Minister, Marian Spychalski, was said to have visited relatives in Israel and was a confidante of Moshe Dayan. The Prime Minister Józef Cyrankiewicz was really 'Zimmerman'. A childless non-Jewish Spanish Civil War veteran was attacked for teaching his children Hebrew.[14] In a rural part of the country, loyal party members convened under the slogan 'Go back to Siam!' Those gathered had not understood the meaning of 'Go back to Zion!' and believed that some sort of error must have occurred – so they changed the slogan accordingly.[15] This bizarre tinkering with reality reached its zenith when the deputy minister for culture commented that:

> It is no secret that many Hitlerite criminals are in the service of the Israeli government. They live on the territory of the state of Israel. I estimate that there are over one thousand experts of the former Hitlerite Wehrmacht who have become advisors to the Israeli army.[16]

World Zionism was said to be mobilizing Polish citizens of Jewish origin and the party secretary, Gomulka privately labelled them a fifth column. The 'Zionists' were seen to be behind dissent and student demonstrations.[17] Andrzej Werblan who was responsible for the Polish party's central committee's ideological programme argued that the problem was in reality 'cosmopolitanism' – and not anti-Semitism.[18] 'No society', he argued, 'can tolerate the excessive participation of a national minority in the elite of power'.[19]

Although this exhibited all the discriminatory techniques observed during the Slansky trial, it did not automatically lead to judicially sanctioned killings, but to imprisonment and departure. Even so, the Orwellian campaign against the Jews in Poland led to a wholesale dismissal of academics, intellectuals, government ministers, diplomats and the eventual exodus of thousands of Jews from the country. These were Polish Jews who had not availed themselves of the opportunity to leave at the end of the 1950s. Many were from pre-war Communist families. They saw themselves as Poles, first and foremost, and committed to a Communist Poland. Their enforced departure to Sweden and Denmark was therefore totally unexpected. It was psychologically devastating.

On the eve of World War II, there were over 3.3 million Jews in Poland. On the eve of the anti-Zionist campaign in 1968, there were approximately 25,000. The expulsion left behind a remnant of a vibrant Jewish community which had existed in Poland for centuries.

In Eastern Europe, dissidence and support for Israel was often closely linked. Opposition to anti-Semitism and human rights for Jews became a cause célèbre – a cause not wholly shared in Western Europe. The Israeli victory in the 1967 war therefore became a reason for celebration by dissidents and human rights advocates – and a defeat for the regimes of the Soviet bloc. Following the Six Day War, a special series of stamps to mark the 700th anniversary of the Altneushul synagogue in Prague was withdrawn and a ban enacted on existing sales.[20] When Czechoslovakia along with the Soviet Union and other Eastern bloc countries broke off diplomatic relations with Israel after the war, over 13,000 students signed a petition calling for its resumption.

Walter Ulbrecht's East Germany overcame its historical sensitivity to the Jewish question during the Six Day War and accorded responsibility to 'the Zionists' for each and every misdemeanour. Given the fact that there were many former Nazi journalists in the East German media, the *Guardian* commented:

> So twisted has been the reporting in the East German press, manipulated with a skill that would have done justice to the propaganda of Goebbels, that even some of the Ulbrecht's regime's most loyal followers are said to have been embarrassed lest the campaign draws accusations of an unbridled anti-Semitism on German soil.[21]

During the Prague Spring of Alexander Dubček, a youth group carried an Israel flag and a placard on May Day 1968 which stated 'Let Israel Live!' Moreover following the Soviet invasion and their summons to Moscow, Dubček and his fellow cabinet members probably averted another anti-Zionist show trial by refusing to leave Moscow without their imprisoned colleague, Kriegel.[22]

The ground had been laid by Dubček's predecessor, Novotny who had warned factory workers against 'the Jew Goldstuecker and his kinsmen'.[23] Indeed Czech ministers had jokingly referred to 'bearded Solomons'. In April 1968, Dubček announced that the party would do its utmost to combat anti-Semitism.[24] The East German press consequently accused 'Zionist forces' of infiltrating and controlling the Czech party.[25]

Western Europe and the Zionists

The Six Day War in 1967 – the fear beforehand of a massacre of the Jews and the exhilaration afterwards of a lightening victory over their enemies – catalysed an awareness among the remnant of Jews who had retained their membership of Communist parties. As with the Molotov-Ribbentrop pact in 1939 or during the Slansky trial in 1952, there was an exodus of Jews from the party.[26] The Soviet invasion of Czechoslovakia in the following year confirmed their decision.

The attention of the European Left in Western Europe was focused on the struggle against colonialism in the developing world and in providing assistance to liberation movements. The use of 'Zionism' as a political tool to often settle internal problems attracted only minimal attention. In this sense, the anti-Zionist campaign in Eastern Europe probably had little direct input into the thinking of the Left in Western Europe. Yet there were often striking points of convergence during the last two decades of the USSR.

One unnoticed side effect of the Six Day War was to replace the now settled Algerian conflict by the Palestinian one in the mindset of the emerging New Left. Now that the PLO was emerging as the standard bearer of Palestinian nationalism, there was a clear reticence to 'defend' Zionism in Western Europe, regardless of a distinct antipathy towards such neo-Stalinist behaviour.

In addition, there was an additional reticence to overtly criticize the Soviet Union since the 'reds under the beds' outbreak in the United States during the 1950s. The Vietnam War – and Israel's more comfortable relationship with the White House exacerbated all this.

Unlike Jean-Paul Sartre's approach, there was little recognition that the Israel-Palestine conflict was complex and not simple. Unlike Sartre, there was an inability to retain two different narratives and to consider the conflict as 'right against right', but instead to pitch one flawed narrative against the other. In part, this was often due to generational experiences – Sartre's and their own. In part, this polarization followed representation from the PLO to include Israel in the anti-colonial discourse. It was clearly an easier choice to wholesale adopt the Palestinian narrative as the history of the Israel-Palestine conflict in contrast to Sartre's complexities.

It was simpler to regard the Jews of Israel as 'Zionist colons' who fitted the traditional colonial template, but who also happened to favour social democracy and collectivism over the politics of reaction. Yet there was also considerable difficulty in rebranding Israelis as Afrikaaner nationalists or French settlers in Algeria. That difficulty resided in the fact that this shift occurred only two decades after the revelations of Auschwitz. As Sartre pointedly asked 'Can the Arabs alter the fact for us that Israelis are still Jews?'[27]

What began as a denunciation of Israel's policies ended by stating that Israel's existence was the source of instability in the Middle East and structurally the built-in cause of inevitable aggression. It was no longer a question of the weakening of an Israel government. After all, at a press conference on 28 May 1967, Nasser commented that the central problem was the existence of Israel.

Such telescoping aligned some on the European Left with their colleagues on the Arab Left. It also opened the way towards identification with Arab

Islamists. As colonialists, the Israelis should just disappear as did the French in Algeria. How this was to be achieved – a one socialist state solution of Jews and Arabs, a democratic secular state with an Arab majority, a voluntary exodus on the Algerian model or an expulsion of those Jews who came after 1917 or after 1948 – all these ideas were mooted as paths out of the morass in the late 1960s. As suppressors of a legitimate liberation movement, the Israelis should leave Palestine just as the Americans would eventually leave Vietnam.

The nature of Arab regimes, it was argued, had changed since 1948. By 1967, the feudal Arab regimes had been replaced by 'progressive' ones. Moreover Israel had also moved closer to the United States. Even so, there was a subtle difference between Soviet hostility towards Israel and the attitude of the Arab Left. The fact that the USSR had supported the Zionist military struggle to secure a state and recognized Israel in 1948, could not be erased. Despite breaking off diplomatic relations with Israel after the 1967 war and the increasing virulence of its verbal and written attacks, the Kremlin did not seemingly wish to see Israel eliminated. Even though Zionism had become an ideological attraction for many Soviet Jews after 1967, the Kremlin's main charge was that Israel was now 'the tool of imperialism'.

The emergence of Palestinian nationalism and its armed struggle was actually greeted rather coolly by the Kremlin. A Soviet peace plan of December 1968 had been rejected by the PLO – and the Kremlin was becoming increasingly irritated by the organization's inability to compromise. It was likened to Trotsky's attitude at Brest-Litovsk.[28] The activities of the PFLP and the DFLP such as the spate of hijackings brought even harsher ideological criticism. Invoking Lenin's 1920 pamphlet, they were accused of being central actors in 'Left Wing Communism: An Infantile Disorder'.[29]

In Sofia, Arab delegates had walked when the leader of the pro-Moscow faction of the Israeli Communist Party, Meir Vilner, rose to address the conference. Israeli Communists were banned from attending the International Youth Festival in Algiers in the summer of 1965. This rejectionism and calls to liquidate Israel were endorsed by Mao's China as part of its ongoing rivalry with Moscow. Thus the Chinese delegation encouraged the exclusion of an Israeli delegation from the Tri-Continental Congress in Havana in January 1966.

Despite its differences with the Arab Left, the Kremlin clearly followed its national interests in the Arab world. The Egyptian Communists were requested to join the Arab Socialist Union. The Syrian Ba'athists were preferred to the Syrian Communists. Similarly the Kremlin maintained a diplomatic silence on the repression and imprisonment of local Communists in Iraq in an attempt to cultivate Saddam Hussein. With the rise of Palestinian nationalism, this extended to arming the PFLP and training PLO fighters in 1970.[30]

The far Left turned a blind eye to the presence of Nazi war criminals in the Middle East and especially in Nasser's Egypt. For example, SS Gruppenfuhrer Alois Mosler, known as Hassan Suleiman in Egypt, was an advisor on the organization of Egyptian youth – yet he was deemed responsible for the deaths of tens of thousands in the Ukraine. Similarly a Gestapo chief, Joachim Gleim, was wanted in Poland, yet he had transferred his expertise to the Egyptian secret police under the alias of Ali al-Nachan.

Algerie Française and the Jewish question

The demise of official Communism after 1956 coincided with the rise of a broad anti-colonialist movement. The Algerian war began in 1954 just as the French were withdrawing from Indo-China, following the defeat at Dien Bien Phu. This war and the broad French resistance to decolonization in Algeria could not this time be justified through opposition to Communism and the Cold War which had been the case in Indo-China. In 1956, France under Guy Mollet extended conscription and started to send those who had enlisted to Algeria. Suez occurred at the same time.

In France, the Section Française de l'International Ouvrière (SFIO) of Guy Mollet had long supported Israel and this approach continued throughout the Suez crisis. There were others on the Left such as Mendès-France of the Radical party who like Bevan in Britain was anti-Suez, but pro-Israel. Mendès-France felt particularly strongly about the question of Algeria and this reflected the views of many on the French Left. The question of Algerian independence fuelled a split in the SFIO and the formation of the Parti Socialiste Unifié (PSU) in 1960. Whereas the SFIO had supported Jewish national aspirations and the establishment of the state, the PSU opposed Mollet and was critical of Israel. The PSU was the third space between the Stalinist PCF and the social democratic SFIO. It also reflected the views of the younger generation and their sensitivity towards nationalist movements in the developing world. Periodicals such as Le Nouvel Observateur now began to raise the Palestinian refugee problem. Following Suez and the emergence of the non-aligned bloc, Israel was now seen to be on the side of the imperialist forces.

When De Gaulle came to power, he sent in even more conscripts to Algeria. However, his volte-face on Algerian independence aligned France with a pro-Arab position. This later evolved into a subsequent break with Israel and an arms embargo. This coincided with an insensitive and probably unintended remark about Jews by De Gaulle which placed the vexed connection between anti-Zionism and anti-Semitism in the arena of public debate for the first time.

It was de Gaulle's comment in November 1967 that the Jews were 'un people d'élite . . . et dominateur' which evoked anti-Jewish stereotypes. De Gaulle's insensitivity conjured up memories of the Vichy years and the racism of the colons of Algeria. Indeed Vichy's initiatives against Jews were strongest in Algeria. The colons went beyond official policy in mainland France and instituted a numerus clausus for Jews not only in universities, but also in primary and secondary schools.[31] Both Xavier Vallat, a former Vichy Commissioner for Jewish Affairs and Yves Moreau, a leader writer for the Communist Party's *L'Humanité* warmed to de Gaulle's sentiments.[32] Significantly, it was the social democrats of the SFIO who attacked De Gaulle. The party had a long history in this regard. It had opposed Daladier's restrictive policies on refugees, experienced the Nazi occupation and the deportation of the Jews. The older Left indeed remembered. The newer Left had no such memory.

The disproportionate number of Jews in the leadership of protests and demonstrations in France in 1968 often originated in the brutality of the Algerian conflict – and regardless of their degree of assimilation, they retained the memory of their parents' experience. Henri Weber's family was part of the Polish-Jewish emigration to France. He saw Algerians arrested and beaten up in the early 1960s and realized that the police had done the same to the Jews in the 1940s.[33] He became a leader of the Jeunesse Communiste Révolutionnaire in 1968.

Their participation in the events of 1968 conversely meant confronting the lingering Vichy mentality as well.[34] It paradoxically reflected their need to escape from the past and to leave behind their status as survivors.

> Survival means having to try not to die. Life is when you are sure of living and have to decide how to live, what you choose as a life and who with. And '68 was the explosion of life rather than (just) survival.[35]

Some Jews such as Alain Krivine, originally a member of the PCF, embraced Trotskyism and was a founder of the Jeunesse Communiste Révolutionnaire. Other Jews who were influenced by the lectures and writings of the philosopher, Louis Althusser, were attracted to Maoism – but often in ignorance of what was actually happening in China. Robert Linhart, a leader of the Maoist Union de la Jeunesse Communiste Marxiste-Leniniste, believed that imperialism would not be defeated by the European countries but only by the struggles of the developing world – of which Algeria and Cuba were prime examples. They were a threat to American hegemony and international capitalism. The central struggle of the developing world was, of course, that of the Vietnamese – and since China was the leading revolutionary power in the third world, this is why they became Maoists.

Many soixante-huitards came from Communist or independent Marxist families. For many, the Shoah – and their parents' treatment in France – was undoubtedly a factor in igniting their political activism. Many had admired the victorious Red Army in vanquishing Nazism and joined the PCF, only to be rudely awakened by the reality of late Stalinism. Even so, the Shoah did not automatically ensure an attachment to Jewish particularism. Fighting in the French resistance did not imply a return to conventional Jewishness and a reintegration into Jewish communal life.

> Every time people spoke to him (Georges Altman, a resistance fighter) about going back to the synagogue, about belonging to the community or making a defence in the name of the Jews, he would say 'Hitler did not win the war! Why do you expect me, out of bravado, to conform to the idea, Hitler had of us? It was not in the name of Jewish identity that we fought Nazism'.[36]

Germany's past and future

In Germany, the situation was uniquely different. Nazism had liquidated the Marxist and social democratic Left on Hitler's rise to power. In post-war West Germany, this ideological vacuum was partly filled by the Frankfurt School of Horkheimer, Adorno and Marcuse as well as by other philosophers such as Ernst Bloch. They elucidated 'critical theory' which evoked both Marxist and Freudian analytical tools so as 'to understand the connection between socio-economic exploitation and psychic oppression under advanced capitalism'.[37]

In 1961, the year of the erection of the Berlin Wall, the German Social Democrats (SPD) expelled its student wing, the Socialistische Deutsche Studentbund (SDS) for arguing for negotiations with East Germany and the denuclearization of both Germanies. The United States deployed nuclear weapons on German soil and this had led to the first big protests since 1945. New tendencies emerged from within the SDS and were influenced by the events of the 1960s and the ideas of student leaders such as Rudi Dutschke who actually had good relations with socialist Zionists. In particular, the affairs of the developing world loomed large.

> We argued that every revolutionary is obliged to go beyond the bounds of bourgeois law if that leads to raising the consciousness of the masses. To accept the legal system in power is to accept the power of the ruling classes. We argued that the Third World and its national liberation movements had taken over the classic

role of the nineteenth century proletariat. In the process of armed struggle, these movements had developed a new morality and ethic, new forms of society and government. But they could only be victorious if open minded people in the First World supported them, paralysed their own system . . . we should interpret these examples in terms relevant for revolutionary change in the First World.[38]

The SDS mounted campaigns about the US presence in Vietnam, the Greek junta and the Shah's repressive regime in Iran. It was, however, the killing of a student demonstrator which catalysed a huge protest under the slogan: 'the students are the Jews of today'. As in France, the past overshadowed the present. The fear of an authoritarian revival, initiated by those who had held office in Nazi Germany, was always present. Yet the accelerating radicalism and theoretical bent of the German students also caused a backlash in that Dutschke's advocacy of direct action similarly conjured up images of the 1920s. In particular, the young Jurgen Habermas who had been influenced by Jewish philosophers of the inter-war period and was highly sensitive to the Jewish question accused the SDS of promoting 'left wing fascism'.[39] Theodor Adorno wrote privately to Herbert Marcuse – both were leading scholars of the Frankfurt School – to express his anguish that their teachings had inspired young people to embark on this road. Adorno, too, was worried that the German student movement was moving towards totalitarianism.

The German taboo about portraying Jews and Israel in a negative light was perhaps for the first time called into question by some on the German Left. Previously lifting the veil from the Judencomplex had been the prerogative of the subterranean far Right who missed the good old days. As in France, the protest movement was a manifestation of the 1960s generation's determination to distance itself from their parents' cultural and political restraints. Too many members of the German establishment were discovered to be former members of the Nazi party, however, nominal. Rolf Hochhuth's controversial play in 1963 about Pope Pius XII's role in World War II similarly pointed an accusing finger at the Catholic Church. All this curdled with the inability of the older generation to adequately explain recent history to their children.

The Six Day War and the rise of the armed struggle by the Palestinian national movement resulted in at least a section of the SDS and other groups on the far Left adopting stringent anti-Israel positions. They forced the Israeli Ambassador to curtail several talks at German universities in 1969. One group, Internationale Solidaritat, was specifically established at the University of Kiel to prevent the Vice-Chancellor of the Hebrew University of Jerusalem from speaking.

Some groups of young Germans believed that it was not enough to support the armed struggle in the developing world from the comfort of post-war

Germany. Such resistance should be brought home to the streets of Berlin as well. A bomb, timed to explode during a crowded meeting to commemorate the anniversary of Kristallnacht at the Jewish community centre in the Fasanenstrasse in West Berlin, failed to detonate. It was believed to have been the work of a group called 'Tupamaros-Berlin', named after the Uruguayan militants. It was further believed that those behind the attempt had been trained in Palestinian camps in Jordan. No one was ever arrested, but a leaflet, entitled 'Schalom und Napalm', which predicted the attack, stated:

> Every memorial ceremony in West Berlin and West Germany conceals the fact that the Kristallnacht of 1938 is now being repeated every day by the Zionists in the occupied territories, in refugee camps and in Israeli prisons. The Jews who were driven out by fascism have become fascists themselves and in collaboration with American capital want to eradicate the Palestinian people. We must smash the direct support of Israel by German industry and government. In this fashion we will prepare the way for the victory of the Palestinian people and force a new defeat for world imperialism.[40]

There was strong support for Arafat's nationalist Fatah as well as for the Marxist Popular Front for the Liberation of Palestine (PFLP) and its ideological splinter, the Popular Democratic Front (DFLP). In part, this was facilitated by the presence of other groups of foreign students, studying in West Germany who identified the Palestinian struggle with their own. Palestinian students, organized as the General Union of Palestinian Students, were also highly active in advocating their cause and promoting their narrative. This solidarity of young Germans occasionally extended to an understanding of the Palestinian bombing campaign in Israeli civilian areas including universities. One leaflet read: 'Only when bombs explode in 50 supermarkets in Israel will there be peace.'[41]

Journalists such as Ulrike Meinhof of the left wing weekly *Konkret* similarly underwent training in Jordan and joined Andreas Baader and Gudrun Ensslin in instigating attacks against the German state and perpetrating acts of terror against German civilians. Following the killing of the Israeli athletes by Palestinians at the Munich Olympic Games in 1973, Meinhof described the dead Israelis as 'Zionist soldiers masquerading as athletes'.[42]

While the Baader-Meinhof group may have been unrepresentative of the German New Left – and particularly over the question of Israel – it did seem to symbolize the fervour with which many young Germans embraced the Palestinian cause and how a backlash to the docile prevailing wisdom, both rhetorically violent and politically abrasive, had been released into the public domain. The Palestinians were viewed as 'the Jews' of 1968.

There were Jews in Israel to be hated for their actions against the Palestinians and there were Jews in the Diaspora to be admired for their persistent existence as the oldest ethnic minority, for their ability to dance on Hitler's grave – those who must be defended against the forces of reaction. The developing world, the Muslim states and the Soviet bloc fortified this crude definition as to which sort of Jew was acceptable – and particularly in forums at the United Nations. This was accentuated by the continuing occupation of the land conquered by Israel during the Six Day War and the subsequent settlement drive.

Israel's support suddenly shrank to the West Europeans and their historically connected former dominions. It was those very countries which had essentially been at the forefront of empire building. In the eyes of the developing world, this further sharpened the image of Israel as a lackey of American imperialism and a colonial implant whereas the Palestinians, fighting occupation and struggling for their freedom, were much more readily identifiable. The 'empire builders', however, were also those who fought Hitler and died in their millions. The Shoah and the fate of the Jews were not a mere footnote of history.

The New Left was unable to accommodate such complexity. In Germany, the contradictions reached their apogee in 1976 when Wilfred Böse and Brigitte Kuhlmann participated in the PFLP's hijacking of a civilian aircraft and landing it in Idi Amin's Uganda. At Entebbe airport, the German revolutionaries sifted the Jews from the non-Jews. The word 'selection' was one which resonated in the European psyche with images of Auschwitz and Treblinka. No European, Jewish or not, could be indifferent.

It was perhaps the symbolism of this incident and the killings at Munich which marked the return to a more rational approach to the Israel-Palestine conflict by the German Left in the latter part of the twentieth century. This differentiated the German Left from other sections of the European Left.

Joschka Fischer, a leading member of the Proletarische Union für Terror und Zerstörung in the 1970s, was so dismayed by the spate of kidnappings and killings that he effectively dropped out of political life. He earned his living as a taxi driver for several years before joining the Greens. Later as German Foreign Minister, he regularly mentioned the legacy of the twentieth century and that it should be more than political lip-service to condemn anti-Semitism.

Yet while the Germans were reticent, the Swedes were not. Under Olof Palme, Sweden led the way in articulating the views of the post-war generation of European social democrats on the Israel-Palestine conflict. Palme's views had been shaped by his travels in the early 1950s throughout Asia and viewing the problems of the developing world. By the early 1960s, foreign aid became an important plank of the Swedish social democrats while proclaiming neutrality between East and West. In 1962, a Swedish government proposal argued for a donation of the equivalent of 1% of GDP. Palme condemned British policy in Malaysia and demonstrated his opposition to the war in Vietnam by appearing with the North Vietnamese ambassador in a huge protest in Stockholm in February 1968. There were increasingly close contacts between the Swedish government and African liberation movements such as Frelimo in Mozambique and Angola's MPLA. While Palme did not renounce his views in support of a social democratic Israel, he expanded them to include recognition of the Palestinians and their right to national self-determination in 1974. This earned him the ire of Golda Meir and the Israeli Right under Menachem Begin. While condemning violence and terrorism and rejecting many aspects of the PLO programme, Sweden cast the decisive vote in favour of inviting the PLO to address the UN Security Council in December 1975.[43]

Notes and Works Cited

1 Christopher Andrew and Vasili Mitrokhin, *The World was Going Our Way: The KGB and the Battle for the Third World* (New York 2005), p. 9.

2 *Great Soviet Encyclopaedia*, vol. 23 (London 1979), p. 745.

3 Andrew and Mitrokhin, op. cit., pp. 231–45.

4 Henry Abramson, *'This is the way it was!': Textual and Iconographic Images of Jews in the Nazi-Sponsored Ukrainian Press of Distrikt Galizien* in ed. Robert Moses Shapiro, *Why Didn't the Press Shout?: American and International Journalism during the Holocaust* (New York 2003), pp. 535–56.

5 Emanuel Litvinoff, *Soviet Anti-Semitism: The Paris Trial* (London 1974), p. 22.

6 *Komsomolskaya Pravda*, 4 October 1967.

7 *Moscow Radio*, 7 September 1967.

8 *Sovetskaya Estonia*, 10 October 1967.

9 *Pravda Ukrainy*, 5 August 1967.

10 *Peace and Progress Radio*, 4 October 1967.

11 *New York Times*, 29 August 1968.

12 *JTA*, 25 March 1970.

13 Josef Banas, *The Scapegoats: The Exodus of the Remnants of Polish Jewry* (London 1979), p. 151.

14 Lendvai, op. cit., p. 147.

15 Banas, op. cit., pp. 57–8.

16 Lendvai, op. cit., pp. 149–50.

17 *Guardian*, 14 March 1967.

18 S. J. Roth, 'The Theory of Polish Anti-Semitism', *Bulletin on Soviet Jewish Affairs*, no. 2, July 1968.

19 Banas, op. cit., p. 153.

20 *Morgen Freiheit*, 16 August 1967.

21 *Guardian*, 12 June 1967.

22 Lendvai, op. cit., p. 280.

23 *Jewish Chronicle*, 26 April 1968.

24 *Rude Pravo*, 10 April 1968.

25 *Neues Deutschland*, 25 August 1968.

26 *Jewish Chronicle*, 16 June 1967.

27 François Bondy, *Communist Attitudes in France and Italy to the Six Day War* in *The Left and Zion: Communism, Israel and the Middle East* ed. Robert S. Wistrich (London 1979), p. 174.

28 Ronald Dannreuther, *The Soviet Union and the PLO* (London 1998), p. 42.

29 Ibid., p. 45.

30 Andrew and Mitrokhin, op. cit., p. 247.

31 Michael R. Marrus and Robert O. Paxton, *Vichy France and the Jews* (Stanford 1995), pp. 191–2.

32 *L'Humanité*, 28 November 1967.

33 Ronald Fraser, *1968: Student Generation in Revolt* (London 1988), pp. 55-6.

34 *Ha'aretz*, 12 May 2008.

35 Virginie Linhart, *Le Jour où mon père s'est tu* (Paris 2008) tr. in www.marxists.org/history/france/may-1968/jews

36 Jean Daniel, *The Jewish Prison: A Rebellious Meditation on the State of Judaism* (New York 2005), p. 60.

37 Fraser, op. cit., p. 49.

38 Bernd Rabehl, Free University of Berlin, Subversive Aktion, SDS in Fraser, pp. 102–3.

39 Fraser, op. cit., pp. 123–4.

40 *Frankfurter Allgemeine Zeitung*, 13 November 1969; Manfred Gerstenfeld, Review of Wolfgang Kraushaar's *Die Bombe im Ju" dischen Gemeindehaus* (Hamburg 2005) in *Jewish Political Studies Review*, vol. 18, nos 3–4 (Autumn 2006).

41 Gerstenfeld, op. cit.

42 Harold Marcuse, *Legacies of Dachau: The Uses and Abuses of a Concentration Camp 1933–2000* (Cambridge 2010), p. 318.

43 Jacob Eriksson, 'Swedish Mediation of the Israel-Palestine Conflict: A Study of the Utility of Small-State mediation and Track III Diplomacy', Ph.D thesis, SOAS, University of London 2011.

15

The changing face of the British Left

A different London

London in the 1980s became the European centre of opposition to Israel's policies – and in a growing number of cases of opposition to Israel as a nation-state. Israel was no longer governed by the Labour Party and its allies. Instead the Likud had become the permanent party of power after 1977. Socialist imagery and visions of making the desert bloom were now seen as past history. Menachem Begin's abrasive style, incendiary language and hardline policies were often accompanied by recollections in the British press of his military opposition to the British in Palestine as the commander of the Irgun Zvai Leumi. In particular, incidents such as the blowing up of the King David hotel and the killing of the two British sergeants lingered in the public memory. The drive to settle the West Bank dramatically accelerated under Begin, now in areas where there were concentrations of Arab population. Triumphs such as the peace agreement with Egypt in 1979 were dimmed by the ill-fated invasion of Lebanon three years later. This war created a deep political schism in Israel which was reflected in the Jewish Diaspora through the formation of groups supporting Peace Now and a preference for the Israeli peace camp in general. For those who had originally opposed the rise of the state of Israel in 1948 and always condemned Zionism, this provided a golden opportunity to recruit and expand. With decolonization entering its twilight phase, despite the notable exception of South Africa, the European Left's attention was gradually shifting onto the Israel-Palestine dispute.

Liberals and centrists who favoured an amelioration of Palestinian sufferings and an outcome, based on a two-state solution, found themselves rubbing shoulders with Trotskyists and Stalinists who wanted nothing of the sort. Both camps were highly critical of Israeli policies.

Yet if Israel had changed, then so had the British Left. Britain's imperial past cemented Palestine to London. The British Empire had been replaced by the multi-national Commonwealth. There was a gradual awakening in British society as to the damage caused by colonialism. Unlike Kenyatta, Nehru, Nkrumeh and other giants of the decolonization era, the remarkable and charismatic figure of Nelson Mandela in the 1990s loomed large. He transcended normal politics in a manner which his predecessors in the 1960s had never done. True, he had spent half a lifetime in prison and he had to heal the wounds of a fractured society, yet his persona was viewed through a non-ideological prism. The political story of Mandela lost its complexity and its nuances. It was reduced to heroic basics for popular consumption.

The Mandela syndrome exemplified the polarizing belief of good and bad, of right and wrong. This retreat from complexity into celebrity was also played out in the arena of the Israel-Palestine conflict. The Palestinians were good guys and underdogs. The Israelis were villains and occupiers.

Britain like other European countries had opened its doors to immigrants from its former colonies to implement a dramatic transition from an all-white society ruling large swathes of the world to a vibrant multi-cultural society whose exemplar was London. This rapid change had taken place in less than 50 years.

The tradition of anti-colonialism was enhanced by this change. The early work of figures such as Fenner Brockway who had done so much to initiate the end of empire was inherited by adherents of the New Left. By the 1980s, the anti-colonial influence of the New Left had permeated the Labour Party and much of liberal discourse.

When the collective which ran the feminist journal, *Spare Rib*, refused to publish responses from Jewish feminists to a critical article by an anti-Zionist Israeli, the bitter debate which followed was not one so much between Jews and Palestinians, but between Jews and activists whose background was in the developing world.

In the 1960s, there had been profound disillusionment with Harold Wilson's Labour governments. In particular, many young people felt Wilson had betrayed them by sitting on the fence on the issue of the American presence in Vietnam. The conflict in particular transmitted the idea that there was a moral corruption in the American model. The United States seemed to be endorsing authoritarian and reactionary regimes, particularly in Latin America – in order to hold at bay the spread of Soviet Communism. In contrast, Che Guevara was seen as trying to fight for the colonized and was transformed into a martyr whose face came to adorn the walls of a million student bedrooms. In the Tet offensive, a third world country inflicted severe casualties on the United States.

Respected thinkers such as Herbert Marcuse had taught that basic human needs had been ruthlessly harnessed to the demands of the socio-industrial complex. Humankind's salvation resided in those, it was argued, who were untainted by either capitalism or Communism. These were the students of the industrialized West and the multitudes of the developing world. This was popularly translated into allegiance to the Palestinian struggle and confrontation with 'technological' Israel. Marcuse, distanced himself from such an interpretation.

The entry into higher education of working-class students in Britain in the 1960s produced a group which was often politically aware due to their background. The conventional student leadership structure, perceived as a stepping stone to a career in the Labour Party, was now often occupied by adherents of the far Left. The Radical Student Alliance was formed in 1967, soon to be supplanted by the Revolutionary Socialist Student Federation and many socialist societies developed in universities. Yet Britain was profoundly different from other European countries because it had abolished military conscription, there was no real history of fascism, collaboration and occupation, no deep-seated tradition in Marxism and no British military participation in the Vietnam War. Moreover, student status was a transient phase. Even so, the Vietnam Solidarity Campaign, founded in the mid-1960s, attracted many concerned students who felt drawn to the issues of the developing world. The VSC called for outright victory for the NLF, the Communists, however, merely wanted 'peace'. There was a willingness to confront the police and skirmishes in Rome, Paris and London were not uncommon.

Tony Cliff of the International Socialist group believed that any criticism in an international crisis should be redirected towards a domestic target. The figure of Ho Chi Minh presented a problem. On the one hand, he was a veteran Stalinist. On the other, he was an icon for national liberation movements and their supporters the world over. The problem was solved by diverting comment towards domestic opinion. Cliff had similarly diverted criticism towards the British and American presence in Korea in the 1950s rather than embrace the North Koreans. He refused in any way to support the Soviet Union and its allies. He did not care for the Prague Spring of 'socialism with a human face' and regarded Dubček's reformist leadership as a means of preventing 'a revolution from below'.[1] Following the Soviet invasion, many concluded that it was now impossible to liberalize a Communist regime from within. This too strengthened the ranks of the Trotskyists and independent Marxist groups generally. All this was embellished by a sense of moral superiority to make a difference in the world – a world which the previous generation was deemed to have failed.

Privileged white minorities still ruled in South Africa and Rhodesia and black nationalists endured long prison sentences. The struggle against apartheid had brought large numbers of South Africans including many Jewish activists to an exile in London. This continued the tradition of South African Jewish radicalism in London which had begun in the 1930s. It also promoted the embryonic comparisons between apartheid South Africa and the changing face of Israel.

In post-1968 Europe, this ongoing transformation of British society proved fertile ground for the far Left. The CPGB and the *Morning Star* tottered on, funded secretly by the Soviet Union with monies laundered by the party's assistant general secretary, Reuben Falber. In contrast, the far Left had capitalized on the excitement of the 1960s. The old slogan 'Be realistic, demand the impossible' still resonated. Tony Cliff had been very successful in expanding his International Socialist group and recasting it as the Socialist Workers' Party in the 1970s. The Militant Tendency of Ted Grant had refined its entryism and quietly secured some MPs. Gerry Healy's sectarian Socialist Labour League had also transformed itself into a party, the Workers' Revolutionary Party (WRP) and with Libyan funding from Colonel Gaddafi was producing a daily newspaper.

The question of whether or not to infiltrate the Labour Party was still one which preoccupied the Trotskyists. Militant had chosen one direction, but Cliff had chosen another as *Labour Worker* changed its name to *Socialist Worker*. As early as 1965, the executive committee of his International Socialism group passed a resolution which set out its clear direction.

> The IS group rejects the Labour party as an instrument for social change, rejects as a milieu for mass conversion to socialist consciousness; and sees in it primarily an area for ideological conflict and a source of individual recruitment to a revolutionary programme.[2]

The International Marxist Group, once the intellectual hothouse of British Trotskyism, kept changing its mind over entryism and this led to splits and fragmentation. One offshoot eventually found a home in the Greater London Council (GLC).

The fractious nature of British Trotskyism, however, prevented any kind of unity and secured its position on the political periphery. However, its ideas on imperialism and colonialism had begun to move from the far Left towards the centre Left.

The rise of Palestinian nationalism under Arafat, coupled with the growing certainty of Israel's permanence in the West Bank and Gaza, had catalysed a disenchantment on Labour's left wing. In post-colonial Britain, they could relate much more fervently to the Palestinians than to the Israelis. In

1969, although unaffiliated to the party, the Labour Middle East Council was established, followed by the Trade Union Friends of Palestine in 1980. Long-time leftist supporters of Israel such as Eric Heffer and born again socialists such as Tony Benn now distanced themselves from Israel. In part, this was also due to the non-realization of the socialist dream in Israel. The kibbutzim had not spread all over Israel. Zionist achievement was now being viewed as entrepreneurial skills and banking expertise. Public ownership was now being replaced by privatization. The gap between the rich and the poor was widening. Israel had not developed into a socialist utopia, but now began to resemble any other West European society.

Citizen Ken

The British Labour Party itself took a distinct move to the Left with the election of the revered Michael Foot in almost a caretaker capacity, following its election defeat in 1979 and the coming to power of Mrs Thatcher. While Foot promoted a two-state solution even though his post-war sympathy for Zionism had long evaporated, the broad shift to the Left brought to prominence a new generation that had neither experienced the fight against fascism nor witnessed the rise of Israel. Their mindset had been fashioned during the decolonization period and thereby had more in common with their counterparts in France whose outlook had been coloured by the Algerian struggle than their parent's generation. Ken Livingstone, elected head of the Greater London Council in 1981, symbolized this dramatic change in Labour Party politics. The GLC began to promote the Palestinian cause and accommodated the Labour Committee on Palestine on its premises.

Livingstone himself had embarked on a six-month trip to Africa including newly independent Algeria and Ghana as a young man in the mid-1960s. He later commented that it had been the combined equivalent of both national service and a university education.[3] With the end of conscription, the openness of the 1960s, the onset of decolonization, the development of multiculturalism in London, it was not surprising that Livingstone had rejected the outlook of his Conservative voting parents.

Livingstone was perhaps the leading figure in the 1980s who provided a bridge for the New Left into the Labour Party. He had come to prominence at a nexus in party politics. The post-war social democracy as exemplified by the Wilson and Callaghan governments had run its course. The weakness of the Labour Left and the militancy of the unions provided fertile ground for the aspirations of the succeeding generation. The advent of Thatcherism provided an identifiable enemy.

Livingstone achieved authority within the GLC by fighting internal battles within the Labour Party rather than by confronting the Tory enemy. He operated a Tammamy Hall type politics which often forged alliances with different Trotskyist groups. Such alliances were recognized as serving the short-term interests of both sides and could be discarded if a better offer arose. Many of these far Left entryists viewed Livingstone as a channel into the Labour Party. For the far Left, Livingstone was a valuable asset. He projected populist views externally and facilitated the prospect of the recruitment of new cadres from within the Labour Party internally. The fact that he denied that he was a Marxist was irrelevant.[4] They in turn provided Livingstone with an activist coterie who would stick with him through every political twist and turn. Unlike his revolutionary partners, Livingstone was in one sense non-ideological and interested mainly in personal advancement. The Trotskyists' sense of Leninist expediency dovetailed with Livingstone's opportunism.

Livingstone grew up in a 'poor white' area of London where there were few Jews. Most Jewish communities were situated north of the river. Moreover the Jews with whom he came into contact in the political arena on the Left had transcended their Jewishness for the revolutionary ideal. His attack on wealthy property developers, the Indian-born Reuben brothers 'Why don't they go back to Iran and try their luck with the Ayatollahs?' sounded very reminiscent of the time-honoured characterization of Jews by the British far Right.[5] Such implicit stereotyping often informed his political understanding. Despite the recent revelations of Mao and Maoism – some 45 million people were estimated to have died during the man-made famine during the Great Leap Forward of 1958–1960[6] – Livingstone would respond to an acerbic criticism about Mao with a deflecting positive comment about the Great Helmsman.[7]

Livingstone's acknowledged boorish attitude towards political opponents and towards Jews who identified with Israel in particular and his approach in diverting any discussion of anti-Jewish behaviourisms became known as the Livingstone Formulation. This essentially brushed away any consideration of a reversion to historic anti-Jewish tropes by suggesting that it was merely a means of deflecting criticism of an Israeli government.

It is defined by the presence of two elements. Firstly the conflation of legitimate criticism of Israel with what are alleged to be demonising, exclusionary or anti-Semitic discourses or actions; secondly, the presence of the counter-accusation that the raisers of the issue of anti-Semitism do so with dishonest intent, in order to delegitimise criticism of Israel. The allegation is that the accuser chooses 'to play the anti-Semitism card' rather than to relate seriously to, or to refute, the criticisms of Israel. While the issue of anti-Semitism is certainly raised in an unjustified way, and may even be raised in bad faith, the Livingstone Formulation may appear as a response to any discussion of contemporary anti-Semitism. [8]

Ironically those British Jews who often raised the issue of contemporary anti-Semitism were on the Left themselves and severely critical of the policies of successive Israeli governments. Livingstone's accession to power in local government coincided with the end of Labour hegemony in Israel and the ascent of Menachem Begin and his Likud party.

It was, however, the ill-fated Israeli invasion of Lebanon in 1982 which tipped the balance. Left wing journalists such as James Cameron who were strong advocates for the Israel of 1948, now for the first time were critical. Although Cameron's views were no different from the Israeli peace camp, from those of Peace Now, he was berated by a Jewish leadership in Britain that defended the Begin government despite the fact that Israel was divided. Cameron wrote:

> I was now the turncoat, the false friend. There are now many like me, berated for saying that the really false friends of dignified Jewry now are the embittered gang whom Israel has chosen to lead it into the shadows. Virtually overnight almost the whole of articulate world opinion changed course. Never in my experience was a switch so simultaneous. In most cases there was regret and sorrow; in others, a hint of relief. It suddenly became acceptable to be anti-Israel, or at least, understandably, anti-Begin.[9]

There was, of course, a considerable difference between anti-Israel commentary and anti-Begin sentiment, between those who wished to weaken a government and those who believed that the state should never have come into existence, between a James Cameron and a Ken Livingstone. Yet the common denominator was opposition to Israel's ill-conceived invasion of Lebanon. This commonality offered the opportunity for the far Left to utilize the broad disillusionment with Israel's action.

Following BBC 2's broadcast of *The Money Programme* in 1983 which alluded to substantial funding of Gerry Healy's WRP by Libya and Iraq, its party organ *Newsline* ran a story entitled 'The Zionist Connection' which conjured up a traditional imagery of Jewish conspirators pulling the strings of power. Ken Livingstone agreed with this line that there was indeed a powerful Zionist connection that ran from the Labour Left through the Thatcher government to the BBC.[10] Livingstone's own journal *Labour Herald* was printed on the WRP's presses. During the Lebanon war, the journal depicted Begin as a Nazi officer amidst a pile of skulls.[11] This kind of caricature had been a feature of Soviet

demonization of Israel. The depiction of Begin ironically prefigured the depiction of Yitzhak Rabin in Gestapo uniform by the Israeli far Right in the weeks
before his assassination.

In 1982, the British Trade Unionists' annual conference overruled its leadership and overwhelmingly condemned the Israeli military action. This was the
first time that the Trades Union Congress was openly critical of Israel. One
major union, the TGWU called for an air and sea boycott while the Labour
Party NEC wanted PLO involvement in negotiations which would lead to the
establishment of a Palestinian state. Support for pro-Palestinian motions at
Labour Party conferences rose from 52.01% in 1982 to 76.92% in 1989.[12]
Speakers who wished to put the Israeli narrative to Labour Party meetings
found it very difficult in Livingstone's London.

Labour under Michael Foot had fragmented through the defection of part
of its right wing and the party generally went from one disaster to the next
until its crushing electoral defeat in 1983. The vacuum created by Foot's
weak leadership was filled to some extent by the ascendency of the entryist
Trotskyists in alliance with the Labour Left to positions of influence. The New
Left had come of political age, however, it allowed the tabloid press to speak
about 'the loony Left' which ran Labour. The replacement of Foot by Neil
Kinnock as party leader meant a determined effort to return Labour to a more
centrist position and to isolate the far Left within. It also meant projecting a
more balanced policy on the Israel-Palestine conflict – one which helped the
party to repair its relations with Britain's Jewish community.

Ken Livingstone was highly adept at weathering all political storms.
Livingstone was a man for all political seasons. On the one hand, he pro-
fessed himself to be an ardent admirer of Gerry Healy, the leader of the Libyan
backed WRP, on the other, he announced that he was 95% Blairite. Over the
years, he would write regularly for both the Murdoch press and contribute to
Tehran's Press TV.

The disillusionment with Israel under Begin by many on the Left and within
Labour's rank and file was matched by a parallel move by many Jews from
the Left towards the Right. In part, this was because they had 'got on' and
changed their socio-economic status even if they had maintained their liberal convictions. Moreover the Conservative party of the 1970s had begun to
lose its anti-Jewish reputation. There were also members of the Jewish intelligentsia who had rejected their past affiliations. Alfred Sherman, a former
Communist, was one of the progenitors of the Thatcherite revolution which
supplanted the sedate one-nation Conservatism of MacMillan and Heath.
This paralleled the rise of neo-conservatism in the United States whereby
former Jewish Trotskyists were its most passionate practitioners. They were
'dissidents from the New Class ideology'.[13]

Even for those who remained decidedly outside the Labour Party such as Tony Cliff's SWP, the advent of Begin's Likud and the invasion of Lebanon in 1982 brought out sinister visions of 'the Zionist'. 'The Zionists, if not for sale, were always for hire'. The Zionists objected to revolutionary socialists organizing the working class against Hitler. The defeat of the German Left in 1933 – and thereby the success of Nazism – strengthened Zionism. The Irgun of Menachem Begin used the Nazi salute.[14] All these factually distorted comments peculated into the centre Left and the Labour Party.

Moreover, in the last decades of the twentieth century, the number of Jewish Labour MPs had decreased dramatically. For the ordinary Labour activist, there were now very few Jewish comrades to fraternize with. Conversely, the Labour Party provided a home for many non-Jewish Jews whose Jewishness was not central to their identity. Israel came to be seen in one-dimensional terms. The conflict with the Palestinians was often stripped of its complexity.

This cultural vacuum in the rank and file of the Labour Party was also filled by newer ethnic minorities whose understanding of imperialism and experience of colonialism placed them much closer to the cause of the Palestinians. Many Muslim immigrants from the Indian subcontinent in particular found a welcome in the Labour Party and an institution to fight for their rights in British society. The agenda of the founding generation of Muslim immigrants was the struggle against racism and working hard for their families. Little was heard about the convoluted problems of Palestine. Kashmir, however, was another matter, literally closer to home. The succeeding generation of British Muslims, often marooned between identities and cultures, thought differently and subsequently acted globally. They would often turn back to the security and comfort of religion as the Rushdie affair indicated at the end of the 1980s.

The lack of knowledge about the Jewish experience and perhaps of Jews per se dovetailed with the fading away of the Old Left as well as an entire generation of Labour Party figures – a generation which had actually lived through the war years, bore witness to the Shoah and understood the significance of the rise of Israel. In contrast, by the first decade of the twenty-first century, the Muslim Council of Britain refused to attend the annual Holocaust Day commemoration because of its desire to promote and publicize the Palestinian Nakhba. New heroes such as Venezuela's Hugo Chavez and Bolivia's Evo Morales were also lauded because of their desire to remain independent of the United States and to solve the disparity between rich and poor in their countries. This desire also led them to be embraced by Ahmadinejad's Iran and to adopt the absolutism and nihilism of Iranian attitudes towards Israel. The attitude of Chavez towards Israel was said to have been influenced by the Argentinian writer and thinker, Noberto Ceresole who held negative views about Jews per se. The Jewish origin of political opponents such as the Governor of Miranda, the Catholic Henrique Capriles Radonski was raised.[15] The Jewish community in Venezuela sought a solution to this unexpected antagonism in emigration. Yet such issues were glossed over by the far Left in Europe in the adulation for Venezuela's new direction.

The arrival of Matzpen

The new London also attracted Israelis who had opposed Zionism and left Israel. They followed in the footsteps of Ygael Gluckstein aka Tony Cliff in 1946. The emergence of the New Left in the 1960s and particularly the resurgence of Trotskyism in Britain attracted several members of Matzpen, the Israeli Socialist Organization. Matzpen had come into existence in September 1962 through ideological disaffection within the Israeli Communist Party and the latter's inability to shake off the dead hand of the Kremlin. The debate had commenced through a discussion about the nature of the Soviet bureaucracy. The denunciation of Stalinism by Khrushchev opened their eyes, but its implicit corollary of peaceful co-existence with the West alarmed them. The persistent Chinese criticism of Moscow of this approach and the alignment of most Western European Communist parties with the USSR effectively forced the split. Writing under the pseudonym, N. Israeli, Moshe Machover and Akiva Orr published their views in a book *Peace, Peace, When There Is No Peace* in 1961. The centrepiece of their argument, albeit in Marxist colouring, was that Israeli history, the war of 1948 and the Suez Campaign of 1956 were not the simplistic renditions of the time. In one sense, it prefigured the revelations of the New Historians some 20 years later. The Cuban and Algerian revolutions were determinants in looking for something different beyond the growing accommodationist approach of Moshe Sneh and Shmuel Mikunis in the Communist Party.[16]

Together with survivors of the Trotskyist movement of the Mandate period, they formed Matzpen.[17] Indeed they spoke of a 'Dor Hamidbar Trotskyisti' – the Trotskyist generation which wandered in the ideological wilderness, forever condemned not to enter the Promised Land of socialism.[18] The first issue of their journal *Matzpen* in November 1962 bore the banner title 'There is an Address'.[19] This appealed particularly to the younger generation of Israeli Marxists who opposed Zionism and found it difficult to relate to the post-Stalinism of the Communist Party. Matzpen promised a return to Leninism, internationalism, Arab-Jewish cooperation and the prospect of revolutionary activity. They wanted greater openness and accountability. They wanted an independent approach when it came to intellectual endeavour. Both Machover and Orr came to London in the 1960s and stayed several decades. This placed them in contact with many groups on the British New Left. They began to act as guides and mentors for the New Left who often understood little about the complexities of the Israel-Palestine imbroglio. As Israelis, they bore the imprimatur of authenticity. As anti-Zionists, they endorsed the New Left's interpretation of Zionism as a settler state. The Zionist state of Israel, Matzpen argued, constituted an obstacle for the Arab struggle against imperialism and its desire for socialist unity. The Zionist state was 'a bridgehead, a political instrument and a destination for immigration of the Jews all over the world'.[20] Yet a Hebrew nation had been established in Palestine according to the Leninist definition. The solution to the conflict was therefore a de-Zionization of Israel whereby Israeli Jews would have a right to self-determination alongside Kurds and South Sudanese within an Arab federated state.

> Will the disposition here be a one-state or a two-state set-up? It will be both and it will be neither. It will be a one-state set-up – in the sense that both national groups will be accommodated, as federated members, in one state. But that one state will not be Palestine; it will be a regional union. And it will be a two-state set-up in the sense that each of the two national groups will have its own canton (in the Swiss sense) or Land (in the German federal sense) where it constitutes a majority of the population. However, no purpose will be served by interposing between these cantons and the federal state an intermediate political entity – let alone one whose borders are those of 'historical' Palestine, created by the British imperialists in 1923. The resolution of the Israeli-Palestinian conflict will not recreate that ill-starred territory as a unitary or binary entity, but will supersede it – as it will also supersede the Zionist state of Israel.[21]

The Hebrew masses were deemed not to be responsible for the deeds of Zionism. Arab nationalists who called for a Holy War to liberate Palestine were condemned. The Six Day War was seen as stemming from Israeli opposition to the left wing Ba'athist coup in Syria at the beginning of 1966 and Matzpen opposed the war itself. Nasser's regime was seen as progressive, but had not as yet achieved a socialist character. With the rise of the PLO under Arafat, Nawef Hawatmeh's Democratic Front for the Liberation of Palestine (DFLP) argued for a dialogue with Matzpen and accused Arab regimes of trying to isolate the Palestinian struggle.[22] The DFLP was the first Palestinian organization to imply a national colouring for the Jews rather than utilizing the hackneyed phraseology of 'coexistence between Muslims, Christians and Jews'.[23]

Matzpen exhibited a profound antagonism towards Marxist-Zionism and groups such as Siah – the Israeli New Left.[24] Indeed Moshe Sneh and Uri Avneri, both perceived as stalwarts of the Israeli Left were labelled 'shame-faced Zionists'. The Histadrut was described as 'a bureaucratic machine which has a department for trade unions'.[25] They also more mildly castigated Rakah, the Moscow-oriented Communist Party of Israel, yet endorsed the party in the 1969 elections.

Outside of Israel, the Paris events of 1968 affected them as much as their British counterparts. Their articles began to appear in journals such as *New Left Review*, *Black Dwarf*[26] and *Red Mole*. They swiftly earned the friendship of Tony Cliff and his followers[27] as well as the International Marxist Group. In Britain, they formed the Israeli Revolutionary Action Committee Abroad and published *Israca* and then *Khamsin*. The activities of the Matzpeniks in London not only influenced the New Left in Europe, but cemented the connection with the Israeli far Left.

Yet sometimes the transmission of such ideas often gelled with the traditional imagery of the Diaspora Jew. The Israeli far Left displayed an ignorance at best, an indifference at worst, towards the propagation of anti-Jewish stereotypes by its counterparts on the British far Left. Jim Allen, a playwright and former SLL entryist into the Labour Party, produced his play *Perdition* in the 1980s. His work focused on the alleged collaboration between Hungarian Zionists and the Nazis in the Kastner affair. However, it often utilized christological stereotypes of Jews involved in conspiratorial activities which led to a public furore and the theatre's withdrawal from the staging of the work. His friend, the acclaimed filmmaker, Ken Loach ascribed this to pressure from a 'clique' who can 'buy their way'.[28]

The Guardianistas

For political activists who cut their teeth during the 1960s, it was only natural that they should find their way into academia, the media, the literary world and the theatre. The *Guardian*, known for its liberal leanings, provided a logical home for many. Yet the paper had long been associated with the Zionist cause. Situated originally in Manchester, it had employed two of the earliest advocates of Zionism in the United Kingdom, Harry Sacher and the leader writer, Herbert Sidebotham. Moreover C. P. Scott, the *Manchester Guardian* editor had introduced Chaim Weizmann, then an academic at the University of Manchester, to many members of the political elite. This enabled Weizmann to take the Zionist cause to the heart of the British establishment. Like the Communists and the Soviet espousal of Israel in 1947, the *Guardian*'s support for Zionism in 1914 could not later be easily disowned.

Scott's successors continued such support – especially as a reaction to the persecution and extermination of European Jews. Yet *Guardian* writers consisted of a mixture of those who were enthusiastic about the Zionist endeavour – and those who were decidedly lukewarm. One editor believed that the *Guardian*'s role in assisting Weizmann was an albatross around its neck.[29]

The *Guardian* generally bemoaned the tragedy of it all and was critical of both sides. Thus an editorial in December 1947 did not argue that Israel should not have come into existence. Indeed it commented on the plight of long-established Jewish communities in the Arab world who were now under threat from Arab nationalists.[30] It castigated Ernest Bevin for his sympathy for the Arab cause and his antipathy towards Jews.[31] It bemoaned the American retreat from partition towards trusteeship. Even so, there was a recurring sentiment which accompanied this that the Jews in 1948 were myopic and headstrong.

It is one of the most unfortunate aspects of this business that it will fatten the neurosis which already torments the Jewish people and blinds their judgement. They will see in it fresh evidence that the Jews alone are always persecuted and betrayed and will be more inclined than ever to listen to those extremists who urge them to put their faith in violence.[32]

Under Alaistair Hetherington who occupied the editorial chair between 1956 and 1975, the *Guardian* applauded 'the sheer drama of the Jewish success in building or rebuilding a homeland . . . and at the same time wishing to see reconciliation of Zionist ambition with Arab rights'.[33] In 1971 Hetherington refused to carry an advertisement styled as an 'open letter to the Jews of Israel and the Western World'. He rejected it on the basis that he did not agree with the contention that the government of Israel constituted a 'dire threat to world peace'.[34]

After Hetherington's departure, the line on the Palestinians under the new editor, Peter Preston, began to reflect the changing position of the British Left on Israel and in particular its support for liberation movements in the developing world including the PLO. The new line was clear as the *Guardian* later commented in its editorial on the fiftieth anniversary of the establishment of the state of Israel in 1998. It pointed out that 'in the 1970s, before it was fashionable to do so, we pioneered the argument that there must be justice for the Palestinians'.[35]

There now co-existed those of the old school, 'more in the C.P. Scott mould' with 'this solid phalanx of left-wing leader writers'.[36]

The Lebanon war of 1982 proved to be a watershed for the *Guardian*. Ariel Sharon's role in the massacre of Palestinians by Christian Phalangists in the Sabra and Shatilla camps during the Israeli invasion of Lebanon in 1982 became a cause célèbre. Yet it was also accompanied by a wider criticism of Israel per se despite the huge Israeli demonstration against the war, following the killings in the camps. One *Guardian* journalist questioned the nature of Israel's judiciary when it attempted to determine responsibility for the atrocity. 'Israel's own Kahan commission found Sharon 'personally' – but 'indirectly' responsible for the massacre, though whether an independent court would be so generous is open to question?[37] Another *Guardian* journalist suggested the contrary view that 'an independent inquiry mildly criticised his role in the atrocity and he was forced to give up the defence portfolio'.[38] Sharon was viewed as being directly involved in virtually overseeing the killings rather than being morally responsible for the outrage. An educational resource in the paper commented that 'he had the power to stop the massacre of Palestinian refugees in neighbouring Lebanon but did nothing'.[39] Yet another commented that 'the massacres by the Israelis and their Lebanese allies at the Sabra and Shatilla camps in 1982 are a wound that has never healed.'[40] The *Guardian* Middle East editor wrote that Sharon 'watched passively as right-wing Lebanese militias massacred hundreds of Palestinian refugees'.[41] Israeli intelligence estimated that 7–800 Palestinians had been killed, the Palestinian Red Crescent put the figure at 2,000 while the *Guardian* quoted 2,500.[42] Such references in the *Guardian* to the Phalangist massacre of Palestinians contradicted the findings of the official Kahan Report[43] in 1983 and were at variance with several highly critical accounts of Israeli actions at the time including the much praised investigative journalism of Schiff and Ya'ari.[44] Lack of familiarity with Middle East history similarly reoccurred in the *Guardian* during the period of the Al Aqsa Intifada. The Temple Mount was 'thought' by Jews to be the site of the Second Temple – thereby leaving leeway for doubt – in spite of all archaeological evidence to the contrary.[45] The Palestinians would have created a Palestinian State after World War I if the British had allowed them to do so – despite the fact that many considered themselves to be part of Southern Syria and strove to unite with their northern neighbour.[46]

Notes and Works Cited

1 David Widgery, *The Left in Britain 1956–1968* (London 1976), p. 438.

2 Ibid., p. 210.

3 John Carvel, *Citizen Ken* (London 1984), p. 39.

4 *Observer*, 14 November 1999.

5 *Times*, 22 March 2006.

6 Roderick MacFarquhar, 'The Worst Man-Made Catastrophe, Ever', *New York Review of Books*, 10 February 2011.

7 *Evening Standard*, 25 October 2010.

8 David Hirsh, 'Accusations of Malicious Intent in Debates about the Palestine-Israel Conflict and about Anti-Semitism', *Transversal*, no. 1 (2010).

9 *Guardian*, 5 October 1982.

10 *Newsline*, 9 April 1983.

11 *Labour Herald*, 7 January 1983.

12 June Edmunds, 'The British Labour Party in the 1980s: The Battle over the Palestinian/Israeli Conflict', *Politics*, vol. 18, no. 2 (1998).

13 Murray Friedman, *The Neoconservative Revolution: Jewish Intellectuals and the Shaping of Public Policy* (Cambridge 2005), p. 188.

14 Tony Cliff, 'Roots of Israel's Violence', *Socialist Worker*, 14 April 2001.

15 *Forward*, 7 June 2011.

16 *Matzpen*, no. 36, June–July 1967.

17 *Ha'aretz*, 14 September 1962.

18 'Matzpen, 'Ten Years of the Organisation', *Matzpen*, no. 67, January 1973.

19 *Al Hamishmar*, 12 November 1962.

20 *Le Monde*, 20 May 1967.

21 Moshe Machover, 'Resolution of the Israeli-Palestinian Conflict: A Socialist Viewpoint', February 2009, http://matzpen.org/index.asp?p=resolution-machover.

22 *Al-Tali'a*, November 1969 in ed. Robert S. Wistrich, *The Left against Zion: Communism, Israel and the Middle East* (London 1979), p. 241.

23 Alain Gresh, *The PLO: The Struggle Within* (London 1985), pp. 40–2.

24 Sharon Rose, 'The Radical Alternative', *Journal of Palestine Studies*, vol. 2, no. 4 (Summer 1973).

25 Interview with Moshe Machover in Nathan Weinstock's *Zionism: False Messiah* (London 1979), p. xxxviii.

26 *Black Dwarf*, 14 June 1969.

27 *Socialist Worker*, June 1968.

28 David Cesarani, 'The Perdition Affair', in ed. R. S. Wistrich, *Anti-Zionism and Anti-Semitism in the Contemporary World* (New York 1990), pp. 58–9.

29 J. M. D. Pringle, *Have Pen, Will Travel* (London 1973), p. 36.

30 *Guardian*, 10 December 1947.

31 *Guardian*, 12 March 1948.

32 *Guardian*, 22 March 1948.

33 Alastair Hetherington, *Guardian Years* (London 1981), p. 250.

34 Alastair Hetherington to Solly Sachs, 22 April 1971 in Geoffrey Taylor, *Changing Faces. A History of The Guardian 1956–1988* (London 1993), p. 169. E. S. 'Solly' Sachs was a Jewish Communist and Trade Union leader from South Africa who was active during the 1960s and 1970s in attacking Zionist ideology.

35 *Guardian*, 30 April 1998.

36 Taylor, op. cit., p. 80.

37 Seumas Milne, *Guardian*, 9 February 2001.

38 Derek Brown, *Guardian*, 5 January 2001.

39 *Guardian*, First Edition (with Channel Four), 10 October 2000.

40 Victoria Brittain, *Guardian*, 26 April 2000.

41 Brian Whitaker and Khaled Dawoud, *Guardian*, 7 February 2001.

42 Derek Brown, *Guardian*, 5 January 2001.

43 The recommendations of the Kahan Report found that Sharon bore 'personal responsibility' and should 'draw the appropriate personal conclusions arising out of the defects revealed with regard to the manner in which he discharged the duties of his office'. Begin was reminded of his authority under Section 21-A (a) of the Basic Law in which he could remove a Minister from office. The official English translation was published in full by the Jerusalem Post; *Jerusalem Post*, 9 February 1983.

44 Ze'ev Schiff and Ehud Ya'ari, *Israel's Lebanon War* (London 1985).

45 *Guardian*, 10 October 2000.

46 Ibid.

16

The campaign against normalization

Boycotts and the intelligentsia

The question of normalizing relations with Israel, following Arafat's and Rabin's handshake, divided Palestinians into advocates and opponents of compromise. A study of several hundred students at Bir Zeit University on the West Bank in 1994 indicated that those of working-class origin were more supportive of cultural cooperation with Israelis. In part, the endorsement of opposition to normalization was a continuation of the boycott enacted during the first Intifada. Working-class Palestinians who often depended on work in Israel for their livelihood actually associated with Israeli Jews in the work-place. They therefore welcomed Oslo and normalization to a much greater extent than did the elite composed of merchants and professionals as well as the intelligentsia.[1]

There was also the question of formulating the meaning of normalization – what was permitted and what was not. Should there be co-operation with the mainstream Israeli peace camp or only those Israelis who sympathized without reservation and identified with Palestinian aspirations? In part, the template for opposing normalization was located in Egypt and Jordan which had signed peace treaties with Israel. In both countries there were substantial parts of the elites and the leftist intelligentsia who opposed any recognition of Israel.

The origin of anti-normalization commenced in Egypt with Sadat's turning away from Nasserism and the Soviet Union in the early 1970s. Instead Egypt turned towards multi-national conglomerates to ensure investment as a means of solving the country's chronic economic problems, a situation made worse by an increasing population. The Camp David peace treaty negotiated with Israel in 1979 was viewed as part of this new direction by many Egyptian intellectuals and professionals. It also allowed them to utilize the Palestinian issue – which no one could quarrel with – as a means of operating publicly yet independently of the military regime which they opposed. This manifested itself in selective refusals to invite Israelis to academic conferences and film festivals. This continued the spirit of the Arab League's economic boycott of Israel which was initiated as early as December 1945.

The lack of contact with Israelis, however, permitted a bubble of isolationism to surface. This also limited different Palestinian voices to be heard, apart from well-known oppositionists such as Edward Said.[2] The opposition to the Oslo accords accentuated this tendency and extended beyond refusals to Israelis to include Palestinians who approved of normalization with Israelis. Said regarded Oslo as the Palestinian Versailles. Thus the General Union of Arab Authors and Writers suspended the membership of the Union of Palestinian Writers and Journalists in 1997 because of its support of normalization of relations with Israel. Naguib Mahfouz, winner of the Nobel Prize for Literature in 1988 supported normalization and was a target for criticism in the Egyptian press. Within the Egyptian media, anti-Zionism occasionally developed anti-Jewish stereotypes. In *al Masry al-Youm* in 2008, Jews were accused of withdrawing $400 billion in the weeks before the collapse of Lehman Brothers.[3] Anti-normalization began to move into the mainstream with the breakdown of the Oslo peace process and undoubtedly with the onset of the al-Aqsa Intifada at the end of 2000. This was manifested by workers and student unions, mosques and human rights groups expanding the anti-normalization circle of activism. Anti-normalization became unquestioned within the Egyptian media. Thus the brutal conflict in the West Bank during the Intifada became a topic for questions in the Egyptian version of 'Who wants to be a millionaire?'[4]

The number of Palestinian students in the West Bank and Gaza had increased exponentially under Israeli rule. At Bir Zeit, the student body was evenly divided in welcoming the Oslo accords – with Marxists and Islamists being strongly opposed. Outside of the Israel-Palestine imbroglio, this mirrored a general trend within the Arab world – a disillusionment with Arab nationalism and the belief that a resurgent Islamism would do better.

The opposition to the Oslo agreement was in general led by a mixture of different Palestinian groups. It was opposed by the Marxists of the PFLP and the DFLP as well by secular intellectuals abroad such as Edward Said, Hisham Shirabi and the poet Mahmud Darwish.[5] They emphasized the weakness of the Palestinians, the downgrading of the right of return and the encirclement of East Jerusalem. Said attacked Arafat for bringing the Intifada to a halt and for failing to coordinate his move with Arab states.

> The PLO has transformed itself from a national liberation movement into a kind of small-town government, with the same handful of people still in command.[6]

The Islamist Hamas similarly had started a campaign against normalization of relations with Israel even before the Oslo accords and thereby forged an alliance with the Shi'ites of Teheran. Hamas sent delegates to a conference 'in support of the Islamic Revolution in Palestine' in the Iranian capital in October 1991. This coincided with the Madrid conference, called by Bush and Gorbachev, which brought together Israel and the Arab states for the first time in decades.

Sheikh Ahmad Yassin, the spiritual mentor of Hamas, sent a letter from his prison cell, exhorting his followers to vehemently oppose Oslo. As a Hamas spokesman commented a week before Arafat and Rabin signed the Declaration of Principles on the White House lawn:

> These developments make Hamas and the other factions strongly believe in our ability to meet our people's aspirations and to lead the people on the path of jihad and liberation.[7]

In April 1994, Hamas introduced suicide bombing into Israeli cities to halt the normalization which Oslo had fostered. A bombing in Afula was followed by attacks on Hadera, Ramla, Jerusalem and the Dizengoff shopping centre in Tel Aviv in the coming months. Hamas was keen to undermine the Israeli peace campaign, but did not move against the PLO which it refused to join. It was eager to disrupt the unwritten normalization of relations between individual Israelis and Palestinians due to proximity and dependency. The bombings in turn led to Israeli closures of the Palestinian territories which prevented Palestinians coming to work in Israel. Between 1993 and 1996, Palestinian workers lost a third of each year.[8] The ensuing unemployment and general economic deterioration in the Palestinian territories created further resentment at the promises of Oslo.

Yet a series of opinion polls suggested that a majority of Palestinians – reaching 71% in August–September 1995 – were willing to support the Oslo accords. At the same time, support for Hamas's Ahmad Yassin dropped to 14% and for the PFLP's George Habash to 7%.[9] The view of the Palestinians in the West Bank and Gaza was in sharp contrast to the Palestinian Diaspora which strongly criticized the Oslo accords.[10] Even so, in January 1994, ten Palestinian organizations which opposed Oslo formed a bloc. This consisted of an uneasy alliance of democratic socialists, nationalists and Islamists. While the PFLP and DFLP eventually came to terms with Arafat, small groups such as the Palestinian Revolutionary Communist

Party which had broken away from the PCP, refused to contemplate any recognition of Israel and any normalization of relations.[11] Secular opponents were gradually squeezed by Arafat's authoritarianism, Israeli military action and the Islamists – and sought refuge in democratization and in NGOs.[12] Liberals and leftists made little headway against Fatah and Hamas – and turned therefore towards the international Left with the idea of opposing normalization with Israel.

Arafat temporarily banned newspapers such as *al-Nahar* and *al-Quds* for their criticisms. The number of armed Palestinian policemen was doubled. The situation was further polarized by the election of a right wing government under Netanyahu, following the assassination of Rabin. The Israeli Right did not believe in Oslo and sought to undermine it. In addition, there was a tremendous increase in the number of settlers in the West Bank. The areas of jurisdiction of existing settlements were changed by the Netanyahu government in 1996 to allow expansion and an intensive programme of by-pass roads was initiated to allow them to be connected to Israel. This in turn led to the fragmentation of the West Bank into a series of enclaves and the loss of territorial contiguity.

Arafat's position was thus considerably weakened by 2000 and even if the Israeli offer by Labour's Ehud Barak at Camp David was a considerable advance on previous negotiations, he was in no position and in no mood to accept it. For a plethora of reasons therefore, Oslo had not improved the hopes for a better life for the ordinary Palestinian Arab. They had been dashed by an array of rejectionist forces from both sides. This allowed Hamas to fill the void of bitterness and to promise a principled way forward. Unlike the first Intifada, the Islamist-led al-Aqsa Intifada was characterized by the use of lethal weapons and suicide bombing. The outbreak of violence catalysed a traditional turn to the Right by the Israeli electorate and the election of the hard-line Ariel Sharon in January 2001. This essentially represented the political demise of the Israeli peace camp due to the Israeli citizen's deep fear of the Islamist suicide bomber. The political ground was cut from beneath their feet. Sharon's crushing of the Islamists militarily led subsequently to a series of centre-right wing governments in Israel that now depended on the far Right to maintain them in power. In Gaza, Hamas eliminated the Palestinian peace camp there following its takeover in 2007. Israel's practice of military deterrence in Lebanon in 2006 and Gaza in 2009 was coupled by the politics of stagnation.

By 2000 there was a general recognition among the Palestinians that the peace process had run its course and that Oslo had failed. The political vacuum which had been created was filled not only by the Islamists, but by that part of the Palestinian intelligentsia that had always opposed Oslo and any hint of normalization of relations with Israel. They mimicked the practice of the Egyptian elite after the Camp David agreement in 1979. One Israeli architect of the Oslo accords bitterly commented:

> The Arabic term for normalisation, 'tatbeeh', now serves as a word of remonstration and criticism against Arab organisations and individuals who maintain ties and relations with Israel and Israelis. It is linked to another concept, that of conspiracy, 'muamara', that has found its way into the discourse. The two terms converge easily among the anti-peace process camp that sees in nearly every Israeli initiative part of a conspiracy, and in normalisation an integral aspect of a grand conspiracy, designed to deliver to Israel, in the course of its transition from wartime military dominance to more subtle control in the post-peace era, social, cultural and economic control of the Arab world.[13]

The polarizing effect of the al-Aqsa Intifada and the Right's political dominance in Israel affected the Left both in Europe and of course, within the Palestinian territories. In 2001, the Palestinian Journalists' Syndicate called for a refusal to participate in meetings with Israelis and thereby 'denying the chance of Israelis of opening up channels of normalization'. Football training sessions between Israelis and Palestinians were stopped.[14]

However, the central vehicle for initiating a boycott of Israel was the Durban Conference of NGOs which was held under the auspices of the UN Commission on Human Rights (UNCHR) in September 2001. The organization had developed during a period of decolonization during the 1960s and particularly in the struggle against apartheid in South Africa. By the 1990s, it had degenerated into a highly politicized tool of a cabal of countries whose trademark was ironically a flouting of human rights. The Durban conference and a parallel forum of NGOs were promoted in particular by the Arab League as the al-Aqsa Intifada commenced. A preparatory conference was held in Teheran and it was here that the declaration of the NGO Forum was broadly formulated. Whereas the Arabs had wanted to reintroduce the 'Zionism is Racism' resolution which had been discarded in the run-up to Oslo, the Iranians injected a less than sedate language into the document: apartheid state, ethnic cleansing, genocide, racism. It also called for 'a policy of complete and total isolation of Israel . . . a cessation of all links: diplomatic, economic, social aid . . .'. The Iranians ultimately refused to permit Jewish NGOs to attend the Teheran meeting despite promises to the UNCHR Commissioner, Mary Robinson. The language of the declaration and the general intimidatory atmosphere shocked Robinson and several Western funders such as the Ford Foundation and the Canadian government. The injection of Islamism into the conference often promoted anti-Jewish rather than anti-Zionist themes. The Protocols of the Elders of Zion was on sale in the exhibition hall. NGOs such as Amnesty International and Human Rights Watch became fellow travellers in all this, genuinely wishing to assist the hard-pressed Palestinians, but blind to other misdemeanours. The UNCHR's role came into question in July 2002, shortly after the Jenin 'massacre' controversy, when the African Union nominated Libya as chair of the UN body. Even Human Rights Watch protested at the inappropriateness of Gaddafi's representative heading the UNCHR. This situation did not last long and the UNCHR finally came to an inglorious end in 2006. Durban had however provided the opponents of Oslo with a platform to move into the mainstream. In this, they were willingly assisted by a network of NGOs whose post-colonial outlook was part of the legacy of the European New Left of the 1960s.

In 2004, several younger academics at Bir Zeit University and Ramallah cultural figures initiated a campaign of boycott, disinvestment and sanctions (BDS). Many of those initially involved had spent considerable time abroad and were influenced by political campaigns for a variety of causes waged in Western Europe and the United States. Quite a few of this elite had been born outside Palestine. This was followed by a call from the Palestinian General Federation of Trade Unions. While its leadership was closely aligned with Fatah, it also utilized the boycott to challenge the old guard in the Palestine Authority.

Guidelines for cooperation with Israelis were formulated and a flow chart with questions such as 'Does the project refrain from condemning the occupation or is it conditional on rejecting the right of return?' A 'yes' took the participant to 'Break Contact'. A 'no' led to a 'Cooperate Carefully'. Such ideological rigidity effectively eliminated a large section of the Israeli peace camp. Other Palestinian voices such as the academic Sari Nusseibeh and the writer Samir el-Youssef who were opposed to such a move were associated with the failure of the peace process and condemned.

There was a broad disdain for the Fatah leadership and Arafat's rule as well as anguish at the arrests of Bir Zeit students by the Israelis and the general difficulty in running the institution during the Intifada. It also represented an opportunity to break with the good intentions of Oslo's perceived utopianism and to present a stand, based on crafted demands. It provided a vehicle to distance that part of the Palestinian Left from the ideological burden of official groups such as the PFLP and DFLP. In one sense, the Bir Zeit group represented a modernization of the Palestinian Left, based on its experience in the West. Apartheid was emphasized therefore and Israel compared to South Africa. Indeed it was argued that Palestinians and Israelis were analogous to Blacks and Whites in South Africa – and therefore any boycott would ultimately be to the benefit of both national groups. The Palestinian nationalist narrative of 1948 was retained. There was no direct mention of a two-state solution. This appealed to the mindset of the far Left in Israel, the Middle East and beyond.

The *Guardian* and normalization

While the *Guardian* greeted the Oslo Accords in 1993, it also gave increasing space to opponents of normalization such as Edward Said. The *Guardian*'s veteran Middle East correspondent, David Hirst, saw Oslo as a means 'to deprive the Palestinians of any sense of historic injustice'.[15]

Edward Said was undoubtedly the most eloquent spokesman for the Palestinian cause in the liberal and left wing press in Europe. Yet for all his brilliance, he appeared to have moved from embracing a two-state solution in 1979 towards a bi-national state on the South African model. He had clearly grown tired of the never-ending deliberations of the PLO bureaucracy and resigned from the PNC in protest against the policies of Arafat and the Arab leadership in attending the Madrid Conference – 'an unseemly rush to discard principles and strategic goals with equal abandon'.[16] The Palestinians had 'ceased being a people determined on liberation; we had accepted the lesser goal of a small degree of independence'.[17]

Said's stand against compromise was widely applauded by the liberal intelligentsia in Europe. His crusading language embellished the prospect of redemptive politics and the dignity of the nation. It simultaneously emphasized victimhood.[18] Part of his appeal was his embrace of areas of universalism within the container of Palestinian nationalism. He presented, as an alternative to Zionism, 'the idea of Palestine, a non-exclusivist, secular, democratic, tolerant and generally progressive ideology'.[19] While a majority of Palestinians, according to opinion polls, was in favour of Oslo, normalization and compromise, Edward Said's approach maintained the ideological purity of the cause.

In 1999, he wrote:

This substitution of a short-range nationalism for a longer social movement is one of the intended effects of Oslo, in effect, to depoliticise Palestinian society and set it squarely within the main current of American style globalisation, where the market is king, everything else is irrelevant or marginal. Just to have a Palestinian institute of folklore research or a Palestinian university or a Palestinian medical association is therefore not enough, any more than nationalism is enough.[20]

As a product of American academia, Said was, like many of his *Guardian* readers, also influenced by the political culture of the 1960s, the New Left and a disdain for fellow travellers of the USSR. In the 1993 Reith Lectures, he viewed any support for Israel from the liberal intelligentsia in the West as 'an abrogation of intellectual responsibility comparable to the connivance of the Old Left with Stalinist crimes'.[21] This further reflected his view that Israelis and Jews were in a state of denial about the past and the present. Said's literary prowess animated his political writings, but it also distanced him from the difficulties of realpolitik. Said's contributions were an example of good passionate writing which were intellectually satisfying.

Like the Egyptian media in the 1990s, the *Guardian* readership was rarely exposed to any other type of Palestinian intellectual. Edward Said's fame, erudition and presumed liberalism dominated. Even the rise of Palestinian Islamism was underplayed. Hamas's introduction of suicide bombing into Israel at the beginning of 1994 was designed to destroy the Oslo Accords and the peace camps in both Israel and Palestine. Such a turn of events was not regarded as central to the success or failure of a peace process as it was seen to be irrevocably flawed – the advent of the suicide bombers therefore could be dismissed as being marginal to the issue. The Islamists succeeded in their political goal and propelled the Israeli Right to electoral victory in 1996.

The failure of Oslo also became synonymous with the corruption of the Palestinian Authority and the ineptitude of Arafat. Opposition to Oslo and Arafat's policies gradually became associated with intellectual honesty – no compromise on the truth of 1948 and the accompanying right to return according to UN Resolution 194. Thus Said dismissed the Abu Mazen-Yossi Beilin agreement in 1996[22] and looked upon supporters of the Israeli peace movement – in particular academics and writers such as Amos Oz and David Grossman – with a particular disdain.

In opposing the Hebron Agreement in January 1997, Said informed *Guardian* readers that

> for the Palestinians, peace with such a state is illusory, not least because Israel is still privileged according to a 'western master-native, highlighting Jewish alienation and redemption' which excludes the Palestinian experience of dispossession and exile.[23]

Such views were echoed in an analysis by the Deputy Foreign Editor of the *Guardian*.[24] It utilized the arguments and material of the Palestinian 'Right to Return' campaign and suggested that approximately 4 million Palestinians would wish to come back.

The *Guardian* also began to dabble in conspiracy inferences.[25] It permitted the inclusion of a half-page advertisement, under the name of Ayatollah Khamenei of Iran, in 1996 on the occasion of the Hajj which implied 'Zionist' control of the US media.[26]

A few years later, 'a shadowy ultra-orthodox Jewish group' was accused of organizing a campaign of vilification and denigration.[27] The impression given was that this was all the work of mainstream Jewish organizations in Britain. Such an attitude pushed some Jewish readers to comment that they felt that they were often differentiated from other ethnic groups and treated as 'fair game for crank provocations'.[28] To be labelled as 'racist' by Asians and Blacks was taken seriously. To be criticized by Jews for insensitivity, subtle discrimination and lack of understanding often invited disbelief and ridicule. This concatenation of criticism persuaded some Jews to ask aloud whether all this was simply a guise for a genteel anti-Semitism on the British model rather than a robust attack on Israeli policies.[29]

The message sent by some *Guardian* contributors was that the supporters of Israel were an internationally powerful group allied with and funded by the forces of reaction. Moreover, the projection of Israeli Jews as a Middle East Goliath helped *Guardian* journalists to psychologically dismiss protests from both Jewish individuals and organizations in Britain as 'resisting pressure'.[30]

The accusation of 'Jewish pressure' was also raised in the *Guardian* by contributors close to Islamist circles who often projected an absolutist view of the Israel-Palestine conflict.[31] Again there was mention of 'shadowy Israeli lobbyists in Westminster'.[32]

The writer Peter Oborne produced a television programme in 2009 about 'the pro-Israel lobby' and attacked it for its efficiency in garnering support from parliamentarians. It was 'well-connected and well-funded' and sent a large number of MPs each year to see Israel for themselves. While he called for greater openness, Oborne also declared that such advocates for Israel had done nothing wrong or illegal and 'there is no conspiracy, and nothing resembling a conspiracy'.[33] One Jewish academic in response commented sarcastically that the reality was that Oborne had set out 'to expose a secretive lobby of rich and powerful Jews who use money and strong-arm tactics to skew British foreign policy in favour of Israel, intimidate MPs, and stifle media criticism of Zionism'.[34] Yet nothing of the kind was uncovered. He further remarked that within minutes of the programme finishing, the comments page of the television station's website carried crude anti-Jewish invective.

In March 2010, a *Guardian* editorial described Israel as 'an arrogant nation that has overreached itself'.[35] Since many Israeli Arabs considered themselves to be members of the Palestinian nation, did this arrogance really only apply to Israeli Jews?

S. mhlne

In 2001, the *Guardian* appointed an adherent of the far Left as its op-ed editor in charge of its 'Comment' page. Thereafter the North Korean Foreign Ministry was quoted approvingly 'that to allow disarmament through inspections does not help to prevent a war, but rather sparks it'.[36] The trial of Milosovic was condemned and NATO's intervention in the Kosovo crisis attacked. In August 2001, the tenth anniversary of the coup against Gorbachev was noted. Glasnost, it was argued, ushered in 'the most cataclysmic peacetime economic collapse of an industrial country in history. Under the banner of reform and the guidance of American-prescribed shock therapy, perestroika became catastroika'.[37] There were also strong objections to attempts to equate Stalin with Hitler even though an estimated 6 million civilians were deliberately killed under Stalinism.[38] Colonialism, it was argued, had as much to answer for as did Nazism and Communism. 'There is no major twentieth century political tradition without blood on its hands.'

This new direction coincided with the entry into the White House of George W. Bush, the attack on the twin towers, Sharon's ascendency and the heat of the al-Aqsa Intifada. The Israel-Palestine imbroglio was covered repeatedly. Although the British journalist, Jonathan Freedland addressed the conflict in his *Guardian* column, it quickly became clear that outside contributors who were representatives of the mainstream peace camps in both Israel and Palestine were rarely asked to write. Instead rejectionist Israelis and Palestinians made their mark. In turn, Freedland organized a meeting of Israeli and Palestinian doves under the aegis of the *Guardian* in June 2002.[39] While this demonstrated that *Guardian* journalists were not a monolithic entity, the essential narrative of outside contributors to the Israel-Palestine conflict during the years of the Intifada in the opinion pages belonged to the far Left with little pretence at offering different leftist views. Thus, for example, the Yossi Beilin-Yasser Abed Rabbo Geneva Initiative was distinctly underplayed and mainly Palestinian critics invited to comment. The advent of suicide bombing by Palestinian Islamists was marked by a dynamic equilibrium of opposition on the one hand against understanding for such events on the other. One writer placed 'suicide bomber' in inverted commas. There were, of course, occasional alternative views, but often from right wing Israelis. Contributors from the mainstream Israeli peace camp disappeared from view, isolated between the righteous views of the official Israeli leadership and the virulence of the rejectionists.

Moreover the politics of 'selective outrage' was practised. While a wave of criticism was directed at Israel, there was minimal coverage of human rights abuses and the marginalization of democratic behaviour in other countries such as China and Russia. This approach to the Israel-Palestine conflict endured for six years. A more rational approach to the Israel-Palestine conflict ensued after 2007 with successor editors. However, the damage done to the *Guardian*'s reputation as a fair-minded publication endured.

The banishment of dialogue

For many groups on the far Left in Europe, the idea of a rapprochement between Arafat and Rabin did not further revolutionary endeavour. It did not fit into the theory of ideological opposition to Zionism. It certainly did not appeal to non-Jewish Jews in that Israel would no longer be considered an aberration. The idea of a state with a Jewish majority – a state based on nationality rather than class was certainly very difficult for some Jewish Marxists.[40] It once again brought up questions of identity. Ronnie Kasrils, a founding member of Umkhonto we Sizwe, a government minister in the new South Africa and a leading member of the country's Communist Party strongly promoted his Jewishness when opposing Israeli policies. Yet such zeal often led into unsavoury characterizations. In 2006, he commented in a *Guardian* interview:

> Israelis claim that they are the chosen people, the elect of God and find a biblical justification for their racism and Zionist exclusivity.[41]

The substitution of 'Jews' for 'Israelis' and 'Jewish' for 'Zionist' sounded remarkably familiar to comments from far Right politicians of the early twentieth century. A similar commentary about 'chosenness' by the Norwegian intellectual, Jostein Gaarder, featured in a commentary, following the second Lebanon war in 2006[42] and by a *Guardian* columnist after the release of Gilad Shalit in October 2011. [43]

The idea of opposition to normalization and selective cooperation with Israelis, depending on whether they conformed to specific political stands, was transmitted to Europe and especially to the United Kingdom which historically had the closest contact with the Palestinians. If in 1993, the opponents of Oslo and normalization had been a small minority in Europe, the deterioration of the situation in the Middle East provided a unique opportunity to work within the larger camp of those who were dismayed by Israeli action and moved by Palestinian suffering. It was no longer a question of the peace camps in Israel and Palestine against their rejectionists, but a polarization into 'Israel versus Palestine'.

Sharon had argued that there could be no negotiations with the Palestinians while there was violence, no matter how insignificant. In parallel, the opponents of normalization had argued that there could be no dialogue without a complete resolution of all outstanding problems. Thus organizations such as Seeds of Peace and One Voice which encouraged young people to engage in dialogue were targeted. All this contributed to the politics of stagnation.

Similarly the Palestinian government of the technocrat, Salam Fayyad which had chosen to work with Western institutions such as the World Bank, dramatically improved the economic situation on West Bank. This persuaded sections of the far Left to quietly support the Islamists of Hamas because the organization personified 'resistance', regardless of its ideological hue. There was, for example, deep resentment at the British Government's Department for International Development in sponsoring Israeli-Palestinian projects and thereby endorsing normalization.

The campaign against normalization blossomed and flourished in Palestine as a result of the suffering and humiliation engendered by the al-Aqsa Intifada. In Britain, Sharon's offensive in Jenin was the immediate cause for 'a restricted call for a moratorium on European research and academic collaboration with Israeli institutions' in April 2002. This dovetailed with the activism of several Muslim Brotherhood adherents. The British call was followed by similar calls from academics in France, Italy and other European countries.

Many of those involved at this time had first cut their political teeth in the 1960s. Several were Jewish, following in the 'as a Jew' tradition of opposing Zionism while proclaiming their Jewishness. The premise of the boycott and the isolation of Israel's academic research community from its colleagues had worked against South African apartheid and many believed that it would ultimately work against Israel. This resonated with many in Britain which had been the traditional home of the struggle against apartheid – and especially by many South African exiles.

It also built on the apartheid analogy which had been propagated in the Soviet press since the 1970s as well as by the Organisation of African Unity. Many African states had, under Arab pressure, broken off formal diplomatic relations with Israel following the Yom Kippur war in 1973.

The ambiguity in the academics' appeal in Europe was superseded by the more radical call for boycott, disinvestment and sanctions by the Bir Zeit group a couple of years later. The spirit of the call was taken up by resolutions in one form or another in successive years at the annual conference of the University and College Union (UCU) of British academics. At first, these moves were instigated by activists who sympathized with the Palestinian cause. With the merger of the two unions which represented both the further and higher education sectors, they were subsequently replaced by Socialist Workers Party (SWP) activists. Out of 120,000 members, only some 10% voted in elections.

While this could be measured largely in public relations terms rather than in concrete political measures, many Jews in Britain and in other European countries psychologically perceived this as the first step towards delegitimizing the state, reversing not 1967, but 1948. This struck at Jewish sensitivities. Despite the fact that there was a long tradition of Marxist Jews who had genuinely opposed Zionism, the repeated argument that anti-Zionism could never be a cover for anti-Semitism did not hold water. In one sense, this evolving environment separated nationally aware Jews from their non-Jewish colleagues. Their fear was that the campaign against normalization between Israelis and Palestinians in the Middle East would ultimately develop into a discrimination against Jews in Europe. And by extension, if Palestinians suffered why should not Jews world-wide do the same? In late 2008, the young Rabbi Gavriel Holtzberg and his wife who offered kosher food and sustenance at a Jewish traveller's house in Mumbai were tortured and killed during the killings by Pakistani Islamists. This was often linked with the siege of Gaza.

What non-Jews understood as standing up for the underdog, supporting human rights and righting a wrong, many Jews conversely believed that what began with the delegitimization of the state would end with the delegitimization of the people. Past history had demonstrated the potency of simplistic distortion and the power of grave accusation with terrible results. Jewish history had taught that to remain passive was not an option.

This was often embellished by Jewish individuals in Europe reacting emotionally rather than politically. Several American Jews erroneously believed that Britain was in the grip of a wave of virulent anti-Semitism, comparable with the 1930s. Robotic emailing campaigns to the *Guardian*, often with the same wording, created entrenchment and resentment rather than dialogue and discussion. The far Right in Israel, only too keen to hit the Left, annexed the issue for its own political purposes. Moreover this was often accompanied by a blurring of the differences between Zionist critics and anti-Zionist opponents by the Israeli Right and a blanket labelling of all as 'self-hating Jews'.

Among liberal opinion, there was considerable resentment at repeated accusations of anti-Semitism which was seen solely through the British experience of combating Nazi Germany. There was often profound irritation with 'Zionists' who provided another narrative which ran counter to sympathy for the hard-pressed Palestinians. Quite often, the only acceptable Jews would be those who denounced Israel per se and the ultra-orthodox who fitted the conventional stereotype of a non-assertive religious group.

More widely there were also intellectuals in European public life who simply did not agree with the boycott initiators that 'exaggerated attention' had been given to academic freedom issues. There was also concern about selective outrage. If this was not the case, there would also have been a boy-cott against American academia for the invasion of Iraq. The strong reaction from many Jews, often opposed to the policies of the Sharon government and its successors, proved to be the fundamental difference between the Israel-Palestine imbroglio and the struggle in South Africa.

The Muslim Brotherhood, Iraq and the European Left

In 1988, the Muslim Brotherhood in Gaza formed a front organization, Hamas, to participate in the first Intifada. The leaders of the revolt against the Israeli occupation were generally local nationalists who carried out their opposi-tion without the use of arms. Its initial success and the independence of its leadership worried the PLO leadership in Tunis. It also worried the Muslim Brotherhood who similarly feared being overtaken by events, but it looked upon the solidarity between the Israeli and Palestinian peace camps with par-ticular disfavour. The establishment of such front organizations on behalf of the Brotherhood spread to Europe in the 1990s where an entryist philosophy was practised with regard to existing Muslim communities.

In Britain, the London-based spokesman for the Muslim Brotherhood established the Muslim Association of Britain (MAB) in 1997. Its co-founders were adherents of the Brotherhood from Iraq, Palestine and Jordan. This capi-talized on Muslim protests against the publication of Salman Rushdie's *The Satanic Verses* in the late 1980s.

The MAB soon joined the Muslim Council of Britain which had been estab-lished at the behest of the British government as a central address for British Muslims. The MAB was perhaps the most politically aware of all Muslim groups and given its ideological origin was keen to assist Hamas in its strug-gle against the Israeli military during the al-Aqsa Intifada.

In April 2002, it was able to organize a large demonstration in London against Israeli attacks on a Palestinian camp in Jenin on the West Bank from where more than 20 suicide bombing attacks on Israeli civilian targets had originated. It was also a base for an active Islamic Jihad unit which was believed to be preparing Qassam missiles to be fired into Israel – as Hamas had done from Gaza. Although half the camp's population left before the Israeli assault, the vicious clash resulted in the deaths of 23 Israeli soldiers and more than 50 Palestinian civilians and combatants and a considerable destruction of homes. Palestinian spokesmen such as Saeb Erekat and Nabil Shaath, however, spoke of a 'massacre' with '500 casualties'. There was clearly a desire to recreate the imagery of the killings in Sabra and Shatilla in 1982 with Sharon once more masterminding the situation. The initial reporting in the broadsheet British press as well as on the BBC therefore related stories of a massacre of an untold large numbers of victims, summary executions and the perpetration of a war crime, citing witnesses who claimed that Israeli troops had piled up dozens of Palestinian corpses before bulldozing homes. A *Guardian* editorial commented:

> Jenin smells like a crime. The stench of decaying bodies left to rot or buried unabsolved under collapsed buildings greets those aid workers and reporters who manage to gain access. What cruel deficit of pity denies those who died the benefit of departing grace? Jenin feels like a crime.[44]

Although the massacre claim was eventually dropped, accusations of disproportionate force remained. In the immediate aftermath of Jenin, the MAB was thereby able to mobilize many young Muslims, alienated and disaffected by British reaction after 9/11 and the invasion of Afghanistan by the United States. The Palestine Solidarity Campaign capitalized on this and asked the MAB to be co-organizers of its annual nakhba demonstration in Trafalgar Square in May 2002.

There was also opposition from Muslims about participating in the protests with non-Muslims. The MAB leadership argued that it was religiously permissible if halal food was provided and men and women were given separate areas. While they argued that they would share platforms with socialists and atheists, this could not be extended to Zionists and Israelis in particular.[45] This was in accordance with Hamas policy not to negotiate with Israel directly – or even with the Israeli peace camp. This had always differentiated the Palestinian Islamists from the Palestinian nationalists of Fatah, but it certainly dovetailed with the BDS approach on normalization of relations with Israel. Yet while the Palestinian group at Bir Zeit and their supporters in the West had made efforts to enlist 'approved' Israelis whose political viewpoints were acceptable, the Islamists made little attempt at dialogue even with the Israeli far Left.

The MAB was subsequently approached by the SWP and the Communist Party of Britain (CPB) to affiliate to the Stop the War Coalition (STWC) in the run-up to the US planned invasion of Iraq. The MAB agreed only to work alongside the STWC and to preserve its own political identity. The first cooperation between the far Left and the Islamists in September 2002 thus occurred at a protest to mark the second anniversary of Sharon's walk on the Temple Mount. While the STWC emphasized the prevention of war in Iraq, the MAB promoted 'Freedom for Palestine'.

The political atmosphere after 9/11 in Britain and the disaffection of second and third generation British Muslims provided this relatively obscure organization with the opportunity to act as the vehicle for protest by a younger generation of the offspring of immigrants who came mainly from the Indian subcontinent. The MAB expressed the anger of British Muslims at a broader political scenario beyond the Israel-Palestine imbroglio. Such disaffection, however, coincided with the al-Aqsa Intifada and Sharon's military initiative against both Arafat and his Islamist opponents. This circle was expanded further just before the invasion of Iraq when Labour party supporters, liberals and an array of leftists joined together with a broad mobilization of Muslims in the United Kingdom and demonstrated in February 2003 in London in probably one of the largest demonstrations since the halcyon days of the 1950s and 1960s. In this fashion, the Muslim Brotherhood transmitted the issue of Palestine to the British Left.

The rise of Islamist movements generally and the historical attitude of the liberal intelligentsia and the political Left had created an ongoing mutual suspicion. On the one hand, King Khaled of Saudi Arabia had spoken in 1979 of the trinity of Zionism, Communism and colonialism, all allied against Arab and Islamic rights and aspirations.[46] On the other, the British academic and political commentator, Fred Halliday, had referred to the Khomeini regime in Iran as 'Islam with a fascist face'. [47] Moreover there was often a blurring of 'Jews' and 'Zionists' in Islamist circles and an indifference to using anti-Jewish stereotypes.

Conversely, others on the European Left viewed Muslim workers as a new proletariat to be cultivated and won over. In Muslim history, it was argued, there were periods of religious intensity, marked by a reoccurring theme of a return to the spiritual purity of the times of the Prophet. Such periods were characterized by revolutionary endeavour against oppressive establishments. One SWP ideologist argued as early as 1994 that:

> Traditionalist Islam is an ideology which seeks to perpetuate a social order which is being undermined by the development of capitalism. There is a corruption of Islam by cultural imperialism.[48]

There was, of course, a conservative exploiting class, but the exploited could rise up and their revolutionary anger could thereby be directed into constructive channels. This was the same sort of argument used by revolutionaries about the Russian peasantry and their attacks upon Jews in 1881.

The far Left in Europe in parallel saw the Oslo Accords as a corrupting influence in the Middle East. The acceptance of Israel, it was argued, was a subterfuge to move the region into the global market. It also opened up the markets of the Islamic world to Israel.

There were other areas of common agreement. Islamists and Trotskyists opposed both East and West – as witnessed by the reaction to both the Soviet and American presences in Afghanistan. Moreover both superpowers had been instrumental in the establishment of Israel in 1948.

The destruction of the Twin Towers accentuated an embedded anti-Americanism. The British SWP issued a statement on 12 September which extended this sentiment to Israel. It commented that as Israel had never shown any compunction about killing civilians in the territories and in Lebanon, it was quite understandable that some angered individuals would take it upon themselves to attack Israel's sponsor, the United States.

The invasion of Saddam's Iraq allowed the far Left in Britain to occupy the political space which was formerly the prerogative of the left wing of the Labour Party. There was great rage against 'liberal imperialism'. In 1956, the Labour Party had organized the protests against the Suez campaign. In 2003, it was an alliance of Trotskyists, Stalinists and Islamists that brought a reputed million people onto the streets of London. Social democracy, it was argued, was now in terminal decline. Yet despite the rebellion of 139 Labour MPs over Iraq, the party did not split.

Lenin's article in 1905 'Socialism and Religion' was dusted off and the early co-operation of Bolsheviks and left wing Muslims in 1917 recalled. The early Soviet state, it was argued, was non-religious rather than anti-religious. The Soviet assault on Muslims in the USSR in the late 1920s was not a faithful development of Leninist policies, but enacted through a coalition of Stalinists, the ultra-left and great Russian chauvinists. The SWP thereby claimed that they were upholding a revolutionary tradition, stretching back to Lenin and Trotsky.[49] There was also a deathly fear of finding themselves on the same side as the imperialists if they rejected Islamist movements. There was criticism of French groups such as Lutte Ouvrière and Ligue Communiste Révolutionnaire by British Marxists that they effectively sided with the Elysee Palace in demanding the banning of the hijab in state schools in France.[50]

With the invasion of Iraq, New Labour was now defined by Blair's support for the war and his identification with George Bush's White House. Ironically many Blairites supported Israel as a means of distinguishing themselves from the failed far Left of the 1980s.

In one sense, the conflict had been transformed into a struggle for the identity of the Labour Party rather than anything which related to the complex brutalities in the Middle East.

Following the train bombings of 7 July 2005 on the London Underground, there was a retrenchment of Muslim activism and a wish not to confront the British establishment in the manner of the MAB. Despite this, there was a growing demand to negotiate with Hamas on the European Left. In part, this was in reaction to Israeli military actions. In part, it was due to a concerted Hamas campaign in Europe to secure recognition. Blair's handling of the Israel-Palestine conflict was highly criticized by Labour Party members when he delayed in calling for a ceasefire during the second Lebanon war in 2006.

The success of the campaign against the war in Iraq War was discussed at length by the far Left and one result of this was the establishment of the Respect party. Yet even by 2006, the days of solidarity and co-operation already belonged to the past. The MAB split, the SWP fragmented and the Respect MP, George Galloway eventually lost his parliamentary seat. In the European elections in 2004, the far Left proved incapable in Europe of capitalizing on the profound antagonism to George Bush's America and to the US invasion of Iraq. Pious Muslims distanced themselves from revolutionary Marxists. Trotskyists were antagonized by Stalinists – and vice-versa. But the issue of Palestine had moved into the centre ground. If in the late 1960s, it had been the prerogative of the International Marxist Group, by 2010 it was being debated in the pages of the *Financial Times*.

Even so, any decline was periodically reversed by events in the Middle East. From 2006 onwards, successive Israeli governments practised the policies of military deterrence as demonstrated by the second Lebanon war and Operation Cast Lead in Gaza. The far Left therefore concentrated on promoting the humanitarian concerns of many Europeans far beyond the Left. Other groups such as the British Muslim Initiative and the Palestine Return Centre emerged with Muslim Brotherhood links. The Palestine Solidarity Campaign, well endowed with SWP members and led by vintage IMG adherents, promoted the Palestinian cause within the British Labour movement. Old themes still remained. In the summer of 2010, the killings on the Mavi Marmara, the lead boat in a flotilla, attempting to reach the shores of Gaza, were therefore compared to the Sharpeville massacre in South Africa in 1960.[51] The sophistication of both Hamas and Hezbollah in managing the media coupled with a growing awareness of the Palestinian question in the West demoted other narratives. It also distracted from a consideration of the central problems of the conflict. The emphasis on the human rights of the Palestinians gained a ready audience in the West while the expansion of the Jewish settlements on the West Bank was little discussed.

Despite a UN report in September 2011 which validated Israel's legal right to prevent vessels from reaching Gaza, the siege of the territory, now under the control of Hamas, was another focus of activity. The flamboyant George Galloway, a long-time stalwart of the British Labour Left and subsequently the Respect party, organized convoys to Gaza through 'Viva Palestina'. It also attempted to develop sympathy for the Palestinian Islamist cause through several Muslim organizations in Britain.

The shape of things to come?

In the twenty-first century, a distinction is made by a growing number on the European Left between 'benign, honest Jews' and 'conniving all-powerful Zionists'. Yet a detailed survey of the attitudes of British Jews in 2010 indicated that 72% categorized themselves as 'Zionists' and 90% viewed Israel as 'the ancestral homeland of the Jewish people'. Would European Jews therefore perceive a crude attack on 'Zionists' as an assault on their identity as Jews? If an attack on the policies of an Israeli government was coloured by time-honoured stereotypes regarding Jews, how would today's Jews understand this?

The far Left in Europe often views those with universalist convictions as upholders of an authentic Jewish tradition. Such 'non-Jewish Jews' are lauded for their courage when criticizing the policies of an Israel government. On the other hand, the views on Israel of non 'non-Jewish Jews' are dismissed as inauthentic and marginal – even though according to the 2010 survey, they represent the overwhelming majority of Jews in Britain.[52] Moreover Jewish community leaders have openly attacked the Netanyahu government[53] and the survey reported that 74% of British Jews opposed the settlement drive on the West Bank. Significantly only 25% of the respondents stated that it was never justified to criticize Israel publicly.

Such reality jars with the perceptions of some on the far Left. To acknowledge that British Jews do not disavow the label of 'Zionist' and identify with the state of Israel, yet are willing to criticize its government, is too perplexing. Once again it proves that it is far easier to bend the Jews to fit theory rather than to examine the reality in which they inhabit.

By extension, such dislocation has also been applied to Israelis. While the epithets of 'imperialist' and 'Nazi' are not scarcities in the far Left lexicon, Israelis are almost never acknowledged as 'Jews'. Would such an admission thereby create an historical context for the emergence of Zionism?

Yet history is important. The memory of World War II has burned brightly for the succeeding generations in European countries which had been occupied by the Nazis. In 2002, the BBC organized a phone-in to discover who was 'the greatest Briton of all time'. Half a million people voted for Churchill, leaving other contenders far behind. This remembrance in Europe naturally links to the extermination of the Jews and to an understanding for the continuation of a state with a Jewish majority. Most social democrats and liberals therefore wished to see reconciliation even if they opposed Israeli government policy. The orthodox Marxist Left never saw the world and the Jews in this light. They opposed Sartre's 'double legacy' view of the conflict. A minority of identifying Jews opposed to Zionism fortified this view.

The far Left has often mistaken Arab nationalism for Arab socialism – and ended up defending the ideologically indefensible. Is there a parallel confusion in the minds of many Muslim activists today in Europe? Did the conquest of the Middle East by the first caliphs in the seventh century bring about Islamization or Arabization? History has forged a synonymity between the two, but is this identification of one with the other theologically true? Conversely has this morphing persuaded the Palestinian Left to view Islamists in a progressive light? A view which has then been passed onto the European far Left in the twenty-first century.[54]

In the 1960s the disdain felt by the New Left for the legacy of Stalinism meant that Soviet subtlety – opposing Zionism but accepting Israel – registered only fleetingly. Indeed by 1967, the French Maoists were already advocating a people's war and the elimination of Israel. The feeling that the creation of Israel in 1948 was a grave error grew in an age of decolonization and rising Palestinian nationalism. This reached its apogee with the removal of the Soviet bloc in 1991. It meant that any recognition that the Jews had a right to national self-determination could similarly be consigned to the rubbish dump of history. It also meant that there were now few restrictions in aligning with the position of the Arab Left that Israel in its current form had no right to exist. And this logically produced an about turn in the uneasy relationship between Marxists and Islamists.

The equilibrium between these different constituent parts of the European Left is affected by many factors, but a continuing one is the unsatisfactory situation in Israel-Palestine and by extension in the wider Middle East – a situation whereby rejectionism has crowded out reconciliation. A just peace between Israelis and Palestinians in the twenty-first century will, of course, deprive some on the far Left of the ability to utilize a situation abroad to serve the cause of revolutionary change at home. Yet this possibility seems unlikely in the second decade of the twenty-first century. Indeed the coming conflict will be a war of missiles. On the Palestinian and Arab side, they will often be fired from the midst of civilian population. Israel's policy of deterrence and retaliation since 2006 indicates therefore that non-combatants will be caught in the crossfire. The spectacle of such death and destruction in turn has become an important card in the game of wooing liberals and social democrats by the far Left.

The polarization between Israelis and Palestinians is welcomed by many on the far Left in Europe. Any reconstruction of the middle ground by the peace camps in both Israel and Palestine is by contrast distinctly unwelcome.

Ironically the polarization between the two national movements has become so severe that a 'peace process' exists in name only. Israelis and Palestinians resemble spectators at a football match – each naturally cheering on their own side. Many, of course, argue that such point scoring is a necessity in order to enlist the support of foreign governments. Yet as history has indicated, this fuels a sectarian discourse by outsiders in Europe which has ultimately little bearing on any future face-to-face negotiations between Israelis and Palestinians. This is where reality is confronted and hard decisions are taken.

The notion of compromise – and living with it – is hard to bear. It will be seen as a betrayal by Palestinian Islamists and by the Palestinian Left. A similar view will be taken by both the far Left and the far Right in Israel. Yet most Israelis and Palestinians do not share such an enthusiasm for ideological purity, but wish mainly for a solution which embraces fairness, an end to violence and the vision of a secure future. If such a solution is located – and is successful in the long term, then the rejectionists in both Israel and Palestine will be rendered impotent. And the far Left in Europe will move on to more lucrative causes.

Notes and Works Cited

1 Mahmoud Mi'ari, 'Attitudes of Palestinians towards Normalisation with Israel', *Journal of Peace Research*, vol. 36, no. 3, 1999.

2 Elliott Colla, 'Solidarity in a Time of Anti-Normalisation', *Middle East Report* no. 224, Autumn 2002.

3 *Wall Street Journal*, 1 December 2008.

4 Colla, op. cit.

5 Amal Jamal, *The Palestinian National Movement: Politics of Contention 1967–2005* (Indiana 2005), p. 120.

6 *Guardian*, 9 September 1993.

7 Ibrahim Ghousheh (Hamas spokesman), 4 September 1993 in As'ad Ghanem, *Palestinian Politics after Arafat: A Failed National Movement* (Indiana 2010), p. 145.

8 Sara Roy, 'Why Peace Failed: An Oslo Autopsy', *Current History*, vol. 100, no. 651, 8 January 2002.

9 Khalil Shikaki, 'The Peace Process: National Reconstruction and the Transition to Democracy in Palestine', *Journal of Palestine Studies*, vol. 25, no. 2, Winter 1996.

10 Wendy Kristianasen, 'Challenge and Counter-Challenge: Hamas's Response to Oslo', *Journal of Palestine Studies*, vol. 28, no. 3, Spring 1999.

11 Anders Strindberg, 'The Damascus-based Alliance of Palestinian Forces: A Primer', *Journal of Palestine Studies*, vol. 29, no. 3, Spring 2000.

12 Ghanem, op. cit., pp. 144–5.

13 Ron Pundak, 'Civil Society Normalisation as a Step towards Peace', *Bitter Lemons* edition 42, vol. 5, 15 November 2007.

14 *Jerusalem Times*, 29 June 2001.

15 *Guardian*, 2 December 1994.

16 Edward W. Said, *The Politics of Dispossession: The Struggle for Palestinian Self-Determination 1969–1994* (London 1994), p. xxxii.

17 Ibid., p. xxiii.

18 Donna Robinson Devine, 'The Middle East Conflict and its Post-Colonial Discontents', *Israel Affairs*, vol. 13, no. 4, October 2007.

19 Said, op. cit., p. xix.

20 Edward W. Said, *The End of the Peace Process: Oslo and After* (London 2000), pp. xviii–xix.

21 Malise Ruthven, *Guardian*, 9 July 1994.

22 Edward W. Said, *Guardian*, 15 February 1997.

23 Ibid.

24 Victoria Brittain, *Guardian*, 26 April 2000.

25 Jemima Khan, *Guardian*, 1 November 2000.

26 *Guardian*, 14 May 1996.

27 Roy Greenslade, *Media Guardian*, 7 May 2001.

28 *Letters to the Guardian*, 13 July 2000.

29 Simon Sebag-Montefiore, *Guardian*, 28 March 2001.

30 Ewan McGaskill, 'Reporting the World' seminar London, 21 March 2001.

31 Faisal Bodi, *Guardian*, 3 January 2001.

32 Faisal Bodi, *Media Guardian*, 21 May 2001.

33 *Guardian*, 16 November 2009.

34 *Guardian*, 17 November 2009.

35 *Guardian*, 24 March 2010.

36 *Guardian*, 10 April 2003.

37 *Guardian*, 16 August 2001.

38 Timothy Snyder, 'Hitler vs. Stalin: Who Killed More?', *New York Review of Books*, 10 March 2011.

39 Daphna Baram, *Disenchantment: The Guardian and Israel* (London 2004), p. 199.

40 *Guardian*, 25 May 2005.

41 *Guardian*, 7 February 2006.

42 *Aftenposten*, 5 August 2006.

43 Deborah Orr, *Guardian*, 20 October 2011.

44 *Guardian*, 17 April 2002.

45 Richard Phillips, 'Standing Together: The Muslim Association of Britain and the Anti-War Movement', *Race and Class*, vol. 50, no. 2, 2008.

46 *BBC Summary of World Broadcasts*, 3 July 1979.

47 *New Left Review*, no. 166, November–December 1987.

48 Chris Harman, 'The Prophet and the Proletariat', *International Socialism Journal*, no. 64, Autumn 1994.

49 Dave Crouch, 'The Bolsheviks and Islam', *International Socialism*, April 2006.

50 Alex Callinicos, 'The European Left Tested Electorally', www.international viewpoint.org December 2004.

51 *Morning Star*, 3 June 2010.

52 David Graham and Jonathan Boyd, 'Committed, Concerned and Conciliatory: The Attitudes of Jews in Britain towards Israel', Institute of Jewish Policy Research, London July 2010.

53 *Jewish Chronicle*, 17 June 2010.

54 *Ha'aretz*, 12 October 2008. See also Tarek Fatah, *Chasing a Mirage: The Tragic Illusion of an Islamic State* (Toronto 2008).

Selected Bibliography

Aberbach, David, ed. and tr. *C. N. Bialik: Selected Poems* (London 2004).

Achcar, Gilbert, ed. *Ralph Miliband and Marcel Liebman: The Israeli Dilemma; A Debate between Two Left Wing Jews* (Monmouth 2006).

Almog, Shmuel, ed. *Anti-Semitism through the Ages* (London 1988).

Andrew, Christopher and Mitrokhin, Vasili, *The World was Going Our Way: The KGB and the Battle for the Third World* (New York 2005).

Andrew, Christopher, *The Defence of the Realm: The Authorised History of MI5* (London 2009).

Anonymous, *The Yellow Spot* (London 1936).

Ascher, Abraham, *Pavel Axelrod and the Development of Menshevism* (Massachusetts 1972).

Attfield, John and Williams, Stephen, eds. *1939: The Communist Party of Great Britain and the War* (London 1984).

Attlee, C. R., *The Labour Party in Perspective* (London 1937).

Banas, Josef, *The Scapegoats: The Exodus of the Remnants of Polish Jewry* (London 1979).

Baram, Daphna, *Disenchantment: The Guardian and Israel* (London 2004).

Baron, Salo W., *The Russian Jew under Tsars and Soviets* (New York 1976).

Beckett, Francis, *Enemy Within: The Rise and Fall of the British Communist Party* (London 1995).

Bialer, Uri, *Between East and West: Israel's Foreign Policy Orientation 1948–1956* (Cambridge 1990).

Black, Robert, *Stalinism in Britain: A Trotskyist Analysis* (London 1970).

Bose, Subhas Chandra, *The Indian Struggle 1920–1942* (New York 1964).

Brady, Robert A., *The Spirit and Structure of German Fascism* (London 1937).

Brailsford, H. N., *The Levellers and the English Revolution* (London 1961).

Branson, Noreen, *History of the Communist Party of Great Britain* (London 1985).

Brockway, Fenner, *Britain's First Socialists: The Levellers, Agitators and Diggers of the English Revolution* (London 1980).

Buber-Neumann, Margarete, *Under Two Dictators: Prisoner of Stalin and Hitler* (London 2009).

Bullock, Alan, *Hitler and Stalin: Parallel Lives* (London 1991).

Cahan, Abraham, *The Education of Abraham Cahan* (Philadelphia 1969).

Callaghan, John, *The Far Left in British Politics* (Oxford 1987).

— *Socialism in Britain* (Oxford 1990).

— *Rajani Palme Dutt: A Study in British Stalinism* (London 1993).

Carr, E. H., *Socialism in One Country* (London 1964).

Carvel, John, *Citizen Ken* (London 1984).

Caute, David, *Communism and the French Intellectuals: 1914–1960* (London 1964).
— *Fanon* (London 1970).
Challinor, Raymond, *The Origins of British Bolshevism* (London 1977).
Cherki, Alice, *Frantz Fanon: A Portrait* (London 2006).
Chernyshevski, Nikolai, *What is to be Done?* (New York 1989).
Chuev, Felix, *Molotov Remembers: Inside Kremlin Politics* (Chicago 1993).
Clarke, Peter, *Liberals and Social Democrats* (Cambridge 1978).
Cohen, Stephen F., *Bukharin and the Bolshevik Revolution* (London 1974).
Cole, G. D. H., *The People's Front* (London 1937).
Collard, Dudley, *Soviet Justice and the Trial of Radek and Others* (London 1937).
Collette, Christine and Bird, Stephen, eds. *Jews, Labour and the Left 1918–1948* (Aldershot 2000).
Colton, Joel, *Léon Blum: Humanist in Politics* (New York 1966).
Cotic, Meir, *The Prague Trial* (London 1987).
Crossman, Richard, *Palestine Mission* (London 1947).
Curtis, Michael and Gitelson, Susan Aurelia, eds. *Israel in the Third World* (New Brunswick 1976).
Daniel, Jean, *The Jewish Prison: A Rebellious Meditation on the State of Judaism* (New York 2005).
Dannreuther, Ronald, *The Soviet Union and the PLO* (London 1998).
Dawidowicz, Lucy, ed. *The Golden Treasury* (New York 1967).
Degras, Jane, ed. *The Communist International 1919–1943: Documents,* vol. 1 (London 1971).
— ed. *Soviet Documents on Foreign Policy, 1925–1932,* vol. 2 (London 1971).
Dewar, Hugo, *Communist Politics in Britain: The CPGB from its Origins to the Second World War* (London 1976).
Dotan, Shmuel, *Adumim: Hamiflagah hakommunistit b'Eretz Yisrael* (Tel Aviv 1991).
Dutt, Rajani Palme, *The Crisis of Britain and the British Empire* (London 1957).
Edmunds, June, *The Left and Israel: Party Policy, Change and Internal Democracy* (London 2000).
Eley, Geoff, *Forging Democracy: The History of the Left in Europe 1850–2000* (Oxford 2002).
Elpeleg, Zvi, *The Grand Mufti: Haj Amin Al-Husseini, Founder of the Palestinian National Movement* (London 1993).
Epstein, Leon D., *British Politics in the Suez Crisis* (London 1964).
Ettinger, Elżbieta, *Roza Luxemburg* (Boston 1986).
Eudin, Xenia Joukoff and North, Robert C., *Soviet Russia and the East 1920–1927* (Stanford 1957).
Fanon, Frantz, *The Wretched of the Earth* (London 1967).
Fatah, Tarek, *Chasing a Mirage: The Tragic Illusion of an Islamic State* (Toronto 2008).
Feuchtwanger, Lion, *Moscow 1937* (London 1937).
Fischer, Ruth, *Stalin and German Communism: A Study in the Origins of the State Party* (Oxford 1948).
Flechtheim, Ossip K., *Le Parti Communisme (K.P.D.) sous la Republique de Weimar* (Paris 1972).

Fonvieille-Alquier, Francois, *The French and the Phoney War 1939–1940* (London 1971).

Foot, Michael, *Aneurin Bevan 1945–1960* (London 1975).

Fourier, Charles, *Oeuvres Completes* (Paris 1846–1848).

Frankel, Edith Rogovin, Frankel, Jonathan and Knei-Paz, Baruch, eds. *Revolution in Russia: Reassessments of 1917* (Cambridge 1992).

Frankel, Jonathan, *Prophecy and Politics: Socialism, Nationalism, and the Russian Jews 1862–1917* (Cambridge 1982).

Fraser, Ronald, *1968: Student Generation in Revolt* (London 1988).

Friedman, Murray, *The Neoconservative Revolution: Jewish Intellectuals and the Shaping of Public Policy* (Cambridge 2005).

Gal, Allon, *Socialist-Zionism: Theory and Issues in Contemporary Jewish Nationalism* (Boston 1989).

Galnoor, Itzhak, *The Partition of Palestine* (New York 1995).

Getz, Marshall J., *Subhas Chandra Bose* (North Carolina 2002).

Getzler, Israel, *Martov: A Political Biography of a Russian Social Democrat* (Cambridge 1967).

Ghanem, As'ad, *Palestinian Politics after Arafat: A Failed National Movement* (Indiana 2010).

Gilbert, Martin, *The Holocaust* (London 1986).

Gilboa, Yehoshua A., *The Black Years of Soviet Jewry* (Boston 1971).

— *Oktobre'im Ivrim* (Tel Aviv 1974).

— *A Language Silenced: The Suppression of Hebrew Literature and Culture in the Soviet Union* (New York 1982).

Gitelman, Zvi Y., ed. *Jewish Nationality and Soviet Politics: The Jewish Sections of the CPSU 1917–1930* (Princeton 1972).

Glotzer, Albert, *Trotsky: Memoir and Critique* (New York 1989).

Goldsmith, Maurice, *Frédéric Joliot-Curie: A Biography* (London 1976).

Gollancz, Victor, ed. *The Betrayal of the Left* (London 1941).

Gorny, Joseph, *The British Labour Movement and Zionism: 1917–1948* (London 1983).

Gorodetsky, Gabriel, *The Precarious Truce* (London 1977).

Gorst, Anthony and Johnman, Lewis, eds. *The Suez Crisis* (London 1997).

Greenberg, Louis, *The Jews in Russia: The Struggle for Emancipation,* vol. 1 (New Haven 1944).

Gresh, Alain, *The PLO: The Struggle Within* (London 1985).

Groves, Reg, *The Balham Group: How British Trotskyism Began* (London 1974).

Gupta, Sobhanlal Datta, *Comintern, India and the Colonial Question 1920–1937* (Calcutta 1980).

Haberer, Erich E., *Jews and Revolution in Nineteenth Century Russia* (Cambridge 2004).

Hanna, Sami A. and Gardner, George, *Arab Socialism* (Leiden 1969).

Harding, Neil, *Leninism* (London 1996).

Hen-Tov, Jacob *Communism and Zionism in Palestine* (Massachusetts 1974).

Herf, Jeffrey, *The Jewish Enemy: Nazi Propaganda During World War II and the Holocaust* (London 2006).

Hertzberg, Arthur, *The Zionist Idea: A Historical Analysis and Reader* (Philadelphia 1997).

Hetherington, Alastair, *Guardian Years* (London 1981).

Hinsler, F. H. and Simkins, C. A. G., *British Intelligence in the Second World War*, vol. 4 (London 1990).

Hirson, Baruch, *Revolutions in My Life* (Johannesburg 1995).

— *The Cape Town Intellectuals: Ruth Schechter and Her Circle 1907–1934* (Cape Town 2001).

— *A History of the Left in South Africa* (London 2005).

Hisin, Chaim, *Mi yoman ehad ha'Biluim* (Tel Aviv 1925).

Hobson, J. A., *The War in South Africa: Its Causes and Effects* (London 1900).

— *Imperialism: A Study* (London 1902).

Holmes, Colin, ed. *Immigrants and Minorities in British Society* (London 1978).

Howe, Stephen, *Anticolonialism in British Politics: The Left and the End of Empire 1918–1964* (Oxford 1993).

Jacobs, Jack, *On Socialists and 'The Jewish Question' after Marx* (New York 1992).

Jamal, Amal, *The Palestinian National Movement: Politics of Contention 1967–2005* (Indiana 2005).

Jones, Bill, *The British Labour Party and the Soviet Union* (Manchester 1977).

Judaken, Jonathan, *Jean-Paul Sartre and the Jewish Question: Anti Anti-Semitism and the Politics of the French Intellectual* (Nebraska 2006).

Kahin, George McTurnan, *The Asian-African Conference* (London 1956).

Kautsky, Karl, *Are the Jews a Race?* (New York 1926).

Kelly, Aileen, *Mikhail Bakunin: A Study in the Psychology and Politics of Utopianism* (Oxford 1982).

Khrushchev, Nikita, *Khrushchev Remembers* (London 1971).

Kimche, David, *The Afro-Asian Movement: Ideology and Foreign Policy of the Third World* (Jerusalem 1973).

King, Francis and Matthews, George, eds. *About Turn: The British Communist Party and the Second World War* (London 1990).

Kirsch, Adam, *Benjamin Disraeli* (New York 2008).

Klier, John D. and Lambroza, Shlomo, *Pogroms: Anti-Jewish Violence in Modern Russian History* (Cambridge 1992).

Klugmann, James, *The History of the Communist Party of Great Britain: Formative and Early Years 1919–1924* (London 1969).

Knight, Amy, *Beria: Stalin's First Lieutenant* (Princeton 1993).

Kochan, Lionel, ed. *The Jews in Soviet Russia since 1917* (Oxford 1970).

Koestler, Arthur, *Darkness at Noon* (London 1940).

— *The Trail of the Dinosaur* (New York 1955).

Kostyrchenko, Gennadi, *Out of the Red Shadows: Anti-Semitism in Stalin's Russia* (New York 1995).

Kovaly, Heda Margolius, *Prague Farewell: A Life in Czechoslovakia 1941–1968* (London 1988).

Laqueur, Walter, (G. Z. Israeli) *MOPS-PCP-MAKI* (Tel Aviv 1953).

— *Communism and Nationalism in the Middle East* (London 1956).

— *The History of Zionism* (London 2003).

Legum, Colin, *Bandung, Cairo and Accra: A Report on the First Conference of Independent African States* (London 1958).

Lendvai, Paul, *Anti-Semitism in Eastern Europe* (London 1971).

Leon, Abram, *The Jewish Question: A Marxist Interpretation* (New York 1970).

Levine-Meyer, Rose, *Inside German Communism: Memoirs of Party Life in the Weimar Republic* (London 1977).

Levy, H., *A Philosophy for a Modern Man* (London 1938).

Liebman, Marcel, *Born Jewish: A Childhood in Occupied Europe* (London 2005).

Litvinoff, Emanuel, *Soviet Anti-Semitism: The Paris Trial* (London 1974).

Loebl, Eugene, *Sentenced and Tried: The Stalinist Purges in Czechoslovakia* (London 1969).

London, Artur, *On Trial* (London 1968).

Lumer, Hyman, ed. *Lenin on the Jewish Question* (New York 1974).

MacDonald, J. Ramsay, *A Socialist in Palestine* (London 1922).

Mackenzie, Norman, ed. *Pilgrimage 1912–1947: The Letters of Sidney and Beatrice Webb* (Cambridge 1978).

Makovsky, Michael, *Churchill's Promised Land: Zionism and Statecraft* (Yale 2007).

Mandel, Ernest, *The Meaning of the Second World War* (London 1986).

Marcuse, Harold, *Legacies of Dachau: The Uses and Abuses of a Concentration Camp 1933–2000* (Cambridge 2010).

Marmor, Kalman, ed. *Aaron Lieberman's Briv* (New York 1951).

Marrus, Michael R. and Paxton, Robert O., *Vichy France and the Jews* (Stanford 1995).

Memmi, Albert, *The Colonizer and the Colonized* (London 2003).

Mendelsohn, Ezra, *Class Struggle in the Pale: The Formative Years of the Jewish Workers' Movement in Tsarist Russia* (Cambridge 1970).

Mendes-Flohr, Paul and Reinharz, Jehuda, eds. *The Jew in the Modern World: A Documentary History* (Oxford 1995).

Merhav, Peretz, *The Israeli Left* (New York 1980).

Merson, Allan, *Communist Resistance in Nazi Germany* (London 1985).

Morgan, Kevin, *Harry Pollitt* (Manchester 1993).

— *Labour Legends and Russian Gold* (London 2006).

Morley, John, *Life of Gladstone* (London 1903).

Namir, Mordechai, *Shlichut B'Moskva* (Tel Aviv 1971).

Nedava, Joseph, *Trotsky and the Jews* (Philadelphia 1972).

Oren, Michael B., *The Origins of the Second Arab-Israeli War: Egypt, Israel and the Great Powers 1952–56* (London 1992).

Orwell, George, *The Road to Wigan Pier* (London 1937).

Overy, Richard with Wheatcroft, Andrew, *The Road to War* (London 1999).

Oxford University Socialist Discussion Group, ed. *Out of Apathy: Voices of the New Left 30 Years On* (London 1989).

Pablo, Michael, *The Arab Revolution* (New York 1959).

Parry, Benita, *Post-Colonial Studies: A Materialist Critique* (London 2004).

Pilzer, J. M., ed. *Anti-Semitism and Jewish Nationalism* (Virginia Beach 1981).

Pinson, Koppel S., ed. *Nationalism and History: Essays on Old and New Judaism by Simon Dubnov* (Philadelphia 1958).

Pipes, Richard, *The Unknown Lenin: From the Secret Archive* (Yale 1998).

Porath, Yehoshua, *The Emergence of the Palestinian Arab National Movement 1918–1929* (London 1974).

Porter, Bernard, *Critics of Empire* (London 1968).

Pringle, J. M. D., *Have Pen, Will Travel* (London 1973).

Radek, Karl, *Portraits and Pamphlets* (London 1935).

Radosh, Ronald, *Commies: A Journey through the Old Left, the New Left and the Leftover Left* (San Francisco 2001).

Rapoport, Yakov, *The Doctors' Plot* (London 1991).

Rees, Tim and Thorpe, Andrew, ed. *International Communism and the Communist International 1919–1943* (Manchester 1998).

Renan, Ernest, *Discours et Conferences par Ernest Renan* (Paris 1887).

— *History of the People of Israel* (Boston 1907).

Rodinson, Maxime, *Cult, Ghetto and State* (London 1983).

Rubenstein, Sondra Miller, *The Communist Movement in Palestine and Israel, 1919–1984* (Boulder 1985).

Sachar, Howard M., *Dreamland: Europeans and Jews in the Aftermath of the Great War* (New York 2002).

Sadat, Anwar, *Revolt on the Nile* (London 1957).

Said, Edward W., *The Politics of Dispossession: The Struggle for Palestinian Self-Determination 1969–1994* (London 1994).

— *The End of the Peace Process: Oslo and After* (London 2000).

Salvemini, Gaetano, *Under the Axe of Fascism* (London 1936).

Sartre, Jean-Paul, *The Spectre of Stalin* (London 1969).

Sebag-Montefiore, Simon, *Young Stalin* (New York 2007).

Serfaty, Simon and Gray, Lawrence, eds. *The Italian Communist Party: Yesterday, Today and Tomorrow* (Westport 1980).

Service, Robert, *Lenin: A Biography* (London 2000).

Shafir, Gershon, *Land, Labour and the Origins of the Israeli-Palestinian Conflict 1882–1914* (Cambridge 1989).

Shapiro, Robert Moses, ed. *Why Didn't the Press Shout?: American and International Journalism during the Holocaust* (New York 2003).

Sheffer, Gabriel, *Moshe Sharett: Biography of a Political Moderate* (Oxford 1996).

Shur, Chaim, *Shomrim in the Land of Apartheid: The Story of Hashomer Hatzair in South Africa 1935–1970* (Givat Haviva 1998).

Simon, Leon, ed. *Ahad Ha'am: Essays, Letters, Memoirs* (Oxford 1946).

Snowman, L. V., ed. *Chaim Nachman Bialik: Poems from the Hebrew* (London 1924).

Spender, Stephen, *Forward from Liberalism* (London 1936).

Spriano, Paolo, *Stalin and the European Communists* (London 1985).

Stillman, Norman A., *The Jews of Arab Lands in Modern Times* (New York 1991).

Strachey, John, *The Coming Struggle for Power* (London 1934).

Stutje, Jan Willem, *Ernest Mandel: A Rebel's Dream Deferred* (London 2009).

Talmon J. L., *Israel among the Nations* (London 1970).

Thomas, Hugh, *The Suez Affair* (London 1986).

Thorpe, Andrew, *The British Communist Party and Moscow 1920–1943* (Manchester 2000).

Todorov, Tzvetan, *Hope and Memory* (London 2005).

Toye, Hugh, *The Springing Tiger* (London 1959).

Traverso, Enzo, *The Marxists and the Jewish Question: The History of a Debate 1843–1943* (New Jersey 1994).

Tsentsiper, Arieh Leib, *Eser Sh'not Redifot* (Tel Aviv 1930).
— *B'maavak L'geula* (Tel Aviv 1956).
Vaksberg, Arkady, *The Prosecutor and the Prey: Vishinsky and the 1930s Moscow Show Trials* (London 1990).
Warner, Geoffrey, *Iraq and Syria: 1941* (London 1974).
Weeks, Albert L., *Stalin's Other War: Soviet Grand Strategy 1939–1941* (Oxford 2002).
Weinstock, Nathan, *Zionism: False Messiah* (London 1979).
Weizmann, Chaim, *Trial and Error* (New York 1949).
Welles, Sumner, *The Time for Decision* (New York 1944).
West, Benjamin, ed. *Struggles of a Generation: The Jews under Soviet Rule* (Tel Aviv 1959).
— *B'derekh l'geula* (Tel Aviv 1971).
— *Bein yayush l'tikva* (Tel Aviv 1973).
Widgery, David, *The Left in Britain 1956–1968* (London 1976).
Wistrich, Robert, ed. *The Left and Zion: Communism, Israel and the Middle East* (London 1979).
— *Trotsky: Fate of a Revolutionary* (London 1979).
— *Laboratory for World Destruction: Germans and Jews in Central Europe* (London 2007).
Wohl, Robert, *French Communism in the Making* (Stanford 1966).
Wood, Neal, *Communism and British Intellectuals* (London 1959).
Wylie, Neville, ed. *European Neutrals and Non-Belligerents during the Second World War* (Cambridge 2002).

Index

Leo Lyons 189